Free and Open Source Software for E-Learning:
Issues, Successes and Challenges

Betül Özkan Czerkawski
University of Arizona South, USA

INFORMATION SCIENCE REFERENCE

Hershey · New York

Director of Editorial Content:	Kristin Klinger
Director of Book Publications:	Julia Mosemann
Acquisitions Editor:	Lindsay Johnston
Development Editor:	Christine Bufton
Publishing Assistant:	Casey Conapitski
Typesetter:	Deanna Jo Zombro
Production Editor:	Jamie Snavely
Cover Design:	Lisa Tosheff

Published in the United States of America by
Information Science Reference (an imprint of IGI Global)
701 E. Chocolate Avenue
Hershey PA 17033
Tel: 717-533-8845
Fax: 717-533-8661
E-mail: cust@igi-global.com
Web site: http://www.igi-global.com

Library of Congress Cataloging-in-Publication Data

Free and open source software for e-learning : issues, successes, and challenges / Betul Ozkan Czerkawski, editor.
    p. cm.
  Includes bibliographical references and index.   Summary: "This book reviews open and free software used in e-learning, examines the pedagogy behind FOSS and how it is applied to e-learning, and discusses the best practices for FOSS through real world examples, providing guidelines for e-learning designers and instructors who use FOSS"--Provided by publisher.
  ISBN 978-1-61520-917-0 (hardcover) -- ISBN 978-1-61520-918-7 (ebook) 1. Computer-assisted instruction--Software. 2. Open source software. 3. Instructional systems--Design. I. Ozkan Czerkawski, Betul, 1969-
  LB1028.5.F734 2010
  371.33'44678--dc22
                        2010010157

British Cataloguing in Publication Data
A Cataloguing in Publication record for this book is available from the British Library.

All work contributed to this book is new, previously-unpublished material. The views expressed in this book are those of the authors, but not necessarily of the publisher.

Table of Contents

Section 3
Implementation Examples

Detailed Table of Contents

Section 1
Introduction to Free and Open Source Software

Köse starts with explaining free and open source software as they apply to Web 2.0 technologies for E-Learning. He argues that Web 2.0 technologies revolutionize E-Learning by emphasizing user control for more personal, social and flexible web contents. He provides definitions of major concepts in FOSS and presents examples from online learning environments. He concludes with a discussion of the future of the Web, including Web 3.0 and Web 4.0 technologies.

The chapter starts with a brief history and a summary of FOSS definition and philosophy. The authors then examine the current literature on the use of Free and Open Source software in education with a particular focus on the promise of E-Learning and emerging technologies to positively shape our educational future. The authors also discuss philosophical, financial, practical, and pedagogical considerations that prompt educators to select free and open source software over propriety software. In conclusion, they discuss the important role FOSS will play in the future with open learning

Section 2
Free and Open Source Software in E- Learning

Chapter 3

Schrynermakers discusses the connections and synergy between constructivist learning theory, open source technologies and student learning. She argues that these connections are problematic as there aren't meaningful links between the first two areas. Therefore, she examines knowledge acquisition process in the 21st century, and then discusses the process of dialectic where learners investigate the truth through discussion. Intrinsic to this discussion is the impact of technology on those interested in pursuing teaching and learning through open source platforms. For example, how has technology enhanced or decreased the dialogue in education? She then follows the linkages between constructivism and open source to look at how both link up to provide support and pedagogical assistance to student learning. The chapter concludes with examples of how the author has integrated constructivist philosophies with open source technology to establish a collaborative and effective learning environment for higher education students

Chapter 4

van Rooij examines the issue of FOSS adoption in U.S. institutions of higher education, where campus-wide deployment of FOSS for E-Learning lags far behind adoption for technical infrastructure applications. In this chapter, van Rooij argues that the gap between the advocacy for FOSS teaching and learning applications and the enterprise-wide deployment of FOSS for E-Learning is a consequence of the divergent perspectives of two organizational sub-cultures – the technologist and the academic – and the extent to which those sub-cultures are likely to embrace FOSS. The author concludes with a few suggestions: collaborative needs analysis/assessment prior to a go/no go adoption decision; and broad dissemination of total cost of ownership (TCO) data by institutions already deploying FOSS for E-Learning enterprise-wide.

Chapter 5

Kurshan, Schreiber and Levy argue that a growing number of education stakeholders are finding that applying an open source approach to content development provides an extraordinary opportunity to change the existing curricula paradigm and expand access to quality learning and the free exchange of knowledge. The authors explore the increased adoption of open and shared educational resources (OSER), using a case study, Curriki, that extends the model further by providing an integrated learning environment and resource repository that is centered on a culture of collective participation.

Section 3
Implementation Examples

This chapter provides a case study from an Australian university, who adopted the open source software, Sakai, as the foundation for the University's new, integrated Online Learning Environment called CSU Interact. In this chapter, Buchan discusses her University's gradual implementation of Sakai course management system first as a pilot project then as a choice of entire University's E-Learning system. She then outlines some of the challenges and successes of the project management methodology and processes which oversaw the successful large-scale implementation of an open-source courseware management solution at the institutional level. In conclusion, Buchan discusses the pedagogical advantages of adopting an open source learning management system as well as the significance of investing human and financial resources into such E-Learning system.

The authors discuss principles of open education and possibilities of implementing these principles for software engineering education on the base of open source software development projects. They present the example of a "Software Engineering" course provided to students of the System Programming sub-faculties of the two Russian top-ranked universities, Moscow State University and Moscow Institute of Physics and Technology.

McGrath discusses usage analysis facilities, as being one of the special considerations when adopting an open source course management system. In his study, McGrath examines how user activity tracking challenges are being met with data mining techniques, in four very different open learning management systems: ATutor, LON-CAPA, Moodle and Sakai. He concludes that as open systems mature in the use of educational data mining, they potentially move closer to the long-sought goal of achieving more interactive, personalized, adaptive learning environments online on a broad scale.

This chapter describes the identification of goals, selection of an Open Source Platform, and the initial implementation stages of an Integrative Knowledge ePortfolio Process (which has both pedagogy and tools) at a midwestern University School of Education. Faculty and students are using the Integrative ePortfolio approach to reflect on, connect, and document their learning and accomplishments over time, and to create an Integrated Professional Teaching Portfolio that showcases their knowledge, skills and contributions to others. Lessons learned during the preliminary phase include the importance of garnering support of adopters, providing sufficient support in order for faculty and students to gain the skills necessary to produce meaningful and dynamic portfolios, and transitioning from multiple ePortfolios to a uniform platform that works across programs.

Chapter 10

This chapter starts with the description of LeMill which is an Open Source Educational Resources (OER) repository where the emphasis has been placed on designing a service to meet the actual needs of teachers preparing for classes. The development of LeMill has utilized open, collaborative, and iterative design methods and many features have been refined or redesigned during the process. Emphasis on design work has helped LeMill avoid and fix problems that are generally problematic for OER repositories because of their origins as learning object repositories. This project is a good example for those who are developing open source projects as it shows how a system flexible and open for formative assessment data provide continuous improvements to the system.

Chapter 11

Swanson, Early and Baumann start with a discussion of second language instruction and some of the barriers that hinder students' oral language performance. Along the same lines, authors argue that many times educators in second language classrooms scramble to squeeze the most out of every minute in the classroom for instructional purposes while trying to increase student achievement. The chapter continues with the presentation of three free and open source software options and findings from two studies of focusing on the use of Audacity which indicates multiple benefits for both teachers and students. The authors conclude with a demonstration of using Audacity for oral language assessment and discuss its implications for the world language classroom.

Chapter 12

James Laffey, University of Missouri, USA
Matthew Schmidt, University of Missouri, USA
Christopher Amelung, Yale University, USA

This chapter first describes how FOSS enables transforming E-Learning from a potentially limiting and constricted framing of the education experience to an emergent and social experience. This chapter identifies several key elements of the FOSS model that position open source initiatives to contribute to the emergent and social nature of experience in E-Learning. The authors also describe several challenges to developing FOSS in a community of educators for E-Learning. These elements and challenges are demonstrated in a brief case report about the development of an open source software system called Context-aware Activity Notification System or CANS.

Chapter 13

Dilek Karahoca, Bahcesehir University, Turkey
Adem Karahoca, Bahcesehir University, Turkey
Ilker Yengin, University of Nebraska-Lincoln, USA
Huseyin Uzunboylu, Near East University, Northern Cyprus

The chapter address the developmental stages and design of the implementation cycles in the Computer Assisted Active Learning System (CALS) for the History of Civilization (HOC) courses at the College of Engineering at Bahcesehir University in Istanbul. The implementation purpose of CALS is to develop a set of tools in a systematic way to enhance students' critical thinking abilities for HOC courses. For this purpose, the authors developed dynamic meta-cognitive maps, movies, flash cards and quiz tools. In order to reduce implementation costs of CALS, open Free and Open Source Software (FOSS) standards and platforms were utilized in the development and implementation cycles. This chapter also highlights the implications of successful development of FOSS for the CALS.

Chapter 14

Lucy Green, Texas Tech University, USA
Fethi Inan, Texas Tech University, USA

Green and İnan report that free and open source Web 2.0 tools present great opportunities for the creation of educational material that reflects best teaching practices for English Language Learners (ELL). To this end, the authors conduct an analysis of second language acquisition (SLA) research that identify the most common components of effective second language teaching practices. They, then, focus on the characteristics of Web 2.0 technologies that might be used to promote educational activities and opportunities that embody effective SLA pedagogical practices while meeting the unique instructional needs of ELL students.

Preface

Technology has become increasingly essential to all aspects of our society, including educational institutions. Today most K-20 schools know the importance of providing students with the skills that are required in the digital age we are living in. However, because commercial or propriety software is so costly, many schools are not able to afford it. Free and open source software is the best solution to this problem.

Open source software is computer software, whose source code is available under a software license that is in the public domain. This permits users to use, edit, and improve the software, and to redistribute it in modified or unmodified forms. Pioneered by Richard M. Stallman, free software was developed in the General Public License (GNU) Project that aimed at developing a Unix-like operating system. Free software is similar in concept to open source, and it refers to the philosophy that freedom users have on accessing, modifying, and redistributing the software. Today, these two terms are used together as Free and Open Source Software or FOSS. Some of the FOSS applications commonly used in education are, but not limited to, Elgg, Moodle, Sakai, Open Office, Drupal, Flickr, YouTube, Audacity, Gimp, and various blog and Wiki programs.

Open source software develops in a community of individuals or companies. Because of the importance of user participation and contribution to the development of the software, no discrimination against individuals or groups is allowed, and users are considered as co-developers. This feature also allows open source software to continually evolve. Unlike beta-testing, open source programs are not rolled out when "perfected".

Use of FOSS in education has increased significantly in the last decade. Thompson (2007) thinks that part of the reason can be found in the Net Generation. "Most "social networking sites such as MySpace and Facebook have had a particularly strong influence in the lives of millions of students" (Thompson, 2007, ¶6). It is a fact that most "students today arrive at their universities as experienced multi-taskers, accustomed to using text messaging, telephones, and e-mail while searching the Internet and watching television" (Roberts, 2005 as cited in Thompson, 2007, ¶8). Moreover, use of FOSS encourages students to be active participants in the teaching and learning process while giving them control in their learning. Since open source encourages user-generated content, students are more actively involved in creating and broadcasting information than in the past.

The implications of free and open software are even more striking for E-Learning. While virtual learning spaces are more prevalent in E-Learning, individual students become the center of E-Instruction; changing the focus from institution to learner. Students adapt distance technologies to meet their needs, rather than adapting to the technologies. A new form of distance education promotes "loosely coupled social software tools, mixed-and-matched and combined together to support online learning communities" (Ozkan & McKenzie, 2007). Thus, FOSS also asserts alternative pedagogies such as constructivism and connectivism which focus on learner-centric online communities rather than E-Learning courses which are more expensive and cumbersome. Traditional E-learning courses that focus on selected content, timetables, and testing become networked-environments where online learners participate in a variety of communities.

Although use of free and open source programs in education has the potential to transform the teaching and learning environment, there is little research on how this can be done. While technologies are readily available for everyone to use, much more attention should be devoted to FOSS pedagogy. The major purpose of this book is to provide information on the possible ways of using FOSS in the context of E-Learning. More specifically, this book will be of value to those who are interested in:

- A review of open and free software that is used in E-Learning,
- An examination of pedagogy behind FOSS and how that is applied to E-Learning,
- A discussion of best practices for FOSS through examples and case studies along with the guidelines for instructors and E-Learning designers who use FOSS, and
- A discussion of opportunities as well as challenges in the use of FOSS.

How this Book is Organized

There are fourteen chapters in this book. Each of the chapters addresses a different aspect of FOSS for E-Learning. The ideas and methods in this book are presented by a number of authors who try to bridge the gap in the literature between teaching and learning and FOSS.

In Chapter 1 entitled, *"Web 2.0 Technologies in E-Learning"*, Köse starts with explaining free and open source software as they apply to Web 2.0 technologies for E-Learning. He argues that Web 2.0 technologies revolutionize E-Learning by emphasizing user control for more personal, social and flexible web contents. He provides definitions of major concepts in FOSS and presents examples from online learning environments. He concludes with a discussion of the future of the Web, including Web 3.0 and Web 4.0 technologies.

Chapter 2, *"What's all the FOSS? How Freedom and Openness is Changing the Face of Our Educational Landscape"* by Huett, Sharp, and Huett starts with a brief history and a summary of FOSS definition and philosophy. The authors then examine the current literature on the use of Free and Open Source software in education with a particular focus on the promise of E-Learning and emerging technologies to positively shape our educational future. The authors also discuss philosophical, financial, practical, and pedagogical considerations that prompt educators to select free and open source software over propriety software. In conclusion, they discuss the important role FOSS will play in the future with open learning.

Chapter 3, *"Lessons from Constructivist Theories, Open Source Technology, and Student Learning"* by Schrynemakers, discusses the connections and synergy between constructivist learning theory, open source technologies and student learning. She argues that these connections are problematic as there aren't meaningful links between the first two areas. Therefore, she examines knowledge acquisition process in the 21st century, and then discusses the process of dialectic where learners investigate the truth through discussion. Intrinsic to this discussion is the impact of technology on those interested in pursuing teaching and learning through open source platforms. For example, how has technology enhanced or decreased the dialogue in education? She then follows the linkages between constructivism and open source to look at how both link up to provide support and pedagogical assistance to student learning. The chapter concludes with examples of how the author has integrated constructivist philosophies with open source technology to establish a collaborative and effective learning environment for higher education students.

In Chapter 4, *"Higher Education and FOSS for E-Learning: The Role of Organizational Sub-Cultures in Enterprise-Wide"*, van Rooij examines the issue of FOSS adoption in U.S. institutions of higher education, where campus-wide deployment of FOSS for E-Learning lags far behind adoption for technical infrastructure applications. In this chapter, van Rooij argues that the gap between the advocacy for FOSS teaching and learning applications and the enterprise-wide deployment of FOSS for E-Learning is a consequence of the divergent perspectives of two organizational sub-cultures – the technologist and the academic – and the extent to which those sub-cultures are likely to embrace FOSS. The author concludes with a few suggestions: collaborative needs analysis/assessment prior to a go/no go adoption decision; and broad dissemination of total cost of ownership (TCO) data by institutions already deploying FOSS for E-Learning enterprise-wide.

In Chapter 5, *"Open and Shared Educational Resources: A Collaborative Strategy for Advancing E-Learning Communities: A Case Exemplified by Curriki"*, Kurshan, Schreiber and Levy, argue that a growing number of education stakeholders are finding that applying an open source approach to content development provides an extraordinary opportunity to change the existing curricula paradigm and expand access to quality learning and the free exchange of knowledge. The authors explore the increased adoption of open and shared educational resources (OSER), using a case study, Curriki, that extends the model further by providing an integrated learning environment and resource repository that is centered on a culture of collective participation.

Chapter 6, *"Developing a New, Dynamic, and Responsive Institutional Online Learning Environment using Open Source Software: A Case Study of a Large Australian University"* by Buchan, provides a case study from an Australian university, who adopted the open source software, Sakai, as the foundation for the University's new, integrated Online Learning Environment called CSU Interact. In this chapter, Buchan discusses her University's gradual implementation of Sakai course management system first as a pilot project then as a choice of entire University's E-Learning system. She then outlines some of the challenges and successes of the project management methodology and processes which oversaw the successful large-scale implementation of an open-source courseware management solution at the institutional level. In conclusion, Buchan discusses the pedagogical advantages of adopting an open source learning management system as well as the significance of investing human and financial resources into such E-Learning system.

Chapter 7, *"Building Open Learning Environment for Software Engineering Students"*, Khoroshilov, Kuliamin, Petrenko, Petrenko, and Rubanov discuss principles of open education and possibilities of implementing these principles for software engineering education on the base of open source software development projects. They present the example of a "Software Engineering" course provided to students of the System Programming sub-faculties of the two Russian top-ranked universities, Moscow State University and Moscow Institute of Physics and Technology.

In the Chapter 8, *"Data Mining User Activity in FOSS/Open Learning Management Systems"*, McGrath discusses usage analysis facilities, as being one of the special considerations when adopting an open source course management system. In his study, McGrath examines how user activity tracking challenges are being met with data mining techniques, in four very different open learning management systems: ATutor, LON-CAPA, Moodle and Sakai. He concludes that as open systems mature in the use of educational data mining, they potentially move closer to the long-sought goal of achieving more interactive, personalized, adaptive learning environments online on a broad scale.

Chapter 9, *"Implementing an Open Source ePortfolio in Higher Education: Lessons Learned Along the Way"* by Brunvard, Luera and Marra, describes the identification of goals, selection of an Open Source

Platform, and the initial implementation stages of an Integrative Knowledge ePortfolio Process (which has both pedagogy and tools) at a midwestern University School of Education. Faculty and students are using the Integrative ePortfolio approach to reflect on, connect, and document their learning and accomplishments over time, and to create an Integrated Professional Teaching Portfolio that showcases their knowledge, skills and contributions to others. Lessons learned during the preliminary phase include the importance of garnering support of adopters, providing sufficient support in order for faculty and students to gain the skills necessary to produce meaningful and dynamic portfolios, and transitioning from multiple ePortfolios to a uniform platform that works across programs.

Chapter 10, *"LeMill: A Case for User-Centered Design and Simplicity in OER Repositories"* by Toikkanen, Purma and Leinonen, starts with the description of LeMill which is an Open Source Educational Resources (OER) repository where the emphasis has been placed on designing a service to meet the actual needs of teachers preparing for classes. The development of LeMill has utilized open, collaborative, and iterative design methods and many features have been refined or redesigned during the process. Emphasis on design work has helped LeMill avoid and fix problems that are generally problematic for OER repositories because of their origins as learning object repositories. This project is a good example for those who are developing open source projects as it shows how a system flexible and open for formative assessment data provide continuous improvements to the system.

Chapter 11, *"What Audacity! Decreasing Student Anxiety while Increasing Instructional Time"* by Swanson, Early and Baumann, starts with a discussion of second language instruction and some of the barriers that hinder students' oral language performance. Along the same lines, authors argue that many times educators in second language classrooms scramble to squeeze the most out of every minute in the classroom for instructional purposes while trying to increase student achievement. The chapter continues with the presentation of three free and open source software options and findings from two studies of focusing on the use of Audacity which indicates multiple benefits for both teachers and students. The authors conclude with a demonstration of using Audacity for oral language assessment and discuss its implications for the world language classroom.

Chapter 12, *"Open for Social: How Open Source Software for E-Learning can Take a Turn to the Social"*, Laffey, Schmidt, and Amelung, first describes how FOSS enables transforming E-Learning from a potentially limiting and constricted framing of the education experience to an emergent and social experience. This chapter identifies several key elements of the FOSS model that position open source initiatives to contribute to the emergent and social nature of experience in E-Learning. The authors also describe several challenges to developing FOSS in a community of educators for E-Learning. These elements and challenges are demonstrated in a brief case report about the development of an open source software system called Context-aware Activity Notification System or CANS (http://cansaware.com).

Chapter 13, *"Computer Assisted Active Learning System Development for The History of Civilization E-learning Courses by Using Free Open Source Software Platforms"* by Karahoca, Karahoca and Yengin, address the developmental stages and design of the implementation cycles in the Computer Assisted Active Learning System (CALS) for the History of Civilization (HOC) courses at the College of Engineering at Bahcesehir University in Istanbul. The implementation purpose of CALS is to develop a set of tools in a systematic way to enhance students' critical thinking abilities for HOC courses. For this purpose, the authors developed dynamic meta-cognitive maps, movies, flash cards and quiz tools. In order to reduce implementation costs of CALS, open Free and Open Source Software (FOSS) standards and platforms were utilized in the development and implementation cycles. This chapter also highlights the implications of successful development of FOSS for the CALS.

Chapter 14, *"Web 2.0 as Potential E-Learning Tools for K-12 English Language Learners"*, by Green and İnan, report that free and open source Web 2.0 tools present great opportunities for the creation of educational material that reflects best teaching practices for English Language Learners (ELL). To this end, the authors conduct an analysis of second language acquisition (SLA) research that identify the most common components of effective second language teaching practices. They, then, focus on the characteristics of Web 2.0 technologies that might be used to promote educational activities and opportunities that embody effective SLA pedagogical practices while meeting the unique instructional needs of ELL students.

It is my hope that the ideas presented in this book show our passion and belief in FOSS for E-Learning. As FOSS mature, it presents many opportunities for those students who are less advantaged in getting a quality education. In addition to bridging existing digital inequities, I also hope that we as educators can begin to start infusing FOSS into the curriculum in meaningful ways in our E-Learning environments that are open to all.

REFERENCES

Özkan, B.C. & McKenzie, B. (2007). Open social software applications and their impact on distance education. In Proceedings of E-Learn World Conference on E-Learning on Corporate, Government, Health Care and Higher Education 2007. (7310-7312) Norfolk, VA: AACE.

Thompson, J. (2007, April-May). Is education 1.0 ready for Web 2.0 students? Innovate 3(4). Retrieved from Internet March 2, 2010 http://www.innovateonline.info/pdf/vol3_issue4/Is_Education_1.0_Ready_for_Web_2.0_Students_.pdf

Betül C. Özkan Czerkawski, Editor
The University of Arizona South, USA

Section 1
Introduction to Free and Open Source Software

Chapter 1
Web 2.0 Technologies in E-Learning

Utku Köse
Afyon Kocatepe Unviersity, Turkey

ABSTRACT

Web 2.0 is the second face of World Wide Web with its revolutionary features and technologies. Web 2.0 takes users to a dynamic environment, where they can build or control more personal, social and flexible web contents. These functions attract educators' attention and enable them to use Web 2.0 technologies in E-Learning activities. As a result of using Web 2.0 technologies, a new generation learning form: E-Learning 2.0 comes to life. This chapter will discuss the roles of Web 2.0 in E-Learning, analyze free and open source E-Learning 2.0 applications, and discuss the future of the Web. The features of Web 2.0 and its popular technologies will be explained first. Later, the roles of Web 2.0 technologies in E-Learning activities and E-Learning 2.0 will be discussed. Following that, free and open source E-Learning 2.0 applications will be analyzed. At last, new generations within the future, Web 3.0 and Web 4.0 will be discussed.

INTRODUCTION

Ways of using the World Wide Web personally and professionally are rapidly changing with the advanced web technologies in recent years. These technologies transform the classical Web into an interactive, dynamic platform and form a new trend in web developing and web designing. Thus, computer users find themselves in a new genera-

tion of the Web. The term "Web 2.0" is used to define this new form of the digital world. Today, the popularity of Web 2.0 and the development of new web applications continue to improve at a rapid rate.

There are many sophisticated Web 2.0 applications that provide collaborative working or social networking platforms for computer users. Web 2.0 technologies also can be used to create personal and interactive technologies or applications. Blogs, wikis, file sharing sites and podcast-

DOI: 10.4018/978-1-61520-917-0.ch001

ing applications are some of Web 2.0 applications that are used all over the world. These applications can be used in different areas to achieve better working standards.

In the last few years, one of the most effective, but least hyped, uses of Web 2.0 technologies is E-Learning (MacManus, 2007). Education activities can be performed easily and efficiently with Web 2.0. Teachers and students embrace some Web 2.0 technologies such as blogging and podcasting. Although not designed specifically for use in education activities, these technologies help teachers and students make E-Learning far more personal, social, and flexible (MacManus, 2007). A new term: "E-Learning 2.0" is used to refer to new ways of thinking about E-Learning activities inspired by the emergence of Web 2.0 (Downes, 2005).

In this chapter, Web 2.0 technologies, their use in E-Learning activities and the free open source applications that are used for educational activities in E-Learning 2.0 will be discussed. The objectives of the chapter are:

- To discuss how Web 2.0 technologies can be incorporated into E-Learning activities.
- To discuss E-Learning 2.0, which is a new form of E-Learning.
- Analyzing some free and open source applications that are used in E-Learning 2.0.
- To discuss the future of Web technologies (Web 3.0 and Web 4.0) in E-Learning activities.

NEW GENERATION OF WWW: WEB 2.0

Web 2.0 is an innovative technology that provides a novel way of learning to the old web platform. It has been defined as the second generation of the World Wide Web. It is important to explain what the terms Web 2.0 and Web 2.0 technologies mean before getting more detailed information on

Web 2.0, and discussing its use in the E-Learning environment.

What is Web 2.0?

Web 2.0 is a word coined and used in an article titled "Fragmented Future" by Darcy DiNucci (1999). Later, it was also used by Tim O'Reilly at O'Reilly Media conference, in 2004 (O'Reilly, 2005; Graham, 2005). Now, the term is mostly associated with Tim O'Reilly. Web 2.0 refers to a new trend after standard web. It is also defined as the second generation of web development and web design (Krish, 2009). One way of explaining the change to Web 2.0 is comparing Web 2.0 with Web 1.0. Web 1.0 is a term that is used to specify the state of the World Wide Web that was used before Web 2.0. In Web 1.0, a few authors were providing content for a wide audience of relatively passive readers. But with Web 2.0, the web is considered to be a platform to generate, re-purpose, and consume shared content. With Web 2.0 technologies, the web also becomes a platform for social networking that enables groups of users to socialize, collaborate, and work with each other. This function is mostly based on existing web data-sharing mechanisms being used to share content, in conjunction with the use of web protocol based interfaces to web applications that

Figure 1. Web 1.0 and Web 2.0

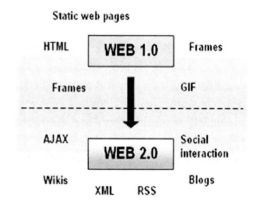

allow flexibility in reusing data and the adoption of communications protocols that allow specialized data exchange (Franklin, & van Harmelen, 2007).

Web 2.0 web sites allow users to take an active part in building and controlling interactive platforms or web site content over the Internet. In Web 2.0, the roles of users are not confined with receiving data from traditional, static web pages. On the contrary, they are encouraged to add or remove data for user-friendly, interactive web pages. On the other hand, they are allowed to create a platform for social interaction or collaborative work.

Web 2.0 Technologies

There are many popular and wide-spread Web 2.0 technologies and applications. Many communities and hosted services like blogs, wikis, podcasting, social-networking and file (video, picture…etc.) sharing sites have been developed and evaluated (Baytak, 2009). To understand Web 2.0 and its technologies better, these communities, services and other technologies that form Web 2.0 must be examined.

Blogs (Weblogs)

A blog is a type of web site that usually includes some data entries, presented in reverse chronological order (Ebner, 2007). The word "blog" comes from a short definition of the word "weblog: a log of the web". The term weblog is coined by Jorn Barger in 1997 (Safran, Helic, & Gütl, 2007). Its short form: blog is coined by Peter Merholz in 1999 (Merholz, 1999; Kottke, 2003). There are some other words derived from blog. "Blogger" is used for the owner of the blog site and writing a contribution is called as "blogging". Another word "blogosphere" is used for defining the collective community of all blogs (Ebner, 2007). Blogs are mostly used as personal online diaries. But they are also used as platforms that provide information or commentary about specific subjects. Blogs

often attract a large and dedicated readership. Because they engage people in knowledge sharing, reflection, and debate (Kamel Boulos, Maramba, & Wheeler, 2006).

Blogs can be categorized according to their subjects or the content they include. They can be explained as below (Wikipedia, 2009):

- **Personal blogs:** It is the most frequent one. It can be a digital diary or a commentary provided by any user.
- **Corporate blogs:** Blogs that are used for business purposes. They are used internally to enhance the communication and culture in a corporation or externally for marketing, branding or public relations purposes.
- **Blogs used for a media:** Blogs can be categorized according to media type. Blogs using videos are called as vlogs. Linklog is the term used for blogs that include only links. Blog sites that include only photos are called photoblogs. There many other types of blogs that are categorized according to the type of media that is used.
- **Blogs by genre:** Blogs that focus on a specific subject can be categorized by their subject names. Examples include travel blogs, fashion blogs, game blogs, political blogs and music blogs.

Figure 2. Blogs can be used as personal diaries on the Internet

RSS (Really Simple Syndication) Services

RSS is an advanced Web 2.0 technology that is used to get new updates about a blog site without opening its homepage. The name RSS is the short definition of "Really Simple Syndication". RSS is not only used for blogs but also used for news sites, product or organization information sites and other sites that update its content regularly. RSS systems include an XML code, which scans the content of a site for updates and then broadcasts the updates to all subscribed users through a feed. In the past users had to bookmark websites in browsers and then open the site again to see what had been added. Now users can use a RSS Reader program or web service to get all the updated contents of their favorite web sites. In order to read the content of a web site, users must enter its URL address to the RSS Reader program. This can be done by clicking on RSS icons that most web sites have.

Wikis

Wiki is a popular Web 2.0 technology among computer users. The word "Wiki" means "fast" in Hawaiian language and it can also be expended as "What I Know Is". The concept of Wiki was first introduced by Bo Leuf and Ward Cunningham in 1995 (Ebner, 2007). Curringham wanted to develop an easy-to-use knowledge management system enabling effective and efficient online collaboration (Ebner, 2007). Wiki is an online system that allows users to create, edit, revise or link articles (Ebner, 2007). It is often used to create collaborative websites and to power community websites. The collaborative encyclopedia Wikipedia is one of the best-known wikis (Ferret, 2006). More than 4 million articles in 100 different languages, outnumbering all other encyclopedias is a magnificent success story (Ebner, 2007).

Both Wikis and blogs have appeared about the same time and both of them offer an easy publishing tool for disseminating information as well as getting feedback to and from the public. So, Wikis are often compared to blogs (Parker, & Chao, 2007).

Blogs are used for mostly personal works while Wikis are mainly used for collaborative works. It is easy to share ideas and knowledge with other people, thanks to Wikis. They are used to get every user on the same page to take an active part in the work. Wikis are also effective applications that increase the user's expertise, productivity, and creativity.

Figure 3. Latest news can be received by using RSS services

Figure 4. Collaborative encyclopedias can be developed by using wikis

According to Doyle (2006), there are some differences between Wikis and blogs; among them being the way they organize their information, the number of users, and what the users intend to achieve. These differences are:

- Wikis typically organize information by using topics while blogs organize information in reverse, chronological order. Since they are reverse chronologically ordered, information in blogs is more of a historical record and rarely changes. Topics in Wikis are expected to evolve and often expand into something of a permanent knowledge base.
- The reverse chronological ordering of blogs makes it difficult to find all postings on a specific topic, and to browse through all postings on that topic. On the other hand, Wikis don't show as easily when information was documented or in what order, but it does show what information is related and make it easy to browse (Woolf, 2006).
- Wikis receive feedback by allowing the public to edit topics directly while blogs provide a mechanism to take readers' comments.
- Wikis encourage knowledge sharing around topics while blogs allow sharing of spontaneous ideas.
- Blogs are better communication tools for disseminating information to people and for enabling feedback while keeping the original text intact. Wikis are better tools when information is intended to be modified and enhanced as part of a collaborative effort (Mader, 2006).

File Sharing Sites

File sharing sites are used to upload, view and share files like pictures, videos and sounds. There are also many web sites that store different file types. A number of developed sharing web sites has been improved especially in the last few years. File sharing sites attract users with their fast and practical file – information sharing roles.

Podcasts

A podcast is a series of digital media files, usually either digital, audio, or video, which is made available for download via the web (Dean, 2008). The term podcast is produced by combining two words: broadcasting and Apple's iPod. Podcasting means broadcasting audio or videos files as online through a subscription feed like RSS. These files can be played on an iPod or MP3 player with podcasting features.

Podcasting began to run in late 2004, though the ability to distribute audio and video files easily has been around since before the dawn of the Internet. Many individuals and groups contributed to the emergence and popularity of podcasts (Wikipedia, 2009).

Podcasting gives many advantages that users can start to podcasting to all over the world, by using only necessary software and a microphone. It is also possible to broadcast radio or television via podcast.

Social Networking Services

Social networking services are used to create online communities where people can communicate and interact with other people. Many social networking services are web based and provide a variety of ways for people to interact, such as e-mail and instant messaging services. Social networking services have encouraged new ways to communicate and share information. Today, these services are growing fast and used regularly by millions of people (Owyang, 2009; Ortutay, 2009).

While social networking services share the basic purpose of online interaction and communication, some specific goals and patterns of usage vary significantly across different services. On the

Figure 5. Social networking sites encourage new ways to communicate

other hand, most of the popular social networking services share similar features: through the site a person offers a "profile" to other people to persue, with the intention of contacting or being contacted by others, to meet new friends or to date, find new jobs and receive or provide recommendations (Gross, & Acquisti, 2005).

Social Bookmarking

Social bookmarking services allow users to bookmark web pages and tag those records with significant words (tags) that describe the pages being recorded. Users can search for bookmarked items by likely tags. Since items have been deemed worthy of being bookmarked and classified with one or more tags, social bookmarking services can be more effective than other technologies like search engines. Users can find other users who use the same tag and who are interested in similar topics. In some social bookmarking systems, users with common interests can be added to an individual's own network to enable easy watching of the other users' tagging activity for interesting items (Franklin, & van Harmelen, 2007).

Collaborative Editing Services

Collaborative editing services provide collaborative working environments where users can control and edit same documents simultaneously. Because most of these services do not allow users to communicate with synchronous voice or video, using third party systems that provide synchronous communication are often needed to coordinate editing activities (Franklin, & van Harmelen, 2007).

Web Widgets and AJAX Applications

A web widget is a type of application that can be used for different purposes on a blog or web page. Scrolling news lines, voting polls and personal calendars are some kind of web widgets. These applications are programmed by using programming languages like DHTML and JavaScript. Web widgets are mostly used personally. But they aren't just for personal use. Businesses also use widgets to track visitors that come to the web site and provide content or information for visitors (Nations, 2009).

AJAX (Asynchronous JavaScript and XML) is a term that defines using some programming techniques like JavaScript, XML and HTML in a cooperation to develop web applications. It is a programming technique rather than web developing or designing. It is possible to create pages that respond to a user's instruction without reloading itself, thanks to AJAX. This feature allows programmers to develop interactive and fast web applications that can not be developed with Web 1.0.

WEB 2.0 AND E-LEARNING

Today, Web 2.0 technologies and applications like blogs, wikis and podcasts are widely used in educational activities. Because of their easy use and rapidity of deployment, they offer the opportunity for powerful information sharing and easy collaboration (Kamel Boulos, Maramba, & Wheeler, 2006).

As a result of combining E-Learning with Web 2.0 technologies, a new form: E-Learning 2.0 is used in education. Web 2.0 technologies in E-Learning will be explained before discussing about E-Learning 2.0.

Using Web 2.0 Technologies in E-Learning

In E-Learning, Web 2.0 and its technologies are mostly used to take advantage of Web 2.0 and ensure successful learning and teaching activities take place. Some technologies like blogs, wikis and podcasting take active roles directly in E-Learning while others are used as extra tools in different educational systems.

Blogs are widely used in E-Learning activities. They are used by teachers to support teaching and learning activities made on the web platform. A general learning community can be created by connecting different blogs. Blogs enable students and teachers to share their own opinions with other class members and support them with commentary and answers given to questions. Additionally, students can increase their writing abilities by using blogs. Blogs also allow students to control their own learning process. Students' motivations can also be increased with the aid of blogs.

Generally, blogs are useful teaching and learning tools because they provide effective environments for students to reflect and publish their ideas. Blogs also provide opportunities for feedback and potential scaffolding of new ideas in that written ideas can be commented on. Furthermore, blogs come with the hyperlink feature, which can be used by students to understand the relational basis of knowledge, knowledge building and definition making (Ferdig, & Trammell, 2004).

According to Ferdig and Trammell (2004), there are four important benefits of using blogs in E-Learning. These benefits are:

- Using blogs helps students to become subject-matter experts. According to Blood (2002), there is a three-step process involved in blogging: scouring, filtering and posting. The user visits multiple web sites relevant to his or her topic to find information they are studying. The user must then filter the results to post the "best" content for readers. With this process, users are exposed to vast amounts of information on their given topic, even if they do not comment on everything they find. Doing this regularly at least once a week creates a repetitive process where the user builds an ever-growing knowledge base on particular topics.

- Using blogs increases student interest and ownership in learning. Technology plays an important role as a motivating tool because of its newness. Contents of blogs are novels for students because they study specific topics that are important to them. Students direct their own learning while receiving information and feedback from other users. They also take ownership of their learning activities.

- Using blogs gives students legitimate chances to participate. While using blogs, students quickly learn that posted content can be read by those other than the teacher and their classmates. Blogs allows the world to grade students and provide encouragement or feedback on their writings.

- Using blogs provides opportunities for diverse perspectives, both within and outside of the classroom. Mainly due to time and curriculum constraints, not every student gets to share his or her ideas in a traditional classroom. Blogs allow all students to participate in a discussion. By using blogs, the classroom also extends from the physical constraints of those who fit in the room and are registered to a limitless international audience.

As previously stated, Wikis are used to view stored articles based on specific subjects. Furthermore, Wikis enable users to add new articles or edit other users' additions. So, Wikis are successful technologies for creating online communities and collaboration environments.

Wikis can be used to provide computer supported collaborative learning. This learning method is the development of collaboration by means of technology to augment education and research. It promotes peer interaction and ensures the sharing and distribution of knowledge and expertise amongst a group of learners (Lipponen, 2002). In collaborative learning, students are the center of learning exercises and they can build on their foundational knowledge (Myers, 1991). An effective platform that ensures online collaborative learning for students can be formed with E-Learning activities.

According to Su and Beaumont (2008), some of the advantages of Wikis are:

- Giving and receiving quick feedback from teachers and other students affects the students' learning experience in a positive way. By using Wikis, it is possible to give feedback to students' work while it is still in the progress.
- It is easy to view other students' works on a typical Wiki platform. Students can learn from others' works in terms of organizing the structure of the writing, putting arguments together, and avoiding similar mistakes other students have made.
- Wiki has tracking facilities on the creation of each Wiki page. For the purpose of assessment, teachers can easily tell when a student's work was completed against the deadline. The history page located on Wikis can help to identify the original student author on a piece of work in the system, which has discouraged plagiarism among students.

- According Salmon's E-Learning model (2006), at the later stages of the learning process students interact with each other actively and collaboratively contributing to knowledge construction. The nature of the Wiki encourages the students to contribute to their own or other students' learning. So, expression of ideas and opinions are encouraged by Wikis.
- Wikis help to promote a sense of authorship. The term authorship means "an explicit way of assigning responsibility and giving credit for intellectual work" (Harvard University, 1999). Students' works on a Wiki system is subjected to public viewing. Authorship is seen by students as a positive way to avoid plagiarism.

Podcasting is another important Web 2.0 technology that is used in E-Learning activities. With podcasting students can begin to learn activities anytime, anywhere. Podcasting also allows students to educate themselves in the most suitable and successful way they choose. In addition to E-Learning, podcasts are also successful at mobile learning (M-Learning) activities. Today, many educators consider podcasting as an exciting learning paradigm of impressive pedagogical potential (Brittain, Glowacki, Van Ittersum, & Johnson, 2006; Cambell, 2005; Cebeci, & Tekdal, 2006; Lazzari, & Betella 2007). By using podcasting technology, it is possible to create learning materials like course lectures, interviews, and workshops reports to meet student's learning or teaching needs (Brittain, Glowacki, Van Ittersum, & Johnson, 2006). Recording lectures as audio format and using them in the learning process provides many advantages to students. Lecture records allow students to control the audio file and rewind it for listening to important parts of lectures again. Furthermore, some students find listening to a subject more effective than reading it in a book (Matthews, 2006).

Watching lesson videos allows students to learn easily with the aid of visual elements. Additionally, students can listen to the audio that is playing on the video. It is important that visually and auditory impaired students find audio recordings or video files more effective and useful in learning activities.

According to Thacker's studies (2007) with Edirisingha and Salmon (2007), some important advantages of podcasting in E-Learning and general learning were identified:

- Podcasting can be integrated to E-Learning activities perfectly.
- Podcasting supplements existing material and resources with a portable and remotely accessible source of information to ensure a high quality E-Learning experience.
- Podcasting allows educators to create digital forms of education materials to provide for students in E-Learning activities.
- Podcasting enables students to replay and review information so that lessons can be learned more easily.
- It is easy and fast to develop E-Learning materials with podcasting.
- Podcasting allows transmitting lesson materials to students who did not take part in past education activities.
- Podcasting provides flexible curriculum pathways to encourage student participation and facilitate success.
- Podcasting allows users to access lesson materials anytime, anywhere.
- Audio and video files that are used in podcasting are more effective in learning activities than reading lesson materials.

The features and functions of traditional E-Learning have changed rapidly with using Web 2.0 technologies in E-Learning activities. Eventually, E-Learning has transformed into a new learning form that includes Web 2.0 technologies. The new form is called as E-Learning 2.0.

E-Learning 2.0

E-Learning 2.0 is a term that is used to define the new form of E-Learning that includes Web 2.0 technologies. The term was first used in an article written by Stephen Downes in 2005. E-Learning 2.0 can be defined more clearly as "the term, which is used to refer to new ways of thinking about E-Learning inspired by the emergence of Web 2.0" (Downes, 2005).

Before E-Learning 2.0, developed systems were based on instructional packets that were delivered to students using Internet technologies and learning strategies were determined by teachers (Wikipedia, 2009). But E-Learning 2.0 allows students to use Web 2.0 technologies like blogs, wikis and podcasts to take an active role in the learning process and determine their own learning strategies according to their interests and needs. Students' learning experiences are based mostly on social interaction and sharing with E-Learning 2.0. Another advantage of E-Learning 2.0 is that shared, remixed, repurposed, and distributed learning contents are emphasized by E-Learning 2.0, rather than being based on a model where the teacher gives learning content to the student (Clarey, 2008).

Web 2.0 technologies are suitable for social interaction and collaborative works. E-learning 2.0 is built around collaboration and it assumes that knowledge is socially constructed. According to E-Learning 2.0, learning activities take place through conversations about lessons and grounded interactions about problems and actions. It is claimed that one of the best ways for learning something is to teach it to others (Brown, & Adler, 2008).

FREE AND OPEN SOURCE E-LEARNING 2.0 APPLICATIONS

There are lots of free and open source E-Learning 2.0 applications and services that can be used by

Figure 6. E-Learning 2.0 and some important features

both teachers and students. Some of these applications and services will be explained under five categories: General purpose E-Learning applications and services, education blogging services, file sharing services, social networking services and special-purpose applications and services.

General Purpose E-Learning Applications and Services

Applications and services in this category contain more than one Web 2.0 technologies and E-Learning materials to provide E-Learning 2.0 experience for users. Some of these applications are listed below:

Eduslide.Open Source

Eduslide.Open Source is a learning management system that was created by The Virtual Training Company located in Virginia, USA. It is possible for teachers to share their knowledge by creating custom courses with Eduslide. Eduslide has many features to create an online learning community. It has different tools such as Wikis, forums, chats and quizzes. Wikis, forums and chat tools can be used for collaboration between teachers and students. Teachers can use integrated project

management tools to control students' learning process. It is also possible for teachers to create lesson objectives for task based learning activities. Eduslide also provides invitation based learning for users. The latest version of the application can be downloaded from the web site address: www.eduslide.org

WIZIQ

WiZiQ is an E-Learning 2.0 platform, where teachers and students can perform live lesson activities. In other words, WiZiQ can be used for creating virtual classrooms on the Internet. Users can interact online by using documents, visual elements, presentations, audio files and video files provided in virtual classrooms. They can also use some features like file sharing, live audio, video communication, and online whiteboard that come with the virtual classroom environments.

WiZiQ is also a social networking platform, where users can search for users that have similar interests and communicate with them to share lesson contents, files and learning experiences on the system. It is also a chance for creating communities that belong to specific subjects and performing activities with the community users.

Yacapaca

Yacapaca is an assessment platform for teachers, which can be used to create, share, set, mark and analyze assessments. It is an E-Learning 2.0 service provided by Chalkface Project Ltd. By using Yacapaca, teachers can create online assessments in specific formats provided by the system. Teachers can use integrated authoring tools to create assessments. Online assessment types provided by the system are:

- Quizzes
- Surveys
- Short and free text tests

- Multiple-choice tests
- E-Portfolios

In addition to creating online assessments, Yacapaca has also some tools for automarking and analyzing assessments. It is also possible to share created assessments with other users on the system. Students can use Yacapaca to create assessments based on a presentation given. Surveys can be used to rate projects developed by students. Furthermore, it is possible for teachers to develop an ongoing project by using E-Portfolio feature.

As a result, Yacapaca is a fast and effective service that allows teachers to create online assessments, grade students and view their statistics. On the other hand, it is some kind of web environment, where students can take tests, submit assignments and receive grades.

KidThing

KidThing is an E-Learning 2.0 application that provides an interactive, colorful and entertaining learning platform for preschool or older age kids. It is a type of software that runs on only Windows operating systems. KidThing can be downloaded from the web site address: www.kidthing.com

KidThing enables parents to download videos, games and some animated learning activity tools for their kids. It is also possible to get free or low-price books from the KidThing system. Additionally, Kids can use the KidThing application to get a secured Internet experience.

KidThing has a simple and fast interface that can be used by kids easily. The interface and some learning materials are designed and developed by using Adobe Flash. KidThing provides an effective and entertaining environment for kids. Provided learning materials like videos, games, animations and books are applicable to kids. Sometimes, well-known foundations make organizations on KidThing to help kids' learning activities and get more learning materials.

Babbel

Babbel is a social language learning community created by Lesson Nine GmbH located in Berlin, Germany. Five different languages can be learned in this service: English, German, French, Italian and Spanish. Babbel is a system that contains Wiki elements.

Babbel has many learning tools that can be used to test reading, writing and listening abilities. Users can write sentences in the chosen language while other users give feedback to the user after checking written sentences for any mistake.

In Babbel, users can search for other users, who have similar interests and want to learn the same language. It is also possible to create communities based on different languages and interests within the system. Another feature that Babbel provides is named as "Tandem Partner". The tandem partner is the user who speaks the language you are learning as a native speaker, and is learning the language that you actually speak.

Palabea

Palabea is another social language learning community where users can learn new languages and communicate with other users. The system is provided in six different languages: English, German, French, Spanish, Chinese and Japanese. Palabea allows for the creating of learning environments for new, different languages that registered users talk. But the importance of these languages in the system is adjusted according to users' additions to Palabea.

Palabea has a fast, simple and user-friendly interface. On this interface, users can execute E-Learning tools easily. These tools allow users to create virtual classrooms, communicate with other users and access to learning materials like podcasts and documents. Some important activities that users can perform on Palabea are:

- Communicating with other users.
- Watching lesson videos, listening to podcasts and reading documents added by other users.
- Uploading and sharing pictures, audio files, video files, and documents.
- Creating virtual classrooms or participating in created ones.
- Organizing lessons.

Education Blogging Services

Services in this category are related to E-Learning 2.0 forms that contain predominantly functions of blogs. Some of these services are:

Edublogs.org

Edublogs.org is a web site that stores many blogs created for teachers, students, academicians, researchers and anyone, who is interested in education, E-Learning. It is possible to create an education blog and share it with other users with Edublogs.org. Blogs created with this service have some different features than other standard blogs on the web because Edublogs.org is improved by educators that know how blogs can be used in teaching and learning activities. While blogging by using Edublogs.org, all posts are automatically spell-checked and can be written by using a complete feature rich editor that allows simple uploading of files and have YouTube, Google Video and more video insertion devices to ensure podcasting.

The most important feature of Edublogs.org is that users can share their knowledge about developing education blogs with other users by using Edublogs.org. This can be done by using the forum or sharing video tutorials. Users can also make collaborative works and help each other for ensuring better education blogs and materials for E-Learning 2.0.

Edmodo 2.0

Edmodo 2.0 is a microblogging platform designed and developed for teachers and students. With Edmodo 2.0, teachers can create some groups for students and combine them in an environment that forms a microblogging network. The term microblogging can be defined as a form of blogging that allows users to send up to 140 character long posts (Williams, 2007).

Edmodo 2.0 comes with many tools that can be used in microblogging activities. The system provides RSS and SMS systems to be used in learning activities. Teachers can post any shared item or content by using RSS feed, thanks to integrated tools in Edmodo 2.0. It is also possible to store lesson files on Edmodo 2.0 system. Teachers can send alerts, events, and assignments to students and create a calendar for future events.

File Sharing Services

This category belongs to services that contain file sharing technologies to be used in E-Learning 2.0 activities. Some of these services are:

Academic Earth

Academic Earth is one of the newest video sharing services that is used for learning specific subjects. It is a website that was launched on March 24, 2009. Academic Earth allows users to watch online video lectures provided by some universities like UC Berkeley, Harvard, MIT, Princeton, Stanford and Yale. Provided videos in the system are categorized in seventeen subject titles as: Astronomy, Biology, Chemistry, Computer Science, Economics, Engineering, English, Entrepreneurship, History, Law, Mathematics, Medicine, Philosophy, Physics, Political Science, Psychology, and Religion. Only lecturers are allowed to add videos in Academic Earth. Users can search for a video belong to a subject by using integrated tools on the interface. It is also possible to search for lecturers and their videos by using system tools. Some videos that can be watched in parts are also provided to users with "Playlist" feature of Academic Earth.

WePapers

WePapers is a file sharing service, where users can search for academic documents or create study groups with other users. WePapers helps users on sharing and expanding their knowledge by using integrated tools. Users can find and download the academic papers that belong to a specific subject. Papers stored on the system are categorized under seven subject titles: Science and engineering, social sciences, art and humanities, computer science, education, health and clinical sciences and agriculture and related sciences. Papers shared on WePapers are also categorized under different titles. These titles define the type of a paper shared. There are eleven paper types: abstract, article, assignment, book, cheatsheet, exam, lecture notes, presentation, research, terms and textbook solutions.

Social Networking Services

This category belongs to the social networking services that enable users for communicating with other users, creating communities or study groups and searching for other users that have similar interests. Some of these services are:

Elgg

Elgg is a social networking service, which was created for education by Curverider Ltd. and open source community. Elgg provides some Web 2.0 technologies such as blogs, file sharing applications, podcasting tools and RSS reader. Users can search for other users by using tag words and create learning communities with them. All stored learning materials can be categorized with tags.

Access permission for learning materials can be adjusted as "public": for all users or "private": for only community users.

The media embedding feature in the system allows users to easily upload their photos, audio, and video files within blog posts, comments and discussion topics. Many different types of files can be imported into Elgg. Elgg also has some tools that can be used for microblogging activities.

Special-Purpose Applications and Services

Applications and services in this category belong to E-Learning 2.0 systems that were developed for special-purposed learning activities. Some of these applications and services are:

TypingWeb

TypingWeb is an online typing tutor that was created by FTW Innovations Inc. Users can test their typing level and learn more about typing by using TypingWeb. The system includes many Web 2.0 technologies that are used for learning activities. According to their typing level, users can take the exercise from the basics of typing to more advanced facets such as problem keys, speed drills, and techniques to reduce the strain that causes Carpal Tunnel syndrome. Some features of TypingWeb are (TypingWeb, 2009):

- Users can use typing courses for beginner, intermediate and advanced levels.
- Users can opt to have lessons e-mailed daily.
- Users can learn to type by typing current news headlines. These types of exercises are updated daily.
- TypingWeb can track users' mistakes and learns most problematic keys. Once enough keys are known, users can enter a custom lesson to work those extra tough letters.

- TypingWeb has a typing test that users can take repeatedly to track their typing progress over time. On this test, users' progress is shown on a graphic.
- TypingWeb provides a printable typing success certificate to users, who successfully completed the typing test five or more times.

Songsterr

Songsterr is a web application which provides an online player for guitar tabs generated by users. It allows users to play well-known songs after learning them from Songsterr. The application has an interface that shows imported tabs with playing functions.

Songsterr allows registered users to search for a song or add a new guitar tab by using the interface. The system has a simple and fast interface that provides an easy-to-use web application for users. Users must prepare their tab in a program named: Guitar Pro to import a new guitar tab to the system. Guitar Pro is a software that has a similar interface with Songsterr. But it has more advanced features to prepare or play guitar tabs. Songsterr can be defined as an online version of Guitar Pro.

Notely

Notely is a web application that can be used by students to organize their learning activities. It is an E-Learning 2.0 application, which was created by a student: Tom Whitson. Notely employs lots of task management tools developed for students. Students can take notes about lessons, organize events, create timetables for education activities and manage their homework by using integrated tools on the system. Some works that students can do on Notely are:

- Creating and organizing timetables for activities.

- Writing and storing notes about lessons.
- Using online notebooks to take notes about lesson activities.
- Organizing works by using To-Do List.
- Organizing homework.

FUTURE OF THE WEB: WEB 3.0 AND WEB 4.0

As a result of rapid improvements, new Web technologies that provide users more advanced and effective Web standards are being developed. It seems that new faces of the Web will make people's daily life simpler and take them to a virtual world, where the physical world can be controlled easier. New Web technologies after Web 2.0 can be defined by using a formula: Web x.x. Nowadays, next generations of the Web: Web 3.0, Web 4.0 and their possible effects on both the physical and digital world are discussed. Their effects on education and E-Learning activities are also an important subject to analyze.

What is Web 3.0?

The term "Web 3.0" can be defined as an evolving extension of the World Wide Web, in which the semantics of information and services on the Web is defined, making it possible for the Web to understand and satisfy the requests of users and machines to use the web contents (Berners-Lee, Hendler, & Lassila, 2001; Herman, 2008). The term "Semantic Web" is also used to define Web 3.0. It is the third generation of the Web, which requires more using of Artificial Intelligence techniques. Web 3.0 derives from Sir Tim Berners-Lee who is the director of World Wide Web Consortium (Herman, 2008).

Web 3.0 technologies comprise a set of design principles, collaborative working groups, and a variety of enabling technologies. Some elements of Web 3.0 are expressed as prospective future possibilities that are yet to be implemented or realized. Other elements are expressed in formal specifications (Herman, 2008). Web 3.0 is all about letting applications and services to understand what the web content means. Since different websites can understand the content coming from other sites, this function of Web 3.0 allows for real data-portability and interoperability. Users can take their web content with them when they go to another web site. Web 3.0 applications and services can understand the meaning of the content and they can work according to users' needs.

Some benefits of Web 3.0 that will be provided to users in the future are:

- Web 3.0 technologies will know users' needs and create interactive platforms according to their needs.
- Information will not be on web pages. They will come in packets of discrete units. Users will merge or cross them according to their needs (Berlinger, 2009).
- Applications and services on the Internet will communicate with each other.
- Information comes to users will be based on tags and search criteria and users will not go anywhere to do their works. They will need only a computer with Internet connection (Berlinger, 2009).
- Information flow will be faster.
- Being on the Internet will be like being on the telephone (Berlinger, 2009).

Using Web 3.0 in E-Learning

In the future, new forms of E-Learning applications and services that include Web 3.0 technologies will be provided for teachers and students. Many Web 2.0 technologies will be transformed into Web 3.0 technologies that will be supported with semantic features.

With Web 3.0, lesson data such as title, time, credits, instructors...etc. and personal data such as education history, learning preferences,

instructional modifications...etc. will become transferable across E-Learning applications and services. This will increase the ability to integrate different applications or services with each other to provide a cross-platform, integrated learning environments. It will also possible to specify students' learning needs with mentioned lesson data and personal data and provide suitable lesson activities and tools for them. There will be an increase in self-organized learning, thanks to Web 3.0 technologies.

E-Learning applications and services will be integrated across devices, with particular emphasis on mobile offerings that fill a void in both frequent off-site, low-commitment interactions. Mobile devices will be more important for E-Learning activities. With Web 3.0, there will need to be ubiquitous access to applications, services and lesson contents, including other users, learning groups and teacher support. As a result of better connectivity through constantly improving line-of-sight (satellite and wireless) networking services, students will have better conditions to take an active part in E-Learning.

For teachers, Web 3.0 applications or services will take data and cooperate to create distributed, adaptive learning environments and especially learning management systems, as well as give information to teachers that can help them scale data-driven, adaptive teaching.

Figure 7. Evolution to the third generation: Web 3.0

15

The Fourth Generation: Web 4.0

Web 4.0 is the fourth generation of World Wide Web after Web 3.0. Almost all features and functions of Web 4.0 are expressed as prospective future possibilities. It is anticipated that Web 4.0 technologies will change all living standards on the world.

The physical world will be connected to a virtual world with Web 4.0. Users will use online operating systems and applications supported with artificial intelligence techniques and more advanced algorithms. Developed applications will have ability to find and correct errors caused on their systems. More effective and advanced devices will be provided to users to control the digital world.

The physical world will be controlled from remote devices and technologies by using Web 4.0 technologies. People will be able to control a TV, washing machine or refrigerator via remote, virtual interfaces. All physical elements in the world will be tagged and controlled. Smart versions of traditional tools will be designed and developed to be controlled with Web 4.0 technologies.

Using Web 4.0 in E-Learning

Web 4.0 technologies will cause a revolution in education methods and activities in the future.

Figure 8. Web 3.0 and Web 4.0

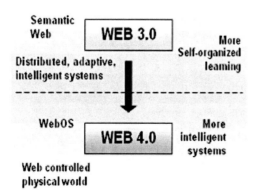

There is not enough information about how education standards will be in the future but some ideas about the future can be expressed according to state of today's technology.

Almost all educational works will be done from anywhere, on anytime by controlling the physical world with remote interfaces. New teaching and learning methods that are suitable for new standards will be developed. Students and teachers will join learning activities from anywhere they want. Perhaps, there is no need to go to schools for education. E-books, electronic lesson materials and more advanced mobile devices will be used instead of books, notebooks and papers. Learning activities will be totally electronic with Web 4.0 technologies.

CONCLUSION

Today, teachers and students are happy with Web 2.0 and Web 2.0 technologies used in education activities. Web 2.0 technologies are widely used in E-Learning activities. It is possible to take active roles in more interactive and effective E-Learning platforms that include social, flexible and interactive web contents, thanks to Web 2.0 technologies.

Web 2.0 technologies like blogs, Wikis and social networking services attract both teachers and students. These technologies have many effective and flexible features that give them advantages of being used for different aims. As a result of using them for educational purposes, a new E-Learning form, which is called as E-Learning 2.0 has been created. Nowadays, E-Learning 2.0 activities are popular among teachers and students.

There are many types of free and open source applications or services that are used for making E-Learning 2.0 activities. Features of Web 2.0 technologies make them more interactive, social and effective for teachers and students. Virtual classrooms, collaborative working groups and communication systems can be created easily by using Web 2.0 technologies. Learning activities are performed in an effective way with these tools. Teachers and students think that E-Learning 2.0 (E-Learning supported with Web 2.0 technologies) is more successful at reaching educational goals rather than standard E-Learning.

It seems that new generations of the Web: Web 3.0 and Web 4.0 will provide more revolutionary web technologies in the future. Web 3.0 will enable web systems to work according to users' needs. People will use Web 3.0 technologies to control many activities in their daily life. After Web 3.0, Web 4.0 will enable users to control the physical world by using remote devices and technologies. All of these changes in web technologies will also affect E-Learning activities in the future. Perhaps, there will be no need to go to schools or use books and notebooks to take an active part in learning activities. Perhaps, student will learn lesson subjects by using intelligent learning systems improved with more advanced artificial intelligence techniques. Improvements in web technologies will show us which changes in our life will occur in the future.

REFERENCES

Baytak, A. (in press). Web 2.0; open opportunities for Turkish universities. *Proceedings of The Academic Informatics 2009 Conference.*

Berlinger, Y. (2009). What is web 3.0?: The psychological experience of using the internet is undergoing slow but constant change. *Web 2.0 Journal.* Retrieved May 15, 2009 from http://web2.sys-con.com/node/236036

Berners-Lee, T., Hendler, J., & Lassila, O. (2001). The semantic web. *Scientific American.* Retrieved May 16, 2009 from http://www.scientificamerican.com/article.cfm?id=the-semantic-web

Blood, R. (2002). *The weblog handbook: Practical advice on creating and maintaining your blog.* Cambridge, MA: Perseus Publishing.

Brittain, S., Glowacki, P., Van Ittersum, J., & Johnson, L. (2006). Podcasting lectures. *EDUCAUSE Quarterly*, *29*(3), 24–31.

Brown, J. S., & Adler, R. P. (2008). Minds on fire: Open education, the long tail, and learning 2.0. *EDUCAUSE Review*, *43*(1), 16–32.

Cambell, G. (2005). There is something in the air: Podcasting in education. *EDUCAUSE Review*, *40*(6), 32–47.

Cebeci, Z., & Tekdal, M. (2006). Using podcasts as audio learning objects. *Interdisciplinary Journal of Knowledge and Learning Objects*, *2*, 47–57.

Clarey, J. (2008). How to implement an effective e-learning 2.0 strategy. Retrieved May 8, 2009 from http://www.brandon-hall.com/publications/learning2.0/learning2.0.shtml

Dean, M. W. (2008). Put your videos on other people's ipods. *O'Reilly Media.* Retrieved May 3 from 2009, http://digitalmedia.oreilly.com/2008/09/04/youtube-rss-ipod-tutorial.html

DiNucci, D. (1999). Fragmented future. *Print*, *53*(4), 32.

Downes, S. (2005). E-learning 2.0. *eLearn Magazine.* Retrieved May 11, 2009 from http://www.elearnmag.org/subpage.cfm?section=articles&article=29-1

Doyle, B. (2006). When to wiki, when to blog. *E-Content: Digital Content Strategies and Resources.* Retrieved May 5, 2009 from http://www.econtentmag.com/Articles/ArticlePrint.aspx?ArticleID=16900

Ebner, M. (2007). E-learning 2.0 = e-learning 1.0 + web 2.0? *The 2nd International Conference on availability, reliability and security* (pp. 1235-1239). Los Alamitos: IEEE Computer Society.

Edirisingha, P., & Salmon, G. (2007). IMPALA podcast models: some examples. Retrieved May 7, 2009 from http://www2.le.ac.uk/projects/impala/documents/IMPALA_podcast_models

Ferdig, R. E., & Trammell, K. D. (2004). Content delivery in the "blogosphere". *The Journal: Transforming Education through Technology.* Retrieved May 16, 2009 from http://www.thejournal.com/articles/16626/

Ferret, L. J. (2006). Wikis and e-learning . In Berman, P. (Ed.), *E-learning concepts and techniques* (pp. 73–74). Bloomsburg, PA: Bloomsburg University.

Franklin, T., & van Harmelen, M. (2007). Web 2.0 for content for learning and teaching in higher education. *JISC: Supporting education and research.* Retrieved May 1, 2009 from http://www.jisc.ac.uk/media/documents/programmes/digitalrepositories/web2-content-learning-and-teaching.pdf

Graham, P. (2005). Web 2.0. *Paul Graham.* Retrieved April 29, 2009 from http://www.paulgraham.com/web20.html

Gross, R., & Acquisti, A. (2005). Information revelation and privacy in online social networks (the facebook case). In S. C. di Vimercati, & R. Dingledine (Eds.), *The 2005 ACM Workshop on Privacy in the Electronics Society* (pp. 71-80). New York: ACM Press.

Harvard University. (1999). Authorship guidelines. *Harvard University Medical School.* Retrieved May 14, 2009 from http://www.hms.harvard.edu/integrity/authorship.html

Herman, I. (2005). W3C semantic web frequently asked questions. *W3C Semantic Web.* Retrieved May 12, 2009 from http://www.w3.org/2001/sw/SW-FAQ

Herman, I. (2008). Semantic web activity statement. *W3C Semantic Web.* Retrieved May 12 from 2009, http://www.w3.org/2001/sw/Activity.html

Herman, I. (2008). W3C semantic web activity. *W3C Semantic Web.* Retrieved May 12, 2009 from http://www.w3.org/2001/sw/

Kamel Boulos, M. N., Maramba, I., & Wheeler, S. (2006). Wikis, blogs and podcasts: A new generation of web-based tools for virtual collaborative clinical practice and education. *BMC Medical Education, 6.* Retrieved April 28, 2009, from http://www.biomedcentral.com/1472-6920/6/41/

Kottke, J. (2003). It's "weblog" not "web log". *Kottke.org.* Retrieved May 2, 2009 from http://www.kottke.org/03/08/its-weblog-not-web-log

Krish Inc. (2009). Web 2.0 design. *Krish Inc: From evolution to acumen.* Retrieved April 29 from 2009, http://www.krishinc.com/web-design-development-services-india/web2.0-design.html

Lazzari, M., & Betella, A. (2007). Towards guidelines on educational podcasting quality: Problems arising from a real world experience . In Smith, M. J., & Salvandy, G. (Eds.), *Human interface and the management of information. Interacting in information environments* (pp. 404–412). Berlin: Springer. doi:10.1007/978-3-540-73354-6_44

Lipponen, L. (2002). Exploring foundations for computer-supported collaborative learning. In G. Stahl (Ed.), *The Computer-supported Collaborative Learning 2002 Conference: Computer support for collaborative learning: Foundations for a CSCL community* (pp. 72-81). Hillsdale: Erlbaum.

MacManus, R. (2007). E-learning 2.0: All you need to know. *Read Write Web.* Retrieved April 28, 2009 from http://www.readwriteweb.com/archives/e-learning_20_all_you_need_to_know.php

Mader, S. (2006). Wiki vs. blog. *Business Blog Wire.* Retrieved May 6, 2009 from http://www.businessblogwire.com/2006/03/stewart_mader_wiki_vs_blog.html

Matthews, K. (2006). Research into podcasting technology including current and possible future uses. Retrieved May 8, 2009 from http://mms.ecs.soton.ac.uk/2007/papers/32.pdf

Merholz, P. (1999). Post on October 12, 1999. *Peterme.com.* Retrieved April 30, 2009 from http://web.archive.org/web/19991013021124/http://peterme.com/index.html

Myers, J. (1991). Cooperative learning in heterogeneous classes. *Cooperative Learning, 11*(4).

Nations, D. (2009). What are web widgets?: How can I use a web widget? *About.com: Web Trends.* Retrieved May 6, 2009 from http://webtrends.about.com/od/widgets/a/what_is_widget.htm

O'Reilly, T. (2005). What is 2.0: Design patterns and business models for the next generation of software. *O'Reilly Media.* Retrieved April 28, 2009 from http://www.oreillynet.com/pub/a/oreilly/tim/news/2005/09/30/what-is-web-20.html

Ortutay, B. (2009). Fast-growing facebook's user base hits 200 million. *Yahoo! Finance.* Retrieved May 21, 2009 from http://finance.yahoo.com/news/Fastgrowing-Facebooks-user-apf-14886318.html?v=6

Owyang, J. (2009). A collection of social network stats for 2009. *Web Strategy by Jeremiah Owyang.* Retrieved May 20, 2009 from http://www.web-strategist.com/blog/2009/01/11/a-collection-of-soical-network-stats-for-2009/

Parker, K. R., & Chao, J. T. (2007). Wiki as a teaching tool. *Interdisciplinary Journal of Knowledge and Learning Objects, 3,* 57–72.

Safran, C., Helic, D., & Gütl, C. (2007). E-learning practices and web 2.0. In M. Aurer (Ed.), *The 10th International Conference on Interactive Computer Aided Learning* (pp. 1(8)-8(8)). Kassel: Kassel University Press.

Salmon, G. (2006). *E-tivities: The key to active online learning. London.* Sterling, VA: RoutledgeFalmer.

Su, F., & Beaumont, C. (2008). Student perceptions of e-learning with a wiki. *SOLSTICE Conference 2008: E-learning and learning environments for the future, 1.* Retrieved May 19, 2009, from http://www.edgehill.ac.uk/solstice/Conference2008/documents/Session5_FrankSu_000.pdf

Thacker, C. (2007). Podcasts in education. *Macinstruct.* Retrieved May 7, 2009, fromhttp://www.macinstruct.com/node/43

TypingWeb. (2009). TypingWeb Features. *TypingWeb: Free Online Typing Tutor.* Retrieved May 13, 2009,from http://classic.typingweb.com/typingtutor/features.php

Wikipedia (2009). Blog. *Wikipedia, the free encyclopedia.* Retrieved May 11, 2009, from http://en.wikipedia.org/wiki/Blog

Wikipedia (2009). Electronic learning. *Wikipedia, the free encyclopedia.* Retrieved May 21, from 2009, http://en.wikipedia.org/wiki/E-learning

Wikipedia (2009). Podcast. *Wikipedia, the free encyclopedia.* Retrieved May 15, 2009, from http://en.wikipedia.org/wiki/Podcast

Williams, D. (2007). Blogging definitions: Types of blogs. *Web design, SEO, blog marketing and social media marketing for your business.* Retrieved May 20, 2009, from http://www.webdesignseo.com/blogging-terms/blogging-definitions-types-of-blogs-part-2.php

Woolf, B. (2006). Wiki vs. blog. *E-Content: IBM Developer Works.* Retrieved May 5, 2009, from http://www.ibm.com/developerworks/wikis/display/woolf/Wiki+vs.+Blog

ADDITIONAL READING

Aroyo, L., & Dicheva, D. (2004). The new challenges for e-learning: The educational semantic web. *Journal of Educational Technology & Society, 7*(4), 59–69.

Baytak, A. (in press). Web 2.0; open opportunities for Turkish universities. *Proceedings of The Academic Informatics 2009 Conference.*

Bruckman, A. (2004). The future of e-learning communities. *Communications of the ACM, 45*(4), 60–63. doi:10.1145/505248.505274

Caladine, R. (2008). *Enhancing e-learning with media-rich content and interactions.* Hershey, PA: IGI Global.

Coleman, D., & Levine, S. (2008). *Collaboration 2.0: Technology and best practices for successful collaboration in a web 2.0 world.* Cupertino, CA: Happy About.

Crane, B. E. (2008). *Using web 2.0 tools in the k-12 classroom.* New York, NY: Neal-Schuman Publishers.

Daconta, M. C., Obrst, L. J., & Smith, K. T. (2003). *The semantic web: A guide to the future of xml, web services, and knowledge management.* Indianapolis, IN: Wiley Publishing.

Davies, J., Studer, R., & Warren, P. (Eds.). (2006). *Semantic web technologies: Trends and research in ontology-based systems.* West Sussex: Wiley Publishing. doi:10.1002/047003033X

Deans, P. C. (2008). *Social software and web 2.0 technology trends.* Hershey, PA: Information Science Reference.

Devedzic, V. (2004). Web intelligence and artificial intelligence in education. *Journal of Educational Technology & Society, 7*(4), 29–39.

Ebner, M. (2007). E-learning 2.0 = e-learning 1.0 + web 2.0? *The 2nd International Conference on availability, reliability and security* (pp. 1235-1239). Los Alamitos: IEEE Computer Society.

Edirisingha, P., Rizzi, C., Nie, M., & Rothwell, L. (2007). Podcasting to provide teaching and learning support for an undergraduate module on english language and communication. *Turkish Online Journal of Distance Education, 8*(3), 87–107.

Elci, A. (2005). A metadata model for e-learning coordination through semantic web languages. *Turkish Online Journal of Distance Education, 4*(3), 12–17.

Esnault, L. (2007). *Web-based education and pedagogical technologies: Solutions for learning applications.* Hershey, PA: IGI Global.

Green, T. D., Brown, A. H., & Robinson, L. K. (2007). *Making the most of the web in your classroom: A teacher's guide to blogs, podcasts, wikis, pages, and sites.* Thousand Oaks, CA: Corwin Press.

Harris, D. (2008). *Web 2.0 evolution into the intelligent web 3.0.* Brisbane, QLD: Emereo Publishing.

Hendron, J. G. (2008). *RSS for educators: blogs, newsfeeds, podcasts, and wikis in the classroom.* Eugene, OR: International Society for Technology in Education.

Herring, S. C., Scheidt, L. A., Bonus, S., & Wright, E. (2004). Bridging the gap: A genre analysis of weblogs. In R. H. Sprague (Ed.), *The 37th Annual Hawaii International Conference on System Science* (pp. 101-111). Los Alamitos: IEEE Computer Society.

Iiyoshi, T., & Vijay Kumar, M. S. (Eds.). (2008). *Opening up education: The collective advancement of education through open technology, open content, and open knowledge.* Boston, MA: The MIT Press.

Jones, B. L. (2008). *Web 2.0 heroes: Interviews with 20 web 2.0 influencers.* Indianapolis, IN: Wiley Publishing.

Jonghe, A. D. (2008). *Social networks around the world: How is web 2.0 changing your daily life?*Charleston, SC: BookSurge Publishing.

Kilian, C. (2007). *Writing for the web 3.0*. North Vancouver, BC: Self-Counsel Press.

Kroski, E. (2008). *Web 2.0 for librarians and information professionals*. New York, NY: Neal-Schuman Publishers.

Lanclos, P. (Ed.). (2008). *Weaving web 2.0 tools into the classroom*. Eugene, OR: Visions Technology in Education.

Lassila, O., & Hendler, J. (2007). Embracing "web 3.0". *IEEE Internet Computing, 11*, 90-93. Retrieved May 3, 2009, from http://www.mindswap.org/papers/2007/90-93.pdf

Lichtman, M. (2009). *Qualitative research in education: A user's guide*. Thousand Oaks, CA: SAGE Publications.

Lytras, M. (Ed.). (2007). *Open source for knowledge and learning management*. Hershey, PA: IGI Global.

Mason, R. (2008). *E-learning and social networking handbook: Resources for higher education*. New York, NY: Routledge.

Mason, R., & Rennie, F. (2007). Using web 2.0 for learning in the community. *The Internet and Higher Education, 10*(3), 196–203. doi:10.1016/j.iheduc.2007.06.003

Mendes, A. J., Pereira, I., & Costa, R. (Eds.). (2007). *Computers and education: Towards educational change and innovation*. London: Springer-Verlag London Ltd.

Mika, P. (2007). *Social Networks and the semantic web*. New York, NY: Springer.

Moo-Young, H. (2006). *Goal oriented learning environments: E-learning strategies for the classroom*. Victoria, BC: Trafford Publishing.

Nardi, B. A., Schiano, D. J., Gumbrecht, M., & Swartz, L. (2005). Why we blog? *Communications of the ACM, 47*(12), 41–46. doi:10.1145/1035134.1035163

O'Reilly, T. (2005). What is web 2.0. *O'Reilly Media*. Retrieved May 5, 2009, from http://oreilly.com/pub/a/oreilly/tim/news/2005/09/30/what-is-web-20.html

O'Reilly, T. (2007). Programming 2.0. *O'Reilly Media*. Retrieved May 9, 2009, from http://radar.oreilly.com/2007/01/programming-20.html

Palloff, R. M., & Pratt, K. (2007). *Building online learning communities: Effective strategies for the virtual classroom*. San Francisco, CA: Jossey-Bass.

Parker, K. R., & Chao, J. T. (2007). Wiki as a teaching tool. *Interdisciplinary Journal of Knowledge and Learning Objects, 3*, 57–72.

Passin, T. B. (2004). *Explorer's guide to the semantic web*. Greenwich, Connecticut, CT: Manning Publications.

Richardson, W. (2008). *Blogs, wikis, podcasts, and other powerful web tools for classrooms*. Thousand Oaks, CA: Corwin Press.

Rosen, A. (2006). Technology tends: e-learning 2.0. *The eLearning Guild's Learning Solutions e-Magazine,* 1-8. Retrieved May 5, 2009, from http://www.readygo.com/e-learning-2.0.pdf

Rosen, A. (2009). *E-learning 2.0: Proven practices and emerging technologies to achieve real results*. New York, NY: AMACOM.

Rosenberg, M. J. (2000). *E-learning: Strategies for delivering knowledge in the digital age*. Chicago, IL: McGraw-Hill.

Safran, C., Helic, D., & Gütl, C. (2007). E-learning practices and web 2.0. In M. Aurer (Ed.), *The 10th International Conference on Interactive Computer Aided Learning* (pp. 1(8)-8(8)). Kassel: Kassel University Press.

Segaran, T. (2007). *Programming collective intelligence: Building smart web 2.0 applications.* Sebastopol, CA: O'Reilly Media.

Solomon, G., & Schrum, L. (2007). *Web 2.0: New tools, new schools.* Eugene, OR: International Society for Technology in Education.

Stauffer, T. (2007). *How to do everything with your web 2.0 blog.* New York, NY: McGraw-Hill Osborne Media.

Steinberg, D. H. (2005). Open source and web 2.0. *O'Reilly Media.* Retrieved May 14, 2009, http://www.oreillynet.com/pub/a/network/2005/10/07/open-source-and-web-20.html

Vossen, G., & Hagemann, S. (2007). *Unleashing web 2.0: From concepts to creativity.* Burlington, MA: Morgan Kaufmann.

Wei-Jane, L., Yi-Ling, L., Kakusho, K., Hsiu-Ping, Y., Murakami, M., & Minoh, M. (2006). Blog as a tool to develop e-learning experience in an international distance course. In Kinshuk, R. Koper, P. Kommers, P. Kirschner, D. G. Sampson & W. Didderen (Ed.), *The 6th International Conference on Advanced Learning Technologies* (pp. 290-292). Los Alamitos: IEEE Computer Society.

Wilen-Daugenti, T. (2008). *edu: Technology and learning environments in higher education.* New York, NY: Peter Lang Publishing.

Yu, L. (2007). *Introduction to semantic web and semantic web services.* Boca Raton, FL: Chapman & Hall. doi:10.1201/9781584889342

Zhang, D., Zhao, J. L., Zhou, L., & Nunamaker, J. F. (2004). Can e-learning replace classroom learning? *Communications of the ACM, 47*(5), 75–79. doi:10.1145/986213.986216

KEY TERMS AND DEFINITIONS

E-Learning: A type of learning that is supported by electronic media, especially by the Internet. In E-Learning, interaction between teachers and students can be made by using special learning and teaching tools on interactive learning platforms.

E-Learning 2.0: A term that is used to define the new form of E-Learning that includes Web 2.0 technologies. E-Learning 2.0 allows students to use Web 2.0 technologies like blogs, wikis and podcasts to take an active role in the learning process and determine their own learning strategies according to their interests and needs.

Free Open Source Application: An application that was developed with open source methodology and has free software rights.

Semantic: A term that is used to define things that work on meanings of words and sentences.

Web 1.0: A term that is used to define past generation of the Web before Web 2.0. Static web pages, simple web contents and less creativity on web design are some characteristics of the Web 1.0.

Web 2.0: The second version of the Web that allows users to work on interactive platforms, make collaborations and create effective web contents over the Internet. Blogs, Wikis, social networking services, and file sharing sites are some popular Web 2.0 technologies that are widely used.

Web 3.0: The third generation of the Web in the future. Web 3.0 includes more intelligent web services and applications that understand users' needs and work according to them. Some features of Web 3.0 are expressed as prospective future possibilities.

Web 4.0: The fourth generation of the Web in the future. Web 4.0 allows users to control the physical world by using more advanced Web technologies. Almost all features and functions of Web 4.0 are expressed as prospective future possibilities.

Web x.x: A formula that can be used to define different generations of the Web. For example, Web 3.0 and Web 4.0 can be used to define next generations while Web 1.0 and Web 2.0 are used to define first and second generations of the Web.

Chapter 2
What's all the FOSS?
How Freedom and Openness are Changing the Face of Our Educational Landscape

Jason B. Huett
University of West Georgia, USA

Jason H. Sharp
Tarleton State University, USA

Kimberly C. Huett
University of West Georgia, USA

ABSTRACT

Philosophical, financial, practical, and pedagogical considerations have prompted educators to take a serious look at Free and Open Source Software (FOSS) as an alternative to proprietary software. To better understand the overall concept of FOSS, this article provides a brief history of FOSS as well as a summary of its definition, philosophy, and major areas of research, including strengths and limitations, diffusion in education and educational uses as well as a look at the opportunities, issues, and challenges associated with FOSS. In conclusion, the authors speculate how FOSS, along with advances in E-Learning and other emerging technologies, will positively shape our educational future.

INTRODUCTION

When writing a chapter about the changing face of education and the important role Free and Open Source Software (FOSS) plays in the future of educating citizens of the planet, one is reminded of the fairytale classic *The Little Dutch Boy.* The tale is based on a Dutch legend about a little boy who notices a small leak in a dyke on his way to school. Risking the wrath of his teachers for being late, the boy opts to plug the hole with his finger until help arrives to patch the leak and save the village. The tale is meant to be an allegory for personal responsibility, timely action, and self-sacrifice. The story illustrates that one individual, no matter how small, can change the course of events for the better.

This fable of individuals with the power to effect positive and dramatic change resembles the birth of FOSS. Visionaries like Richard Stallman and Linus Torvalds were among the first of the "computer generation" to dare to ask us to imag-

DOI: 10.4018/978-1-61520-917-0.ch002

ine a world where *free* and *open* are fundamental *rights*. They are notables, in a cast of thousands, who have unleashed nothing short of a growing tsunami in education. However, such change is continually being met by strong opposition.

Deep-rooted educational systems, rife with self-interested reasons to perpetuate the status quotient, refuse to acknowledge that our learning landscape has been fundamentally altered. This is understandable to some extent since the basic philosophy underlying the FOSS movement is a radical one: something for nothing. It goes against what most people have been taught since grade school. But, in this case, *nothing* turns out to be something extraordinary.

The world of education is being radically altered and that change is driven by technology, openness, and unprecedented access to knowledge. Futurist James Canton (2006), finds the sorry state of the American educational system to be one of the biggest threats to our future prosperity and states "the quality of public education, in crisis today, will either propel or crash the future aspirations of the American workforce" (p. 332). According to Dr. Curtis Bonk (2009) in his recent book *The World is Open*, control over the learning process is being abolished at the institutional level and placed into the hands of the individual, and "the abolitionists are the advocates of open access, open source, and open educational resources" (p. 181). The question is not *if* we have to change to keep up with the free, informal, immediate, open, and portable world of learning, but *when*. So much of what we have been doing with technology in education is little more than window dressing. We use technology, at the basest of levels, to repackage and "pretty up" a failing system in a futile attempt to make it seem new and fresh. We barely scratch the surface of what is possible let alone what is now *required*.

In this chapter, we will examine the literature written on the use of Free and Open Source software in education with a particular focus on the promise of E-Learning and emerging technolo-gies to positively shape our educational future. Several reasons have prompted educators to take a serious look at FOSS as an alternative to proprietary software--which is currently the most predominant type of software used in education. These reasons include philosophical, financial, practical, and pedagogical considerations. In order to better understand the overall concept of FOSS, we provide a brief history as well as a summary of its definition and philosophy. After this foundation has been established, we focus on some major areas of research dealing with FOSS. These include strengths and limitations, diffusion in education and educational uses as well as a look at the opportunities, issues, and challenges associated with FOSS. In conclusion, based on a synthesis of published research and our own experiences, we speculate about the important role that FOSS will play in the future of open learning. This is indeed an exciting time for education, and while there is no reason to fear a changing educational world, there is every reason to understand it and prepare for it.

HISTORY OF THE FREE AND OPEN SOURCE MOVEMENT

Before discussing the history of the free and open source software movement, it would be helpful to define what we mean by "free" and "open source." Remidez, Laffey and Musser (2001) explicitly state that "the open-source model is not a set model or procedure for developing software. It is closer to a philosophy than a process" (p. 2). At the heart of open source software philosophy is the concept of "free," not necessarily in financial terms, although many open source software applications are free of charge, but more so in the sense of freedom to examine the source code, to make modification, and to redistribute the software to others who have the exact same freedom (Hart, 2003; Moyle, 2003). The *GNU Operating System* website (2009) explains *free* this way:

"free software is a matter of liberty, not price. To understand the concept, you should think of free as in free speech, not as in free beer" (GNU Operating System, (p. 2). So while most open source and free software programs are devoid of cost, free in this instance more aptly refers to a philosophy of freedom. However, as Bonk (2009) points out, while technically two separate movements, on a practical level, the open source movement and the free software movement overlap one another considerably. And, for the purposes of this chapter the terms free, open source, and FOSS are used interchangeably.

Although definitions vary slightly from author to author, the majority agree that open source software can be defined as software whose source code is freely available to the user to examine, modify, and redistribute (Bretthauer, 2002; Hart, 2003; Herbert, 2001; Kim, 2002; Moyle, 2003; O'Dell, 2004; Remidez, Laffey & Musser, 2001; Tong, 2004; Warger, 2002). Moyle adds another component to the definition by including that it is "open, unrestricted, and available by downloading from the Internet" (p. 4).

FOSS contrasts sharply with proprietary or closed-source software, which by nature does not make the source code available. Moyle adds that closed source software "cannot be opened, viewed, customized or reauthored to meet specific requirements of individual locations nor can it be manipulated in order to fix bugs" (p. 10). FOSS proponents are also quick to point out what open source is not. It is not shareware, public-domain, or freeware (Bretthauer, 2002; Moyle, 2003; "Working with Open Source," 2004;). These types of software, although they may be downloaded for free, do not typically allow access to the source code—the very definition of open source software.

Bretthauer (2002) contends that although the term itself was only coined in 1998, the roots of open source software can be traced back at least 30 years. Bonk (2009) connects the FOSS movement to the "hacker" culture that originated at MIT in the late 1950s: "This hacker culture had a firm belief in knowledge sharing and helping others, including exploration of computer programming secrets and free access to computers" (p.143). For O'Dell (2004), the major stepping off point for the open source movement began in 1989 with the release of the World Wide Web specification by Tim Berners-Lee and the team at CERN. O'Dell cites the impact of the Internet as possibly the most important factor for the success of the open source movement. In fact, O'Dell (2004) states, "I think it is fair to say that without the Internet, the open source movement would not exist today" (p. 3). The second factor that O'Dell attributes to its success is its economic viability which has been accomplished based on one of three models: (1) income derived from providing support services, (2) vested interest, which means by using open source solutions, companies save money and pass the savings on to the customer, or (3) the concept that a product will continue to be used while it has sufficient interest and a community to work on it. Perhaps most famously, the release of Linux 1.0 in 1994 by Linus Torvalds officially spurred the open source movement toward the mainstream. Bretthauer (2002) summarizes the history of the FOSS movement by commenting that it "began as an assumption without a name or a clear alternative"; but, over the last thirty years, "it has produced some of the most stable and widely used software packages ever produced" (p. 3).

FOSS PHILOSOPHY

Ultimately, the philosophical difference between open source and proprietary software is the issue of control. Where by definition, open source software allows for access, modification, and redistribution, proprietary software does not (Coppolla & Neelley, 2004). In fact, the makers of proprietary software have gone to great lengths to restrict access to the source code by creating intricate and complicated license agreements. Herbert (2001) contends that open source as a philosophy is applicable to a wide range of technology areas. In its purest form, open source is an approach that is more interested in serving the public good than it is in the bottom line (Hart, 2003; Moyle, 2003). The goal is to create a quality piece of software that will find broad application among users (Hart, 2003).

But, how is this possible? No discussion about the history of open source would be complete without asking the question: What motivated people like Linus Torvalds, a 21-year-old computer science student in Finland, to create software that could be used and modified by anyone for free? Such a concept was basically unheard of in the business and education worlds. It was also a direct challenge to the software giant *Microsoft* and the current marketplace. In September of 1991, companies like *Microsoft* probably felt they had little to fear from upstarts like Torvalds; they were wrong.

If you have ever worked around computer geeks, you probably understand that many in the "hacker" culture do not need a reason to challenge the establishment: the establishment is reason enough. George Mallory the legendary English mountaineer was once asked the question: "Why do you want to climb Mt. Everest?" To which he famously replied, "Because it is there." Interviews with Torvalds indicate a similar stance on taking on *Microsoft* with the first open source operating system (Bonk, 2009). In one of the few studies encompassing motivation in open source development, Bonaccorsi and Rossi (2003) identified several motivational factors including (1) intellectual gratification, (2) demonstration of an art form, (3) pleasure of creativity, (4) notice by software firms, and (5) satisfaction of a demand. Edwards (2001) corroborates these findings by listing influence, recognition, and reputation as motivating factors. He also proposes an additional factor as personal need. Simply put, programmers truly have a need to solve problems, even if it is for free.

With FOSS creators and participators, there appears to be no real motivation for profit, an inherent sense of cooperation and coordination, a shared sense of purpose, and a genuine desire to just do something "neat." Within the FOSS culture, you have a successful, functioning, community that has no formal hierarchical coordination or infrastructure. The crux of this work is that to understand the open source phenomenon one must also have an understanding of the communities in which the software is developed. The idea is that the learner, the individual new to the community, must be viewed as a legitimate participant with all the rights and privileges as the other members. Now, this does not necessarily mean the learner will have the same responsibilities or authority as insiders. What it does mean, however, is that in order for the learner to become a practitioner, the learner must be given the chance not only to observe the work that is happening in the community, but also to participate in the work. Edwards (2001) asserts, "completion of this process and transformation of the learner into an insider requires that the insider must allow the learner legitimate peripheral participation" (p. 20). This kind of informal and cooperative partnership is very impressive when you think about it.

The fact that such a movement led to software that now runs more than half of the world's servers, has an almost a 20% market share of cell phone operating systems, commands at least a 30% share of a ballooning Chinese software market, and is used as the operating system for 443 of the top 500 supercomputers in the world, is nothing short of amazing (Bonk, 2009; Wikipedia, 2009).

What undoubtedly seemed like Utopian silliness born out of the geeky, hacker culture to most working at *Microsoft* almost 20 years ago, now seems poised to revolutionize the way we conduct business and education.

THE ADVANTAGES AND LIMITATIONS OF OPEN SOURCE SOFTWARE IN EDUCATION

Advantages of Open Source Software

The advocates of open source software in education point to its many strengths when presenting it as an alternative to proprietary software. With the rising price of proprietary software and its associated license fees, one of the primary strengths for open source is its low cost of entry (Chauhan, 2004; "Working with Open Source," 2004; Moyle, 2003; Tong, 2004). O'Dell (2004) asserts that for many the decision to adopt open source simply boils down to the price. He states "most budgets can handle free quite nicely" (p. 5). Gonsalves (2003) follows up this argument by commenting that "for cash-strapped schools, open source technology may offer an appealing choice over costly proprietary software" (p. 9). Hart (2003) points to lack of money as a significant problem facing a large number of schools today. He concludes that, "a school can save a huge amount of money by using open source" (p. 12). Finally, according to Whitehurst (2009), "open source is now recognized in institutions of higher education as a viable technology solution that provides superior value at a fraction of the cost of proprietary applications" (p. 70). Consequently, the savings can be used for other technology-related expenses such as hardware upgrades and staff development and training.

Flexibility and access also factor into the cost equation. Open source software will effectively run on older computers ranging from 486s to early Pentium machines, which are still found in many educational settings (Gonsalves, 2003), making it a more flexible option for schools short on funding. In addition to hardware flexibility, Herbert (2001) points out that flexibility extends into the software area as well. This is due to the nature of the open source licensure which does not lock

the user into any contractual obligations. Warger (2002) comments that "one of the alluring promises of open-source is return of control" (p. 19) to the end user. Schools can upgrade or abandon the software without added expense, fear of penalty or contract violations.

Older machines and a lack of resources and availability can create a separation between those who have access to technology, and those who do not. This is often referred to as the "Digital Divide." Hart (2003) asserts that due to its lower cost of entry, ability to run on older machines, and inherent flexibility, "open source does a lot to bridge this gap" (p. 15). Beyond the United States, the fact that the system requirements and cost of open source solutions are lower is "particularly important in helping us bridge the digital divide in countries where computers are a scarce and treasured commodity" (Halse & Terzoli, 2002, p. 8).

In addition to cost savings, greater flexibility and improved access, we have seen the quality of open source software improve dramatically in the past decade. Herbert (2001) goes as far as to say that regardless of cost benefits, "it is the quality of the software that is the primary reason for the ongoing success of open source" (p. 4). This emphasis on quality comes from the collaborative nature of open source and the idea of what Raymond (1999) calls *Linus' Law*, which states, "given enough eyeballs, all bugs are shallow" (p. 6). That is, the more people or "eyeballs" involved in the design and development, the better the end product. Chauhan (2004) and Tong (2004) agree that the quality is due to the overall philosophy of open source which allows many skilled individuals to modify and then redistribute the code.

We are also seeing these communities of designers and developers become better organized in offering support for their products. Support has always been available via the Internet through various development communities and forum boards, but traditional support, similar to that provided by proprietary software distributors, in which a fee is paid for "helpdesk style" support is now available and growing (Hart, 2003; Herbert, 2001; Moyle, 2003). However, organized support is still relatively inadequate for many average users and this highlights what is probably the number one limitation of FOSS.

Limitations of Open Source Software

Perhaps the most often cited drawback of open source is the lack of support. There is no single organization responsible for support and thus no 800 number to call when a problem is encountered (Gonsalves, 2003; Moyle 2003). A closely associated limitation is the lack of support documentation in comparison to documentation available for proprietary software (O'Dell, 2004). The issue of support is not limited to external support, but also includes the local technology staff as well. Most schools simply do not have access to support staff knowledgeable enough in FOSS to support it adequately.

Assuming that a local technology staff exists (and this is a big assumption), it is not only a matter of the staff possessing the technical skills to support an open source software environment, but also a matter of the attitude of the staff. Individuals working in an open source environment must possess an attitude of collaboration and a willingness to ask questions when confronted with an unknown. Many support staff members are reluctant to do this for fear of looking incompetent ("Working with Open Source," 2004). They must also be able to mitigate problems as they arise and find potential workarounds for issues that, given the nature of FOSS, will often not have immediate solutions available.

For schools, this question of immediate support is particularly challenging. When a school purchases proprietary software, there are established support expectations. During the initial deployment, setup and training stages of propriety software adoptions, schools may rely heavily on centralized and well-established technical support channels. With FOSS deployment, users and sup-

port personnel have a more active role in reporting bugs, requesting new features, enhancements, and customizations as well as being generally asked to "get into the spirit of things" and be more patient with, and participative in, the entire process.

Therein lies the rub. Many times, the decision to go with proprietary software over FOSS is based almost entirely on the expectation of proprietary software to function properly every time with minimal and predictable user feedback and to provide access to a dedicated support structure for rapid solutions to any problems that arise. Add to this the concept of "total cost," and one can see why many in education are reluctant to adopt FOSS. While the entry cost for open source is low, this may not be the case with *total cost* of ownership. This is due primarily to the fact that technical staff will require more extensive training, and the time and money involved in this process may exceed the initial savings of software purchases (Warger, 2002; "Working with Open Source," 2004). Other limitations include a steep learning curve for some open source applications and the fact that open source applications lack the slick user interfaces of many proprietary software packages ("Working with Open Source," 2004). While FOSS is not the "leap of faith" it once was, for many schools the remaining unknowns are still too much to swallow.

Although open source software does possess some limitations, Gonsalves (2003) still asserts that "the potential cost savings is attractive enough to consider open source, especially if a school has a strong technology team in place" (p. 9). Warger (2002) echoes these sentiments by stating, "despite all the obstacles, open-source has the potential to strongly influence the future of software development and support in the academic world" (p. 20). In other words, the time has come to give FOSS a second look.

Why Open Source? Why Now?

So, assuming you can make open source software work in an educational setting, should you? This question is more nebulous and brings forward some pedagogical concerns. Is one better off teaching concepts or specific software? There can be little doubt that certain software packages dominate in the marketplace. Take for instance, the most used and most popular of the office applications: the *Microsoft Office Suite*. According to Forrester Research, "Eighty percent of enterprise customers are still using some version of *Microsoft Office* for worker productivity and collaboration, with only 8 percent using alternatives…" (Montalbano, 2009, para. 2).

With such dominance in the marketplace, one could easily argue that teaching certain software applications is more valuable than teaching concepts. Couple this with the negative perceptions of open source (Moyle, 2003) and the general lack of understanding about FOSS, and the result is many parents want their children learning the software they will be using in the "real world" and may feel their children are being placed at a disadvantage by using FOSS alternatives (Hart, 2003). In truth, this is an issue which can be argued either as a strength or weakness (Hart, 2003; Moyle, 2003). Hart (2003) argues that "it is far better to teach the concepts behind word processing than it is to teach a particular program" (p. 20). Tong (2004) relates the pedagogical advantage of open source to the teaching of computer literacy. He asserts that "it is not important which operating system, word processor, email client, Web browser and spreadsheet used" (p. 30). Rather, one should focus "on the teaching of the basic principles and concepts and avoid narrow exposure to only proprietary software from specific vendors" (p. 31).

Given the rapidly changing nature of technology, the propensity for software to be replaced regularly when a newer, better, faster, and in some cases, revolutionary, option comes along, it would seem that mastery of single software programs would not well-serve students in the changing world of tomorrow. The general philosophy behind FOSS is one of inquiry, collaboration, and creativity, and these are skills most would agree we should be fostering in modern learners. Thomas Friedman (2006), in his best seller *The World is Flat*, repeatedly reminds readers that the only security they, or their children, really have in the hot, flat, and crowded world of tomorrow is their ability to learn how to learn. If one agrees with this assertion, then it should follow that using FOSS to teach and to learn concepts that inspire, transform, and promote creativity, collaboration and innovation is more important than teaching mastery of single, currently-relevant programs. We need to think of FOSS *as education* and not just hardware or software used *in education*.

FOSS in Education

Free and Open Source Software (FOSS) has recently entered the conventional mainstream. While there have been communities of people working together on software development projects for decades—even before the Free Software Movement began in the 80s—the idea of free and open source software in education is a fairly new idea. This is a little ironic given that anyone who uses the Internet very likely makes use of FOSS regularly. From domain names that use the standard open source Berkeley Internet Name Daemon (BIND) to web pages served using Apache to a quick Google search on a Firefox browser, teachers, students, and administrators are relying on FOSS to help them complete daily tasks and manage their lives. Without FOSS, the Internet, as known today, would not exist. Still, most educators are unaware of the role FOSS plays in our daily lives and are ill-informed about its power as a pedagogical tool.

The world of school-based education tends to be conservative, so it is no surprise that the majority of software applications found in U.S. schools, and most schools outside the U.S., are proprietary in nature. The idea that FOSS could be a viable solution for educational needs, from operating systems to desktop applications, is gaining momentum but is still a fairly radical concept for most educational institutions. With the recent economic downturn (2009-2010) and its resulting budget cuts at all levels of education, the financial benefit of adopting FOSS is gaining recognition as a key selling point and has, indeed, been one of the primary reasons for its recent educational implementation. As van Rooij (2007) states, "Open Source software is being touted as the key to building integrated learning environments that serve the academic and the business needs of the institution, within the confines of resource and budgetary constraints" (p. 192).

However, while budgetary consideration may be the "foot in the door" of education for FOSS, free and open source represents a transformative force in education which could potentially alter the way that curricula is developed and signal a significant change in the way that education is conducted (Whitehurst, 2009). Szulik (2007) asserts, "more than ever... the philosophy of open source is changing the world" (p. 4). Potentially, this is very good news for both the open source community as well as students at all levels of education. As Watson, Boudreau, York, and Greiner (2008) state: "The power of technology is released when it enables new and more productive roles and transforms organizational structures" (p. 82). This is no more true, and necessary, than in the application of FOSS, and the emerging E-Learning technologies that complement it, to our educational structures.

Proponents of FOSS in schools say that its ideals of openness and freedom and self-sufficiency are a good complement to what education at least *should* be. If we are to foster in our students the development of critical thinking and problem-solving and teach the skills and dispositions needed in this century, then students need a wide range of tools available to them, and they should not be limited by the dependencies that many adults in the education system may have on proprietary software. Further, using technology and understanding technology are two different things. A dependency on proprietary software encourages

only use of the technology. The philosophy of FOSS with its emphasis on collaboration and development promotes understanding.

FOSS as Education

Educational technologist Steve Hargadon (2006) sees two ways of characterizing FOSS in education. He uses the expression "FOSS *in* Education" to describe the use of free and open source applications in educational settings. This would include such activities as using the spreadsheet feature in *OpenOffice* to calculate grades, or creating a picture in *TuxPaint*. Hargadon (2006) uses the expression "FOSS *as* Education" to describe the less common practice of using FOSS applications in education courses. With FOSS *as* Education, students work with the source code and collaborate in a community of practice, which may include the larger open source community surrounding a given software application. Unfortunately, outside of the field of computer science, one does not currently see students often working with source code. However, we can learn from what is happening with FOSS in computer-related disciplines and speculate about FOSS's potential impact as positive force for change.

Initiatives to teach FOSS as education tend to be started at the grassroots level, by individual teachers or by groups of teachers, and often in partnership with companies. One such example is *Google's Summer of Code* program. In this program, high school and college students from around the world are brought together through the Internet to collaborate on open source projects. Another Google initiative, known as the *Google Highly Open Participation Contest*, challenges pre-college students to write code, to produce documentation, and to participate in other social constructivist-style "FOSS as education," activities. Projects such as these highlight a reoccurring theme across the current FOSS literature: the ability for open source to expose students to real-world problems in order to better prepare them for the business world or other professional domains. As Whitehurst (2009) affirms, "open source amplifies a 'hands-on' approach to learning by connecting students to a community of users in an effort to solve problems" (p. 70).

FOSS also represents a break from the traditional approach to software development and encourages an ethic of sharing and collaboration as part of the educational process (Morelli et al., 2009). According to Watson et al. (2008), participating in software development projects and tools via websites such as *Sourceforge* can "allow students to be involved in a project that more closely resembles commercial software development environments than the typical class assignments" (p. 80). In a study, including chief academic officers conducted by van Rooij (2007), the findings indicated that "the strongest positive influence (52.6% stating strong positive/positive influence) on CAO consideration of open source for teaching and learning is the ability of open source to support active learning, so that students are engaged in real-world tasks, practice and reinforcement" (p. 201). FOSS provides "a model for the creation of self-learning and self-organizing communities" (Sowe & Stamelos, 2007, p. 425). Open source distributed virtual communities afford the opportunity for apprenticeship and participating in "real-world" experiences. These communities of practice "allow new students to engage in 'learning to be' even as they are mastering the content of a field" (Brown & Adler, 2008, p. 20). In other words, FOSS *as* education may be more important and valuable than FOSS *in* education.

For example, would offering students the opportunity to develop FOSS applications within a real-world environment motivate them in to excel in their coursework? Would coupling FOSS to relevant real-world projects serve to change the way we conduct education at all levels? Instead of continuing the "supply-push" model of twentieth century education where proprietary suppliers push their needs on the education system, Brown

and Adler (2008) suggest that a new pedagogical approach, "demand-pull" be implemented for the Twenty-First Century "based on providing students with access to rich (sometimes virtual) learning communities built around practice" (p. 30) so they can pull information and learning opportunities based on their needs. Real-world problem solving is what Friedman (2006) had in mind when he talked about teaching students to learn how to learn as well as how to be creative, flexible and open to new ideas and new ways of doing things. The coming century will demand that learners combine unprecedented access to knowledge with creative thinking (generating new ideas) and critical thinking (analyzing and evaluating ideas). FOSS as education encourages learners not only to access information but also to process it, critically analyze it, and make something new with it. The suggestion, therefore, is that the introduction of FOSS software and its associated philosophy into curricula at all levels of education could represent a quantum and necessary shift to a learning paradigm that is more relevant, more adaptive, more continuous: in other words, a true 21st century learning environment.

THE FUTURE IS OPEN

Who could have anticipated 100, 50, or even 25 years ago, that a learner, sitting in isolation, in front of a device no bigger than a stack of books would be able to access practically limitless knowledge and create a personalized learning environment that literally knows no bounds? Without question, unprecedented instant access to information and a new sense of openness and collaboration is changing the educational landscape. Unfortunately, the current classroom model is the educational equivalent of Ford's *Model T* automobile. It was arguably fine for 100 years ago but has little place in the modern world other than as an anachronistic curiosity.

Modern learners are being continually connected to new and ever-evolving content that addresses their personal learning needs in ways unimagined just a few years ago. There is a raw sense of empowerment in the learning process that is sweeping the world. This newfound freedom is equalizing the educational playing field between social classes and between countries and is placing control of the learning process in the hands of the individual—where many argue it rightly belongs.

Free and Open Source Software is helping to drive this new participatory culture of learning. Unfortunately, the concepts of learner-centered instruction, empowered learning, and open access are not making their way into our brick-and-mortar schools at anything resembling an appropriate pace. Generally speaking, we have a current system with a vested interest in perpetuating the status quotient. That is not to say that there are not isolated cases of individual teachers and schools bucking the system and doing innovative things. However, there is most certainly a disconnect between what we *know* is happening in the real world and what we *do* in our classrooms at all levels of instruction.

Most people would admit the current educational system needs changing, but they can cite a list of reasons—from lack of funding and technology training to classroom management issues and teachers unions—as to why change does not happen. Regardless, the truth is this: there is no technology revolution in education inside the walls of our schools. It is as if the schools exist in a vacuum, suspended in time, while the world streaks by. Walk into any classroom today and chances are it is going to look almost exactly like it looked 100 years ago: teacher on the front stage, students in desks, eyes forward, dozily accepting their role as passive learning receptacles. One hundred years ago, students clustered around typewriters typing papers. Today, they cluster around laptops doing the same thing, but, the use of the technology has not changed. Whether they are banging away on an *Underwood Typewriter* or a new *Apple Macbook*, it is still only a word processing tool. There is little real effort on a system-wide basis to *access* and *participate* in the free and unique learning opportunities that technology brings to students regardless of age, race, background, or financial status. Robert Reich (1992), Secretary of Labor in the first Clinton presidency wrote in his book *The Work of Nations*:

[In the current classroom model] Children [move] from grade to grade through a preplanned sequence of standard subjects, as if on factory conveyor belts. At each stage, certain facts [are] poured into their heads. Children with the greatest capacity to absorb the facts, and with the most submissive demeanor, [are] placed on a rapid track through the sequence; those with the least capacity for fact retention and self-discipline, on the slowest. Most children [end] up on a conveyor belt of medium speed. Standardized tests [are] routinely administered at certain checkpoints in order to measure how many of the facts [have] stuck in the small heads, and product defects [are] taken off the line and returned for retooling. As in the mass-production system, discipline and order [are] emphasized above all else. (p.60)

The point to be taken is that American school systems, and many of those abroad, were never designed to support open, collaborative learning. They were designed to serve the needs of a society and not to support personalized, learner-centered instruction. Given this, it is easy to understand the resistance to change, as it would require a rethinking of the entire institutional setup. But, rethink we must.

Real, modern learning is messy. The current educational system is insular and controlling, and it is doing a disservice to our students. Bonk (2009) points out that just years ago, "educational institutions were not expected to share their courses and course materials with competing institutions or with learners not enrolled in their programs" (p. 16). Now, openness is becoming the norm.

The culture of sharing that marks the history of the Free and Open Source Software movement has spread beyond the realm of software development (Bonk, 2009). It can be seen in the idea of Open Education, under which title we include such things as open courseware, content management systems, and communities of practice. We are already seeing exemplary universities such as UC Berkley, MIT, Utah State, Tufts, and Carnegie, offering full courses, taught by noted educators, in a huge range of subjects for free on the Web. According to Bonk (2009) as of 2008 "there were more than one hundred universities placing their content on display for millions of spectators without charging any admission fees" (p. 175).

Programs such as Europe's *Openlearn* and Rice Universities' *Connexions,* with its nearly 15,000 learning modules, are allowing users not only to select material from a variety of disciplines, but also to create new customized courses for individual learning needs. In the K-12 sector, open content repositories like *Curriki* are allowing educators and students access to world-class educational materials as well as the ability to collaboratively build on and review material that has already been uploaded. What happens to our current educational institutions when *open* learning begins to be a viable option for students at all levels? For the first time in our history, the educational establishment is facing real competition, and it is not from the school in the next county or the regional university down the road. It is coming from the Web.

Combine all of this with the literal explosion of online (E-Learning) enrollments at all levels of education and the recent systematic meta-analysis of the research literature from 1996 through 2008 by the U.S. Department of Education that found for the first time that "…on average, students in online learning conditions performed better than those receiving face-to-face instruction" (Means, Toyama, Murphy, Bakia, & Jones, 2009, p.ix), and one has nothing short of a modern learning renaissance. And, the Obama administration supports this cultural shift. Current Secretary of Education Arne Duncan said of the report:

This new report reinforces that effective teachers need to incorporate digital content into everyday classes and consider open-source learning management systems, which have proven cost effective in school districts and colleges nationwide. We must take advantage of this historic opportunity to use American Recovery and Reinvestment Act funds to bring broadband access and online learning to more communities (U.S. Department of Education, 2009, para. 3).

President Barack Obama is also calling for federal funds to be used in the creation of free and open courses at community colleges and high schools (Inside Higher Ed, 2009). For the first time in the history of this country, we have politicians who are not only taking notice of the sweeping changes taking place in education, but who are also willing to speak out for and fund a new generation of learners who want new, more open, and personal ways to access educational opportunities.

While politicians are committed to working with institutions, the real truth may be that institutions are fighting a losing battle for control over the learning process. Control is shifting into the hands of learners where innovation, creativity, and self-determination could do more to shape a person's future than a degree from a brick-and-mortar institution. Right now, much of the available content is un-credentialed and lacks accreditation; however, is it really so far-fetched to imagine a future where institutions will arise with the sole purpose of cobbling together a individualized, world-class education with classes from Harvard, Yale, MIT, Cambridge, The Open University, or any number of possible learning opportunities and then issuing an accredited degree upon successful completion of the course of study—all for FREE? Think of how the world will change when a boy from a remote village in Afghanistan with a $100 laptop and satellite Internet connection will be afforded the same learning opportunities as a wealthy student from London. Right now, the world is open when it comes to learning for learning sake. Soon, it will be open and accredited for formalized learning as well.

Concepts of openness, access, E-Learning, mobile technologies, and personal learning environments that were unthinkable just a few years ago have now gone mainstream. FOSS is a driving force behind much of this change. However, adapting the concepts of freedom and openness to change the face of our current educational landscape is no small task, and educational institutions must begin to adapt or run the risk of becoming irrelevant.

We began this chapter with the story of *The Little Dutch Boy*. We now return to that story from a different viewpoint. In this new telling, the little boy is representative of an entrenched educational bureaucracy futilely trying to plug a growing number of leaks in the dyke protecting them from the wave of free and open technological change crashing against their walls. There are not enough fingers and toes in the entire village to plug the leaks of change. The leaks are becoming a stream, the stream will become a gush, and the gush will become a flood that sweeps away all that has come before. Those living "behind the dyke" are going to be forced to change whether they like it or not. It is the authors' hope that when the dyke breaks, we will be prepared to surf our way through one of the most exciting times for education in human history.

REFERENCES

Allbritton, D. W. (2003). Using open-source solutions to teach computing skills for student research. *Behavior Research Methods, Instruments, & Computers, 35*(2), 251–254.

Bonaccorsi, A., & Rossi, C. (2003). Why open source software can succeed. *Research Policy, 32,* 1243–1258. doi:10.1016/S0048-7333(03)00051-9

Bonk, C. (2009). *The world is open: How web technology is revolutionizing education.* San Francisco: Jossey-Bass.

Bretthauer, D. (2002). Open source software: A history. *Information Technology and Libraries, 21*(1), 3–10.

Brown, J. S., & Adler, R. P. (2008). Minds on fire. *EDUCAUSE Review, 43*(1), 16–32.

Canton, J. (2006). *The extreme future: The top trends that will reshape the world for the next 5, 10, and 20 years.* New York: Penguin Group.

Carmichael, P., & Honour, L. (2002). Open source as appropriate technology for global education. *International Journal of Educational Development, 22,* 47–53. doi:10.1016/S0738-0593(00)00077-8

Chauhan, A. (2004). Open source and open standards in higher education. *ACET Journal of Computer Education and Research, 2*(1), 1–3.

Coppola, C., & Neelley, E. (2004). Open source – opens learning: Why open source makes sense for education. *The r-smart group.* Retrieved September 9, 2009, from http://www.rsmart.com/assets/OpenSourceOpensLearningJuly2004.pdf

Dunlap, J., Wilson, B., & Young, D. (2002, June 24-29). Xtreme learning control: Examples of the open source movement's impact on our educational practice in a university setting. In *Proceedings of the ED-MEDIA 2002 World Conference on Educational Multimedia, Hypermedia & Telecommunications* (pp. 2-7).

Edwards, K. (2001). Epistemic communities, situated learning and open source software development. In *Proceedings of the Workshop on Epistemic Cultures and the Practice of Interdisciplinarity,* Trondheim, Norway. Retrieved September 9, 2009, from http://opensource.mit.edu/papers/kasperedwards-ec.pdf

Friedman, T. (2006). *The world is flat: A brief history of the twenty-first century (updated and expanded edition)*. New York: Farrar, Straus, and Giroux.

GNU Operating System. (2009). *The free software definition*. Retrieved September 9, 2009, from http://www.gnu.org/philosophy/free-sw.html

Gonsalves, A. (2003). The Linux alternative. *Technology & Learning, 23*, 9–12.

Halse, G., & Terzoli, A. (2002). *Open source in South African schools: Two case studies*. Retrieved September 9, 2009, from http://www.schoolnetafrica.net/fileadmin/resources/Open_Source_in_South_African_Schools.pdf

Hargadon, S. (2006, October 23*). Interview with Martin Dougiamas, creator of Moodle*. Retrieved September 9, 2009, from http://www.stevehargadon.com/2006/10/interview-with-martin-dougiamas.html

Hart, T. (2003). *Open source in education*. Retrieved September 9, 2009, from http://www.portfolio.umaine.edu/~hartt/OS%20in%20Education.pdf

Herbert, M. (2001). *Open source in education: An overview*. Retrieved September 9, 2009, from http://people.redhat.com/mherbert/papers/RHPaper1.pdf

Inside Higher Ed. (2009, June 29). *US Push for Free Online Courses*. Retrieved September 9, 2009, from http://www.insidehighered.com/news/2009/06/29/ccplan

Kim, A. (2002). Open source presents benefits to educators. *T.H.E. Journal, 30*(1), 1–3.

Lakhan, S. E., & Jhunjhunwala, K. (2008). Open source in education. *EDUCAUSE Quarterly, 31*(2), 32–40.

Means, B., Toyama, Y., Murphy, R., Bakia, M., & Jones, K. (2009). *Evaluation of evidence-based practices in online learning: A meta-analysis and review of online learning studies*. Washington, DC: U.S. Department of Education. Retrieved September 19, 2009, from http://www.ed.gov/rschstat/eval/tech/evidence-based-practices/finalreport.pdf

Montalbano, E. (2009). Forrester: Microsoft office in no danger from competitors. *PC World*. Retrieved September 9, 2009, from http://www.pcworld.com/businesscenter/article/166123/forrester_microsoft_office_in_no_danger_from_competitors.html?tk=nl_dnx_h_crawl

Morelli, R., Tucker, A., Danner, N., De Lanerolle, T. R., Ellis, H. J. C., & Izmirli, O. (2009). Revitalizing computing through fee and open Source software for humanity. *Communications of the ACM, 52*(8), 67–75. doi:10.1145/1536616.1536635

Moyle, K. (2003). *Open source software and Australian school education: An introduction*. Retrieved September 9, 2009, from http://www.educationau.edu.au/jahia/webdav/site/myjahiasite/shared/papers/open_source.pdf

O'Dell, R. (2002). Using Open Source in Education. *T.H.E. Focus*. Retrieved September 9, 2009, from http://www.thejournal.com/thefocus/12.cfm

Raymond, E. (1999). *The cathedral and the bazaar*. Retrieved September 9, 2009, from http://www.catb.org/~esr/writings/cathedral-bazaar/cathedral-bazaar/

Reich, R. (1992). *The work of nations: Preparing ourselves for 21st century capitalism*. New York: Alfred A. Knopf, Inc.

Remidez, H., Laffey, J., & Musser, D. (2001). Open source and the diffusion of teacher education software. In J. Price, et al. (Eds.), *Proceedings of Society for Information Technology and Teacher Education International Conference 2001* (pp. 2774-2778). Chesapeake, VA: AACE

Sowe, S. K., & Stamelos, I. G. (2007). Involving software engineering students in open source software projects: Experiences from a pilot study. *Journal of Information Systems Education, 18*(4), 425–436.

Szulik, M. J. (2007). Open for change. *EDUCAUSE Review, 42*(1), 4–5.

Technology: Measuring Impacts and Shaping the Future, Washington, DC.

Tinker, R. (2000). *Ice machines, steamboats, and education: Structural change and educational technologies.* Paper presented at the Secretary's Conference on Educational

Tong, T. (2004). *Free/open source software in education.* Retrieved September 9, 2009, from http://www.iosn.net/education/foss-educationprimer/fossPrimer-Education.pdf

U.S. Department of Education. (2009, June 26). *Analysis of controlled studies shows online learning enhances classroom instruction.* Retrieved September 9, 2009, http://www.ed.gov/news/pressreleases/2009/06/06262009.html van Rooij, S. (2007). Open source software in US higher education: Reality or illusion? *Education & Information Technologies, 12*(4), 191-209.

Warger, T. (2002). The open-source movement. *EDUTECH Report, 18*(2), 18-20. Retrieved September 9, 2009, from http://net.educause.edu/ir/library/pdf/eqm0233.pdf

Watson, R. T., Boudreau, M., York, P. T., & Greiner, M. (2008). Opening the classroom. *Journal of Information Systems Education, 19*(1), 75–85.

Wheeler, B. (2004). Open source 2007: How did this happen? *EDUCAUSE Review, 39*(4), 12–27.

Wheeler, B. (2007). Open source 2010: Reflections on 2007. *EDUCAUSE Review, 42*(1), 48–67.

Whitehurst, J. (2009). Open source: Narrowing the divides between education, business, and community. *EDUCAUSE Review, 44*(1), 70–71.

Wikipedia. (2009). *Open Source.*

Working with Open Source. (2004, March)... *EDUTECH Report, 20*(3), 1–7.

Section 2
Free and Open Source Software in E- Learning

Chapter 3
Lessons from Constructivist Theories, Open Source Technology, and Student Learning

Gladys Palma de Schrynemakers
Long Island University, USA

ABSTRACT

There has been a great deal written about the three subjects discussed in this chapter. One of the challenges, however, is establishing meaningful links between the first two, constructivism and open source, so that the synergism between them can provide faculty with the tools to create the best possible learning environment for students. Herein, therefore, we examine these connections, first by an overview of how students acquire information and thus learn about themselves and others in the 21st century. From here, the discussion moves on to shed light on the deeply-rooted need of individuals to understand themselves and the world through dialectic, that is by investigating truths through discussion. Intrinsic to this task is an examination of the impact of technology on those interested in pursuing teaching and learning through open source platforms: How, for example, has technology abetted or truncated that dialogue in education? We then follow the linkages between constructivism and open source to examine how both link up to provide support and pedagogical assistance to student learning. The chapter concludes with examples of how the author has integrated constructivist philosophies with open source technology to establish a collaborative and effective learning environment for college students.

INTRODUCTION

Twenty-first century students, characterized at different times and places as the x, y, or, z generation or whatever run of the alphabet happens to be today's current fashion, think of themselves as communicators in cyberspace. For this generation, the worldwide social networking system places young people at the vanguard of communicating about who they are—their identity, knowledge of others, social interactions, and understanding of world events—with their contemporaries in real time. Equally important to these students is the ability to filter all they do through their digital

DOI: 10.4018/978-1-61520-917-0.ch003

social networking, which can literally span the globe.

The need for electronic verification of self through social networking may represent the purest form of Erving Goffman's theory of how individuals present themselves to their peers, i.e., by creating digital self-impressions. We know that learning may occur in many ways, including personal exchanges and direct observations For example, the best way to a learn a language is to interact in an environment where others speak the language and you are able to use that language to connect with people and produce successful outcomes. In a real way, we are re-learning the art of conversation through social networking, where communication may be less poetic and more truncated but where students are comfortable—and, yes, happy. Concomitantly, we are moving away from lecture halls, cafeterias, etc., and learning and socializing within our digital communities.

Students attending today's colleges and universities are looking for and often indeed requiring the same personalization, connection, and flexibility in their educational experience. Because garnering and assimilating information in today's world are instantaneous activities, forward-looking companies like Google and Apple have developed and incorporated social networking into their vision and production. For instance, Google, through its recent addition of a function entitled "scholarly articles," provides its users with built-in academic references. In another example, Apple's iPod revolution is leveraging the business of teaching and learning with its creative iTunes U. In 1990, Apple launched its first TED (Technology Entertainment Design) Talks conference in California to facilitate, in part, building alliances with learning institutions and being responsive to the educational needs of students. Now an annual conference devoted to the sharing of innovative ideas through its own website, YouTube, and iTunes, the conference continues to clarify the dynamics and challenges of the growing collaborations between social

networking and educational success. No doubt, these powerful cooperative relationships will result in exciting learning outcomes as today's students become more competent with integrating social networking into learning experiences and classroom lessons. In fact, having the ability to select any topic of interest within a matter of minutes, listen to lectures, view videos, or download relevant research information spawns new learning strategies; furthermore, using this multi and mixed media to learn and synthesize new information fosters the potential for community learning by sharing student responses online, e.g., by postings on Wikipedia. In an environment of instant information, students are searching to become more involved and empowered and thus are receptive to change that allows for greater creativity and flexibility. Being able to be proactive in communicating their identities and knowledge in their own voices and connecting and contributing these voices to a larger arena and having them become a part of a larger context will, I believe, have a salutary effect on student outcomes. Patricia Hill Collins (1990) writes about this need to voice the "I" and communicate it to the "we": "So the voice that I now seek is both individual and collective, personal and political, one reflecting the intersection of my unique biography with the larger meaning of my times."

Therefore, the faculty who are truly interested in engaging students in active learning must embrace technology as the new medium of communication and use this medium as a way of teaching and helping students progress from the individual to the collective. Beyond simply representing an avenue for communicating ideas, the medium is one where new ideas can emerge. Technology is a compelling resource for students because it offers them much more than information acquisition: it is a responsive educational "opportunity" for students to become active participants in the creation of knowledge. But simply having the technology and the various sources obviously is not enough, particularly if the technology is not wedded to a strong philosophical base. Jean-Francois Lyotard (1991), in his Postmodern Condition: A Report on Knowledge, describes the importance of the philosophical platform with regards to technology:

The relation to knowledge is not articulated in terms of the realization of the life of the spirit or the emancipation of humanity, but in terms of the users of complex conceptual and material machinery and those who benefit from its performance capabilities. They have at their disposal no metalanguage or metanarrative in which to formulate the final goal and correct use of that machinery. (p.52)

The use of technology clearly therefore must be built on an intellectual foundation that fosters individual knowledge and contributes to and sustains collective understanding, or it runs the risk of merely being "machinery," as Lyotard concludes. Equally important to the discussion of the philosophical foundation is the selection of technology that will sustain that foundation, that is, the choice of a technological platform with the capability to sustain and support students—as they write individual narratives, contribute to a learning dialog, and learn from a metanarrative. Carol Gilligan (1993) describes this education through the development of voice: "A voice is a powerful psychological instrument and channel, which connects the inner and outworlds...[and] this ongoing relational exchange among people is mediated through language and culture, diversity and plurality."

The philosophical underpinning of the partnership between technology and education, discussed herein, is one that incorporates the individual and collective voice, that is, the educational philosophy known as constructivism. Supported and advocated by researchers known as developmentalists—including Jean Piaget, Erik Erikson, Carol Gilligan, and Robert Kegan, who have studies the interaction of individuals and the environments in which they live—constructivism is pivotal to

the discussion that follows. Piaget's work dealt with cognitive development, focusing primarily on how infants moved from their totally subjective world to one that incorporates and understands objective reality. He supposed that each cognitive structure provided operations or capacities that serve as building blocks for making sense of the world, that is, for "constructing" a type of external reality. Yet those operations correspondingly structure an inner world or self as well, based on the interactions between self and other, a subject and object, inside and outside, permitting the individual to know the world (Crittenden, 1992). Robert Kegan, in studying human development, noted that the concept of development was not a static condition, but a gradual evolving one, where the individual was unfolding through chronological and experiential maturation. The constructive-development framework studies the phenomenon in nature that Kegan (1982) calls the evolution of meaning. Kegan speaks of constructing a framework for the making of meaning, so as individuals develop they have an internal device for dealing with new experiences and information. It is, therefore, in the contextual framework of constructivism, which is derived from social psychology, where the individual and communal commitments are bridged; for constructivists, as with social psychologists, an individual is interactively connected to a larger societal context. In fact, Erik Erikson (1968) defines identity as "... characterized by the actually attained forever to-be-revised sense of the reality of the self within social reality."

One is then left to consider what technology would best support the type of learning that Dewey (1916) describes as "backward-forward," i.e., the inextricable connections that must be forged between the individual and the subject matter for learning to occur. *I* take the position that Open Source is such a platform. Open Source is defined (Wikipedia, 2009) as "an approach to the design, development, and distribution of software, offering practical accessibility to a software's source code." In fact, the President's Information Technology Advisory Committee in 2000 endorsed the platform by calling it a "viable strategy for producing high-quality software through a mixture of public, private and academic partnerships...." When referencing Open Source, the Committee defined Open Source as, "...a generic term for software that is intended to be distributed to anyone who wants it, possibly under certain conditions determined by a licensing agreement. With the explosive growth of the Linux open source operating system over the last several years, the term has become increasingly commonplace." All very technical definitions that put simply say that open source is a platform that allows individuals to look at the program, review its progress, make changes, and distribute the new program. Russell Pavlicek (2000) outlines four major benefits of Open Source Technology.

1. Open Source emphasizes quality
2. Open Sources stresses flexibility
3. Open Source decreases development time
4. Closed Source is characterized ad non-competitive...

Clearly, a learning model like constructivism, which for the most part is adapted in higher education through experiential learning, requires a technological platform with the flexibility and adaptability of Open Source; what is more, in the world of Open Source there exist countless choices for educational use.

No discussion of Open Source is complete without examining and evaluating its efficacy on student learning and the academic programs that develop an experience using the scaffolding approach towards that learning. One might argue that the technology has finally opened the door to constructivism and action-oriented learning. "Knowledge building is an active construction performed by learners based on the interaction with their environment." (Schroeder & Spannagel 2006) What better way exists than to engage in

meaningful interaction than through blogging, collaborative work in group assignments, and in on-line peer tutoring groups? The fact that all this could be accomplished through the use of open source is a cognitivist's dream. In fact, the flexibility that open source course management systems have provided has set the stage for a myriad of pedagogical possibilities. Moreover, the potential for students to construct individual and collective meaning/understanding through digital active learning is unlimited.

What open source technology provides is a medium or a technological link to theoretical notions reflecting on how individuals understand, process, and create new knowledge or build on existing comprehension. Inherent in the design of the instruction of open source are the elements essential to the constructivist notion of learning. Bedmar, Cunningham, Duffy, and Perry (1992) suggest that, for the individual to learn within the theoretical framework known as constructivism, there are elements necessary to instructional design, including analysis, synthesis, and evaluation. Therefore, whenever designing an educational environment for an open source course, the instructor must include these key three factors into the design protocol. The "link" between the learning and the technology establishes a clear framework for the instructor to build an environment where students can analyze information through synthesis, create new paradigms by combining and reconfiguring different ideas, and thereafter evaluate whether these new ideas have value or need to be explored further.

One example of what Schroeder and Spanngel (2006) refer to as "construction performed by learners" provided the basis for an assignment that the author designed for a graduate Urban Studies class. The class project, taught from an interdisciplinary perspective, that is, one melding concepts/theories from urban planning, sociology, and film studies, required students to view clips from Spike Lee's explosive film, "Do the Right Thing" and read an excerpt of his production notes. Students were then asked to create a digital collage or short film about a city block, produce an explanatory narrative, and, in a collaborative undertaking, blog about the process and each other's submissions. The results exceeded the expectations of both professor and students, principally because participating students were able to dialogue effectively about the process of selecting a location and the medium—photographic collage or a moving collage—most consistent with what they wished to portray. Equally important to creating something of value for this learning experience was the goal of elevating students' cognitive skills as they labored to connect the visual with written aspects of the assignment. This effort was advanced because students were learning not only to create narratives from visual images, but also were reflecting on their decision-making processes. Beyond the constructivist philosophical underpinnings so far discussed, we, as instructors, wish to move our students from simply appreciating a basic understanding of subject matter to deeper levels of understanding, for example, those found in Bloom's Taxonomy, namely, application, analysis, and synthesis and in the end the evaluation of knowledge. It appears that open source learning moves the locus of control away from the professor formulating the content, delivering the content, and asking simply for student response to the student, who becomes an empowered learner through active learning. In many ways, the use of open source technology is in harmony with Dewey's (1938) notion of the need for a learner to have an intimate and a necessary relation to the "idea" or concept being learned and the process of actual experience and learning.

AN OVERVIEW OF THE PRINCIPLES OF OPEN SOURCE AND LEARNING

As mentioned earlier Open Source is a delivery system for technology that does not require the sophistication of a computer programmer. Edu-cators and students, however, wish to know how this platform effectively supports student learning, specifically the higher level learning skills that Bloom outlines as application, analysis, synthesis, and evaluation of knowledge. The Open Source learning environment includes Moodle, EduCreate, Eduspaces, Covidia, and LogiCampus, to name a few. The feature common to all is software with user friendly language, which can be modified to address user learning needs. Moore (2002) notes that Open Source provides a forum for student learning in as much as students are critical voices in the process of change: "Students figure as an integral part of this development process, just as they do in a good open, face-to face exchange of ideas in a physical space. Indeed, success will depend on participation by students as they simultaneously solve problems, make critical evaluations, and help accomplish the work at hand." (p.48) Consistent with this view of student involvement, Professors Perkins and Hartman, at a recent Society of Geological Society meeting (2007), lectured on the role students have in mapping out their own connections for learning.

Students are responsible, in large part, for directing class activities and assessment. They provide *Just-In-Time-Teaching* feedback on reading and homework before every class through *Moodle*. Instructors use the feedback to plan class activities. This means that students' outside-of-class preparation fundamentally affects what happens during class. Learning and goals assessment are accomplished using carefully designed rubrics developed for each activity. Students have the rubrics ahead of time so they know exactly what the goals are, and can use the rubrics to assess themselves. Our end game is to involve a generally reluctant student body into active and reflective participation.

Perkins and Hartman describe how students—using Moodle (Modular Object-Oriented Learning Environment), a popular Open Source course management system—actively navigate the course and reflect on and assessing their own learning.

There are no mysteries here that the professor unravels because students understand the learning goals and expectations of the course and thus become "active and reflective" learners

Evidently, Open Source advances student learning by creating an environment for students to map a clear and precise route to their own acquisition of knowledge. And in many instances, it also brings about a learning environment and experience for the professor. By design, this technology not only offers a forum for consequential dialogue between the professor and students, but also leads to a vigorous engagement with content. This, in turn, has the potential for creating new knowledge for those involved in the course and for the learning community.

AN OVERVIEW OF THE PRINCIPLES OF CONSTRUCTIVISM AND LEARNING

Reviewing constructivist theories is in many ways analogous to examining the different digits of the hand. We instantly recognized that, while each finger has distinctive features and, at times, very individual purposes, together they work towards a collective purpose. Such is the case for the theories of constructivist thinkers, each adding its own distinct fingerprint, yet in totality achieving a comprehensive understanding of how human learning is accomplished. Constructivists like John Dewey, Jean Piaget, Lev Vygotsky, Jerome Burner, and Howard Gardner have described human cognition in the context of the connections individuals make. In other words, they all agree that the act of learning is not passive but built on a foundation of cultural constructs and previous experiences. Culture and preceding knowledge, therefore, help us to configure new information or reconfigure old information.

Constructivism is an interdisciplinary notion about learning that takes into account how individuals create meaning. For Lev Vogotsky,

meaning was the connection between language and cognition, which was influenced by the individual's personal culture. Jerome Burner (1987) expanded on Vogotsky's idea when he wrote about Vogotsky's work: "...his educational theory is a theory of cultural transmission as well as a theory of development. For 'education' implies for Vogotsky not only the development of the individual's potential, but the historical expression and growth of the human culture from which Man springs" (pp.1-2). The "growth of human culture," therefore, rests not only with the improvement of the individual, but also with the intellectual enrichment of humanity. Vogotsky's idea of learning was very similar to Burner's vision of how an individual pieces together new information and integrates that information using her own past and current knowledge. Burner referred to this newly transformed information as "paradoxical intent." In effect, the teacher's task is to introduce a concept to her students; however, if the student simply captures the information in the exact way it was transmitted, then there is no real learning on the student's part. All the student can hope to do is remember or memorize the concept as a factoid.

True learning only happens when the individual processes the concept through the lens of her own experience and knowledge. And the knowledge the individual possesses is exclusive and singular to that individual, because it is based on her own experiences and understanding of the world. In fact, Burner (1962) went further, by saying, "No person is master of the whole culture; indeed, this is almost a defining characteristic of that form of social memory that we speak of as culture. Each man lives a fragment of it. To be whole, he must create his own version of the world, using that part of his cultural heritage he has made his own through education" (p.116). Therefore, learning requires the assimilation of information into understanding, which can only properly occur through the metaphor of the individual lens that focuses on one's own culture and understanding of events. This insight is consistent, I believe, with Piaget's view of assimilation and accommodation, but both are forms in which one connects new information to existing knowledge and understanding. However, there are differences to consider: Piaget, who is regarded as a constructivist, paid more attention to neurological connections, while Bruner and Vogostsky concentrated on socialization and learning. But it was John Dewey's theory of understanding and his application to learning that forged the best connection between constructivism and the open-source learning environment.

Dewey's idea of constructed learning is inextricable bound to an open-source learning environment, where "there is an intimate and necessary relationship between experience and education" (p.7). The intimate relationship that Dewey speaks of cannot always be achieved through traditional mediums. For example, I have been using WebCT in my courses for the last decade and, I believe, never fully achieved the "intimate and necessary" synergy that Dewey wrote about. This platform, WebCT, suffers from one- dimensionality and can be described as an expanded lecture that allows for a very limited question and answer format. For example, the professor first posts a question based on a lecture, reading, etc., to which each student responds individually; and the professor then grades the student's work and returns the post (similar to the traditional handing in of assignments). Clearly, the student's response is limited to answering the question(s) framed by the professor, with little or no opportunity existing for the student to expand her own understanding of the assigned material beyond the information presented by the professor. However, using open-source learning, the traditional constructivists can directly connect with student needs in the 21st century. Noted psychologist and author Howard Gardner (2008) referenced this need when he wrote about how knowledge is being constructed and shared in the new century: "…the ability to survey huge bodies of information—print and electronic—and to organize that information in useful ways looms more important than ever" (p.11). Likewise, the need

to manage and coordinate vast and multi-media information is referenced in Gardner's 5 Minds for the Future (2008), where he expressly focuses on two specific types of intelligence that are central to the constructivist paradigm—a synthesizing mind and a creative mind. The synthesizing and creative minds are two of five intelligences that Gardner addresses and are the focus of this discussion because they are essential to the constructivist approach. One example of these forms of intelligences, synthesis and creativity, is embodied in the imagination and resourcefulness of Steve Job, the creator of Mac. Apart from creating a new operating system that revolutionized the computer industry, he synthesized new and existing information to craft an innovative platform for the delivery of music—that allows an individual to use a multi-media platform to search the web, speak on the telephone, e-mail, listen to music, type memos, etc. To take existing information and integrate it into one's own experience and thereafter construct fresh and, at times, never before conceived information and then channel it into new constructs and paradigms is building knowledge. For the 21st century learner, learning in an open source environment is resilient and addresses the complexities of managing information in practical ways.

CONSTRUCTIVISM AND OPEN SOURCE

Simply stated, constructivism is the building of knowledge using one's experience as a foundation. Open source learning depends on relatively new media-based platforms that students can easily access to craft new learning. Lifton (1993) may have understood this on some level when he defined the post-modern person as having to be protean, that is, versatile: "…[it] is a balancing act between responsive shapeshifting, on the one hand, and efforts to consolidate and cohere, on the other" (p.9). This shapeshifting, consolidation, and coherence combine to produce the precise environment that open source affords learners. It is a new but nevertheless "natural" setting, where professors can forge a learning rich experience that makes use of texts, videos, images, etc—one that results in a learning community, where students connect in ways not possible in the classroom or even in physical experiential activities.

The open source environment prepares students to be active participants in their learning—the central underpinning of constructivist learning theory—and establishes a conceptual learning framework within the context of a learning community, where professors and students are embedded in a culture of collective learning and comprehension. In this environment, program and course subject matter, instruction, and learning are linked to student experience and are shared reflectively by all participants. The open source platform also provides students a feel for what Maxine Greene (1988) embraces as the dialect of freedom, namely, "…that a person struggling to connect the undertaking of education… to the making and remaking of a public space, a space of dialogue and possibility," (p. *xi*) will find an enhanced sense of solidarity with her learning community. In this educational setting, the professor is the facilitator of the discourse that occurs through a medium that invites students to take on individual and collective roles in the learning endeavor. Thus, the focus shifts from the professor as locus of learning to the student; that is, once the student is at the center of the learning, she is no longer simply memorizing, reciting, and labeling information. Instead, she can move to the upper levels of Bloom's famous taxonomy that includes synthesis, analysis, and application, which better prepares the student to utilize the two of the five intelligences that Gardner deems necessary for the 21st century citizens. But beyond simply providing the student with a means to take hold of her own learning, the open source platform also is a channel for assisting the student to grow as an individual, where " …the

lives and selves we construct are the outcomes of this process meaning-construction" (Bruner, 1990, p.138). Only then does the content shift from simply learning a subject, studying a major, or completing a degree to the approach in William Perry's (1970) Scheme of Intellectual and Ethical Development. Perry's "constructed knowledge" provides a powerful working explanation about how the student incorporates knowledge from others, integrates it into her own personal experience, and reflects on this learning.

So, how does the open source environment set the stage for higher levels of learning? It does so by breaking down the intimidating barriers that traditionally block or discourage collaborative learning and by establishing a social group within the design of the course that improves the coherence and integrity of learning. In fact, the look and feel of most open source networks is purposely designed to simulate social networking through vehicles like Facebook and My Space. For example, using open source, the student is able to post bios like those appearing in social networking systems, where one can introduce oneself to the new community. Many times, this initially includes personal information, individual goals, and expectations for the course and thereafter subsequent learning. Networking of this sort not only makes opportunities available for the professor and classmates to share individual and collective learning goals, but also provides the professor with invaluable information about how to formulate or complete the learning landscape of the course. Moreover, this initial sharing of self, including background and course expectations, engages the student in her first reflective experience in the course and thereby constructs a pathway for reflecting about her learning goals and mapping a strategy for achieving them—all within the framework of her personnel narrative or, in the language of social networking, in her "profile."

The posting of that initial profile can become fertile ground for self and course assessment, which will be discussed elsewhere. For example, in an interdisciplinary, writing intensive course the author teaches, entitled the Idea of the Human, students are required to post an initial "profile" of themselves or a digital portrait that must include both narrative and visual elements. Students must then develop this portrait to reflect their family histories, cultural and/or ethnic backgrounds, interests, and academic and professional aspirations. These portraits serve as a springboard for the first reflective assignment, one that asks students to review their portraits and compose a definition of what it means to be human using this information. The students are then expected to comment on at least two other portraits. Consequently, prior to any class lecture or reading about what it means to be human, students have expanded their understanding of humanness, based, in part, on their own life experiences as well as those of their classmates. They begin to understand that this notion of what it means to be human has many components, including social and cultural, physical and physiological, and ethereal. They also come to appreciate that commonalities can and do exist among classmates who come from different backgrounds. Students must reflect on their original portraits many times during the semester, e.g., after selected readings, class discussions, and experiential explorations, and make whatever changes they deem appropriate and also comment on the transformations of their classmates. All together, the portrait each paints is a work that grows in character and strength but will never be completed.

Successfully linking an Open Source technology like Moodle and the Constructivist pedagogy to a collaborative learning strategy forges a synergy that benefits students and instructors alike. As a doctoral student in computer science, Martin Dogiamas, the creator of Moodle, saw the shortcomings of commercial course management systems, which he found to be limited to the programs constructed by the designers. Dogiamas (1998) considered what philosophical, psychological, and pedagogical antecedents were critical to the

creation of an open source like Moodle: "A constructivist perspective views learners as actively engaged in making meaning, and teaching with that approach looks for what students can analyse, investigate, collaborate, share, build and generate based on what they already know, rather than what facts, skills, and processes they can parrot. To do this effectively, a teacher needs to be a learner and a researcher, to strive for greater awareness of the environments and the participants in a given teaching situation in order to continually adjust their actions to engage students in learning, using constructivism as a referent." Embedded in Moodle was a synergistic connection between technology and teaching and learning that proved to be dynamic and responsive to an-ever changing learning environment. Antonenko, Toy, and Niederhauser (2004) analyzed Moodle through the constructivist lens developed by Hannafin and Land (1997), which focused on five core foundations for a student-centered learning environment, i.e., psychological, pedagogical, cultural, technological, and pragmatic, and found all five fixed in Moodle.

CONSTRUCTIVISM AND ITS USE IN INFORMING INSTRUCTIONAL PRACTICES IN THE OPEN SOURCE ARENA

The use of technology within a constructivist framework in the blended learning arena has many implications for instructional practice. For example, such technologies can generate enormous conceptualizing power and thus guide our thinking to a deeper and more complex understanding of student learning, unfettered by one-dimensionality or tied to any one teaching style or method of assessment. Peter Honebein (1996) outlined seven comprehensive goals for learning environments that are essential for effective pedagogy in an open source environment. These goals are presented below along with the author's strategies for achieving some of them in her college classes.

1. Provide students with the experience to construct their own knowledge. This is a challenging notion for most faculty, since they are asking students to decide what methods are to be used to learn a subject. For example, as part of my course, students are asked to visit the American Museum of Natural History and select an artifact and then to present it as part of an exhibit room, where they are free to design their presentations as they see fit. The only requirement is the presentation must include narrative about the artifact, e.g., country of origin, culture, and usage. All students include their presentations as part of an exhibit. Students can be creative in their presentations, including music and dance from the culture and time period of their artifacts and can fashion original stories about the artifacts.

2. Provide experience in and appreciation for multiple perspectives. Assignments like the one mentioned in goal 1 allow students to experience different cultures through new and interesting ways. By designing an appropriate setting for presenting the cultural artifact, students are exposed to and learn about the culture, history, customs, and practices. Students are required to consider the virtual presentations of their classmates, which may assist them in better understanding their own artifacts, even as it allows them to reflect on the other presentations and cultures.

3. Embed learning in realistic and relevant contexts (an essential part of constructive theory). This is an issue that is particularly evident in mathematics and science courses, where students are rarely, if ever, provided with the relevant connections among the sciences. Scientists themselves admit to this critical disconnect. For example, in Natalie Angier's text, The Cannon (2007), Andrew Knoll, a professor of natural history at Harvard University, concluded that "the average adult American today knows less biology than an average ten-year old living in the Amazon, or than the average American of two hundred years ago" (p.22). Angier proceeds to interview a number of noted scientists in the all the aforementioned fields and all point to the same problem with science education, namely, the disconnect that exists between the material and real and relevant situations.

4. Encourage ownership and voice in the learning process. Students in a learning environment are able to design and construct their own projects and communicate with classmates through multiple mediums, which stimulate goal-directed exploration and engagement in social, educational, and ethical problems. Students can also become architects of their own learning as learning grows to be a part of their personal topography. Gone are the days of John Locke's concept of education, where students are considered to be blank slates that professors fill with knowledge.

5. Embed learning in social experience. First types of learning are normally guided by one's social experiences, which encompass all kinds of connections with the world; for example, children learn their first language during immersion in social learning experiences. One of the author's first forays into open source was Elgg, which is often referred to as a "social networking framework." True to its name, Elgg allows students to function in a social networking milieu as an alternative portfolio system that "follows a constructivist paradigm, allowing the user to completely control and manage [her] e-portfolio" (Tosh & Werdmuller, 2004, p.2).

6. Encourage the use of multiple modes of representation. With open-source, students

have the capability of presenting information in many ways. For example, in my Reality Television course, final projects varied widely, from the creation of theme songs for reality television shows to videotaped try-outs to "Who Wants to be a Millionaire," to the creation of a show based on Spoken Word. Moreover, the range and creativity of modes of presentation challenged students to find real connections and applications to the theoretical foundations in every project.

7. Encourage self-awareness in the knowledge construction process. This particular goal really permeates throughout the entire student experience. As students interact with each other, they are able to reflect about their experiences and their learning and become conscious of the learning process because they are in control of their learning. "Human beings are most likely to learn deeply when they are trying to solve problems or answer questions that they have come to regard as important, intriguing, or beautiful"(Bain& Zimmerman, 2009. p. 11)

Honebein's goals can and should be applied to any learning situation because the embedded goals specifically relate to the open source environment, where students have the freedom and flexibility to achieve all the outlined aims. The open source not only provides for a learning rich environment that goes beyond a simple e-portfolio, but also becomes a three-dimensional portrait for student learning. In an open source environment students are able to explore, cooperate, collaborate, problem-solve, apply information, and, more importantly, participate in social discourse about their experiences. For example, in a course entitled *Reality Television: Somebody is Watching Me*, taught by the author, the three-dimensionality of student learning became a central component of the collaborative learning environment. Students in the class were involved in blogging about their attending the premier of the reality television

show, *NYC Prep hosted by the Paley Center for Media in New York City.* They were required to write about their experiences, in the context of theoretically based readings and class discussions. The assignment for the experience stated,

NYC Prep is a new reality T.V. show. Based on our visit to the opening event and reading Chapter Four: Performance and Authenticity, please do the following:

Post a blog that incorporates the chapter concepts on paradoxes and authentic behavior, using examples from NYC Prep.

Examples of Initial Student Blogging

NYC prep is a reality show that reveals the lives of the upper west side community. It shows another world and culture that we normal people will never be exposed to. In this show we have six "young adults" as the producers call them who have never worked a day in their lives and wouldn't know what to do if daddy's money was all of sudden gone from their lives show us the daily lives of the rich and clueless. Hill states that, "these entertaining elements of reality TV are borrowed from fictional genres, such as soap operas, and serve to put the popular into popular factual television." (pg. 58) and that is exactly what NYC prep is. It's a generic copy of soap operas such as "Gossip Girls", "The Breakfast Club" and "My so called life". Every character in this show are amplified personalities that the producers as well as we the watchers want to see, which decreases the authenticity of this show to about zilch. We have PC the bad boy who really only wants to be loved, Camille the overachiever who really is an eccentric nut, Taylor the wanna be that desperately wants to fit in by marrying a sugar daddy instead of by doing it on her own, Jessica the over achiever who wants nothing but to be loved by the bad boy PC, Sebastian the bubbly headed blonde who by the age of 18 will probably have more visits to the clinic than the Hilton sisters, and of course there is Kellie the empty headed brunette with the attention span of a two-year old. Put all these characters together and you get an episode of any fictional show about the lives of privileged teenagers.

At the premiere, when Camile was asked how she felt about her imprudent behavior being viewed by college admissions officers and parents her response was that "people realize there is a difference between reality and reality TV." Despite the producers claim that the show is completely unscripted, when I heard Camile's response I immediately felt that she pretty much confirmed that what we are watching is not all that real. Hill refers to Goffman's claims where "we are all performing all of the time on various different audiences, such as our boss or our family. For Goffman, our houses cars, clothing, and other such everyday items are 'props' and 'scenery' required for the 'work of successfully staging a character'" (73). Throughout the premiere I consistently saw how the cast played up to the persona expected of them whether it was sex crazed Sebastian or ditzy Taylor they did a good job at 'staging their character' (73). Also, even though the cast members shun the Gossip Girl series and say they are nothing like them I found it extremely interesting to note that the cast of NYC Prep correlates perfectly with the Gossip Girl cast as far as character personalities go. For example, Taylor correlates to Jenny Humphrey the underprivileged girl from Brooklyn who has to kiss up to the rich kids in order to gain acceptance. Although based on Hill's interpretation of authenticity NYC Prep may not be authentic, there was a moment when I really thought that Kelli was well being real. The moment when Kelly was telling the camera about how she lives alone with her older brother because her parents live in the Hamptons and how they order takeout every night was too much. When she opened her fridge door and there was nothing but Poland Spring bottles I pitied her because although she

is financially dependent, she is a kid that is made emotionally independent and is lacking the guidance that only a parent can offer. What's interesting is that reality tv producers desire this effect, as Hill states, "Inevitably, audiences draw on their own personal experience of social interaction to judge the authenticity of the way ordinary people talk, behave, and respond to situations and other people in reality programmes" (78).

Examples of Blogs with Commentary

In chapter 4, it states, "Just as the development of photographic techniques is connected with the changing ways we look at photographic images, so too is the development of production techniques within reality programming connected with the changing ways we look at television images." (p.59). What I think this statement is trying to say is that although we call it "reality TV", producers and camera people have the ability and technology to manipulate what we see. In NYC Prep, these kids are not followed around 24/7, they are only shot when they are available. The whole "authenticity" part of this show is taken away by the fact that producers and people in charge of the show have to "plan" a week in advance what they and the kids are going to be doing, and also they have to plan and get permission to shoot the camera at places the kids eat and hang out. I would think that reality TV is about going with flow and having no "plans" of what is going to be happening. Basically, we only see what the producers think are "juicy" enough to keep the show running and whatever they are allowed to record. And since the cast has to know when they will be taped, wouldn't that affect the way they behave? I think knowing the fact that you're being recorded changes the way you behave in front of the camera- well at least for most people.

Response #1
I definitely agree with your statement. Of course when you are being recorded most people will put

on a certain persona that may show something different about them and what the public would be most interested in. The whole reality television is mostly based on what really attracts the public and to get the most viewers to watch the show. NYC Prep shows a typical teenage life that people that age would want to portray and they will attract many people in that age group.

Response #2

I also completely agree with **** statement. What I found interesting was how the cast entered the building before the show and how they presented themselves during the panel and during the show. When Camille and Sebastian entered the building I thought they were cute little kids; they were standing on the side and looked kind of quiet and uncomfortable. The moment I saw them speaking on the show my thoughts of them changed and they were no longer cute little kids but rather spoiled obnoxious kids. They truly were living up to the persona that was expected of them when being filmed and when they were speaking during the panel. Additionally, the producers claimed that NYC Prep is totally different than Gossip Girl, but after watching three episodes of Gossip Girl last night the cast in NYC correlate perfectly to the cast in Gossip Girl. Personally, I view NYC Prep as a knockoff Gossip Girl series....

Response #3

There are various people that surround us and as we look around we are all different. As we discussed in class the NYC Prep reality TV show made most of us feel different compared to those people that are similar to the characters in the show. We would say their lives and the show are diverse because they are aware that they are exposing their lives to the public. There may be some of the things that are true and some or most that are staged to attract the viewers. I would agree with the author in Reality TV because it states that "Most viewers argue that the only way ordinary people will be themselves on television is if they don't know

they're on television..." (65) When the interviews started with the cast from NYC Prep PC mentioned that people wouldn't want to see them studying or "writing our beautiful essays." This basically explains that the show only reveals the things that they would have fun or engage in. I really didn't like the part where Taylor the 15 year old was disrespecting her mother in front of the public. It shows how these kids do not know what is most valuable in life and how family is important. They believe "status" is the most important thing and being able to fit in.

Reading these posts and viewing the videos students posted for this assignment provided the author with a clear perspective about how the students were connecting theory and experience through open source technology. As a professor, I found it to be an invaluable tool, helping me to tweak readings, assignments, and other experiences in real time and thus elevate student outcomes. It provided students with an opportunity to position their understanding of text and experience in the context of the shared learning goals of the course.

Professors can now review a complete picture of student learning, whether it is through on-line quizzes, blogs, wikis, and audio or visual presentations. The open source arena positions the professor as a facilitator and addresses student learning in a formative way. And we are no longer held hostage to the results of a quiz or exam, given the second or third week in the semester; instead, open source allows for real-time evidence of student learning and, when called for, real-time interventions by the professor. This makes it possible for professors to assess student learning concurrently and provide timely guidance and direction, e.g., through Wiki practices using group course notes, posted outlines, and student course notes. In this format, faculty can review the group course notes, clarify points, or ask students to explain notes for each other. Wiki's have limitless capabilities to assist in interactive student learning and, if used effectively, can create a setting for faculty to assess student learning formatively. The function of the lecture notes then becomes the meta-narrative for the course that each student has a role in shaping and sharing with all participants.

LESSONS LEARNED FROM THEORY, OPEN SOURCE AND PRACTICE

Throughout this chapter, I have attempted to weave a tapestry of learning from whole threads that connect traditional constructivist theories to the technology known as open source. The fabric that has emerged is a natural one because the design of open source networks is simpatico to how human beings learn best, that is, through social networking. In examining the literature connecting open source technology to constructivist approaches, one is struck by their compatibility and synergy and by the efforts of researchers to understand the solidarity inherent in this mutualistic association. These efforts, however, too often result in elaborate correlations and complex charts and diagrams to outline obvious ties. I, on the other hand, have tried to make the relevant connections by presenting how students in my blended learning courses, graduate and undergraduate, use the open source platform to improve their learning. Such examples were purposely connected to the theoretical underpinnings in constructivist theory so the reader could appreciate their impact on student learning in real world educational illustrations.

When constructivism is allied to the practice of open source technology, students indicate the path to learning for the professor by mapping the routes best suited to their own experiences. To exclude the students and their experiences from discussions about theory, research, or the technology is simply pointless. It is as Maxine Greene (1995) describes: "...becoming literate is also a matter of transcending the given, of entering a field of possibilities. We are moved to do that, however,

only when we become aware of rifts, gaps in what we think of as reality" (p.111).

REFERENCES

Angier, N. (2007). *The Canon A Whirligig Tour of the Beautiful Basics in Science*. New York: Mariner Book.

Antonenko, P., Toy, S., & Niederhauser, D. (2004). Modular Object-Oriented Dynamic Learning Environment: What Open Source Has to Offer. In Contemporary Instruction Concepts. Retrieved September 22, 2009, from http://contempinstruct. com/books/open%20source%20moodle.pdf.

Bain, K., & Zimmerman, J. (2009). Understanding Great Teaching. *Peer Review Emering Trends and Key Debates in Undergraduate Education*, *11*(2), 9–12.

Bednar, A., Cunningham, D., Duffy, T., & Perry, J. (1992). Theory into Practice: How Do We Link? InT. M. Duffy I D.H. Jonassen, (Eds.), *Constructivism and the Technology of Instruction*. (pp. 17-31). New Jersey: Lawerence Erlbaum Associates, Publishers.

Bruner, J. (1987). Proglogue to the English edition. In L.S. Vygostsky, *Collected works* (Vo.1., pp.1-16)(R. Rieber & A. Cartom, Eds.: N. Minick, Trans). New York: Plenum.

Bruner, J. (1990). *Acts of Meaning*. Boston, MA: Harvard University Press.

Colins, P. H. (1990). *Black Feminist Thought*. New York: Routledge.

Crittenden, J. (1992). *Beyond Individualism: Reconstituting the Liberal Self*. New York: Oxford University Press.

Dewey, J. (1916). *Democracy and Education*. New York:Macmillan Company. (Macmillan Paperback Edition 1961.)

Dewey, J. (1938). *Experience and Education.* London: Collier Macmillian Publishers.

Dougiamas. (November 1998). A Journey into Constructivism. In Dougiamas. Retrieved September 21, 2009, from http://dougiamas.com/writing/constructivism.html.

Eriskon, E. H. (1968). *Identity: Youth and Crisis.* New York: W.W. Norton, &Co.

Gardner, H. (2008). *5 Minds for the Future.* Boston, MA: Harvard Business Press.

Gilligan, C. (1993). *In a Different Voice.* Cambridge, MA: Harvard University Press.

Greene, M. (1988). *The Dialectic of Freedom.* New York: Teachers College Press.

Greene, M. (1995). *Releasing the Imagination.* San Francisco, California: Jossey-Bass.

Hannafin, M. J., & Land, S. M. (1997). The foundations and assumptions of technology-enhanced, student-centered learning environments. *Instructional Science*, *25*, 167–202. doi:10.1023/A:1002997414652

Honebein, P. (1996). Seven goals for the designing of Constructivist Learning environments . In Wilson, B. (Ed.), *Constructivists learning environments* (pp. 11–24). New Jersey: Educational Technology Publications.

Kegan, R. (1982). *The Evolving Self.* Cambridge, MA: Harvard University Press.

Lifton, R. (1993). *The Protean Self.* New York: Basic Books.

Lyotard, J. F. (1991). *The Postmodern Condition: A Report on Knowledge.* Minneapolis, MN: University of Minnesota Press.

Moore, A. H. (2002, September/October). Open Source Learning. *EDUCAUSE Review*, 42–51.

Pavlicek, R. (2000). *Embracing Insanity.* Indianapolis, IN: Sams.

Perkins, D., & Hartman, J. *(October, 2007).* Transparent Teaching: An Open- Source code for student learning. *Presentation at the Annual Geological Society Meeting. Colorado, Denever.*

Perry, W. (1970). *Forms of Intellectual and Ethical Development in the College Years: A Scheme.* New York: Holt, Rinehart, and Winston.

President's Information Technology Advisory Committee. (2000, October). Developing open source software to advance high end computing: Report to the president. Arlington, VA: National Coordination Office for Information Technology Research and Development. Retrieved September 3, 2009, from http://www.nitrd.gov/pubs/pitac/pres-oss-11sep00.pdf.

Schroeder, U., & Spannagel, C. (2006). Supporting Active Learning Process. *International Journal on E-Learning*, *5*(2), 245–264.

Tosh, D., & Werdmuller, B. (2004). E-portfolios and weblogs: One vision for ePortfolio development. Retrieved September 21, 2006 from http://www.eradc.org/papers/ePortfolio_Weblog.pdf

Wikipedia: The free encyclopedia. (2009, September 5). FL: Wikimedia Foundation, Inc. Retrieved September 5, 2009, from http://www.wikipedia.org

KEY TERMS AND DEFINITIONS

Cognitive Development: A theoretical approach to the acquisition of knowledge.

Constructivism: The building of knowledge using one's experience as a foundation.

Course Management System: Software that assists in organizing and delivering course content.

Cultural Construct: Connections made about race, gender, age relating to a specific culture.

Learning Environment: A setting that is supportive of student learning.

Open Source: Software with user friendly language, which can be modified to address user learning needs.

Chapter 4

Higher Education and FOSS for E-Learning:
The Role of Organizational Sub-Cultures in Enterprise-Wide Adoption

Shahron Williams van Rooij
George Mason University, USA

ABSTRACT

This chapter examines the paradox of FOSS adoption in U.S. institutions of higher education, where campus-wide deployment of FOSS for e-learning lags far behind adoption for technical infrastructure applications. Drawing on the fields of organizational management, information systems, and education, the author argues that the gap between the advocacy for FOSS teaching and learning applications and the enterprise-wide deployment of FOSS for e-learning is a consequence of the divergent perspectives of two organizational sub-cultures—the technologist and the academic—and the extent to which those sub-cultures are likely to embrace FOSS. The author recommends (a) collaborative needs analysis/assessment prior to a go/no go adoption decision, and (b) broad dissemination of total cost of ownership (TCO) data by institutions deploying FOSS for e-learning enterprise-wide. This discussion satisfies e-learning administrators and practitioners seeking research-based, cross-disciplinary evidence about the FOSS decision-making process and also assists educators in graduate degree programs seeking to expand student knowledge of e-learning technology options.

INTRODUCTION

Higher education has been delivering courses and programs via e-learning in a variety of disciplines and fields for more than a decade. In its sixth annual report on the state of online learning in U.S. higher education, the Sloan Consortium reports that more than three quarters of all public institutions in the U.S. are either engaged or fully engaged in offering education online and that future enrollment growth will be fueled by adults seeking to switch or advance careers in a changing labor market, as well as by the rising costs of commuting (Allen & Seaman, 2008). As noted by the Gartner Group (Zastrocky, Harris, & Lowendahl, 2008), e-learning has become

DOI: 10.4018/978-1-61520-917-0.ch004

mainstream and is now part of higher education's effort to meet student needs.

As new information and communications technologies (ICTs) continue to emerge, institutions of higher education are increasingly faced with the need to anticipate what impact these new technologies will have on teaching, learning and research. The technology expectations of students who were born digital (Palfrey and Gasser, 2008; Caruso and Salaway, 2008), as well as the financial challenges posed by the current economic downturn, are forcing institutions to improve efficiencies and enhance organizational performance while adopting new technologies to remain competitive. Free/Open Source Software (FOSS)–software that is distributed with its source code according to the criteria established by the Open Source Initiative (Open Source Initiative, 2006) - is already recognized by the U.S. Government as a means of advancing infrastructure efficiencies in a time of flat budgets (Beizer, 2008). There are also indications that the new Administration will strengthen government commitment to FOSS. In higher education, campus-wide FOSS adoption for technical infrastructure applications (e.g., databases, operating systems) reflects this same commitment. However, campus-wide adoption of FOSS for e-learning is still limited, despite the use of selected FOSS applications by individual faculty or departments (Williams van Rooij, 2007a; Green, 2008).

In this chapter, the author draws on the fields of organizational management, information systems, and education to examine this gap. The author argues that the gap between the advocacy for FOSS teaching and learning applications and the enterprise-wide deployment of FOSS for e-learning is a consequence of the divergent perspectives of higher education sub-cultures, particularly the technologist and academic sub-cultures. Those divergent perspectives determine the extent to which the two sub-cultures are likely to embrace FOSS for e-learning. Recommendations for closing the gap are also discussed. The

chapter concludes with emerging trends in FOSS for e-learning and suggests opportunities for future research.

BACKGROUND

Before addressing the role of organizational sub-cultures on U.S. higher education adoption of FOSS for e-learning, a clarification of the terminology used in this chapter is in order, particularly regarding e-learning, and the various e-learning technologies. The concepts of organizational culture, sub-culture, and technology adoption will then be addressed.

E-LEARNING

The term "e-learning" first appeared in a 1999 White Paper published by SmartForce, a consulting company that developed electronic learning solutions for corporate and government clients (Priest, 1999). The term initially meant learner-focused training and skills development for corporate knowledge workers delivered via the Internet, an organization's intranet, or other similar means. That is probably why the term e-learning is deemed to be a business term by some in the field of education (Berge, 1998). Moore (2003) addresses the terminology issue by differentiating between generic and subordinate concepts. For Moore, distance education is a generic term for all forms of education in which all or most of the teaching is conducted in a different physical space than the learning, with the result being that all or most communication between teachers and learners is through a communications technology. Subordinate concepts include (a) e-learning and tele-learning, which emphasize the use of a particular communications technology, (b) distributed and distance learning, which focus on the location of the learning, and (c) open and flexible learning, which point to the relative freedom of distance learners to exercise more control over their learning than is normal in commercial education. Like Moore, some scholars (Dabbagh & Bannan-Ritland, 2005; Mayer, 2003; Wentling, Waight, Gallaher, La Fleur, Wang, & Kanfer, 2000) define e-learning as instruction delivered via electronic means that are dependent on networks and computers, but also include a variety of channels (e.g., satellite, wireless) and technologies (cell phones, PDAs, etc.).

E-Learning is sometimes deemed to be synonymous with online learning, cyber-education and e-training. However, a distinction can be made between a purely online format, where at least 80% of the content is delivered online, and hybrid formats, where 30%-80% of the content is delivered online (Allen & Seaman, 2008). This is also the definition underlying the annual review of learning technologies conducted by EDUCAUSE (2008). It is this latter, broader definition – at least 30% of the instruction delivered via electronic means - that serves as the working definition of e-learning throughout this chapter.

E-LEARNING TECHNOLOGIES

There is a wide variety of technologies available that enable e-learning. These include, among others, multimedia software tools to create audio/visual files; e-commerce applications that enable transaction processing and electronic payment, and asynchronous (not "real-time") and synchronous (real-time) communication and collaboration tools for information sharing and group discussion (Zhang & Nunamaker, 2003). The mutlimedia tools are available as desktop applications that individual users can load onto their PCs/Macs and used by anyone skilled in using basic desktop productivity tools (e.g., spreadsheets, word processing, slides for presentations). To facilitate ease of use as well as stimulate usage of multiple products, vendors bundle several of their applications into a single platform. Adobe (http://www.

adobe.com) is among the vendors well-known for bundling mutliple applications for creating multimedia. These applications can also reside on an institution's servers, so that multiple users can access them and create multimedia e-learning applications from their desktops without having to purchase individual licenses or upgrades when new versions of the software are released. E-commerce applications, conversely, are server-based infrastructure software applications used by the institution's technology staff. Part of the institution's backend systems, these applications require technical expertise to use and maintain, and help manage the administrative side of e-learning.

In the late 1990s, the multimedia tools were integrated into single, stand-alone Web-based course management systems that were orignially intended as administrative support for classroom instruction, but which have since evolved into enterprise-wide learning management systems (LMS) that also include social software tools such as blogs and wikis, as well as interfaces to an institution's student information and financial administrative systems. The dominant commercial LMS provider to higher education is Blackboard, having acquired WebCT, its largest competitor, in 2006. Blackboard is now in the process of acquiring Angel Learning, another LMS competitor. The leading FOSS LMS products are Moodle (http://www.moodle.org), originally developed in Australia, but currently with a global user base that includes nearly 30,000 registerd sites, one million courses, and available to anyone for downloading, and; Sakai (http://www.sakaiproject.org), a platform developed by a group of U.S. institutions that includes generic collaboration tools along with teaching and portfolio tools available under an Education Community License. Moodle is built on FOSS technologies such as PHP, while Sakai is largely Java-based. Other FOSS LMS products include Claroline (http://www.claroline.net), available in more than 35 languages and used in 80 countries; LRN (http://www.dotlrn.com), a system that has e-commerce and project management applications built in; ATutor (http://www.atutor. ca), developed in Canada and includes more than 17,000 registered user sites, and; Bodington (http:// www.bodington.org), developed in the U.K. and implemented at the University of Leeds and the University of Oxford. The Western Cooperative for Educational Telecommunications (WCET) provides reviews and product comparisons to assist decision-makers in selecting the LMS – commercial or FOSS - that meets their institution's e-learning needs (EduTools, 2009).

Nearly all (97.5%) institutions of higher education have deployed at least one LMS campus-wide (Green, 2008), enabling them to maximize the use of technology investments to support multiple instructional models. Further, more than 3 in 4 (76.9%) have standardized on a single LMS enterprise-wide, primarily a commercial vendor product (EDUCAUSE CORE Data Service, 2007). Consistent with higher education's tradition of shared governance (American Association of Univeristy Professors, 2009), the decision to acquire and/or support enterprise-wide e-learning systems such as LMSs is made by the Chief Information Officer (CIO) and his/her staff in collaboration with the Chief Academic Officer (CAO), department chairs, and faculty (Green, 2004), although the final decision and funding usually resides with the technologists.

A recent addition to the discussion about e-learning technologies is the focus on learning objects, or digital resources that are stored in repositories and can be accessed and reused in various instructional contexts. Learning objects can be small (e.g., digital images, video or audio snippets, small chunks of text) or large (e.g., entire web pages that combine text, images and other media or applications), all of which can be delivered across the network on demand (Wiley, 2000). Some of the well-known repositories offering free learning objects include MERLOT (http://www. merlot.org) and MIT's OpenCourseWare (http:// ocw.mit.edu). However, this chapter focuses on enterprise-wide e-learning LMS systems and thus, does not address learning objects.

ORGANIZATIONAL CULTURE AND SUB-CULTURES IN HIGHER EDUCATION

Adoption of new technologies requires change and change puts pressure on an organization's culture. Organizational culture refers to the values, symbols, beliefs, stories, heroes, rites and shared assumptions that have special meaning for an organization's employees (Hofstede, 1980; Schein, 1985-2005; Parker, 2000; Hill & Jones, 2001). Organizational cultures are composed of discrete sub-cultures or clusters of ideologies, cultural forms and practices, the most distinctive sources of which are people's occupations. Centered around defined, interrelated tasks that create self-definitions and self-perceptions as well as perceptions of relationships to other sub-cultures, occupational sub-cultures can serve as potential sources of conflict concerning decisions about such issues as the allocation of resources, future goals, changes in practices, and criteria used to evaluate performance (Trice & Beyer, 1993).

In his case study of a state college, Tierney (1988) noted that like in the private sector, higher education decision-making is influenced by organizational culture and sub-cultures, with an institution's specific mission contributing to the intensity of that institution's belief system. Understanding the culture and various sub-cultures provides administrators with information about how to increase performance and decrease conflict in particular groups. Smart and St. John (1996) examined the linkage between organizational culture type, culture strength – the degree of congruence between espoused beliefs and actual practices – and institutional effectiveness based on Cameron and Ettington's (1988) typology of higher education cultures. Analyzing 334 institutions across the U.S., Smart and St. John concluded that the clan culture, characterized by a mentor/ facilitator leadership style, bonding mechanisms emphasizing loyalty and tradition, and a strategic emphasis on human resources and cohesion, was the most prevalent, but that regardless of culture type, institutions with the strongest cultures – i.e., those with congruence between espoused beliefs and actual practices – were the best performers.

These early studies tend to view higher education culture and sub-cultures as static, almost monolithic constructs. Recent studies recognize that organizational cultures and sub-cultures are affected by changes in the environment in which the organization operates (Reschke & Aldag, 2000). Consequently, higher education culture and sub-cultures are affected by a myriad of changes that have taken place over the past decade, ranging from changes in student demographics and changes in the expectations of external stakeholders, to changes in the technology choice set available for remaining competitive and achieving an institution's mission.

CULTURE, SUB-CULTURES AND TECHNOLOGY ADOPTION

The impact of culture on technology adoption decision-making has attracted the interest of scholars and practitioners. Huang, Newell, Galliers, and Pan's (2003) study of the relationship between organizational sub-culture inconsistencies and the adoption of component-based software development methods indicate that the clashing values of organizational sub-cultures hinder the collaboration and communication necessary to effectively integrate technologies like component-based software development. In a study of individual work groups within the technology occupational sub-culture, Von Meier (1999) identifies two different cultural interpretaions of proposed technologies – that of engineers vs that of operators – that contributed to conflict and resistance to adopting certain technologies.

Research has shown that new technology adoption in the public sector – to which higher education belongs - has been slower than in the private sector, with constraining organizational cultures and risk aversion among the key barriers (Albury, 2005; Gallaher & Petrusa, 2006). Successful technology adoption and implementation tend to occur in cultures that emphasize learning and development, participative decision-making, power sharing, support and collaboration, product and process innovation, and tolerance for risk and conflicts (Ke & Wei, 2008; Obendhain & Johnson, 2004; Frambach & Schillewaert, 2002; Johnson, 2000). As with other service organizations in the public sector, higher education adoption of FOSS applications for e-learning enterprise-wide can be particularly challenging due to higher levels of public scrutiny and calls for evidence of organizational effectiveness. Such challenges also place pressure on organizational sub-cultures– particularly the academic and the technology occupational sub-cultures – to compete for scarce resources and capitalize on existing competencies with as little risk as possible.

A key input to the technology adoption decision-making process is the evaluation of available talent. Organizational culture and sub-cultures also serve as lenses through which current and potential employee competencies as well as adoption risks are evaluated. Employee competencies encompass the personal experience, knowledge, skills and abilities that are observable in the performance of certain activities and the achievement of certain results (Escrig-Tena & Bou-Llusar, 2005). The occupational sub-culture of technologists must be perceived as possessing the knowledge necessary to deploy and maintain a new technology (Kamal, 2006). For the academic occupational sub-culture, the ability to capitalize on the maximum learning affordances offered by various technologies based on solid pedagogy as well as on awareness of available technologies (Dabbagh & Bannan-Ritland, 2005) is a key input to adoption. Additionally, the cultural context shapes the level of risk associated with new technology adoption. If the context is unstable, highly politicized, or resistant to change, the management of a project to adopt a new technology will be perceived as highly complex, reducing commitment and resources needed for success (Wallace, Keil, & Rai, 2004).

There is some evidence to support the concept of sub-culture competition in higher education. For example, Bergquist and Pawlak (2008) identify six cultures within higher education – collegial, managerial, developmental, advocacy, virtual, and tangible – that impact change efforts. The collegial faculty culture that emphasizes professional autonomy and consensus-building may conflict with the managerial administration culture that focuses on goals, outcomes, efficiency and accountability. Smith (2006) examines the impact of the faculty sub-culture on the adoption of technology in the classroom of a large mid-Western public university. Drawing on Rogers' diffusion of innovations theory (1995), Smith notes that the academic sub-culture, of which the faculty is a part, tends to support a conservative diffusion of technology unless it is essential to the content of the course or it is supported financially by the administration. In depth research on the relationship between the academic and technology sub-cultures in the context of FOSS adoption is limited, however.

What has gained attention is an array of beliefs, attitudes and opinions about the causes of competition between the academic and technologist sub-cultures. Anecdotes in the trade press that characterize higher education information technology (IT) departments as toxic and regressive influences who place ease of support and centralization above user needs (Carnevale, 2007) have raised the temperature on the discussions about this clash of occupational sub-cultures. Fernandez (2008) states that the growing gap between faculty and IT staff salaries and budgets, coupled with higher education's increasing adoption of the language and models from the business world, have further contributed to sub-culture competition, and calls for technologists to take the first step by better

understanding the academic sub-culture. Interestingly, much of the current discussion focuses on the technologists' need to change, with little comment about how academics can contribute to bridging the sub-cultural divide.

FOSS FOR E-LEARNING ENTERPRISE-WIDE

The Academic Sub-Culture

Members of the academic sub-culture include faculty, non-technical instructional and research support staff (e.g., instructional designers, library staff), and other non-technical staff under the Chief Academic Officer (CAO). Although institutional characteristics (Carnegie classification, number of students, public vs. private, for-profit vs. nonprofit, etc.), culture, discipline, and other factors provide the context in which the academic sub-culture exists, concepts basic to this sub-culture include the pursuit and dissemination of knowledge through teaching and research, academic honesty, and academic freedom (Umbach, 2007; American Association of Univeristy Professors (AAUP), 2009). Commitment to these basic concepts means understanding the impact of technology on the processes of teaching and learning, on the role of sub-culture members, particularly the faculty, and on how student performance is assessed.

Incorporating technology into instruction has meant re-examining the instructional development process and the nature of the environment in which students learn, including the setting or "space" in which learning is fostered and supported (Wilson, 1996). It has also meant addressing the expectations of a different demographic in which the majority of learners is non-traditional: Older, employed, not dependent on parents, and seeking engagement as well as knowledge (National Center for Education Statistics, 2009). This re-examination of instructional process, of the learning environment, and of the learner, is part of the constructivist perspective on learning. Constructivism holds that learners build their own personal interpretation of the world based on their own experiences. Because there are so many ways of structuring the world and its entities – i.e., there are multiple perspectives – learners make their own meaning rather than having it imposed from some external, independent reality (Duffy & Jonassen, 1992). Thus, the pedagogical goals of a learning environment grounded in constructivism must provide these multiple perspectives and enable learners to make their own meaning by providing multiple modes of representation (Honebein, 1996). Technology's potential lies in the extent to which it enables the creation of a learning environment grounded in constructivism (Domine, 2006).

The academic sub-culture's experiences with commercial e-learning systems, particularly LMSs deployed campus-wide, have been mixed. Institutions have traditionally adopted these systems to provide an entry point into using technology in instruction and have increasingly relied on them to support a variety of instructional models (Morgan, 2003). Although these systems offer pedagogical affordances that can shape pedagogical models and inform the design of e-learning (Kozma, 1994; Jaffee, 2003; Frielick, 2004; Dabbagh, 2004), the default design of these systems has been criticized for limiting instructional creativity by forcing instructors who are novice users of these systems into the traditional lecture-based model of instruction and for lacking good value-added development resources to supplement the limited instructional design skills of the average faculty member (Lane, 2008; Sclater, 2008; Carmean & Haefner, 2003). In a review of the literature, Papastergiou (2006) states that although students and faculty have positive attitudes towards LMS-based learning and faculty can apply participatory, constructivist approaches to learning in commercial LMSs, increased faculty workload, limited assessment capabilities, the inability to support subjects that involve hands-on tasks, and the need

for more sophisticated collaborative capabilities beyond discussion boards are all weaknesses of commercial LMSs.

There is also evidence to refute these criticisms of commercial LMSs. Studies of individual courses using Blackboard or WebCT have found that those technologies enhanced the learning experience by enabling collaboration, the development of a sense of community, and the inclusion of constructivist strategies of collaborative learning into the instructional environment (DeNuei & Dodge, 2006; Gill, 2006; Iyer, 2003). As noted by Sclater (2008), LMSs are pedagogy-neutral; the combined forces of instructor as subject matter expert, instructional designer, and multimedia specialists define the instructional approaches and pedagogical models to be used, all of which are informed by the pedagogical affordances of the LMS.

Why, then, do novice faculty settle for the default design of commercial LMSs? Why not seek out instructional designers, multimedia specialists, and other instructional resources that would assist them in identifying the pedagogical affordances offered by commerical LMSs? Although most institutions offer assistance and support to faculty seeking to learn to use these systems, that assistance tends to focus on how the systems work and on teaching system features rather than on the pedagogical affordances that these systems offer. Woolsey (2008) found the following:

The new media resource groups that have emerged on campuses struggle to collaborate with faculty. The hierarchies that divide faculty and staff prevent equal collaborations between form and content, and so the assistance that staff can provide faculty is typically limited to technical assistance rather than to significant experimentation and imaginative explorations of explanations and learning activities in a content domain. Collaborations between faculty and new media experts and craftsmen more often than not disintegrate, as an equal footing for "form and content" in a design activity is difficult to maintain. (p. 215)

FOSS has the potential to bridge this collaboration gap. There is synergy between FOSS' adaptability and reusability principles and the academic sub-culture's constructivist principles that drive the design of e-learning environments. Koohang and Harman (2005) see FOSS as a metaphor for e-learning in that they both involve naturalistic processes that are embedded in the same milieu – the digital world and the human mind – and share the same philosophical foundation of constructivism, with common elements such as collaboration, cooperation, knowledge construction, and problem-solving. As such, constructivist faculty would tend to prefer FOSS LMSs over commercial LMSs. In a survey of 271 U.S. higher education CAOs representing a variety of Carnegie classifications (Williams van Rooij, 2007a), the strongest positive influence on CAO consideration of FOSS for e-learning is the ability of FOSS to support active learning, so that students are engaged in real-world tasks, practice and reinforcement. Other key considerations include FOSS' ability to support (a) ownership of learning, to facilitate students taking control of their own learning, (b) social learning, to facilitate reciprocity and cooperation among students, faculty and discipline experts, (c) contextual learning, to facilitate new knowledge built on students' existing knowledge and integration of new knowledge into the students' world, and (d) engaged learning, to create a high-challenge, low-threat learning environment for students with diverse talents and ways of learning. In follow up phone interviews with selected CAOs, participants stressed the pedagogical fit of FOSS LMSs versus commercial LMSs in terms of the ability to customize to get the functionality you need (and not what you don't), as well as the ability to work with other institutions similar to one's own to enhance teaching and make outcomes demonstrable internally and externally (Williams van Rooij, 2007b).

There are many published examples of successful e-learning practice using FOSS applications in a variety of disciplines, some of which have been published on their respective FOSS community web sites. Evidence of success is important to the academic sub-culture, particularly for faculty transitioning into e-learning (Sclater, 2008), but also for non-technical support staff seeking to build their own best practices inventory. Although constructivism is not the sole perspective in the academic sub-culture and faculty seek to ensure that technology remains in the service of pedagogy, and not the other way around, the academic sub-culture responds favorably to FOSS for e-learning when, like any technological change, it is (a) evident, so that there is an awareness of FOSS and of how FOSS is being used for e-learning, (b) easy to use, without having to choose from a host of features, functions, and complex user interfaces, and (c) essential, so that the what's-in-it-for-me (WIFM) is clear, rather than being a mandate from above (Haymes, 2008).

Despite the academic sub-culture's tendency to look favorably upon FOSS for e-learning, the decision to adopt and deploy FOSS for e-learning enterprise-wide requires the support of the institution's technologists. A closer look at the technologist sub-culture reveals diverging perspectives that underlie the gap between FOSS advocacy and the realities of campus-wide adoption of FOSS for e-learning.

The Technologist Sub-Culture

Members of the technologist sub-culture include the institution's information technology (IT) staff, academic computing as well as administrative computing, and the technical instructional and research support staff under the Chief Information Officer (CIO). As with the academic sub-culture, the technologist sub-culture operates within the context of its institution. Traditionally, this sub-culture has focused on maintaining an institution's cyber-infrastructure efficiently and effectively –

what Fuchs (2008) calls "keeping the lights on" - and providing innovative technology platforms that support collaboration and strategic agility in teaching, learning and research. As the pace of technological innovation has increased, the essence of this sub-culture, i.e., what it means to be a technologist, is also changing. Keeping abreast of emerging technologies means that there is more to think about and process, more perspectives to consider, more complexity to IT as an occupation and contributor to the education experience (Alexander, 2009). The potential of cloud computing – providing commonly used business and instructional applications online that are accessible via a standard browser but are stored on host servers – the uncertainties about the size and depth of the future IT talent pool, as well as the competencies that define the occupation are examples of factors contributing to this complexity. The challenges facing this sub-culture are clearly reflected in the results of EDUCAUSE's survey of the top ten issues of concern to higher education technology leaders over the past five years (Allison, DeBlois, & EDUCAUSE Current Issues Committee, 2008). Funding remains an on-going concern. E-learning has risen to the top ten, reflecting the emerging influence of instructional technology and design both as a key element of the IT organization's mission and as an expanding niche of the profession. As a mission-critical application supporting all of the institution's instructional models, including e-learning, the LMS is inexorably intertwined with the number one issue keeping technologists up at night: Security and risk management. Consequently, the technologist sub-culture faces the challenge of managing risk while enabling the academic sub-culture to capitalize on the affordances offered by these systems (Lambert, 2008).

Can FOSS help the technologist sub-culture address these challenges by providing the flexibility needed to maintain the correct balance between technological innovation and pedagogy for e-learning? When it comes to FOSS advocacy,

CIOs and Chief Financial Officers (CFOs) of large research institutions have been among the most vocal FOSS proponents. These institutions tend to have a history of in-house software development, so that the adaptability of FOSS source code fits well with current development paradigms at those institutions. Using the case study method, Eduventures analysts Burdt and Bassett (2005) investigate the motivations and decision-making rationales of eight senior IT administrators. Study participants mention cultural fit between FOSS as a social movement and public education as one of the reasons for institutions of higher education to explore FOSS. Similarly, more than half (58%) of the 257 higher education Chief Financial Officers participating in a survey sponsored by the National Association of College and University Business Officers (NACUBO) state that the freedom to modify software source code was the primary reason for their interest in adopting FOSS applications (Hignite, 2004).

The FOSS software development paradigm is also cited by this group of advocates as an advantage of FOSS over commercial vendor-produced software. Drawing on Raymond's (2001) metaphor of the cathedral (commercial software) and the bazaar (FOSS), community oversight is deemed a key driver to maintaining quality and innovation in FOSS. In a keynote presentation at the 2004 EDUCAUSE conference, H.D. Lambert, VP and CIO of Georgetown University, defines FOSS as producer universities and (possibly) vendors working together with stakeholders on innovative software that fulfills academic priorities. Lambert later (2005) proposes that institutions focus on the scholarly information systems where FOSS already has a foothold (portfolios, course management systems, etc.), while working to open up the Student Information Systems environment using collaborative development and FOSS standards. Lambert warns, however, that higher education still needs to work with the vendor community to minimize risk and must establish a new organizational vehicle for the community to address challenges and barriers.

FOSS' lower total cost of ownership is cited as a particular advantage by FOSS advocates in the technologist sub-culture. Total cost of ownership (TCO) analysis is used to support acquisition and planning decisions by taking into account the life-time costs of acquiring, maintaining, and changing software systems, and includes the obvious costs, such as vendor license fees and maintenance contract costs, as well as hidden costs, such as internal staffing and training (Sen, 2007; Karsak & Ozogul, 2009). However, there is little solid evidence to support the contention that FOSS is less expensive to use than commercial software. In the July 2006 issue of the trade publication *Campus Technology*, the CIO of a private Masters institution with an enrollment of 3,500 students purports to have saved 20% in annual maintenance costs by switching from vendor products to FOSS (Villano, 2006). What is not stated is what type of FOSS software (infrastructure level vs. application level) the institution uses or the number and skill set of the institution's programmers. In a survey of 195 CIOs conducted by the IMS Global Learning Consortium, an international educational technology standards organization, more than half (57%) of the respondents purport to have seen cost of ownership improvements since replacing vendor products with FOSS software applications (Abel, 2006). However, the applications adopted include a mix of desktop (e.g., MyOffice), user interface (e.g., uPortal), and teaching/learning applications (e.g., Moodle), all with adoption rates of ≤24% of the total survey sample. Similarly, Green (2004) notes that greatest support for FOSS is among re-search universities, with FOSS perceived as being a viable alternative for learning management systems. These results remain relatively unchanged in Green's annual surveys through 2008.

Advocacy vs. Reality

In marked contrast with the enthusiasm of tech-nologists at large research institutions is the cau-tious pragmatism of technologists at most other types of institutions. As part of his annual survey of more than 500 higher education CIOs, Green (2008) asks about the adoption of FOSS LMS as the campus standard. Only one in seven (13.8%) report adopting a FOSS LMS as the single campus standard, although this represents an increase from 10.3% in 2007 and 7.2% in 2006. The growth in FOSS adoption has largely been at the expense of Blackboard; however, Blackboard remains the single campus standard at more than half (56.8%) of the institutions participating in the survey.

The literature is generally consistent in identi-fying the barriers to enterprise-wide FOSS LMS adoption, barriers that have also been identified for other non-technical FOSS applications. Spe-cifically, the barriers include (a) the difficulty in calculating the true cost of ownership of FOSS LMSs, (b) the lack of formal support mecha-nisms, (c) the need for highly skilled and highly motivated technical personnel, (d) the lack of efficient tools for migrating from commercial LMSs, and (e) the lack of interoperability with other campus systems (Molina & EDUCAUSE Evolving Technologies Committee, 2006; EDU-CAUSE Constituent Group, 2008; Williams van Rooij, 2007b). Intellectual property rights and identifying what software solutions have been patented – think of the Blackboard-Desire2Learn litigation – are also barriers to the building of a stable development and support community, along with uncertain funding sustainability, particularly for FOSS applications created with grant funding (Lakhan and Jhunjhunwala, 2008; Dalziel, 2003).

There are commercial vendors that assist insti-tutions wishing to migrate to FOSS for e-learning but lack the technical infrastructure to do so on their own. The Moodle Partners group (http://moodle.com/partners/list/) offers a range of services such as hosting, customization, technical support, and courseware development, to institutions seeking to implement Moodle enterprise-wide. Unicon (http://www.unicon.net) and rSmart (http://www.rsmart.com) offer a range of services to institutions seeking to implement Sakai. However, there is limited hard data to support the cost-benefit of these services vs. that of commercial LMS or vs. the development of in-house talent.

The paradox of enterprise-wide FOSS for e-learning lies in the convergence of FOSS and academic sub-culture principles on the one hand, and the divergence of technologist sub-culture development paradigms – in-house vs. vendor-provided – as lenses through which enterprise-wide technology deployment is evaluated. A visual representation of the gap between the advocacy for FOSS teaching and learning applications among the two sub-cultures and the enterprise-wide deployment of FOSS for e-learning is shown in Figure 1.

SOLUTIONS AND RECOMMENDATIONS

Although this chapter focuses on only two of the higher education sub-cultures, it offers some approaches to promoting FOSS for e-learning enterprise-wide.

Collaborative needs analysis/assessment. Long before any go/no go decision about FOSS vs. commercial systems for e-learning is made, representatives of both the academic and technology sub-cultures should work together to document and analyze user requirements from the perspectives of faculty, their instructional support teams, and even students. This enables faculty and instructional support professionals to identify the pedagogical affordances of technology that can shape pedagogical models and inform the design of e-learning. Approaches to identifying the pedagogical affordances of various technologies have been well documented (Bower, 2008; Suthers, 2006; Resta & Laferriere, 2007; Grainne & Dyke, 2004). Clearly defined user requirements then inform development of the technical system requirements.

There are published guidelines to assist institutions in conducting FOSS assessments. For example, the Business Readiness Rating (Business Readiness Rating, 2006) provides a framework advanced by developers from education and industry to assess the organizational fit of FOSS based on seven weighted criteria: Functionality,

Figure 1. Perspectives on FOSS for e-learning enterprise-wide: academic vs. technologist sub-cultures

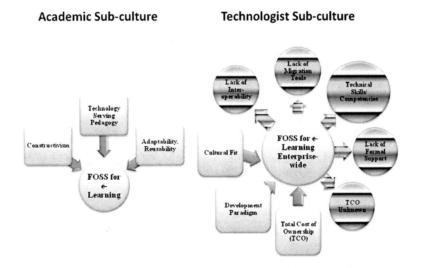

65

including communication, collaboration, learner assessment, and instructional management tools; usability, particularly the ease with which faculty and students can become proficient in using the software; the availability and quality of user-maintained documentation for system administrators, faculty, and students; the size and activity level of the developer community, as measured by the e-mail forums and number of people contributing code; the number and severity of security alerts and the speed with which they are addressed; the amount and quality of volunteer and commercial support available, and; the number and size of current installations at other institutions. Developed by the Navica company but available to the public is the Open Source Maturity Model (Navica, 2008), another FOSS assessment model. This model enables organizations to self-identify as to how they rate themselves in terms of overall maturity in information technology adoption. Based on where they fall in the maturity rankings, organizations then assess FOSS systems on features/functions, support, documentation, training, product integration, and available professional services. Individual institutions have placed their own FOSS assessment models and migration experiences in the public domain (Chao, 2008; O'Laughlin & Borkowski, 2008; Uys & Morton-Allen, 2007), although there is room for improvement in terms of the number of institutions contributing hard data about their assessment and implementation approaches and experiences.

Dissemination of TCO data. To better understand the true total cost of ownership, institutions that have already deployed FOSS LMSs for e-learning enterprise-wide need to place hard data about support costs in terms of hours, skills/competencies, services provided to faculty, students and other instructional support staff, migration costs, documentation, deployment methods used (e.g., in-house vs. third party vendor services), etc., in the public domain. This would also enable institutions to compare current costs with the costs of migrating to FOSS. Sharing of TCO data is potentially challenging given the different

ways in which institutions calculate and track financial data (Wheeler and DeStefano, 2007). Nevertheless, case studies from "live" FOSS LMS sites can provide some starting points for other institutions seeking to explore the cost-value of enterprise-wide FOSS for e-learning.

FUTURE RESEARCH DIRECTIONS

Adoption of FOSS for e-learning in U.S. higher education lags well behind that of other countries. Results of a periodic survey of open and closed source software conducted among more than 450 further and higher education institutions in the U.K. (Cornelius, 2006) indicate that the use of Open Source is on the rise at U.K. institutions, with 77% of U.K. further and higher educational institutions considering Open Source in the software selection process and 25% mentioning Open Source in institutional policy. With respect to survey questions about virtual learning environments and LMSs, Open Source dominates, with the Moodle adoption at 39%, followed by Blackboard (19%) and WebCT (9%). The 2008 survey indicates an increase in these adoption trends (Canas, 2009). Consistent with European goals for free software development, deployment and collaborative research, and the European Union's desire to maintain its lead in the Open Source arena, the University of Maastricht in The Netherlands and the University of Cambridge in the U.K. established a consortium focused on Open Source projects, including the single largest knowledge base on Open Source usage and development worldwide (Ghosh, 2006).

The absence of hard data about the level of effort and resources required to successfully deploy FOSS for e-learning enterprise-wide is a barrier to resolving the gap between FOSS advocacy and the adoption realities in the U.S. This suggests opportunities for further research about (a) how institutions can assess their own sub-cultures, and the impact of those sub-cultures on perceptions of staff competency, and perceptions of risk tolerance in decision-making about adopting FOSS for e-learning enterprise-wide, (b) developing a working model of critical success factors for enterprise-wide FOSS deployment for e-learning, so that institutions have concrete criteria for attracting and developing internal talent that is perceived as being competent to deploy and maintain FOSS e-learning applications, and (c) successful models of academic-technologist collaboration prior to go/no go adoption decisions. Evidence-based models should also include data from institutions that utilize third party commercial vendors for FOSS implementation and maintenance services, as well as institutions utilizing in-house talent and resources.

CONCLUSION

This chapter offered research-based insights into the role of organizational sub-cultures as challenges and opportunities for the adoption of FOSS for e-learning enterprise-wide. It provides e-learning administrators and practitioners with recommendations for addressing the challenges and capitalizing on the opportunities. It also provides educators who use FOSS applications with guidelines for teaching instructional technology graduate students to consider the organizational context when evaluating FOSS as an alternative or complement to commercial vendor LMSs. It is hoped that this chapter will contribute to the ongoing dialog about how e-learning professionals can capitalize on the affordances offered by FOSS applications for designing instruction for the e-learning environment.

REFERENCES

Abel, R. (2006, June 29). *Best practices in open source in higher education.* Retrieved May 26, 2009, http://www.a-hec.org/open_source_state.html

Albury, D. (2005). Fostering innovation in public services. *Public Money & Management, 25*(1), 51–56.

Alexander, B. (2009). Apprehending the future: Emerging technologies, from science fiction to campus reality. *EDUCAUSE Review, 44*(3), 12–29.

Allen, I., & Seaman, J. (2008). *Staying the course: Online education in the United States, 2008.* Retrieved May 18, 2009, http://www.sloan-c.org/publications/survey/index.asp

Allison, D., DeBlois, P., & EDUCAUSE Current Issues Committee. (2008). *Current issues survey report, 2008.* Retrieved May 18, 2009, from http://www.educause.edu/EDUCAUSE+Quarterly/EDUCAUSEQuarterlyMagazineVolum/CurrentIssuesSurveyReport2008/162861

American Association of Univeristy Professors (AAUP). (2009). *Informal glossary of AAUP terms and abbreviations.* Retrieved May 27, 2009, from http://www.aaup.org/AAUP/about/mission/glossary.htm

Beizer, D. (2008). *5 tech tools with lasting appeal.* Retrieved June 1, 2009, from http://fcw.com/articles/2008/08/29/5-tech-tools-with-lasting-appeal.aspx

Berge, Z. L. (1998). Conceptual frameworks in distance training and education . In Schreiber, D., & Berge, Z. (Eds.), *Distance training: How innovative organizations are using technology to maximize learning and meet business objectives* (pp. 19–36). San Francisco: Jossey-Bass.

Bergquist, W., & Pawlak, K. (2008). *Engaging the six cultures of the academy.* San Francisco: Jossey-Bass.

Bower, M. (2008). Affordance analysis-matching learning tasks with learning technologies. *Educational Media International, 45*(1), 3–15. doi:10.1080/09523980701847115

Burdt, C., & Bassett, E. (2005). *Open source in Higher Education: Decision-making for open source adoptions*. Boston: Eduventures.

Bureau of Labor Statistics. (2008). *Human resources, training, and labor relations managers and specialists*. Retrieved from http://www.bls.gov/oco/ocos021.htm#training

Bureau of Labor Statistics. (2008). *Instructional Coordinators*. Retrieved May 4, 2009, from http://www.bls.gov/oco/ocos269.htm#outlook

Business Readiness Rating. (2006). *Business readiness rating for open source*. Retrieved June 2, 2009, from http://www.openbrr.org/wiki/index.php/BRRWhitepaper

Cameron, K., & Ettington, D. (1988). The conceptual foundations of organizational culture . In Smart, J. (Ed.), *Higher education: Handbook of theory and research* (pp. 356–396). New York: Agathon.

Canas, R. (2009). *OSS watch national software survey 2008*. Retrieved June 5, 2009, from Open source Software Advisory Service: http://www.oss-watch.ac.uk/resources/

Carmean, C., & Haefner, J. (2003). Next-generation course management systems. *EDUCAUSE Quarterly*, *26*(1), 10–13.

Carnevale, D. (2007, June 22). The most poisonous force in technology. *The Chronicle of Higher Education*, *53*(42), A37.

Caruso, J., & Salaway, G. (2008). *The ECAR study of undergraduate students and information technology, 2008*. Boulder, CO: EDUCAUSE Center for Applied Research.

Chao, I. (2008). Moving to Moodle: Reflections two years later. *EDUCAUSE Quarterly*, *31*(3), 46–52.

Cleary, Y., & Marcus-Quinn, A. (2008). Using a virtual learning environment to manage group projects: A case study. *International Journal on E-Learning*, *7*(4), 603–621.

Cornelius, B. (2006). *OSS watch survey 2006*. Retrieved June 5, 2009, from http://www.oss-watch.ac.uk/studies/survey2006/

Dabbagh, N. (2004). Distance learning: Emerging pedagogical issues and learning designs. *Quarterly Review of Distance Education*, *5*(1), 37–49.

Dabbagh, N., & Bannan-Ritland, B. (2005). *Online learning: Concepts, strategies, and application*. Upper Saddle River, NJ: Pearson Education, Inc.

Dalziel, J. (2003). Open standards versus open source in e-learning. *EDUCAUSE Quarterly*, *26*(4), 4–7.

DeNuei, D., & Dodge, T. (2006). Asynchronous learning networks and student outcomes: The utility of online learning components in hybrid courses. *Journal of Instructional Psychology*, *33*(4), 256–259.

Domine, V. (2006). Online pedagogy: Beyond digital "chalk and talk." . *Academic Exchange Quarterly*, *10*(1), 48–51.

Duffy, T., & Jonassen, D. (1992). Constructivism: New implications for instructional technology . In Duffy, T. (Ed.), *Constructivism and the technology of instruction: A conversation* (pp. 1–16). Hillsdale, NJ: Lawrence Erlbaum Associates.

EDUCAUSE Constituent Group. (2008, October 20). *2008 Openness Constituent Group Meeting*. Retrieved June 1, 2009, from http://www.educause.edu/wiki/Openness

EDUCAUSE CORE Data Service. (2007). *Fiscal year 2007 summary report*. Retrieved May 27, 2009, from http://net.educause.edu/apps/coredata/reports/2007/

EduTools. (2009). *Welcome to EduTools.* Retrieved May 27, 2009, from http://www.edutools.info/index.jsp?pj=1

Escrig-Tena, A., & Bou-Llusar, J. (2005). A model for evaluating organizational competencies: An application in the context of a quality management initiative. *Decision Sciences, 36*(2), 221–257. doi:10.1111/j.1540-5414.2005.00072.x

Fernandez, L. (2008). An antidote for the faculty-IT divide. *EDUCAUSE Quarterly, 31*(1), 7–9.

Frambach, R., & Schillewaert, N. (2002). Organizational innovation adoption: A multilevel framework of determinants and opportunities for future research. *Journal of Business Research, 55*(2), 163–176. doi:10.1016/S0148-2963(00)00152-1

Frielick, S. (2004). Beyond constructivism: An ecological approach to e-learning. In *Beyond the comfort zone: Proceedings of the 21st ASCILITE Conference* (pp. 328-332). Perth, Australia: University of Western Australia.

Fuchs, I. (2008). Challenges and opportunities of open source in higher education. In Katz, R. (Ed.), *The tower and the cloud: Higher education in the age of cloud computing* (pp. 150–157). Boulder, CO: EDUCAUSE.

Gallaher, M., & Petrusa, J. (2006). Innovation in the U.S. service sector. *The Journal of Technology Transfer, 31*(6), 611–628. doi:10.1007/s10961-006-0018-4

Ghosh, R. (2006, June 14). *Who is behind open source? Presentation at the Gartner Open Source Summit, Barcelona, Spain.* Retrieved June 5, 2009, from http://www.flossproject.org/papers/20060614/RishabGHOSH-gartner2.pdf

Gill, T. (2006). The memory grid: A glass box view of data representation. *Journal of Information Systems Education, 17*(2), 119–129.

Grainne, C., & Dyke, M. (2004). What are the affordances of information and communication technololgies. *ALT-J: Research in Learning, 12*(2), 113–124.

Green, K. (2008). *The 2008 national survey of information technology in U.S. higher education.* Encino, CA: The Campus Computing Project.

Green, K. C. (2004). *Campus computing 2004: The 15th national survey of computing and information technology in American higher education.* Encino, CA: The Campus Computing Project.

Haymes, T. (2008). The three-e strategy for overcoming resistance to technological change. *EDUCAUSE Quarterly, 31*(4), 67–69.

Hignite, K. (2004, August). *An open mind on open source.* Retrieved May 25, 2009, from http://www.nacubo.org/Business_Officer_Magazine/Magazine_Archives/August_2004/An_Open_Mind_on_Open_Source.html

Hill, C., & Jones, G. (2001). *Strategic management theory-An integrated approach.* Boston: Houghton Mifflin.

Hofstede, G. (1980). *Culture's consequences: International differences in work related values.* Thousand Oaks, CA: Sage Publications, Inc.

Honebein, P. (1996). Seven goals for the design of constructivist learning environments. In Wilson, B. (Ed.), *Constructivist learning environments: Case studies in instructional design* (pp. 11–24). Englewood Cliffs, NJ: Educational Technology Publications.

Huang, J., Newell, S., Galliers, R., & Pan, S. (2003). Dangerous liaisons? Component based development and organizational subcultures. *IEEE Transactions on Engineering Management, 50*(1), 89–99. doi:10.1109/TEM.2002.808297

Iyer, H. (2003). Web-based instructional technology in an information science classroom. *Journal of Education for Library and Information Science, 44*(5), 296–315.

Jaffee, D. (2003). Virtual transformation: Web-based technology and pedagogical change. *Teaching Sociology, 31*(2), 227–236. doi:10.2307/3211312

Johnson, J. (2000). Levels of success in implementing information technologies. *Innovative Higher Education, 25*(1), 59–76. doi:10.1023/A:1007536402952

Kamal, M. (2006). IT innovation adoption in the government sector: Identifying the critical success factors. *Journal of Enterprise Information Management, 19*(2), 192–222. doi:10.1108/17410390610645085

Karsak, E., & Ozogul, C. (2009). An integrated decision making approach for ERP system selection. *Expert Systems with Applications, 36*(1), 660–667. doi:10.1016/j.eswa.2007.09.016

Ke, W., & Wei, K. (2008). Organizational culture and leadership in ERP implementation. *Decision Support Systems, 45*(2), 208–218. doi:10.1016/j.dss.2007.02.002

Koohang, A., & Harman, K. (2005). Open source: A metaphor for e-learning. *Informing Science Journal, 8*, 75–86.

Kozma, R. (1994). A reply: Media and methods. *Educational Technology Research and Development, 42*(3), 11–14. doi:10.1007/BF02298091

Lakhan, S., & Jhunjhunwala, K. (2008). Open source software in education. *EDUCAUSE Quarterly, 31*(2), 1–11.

Lambert, H. (2005). *Collaborative open source software: Panacea or pipe dream for higher education?* Retrieved May 26, 2009, from http://www.educause.edu/ir/

Lambert, H. (2008). Managing risk and exploiting opportunity. *EDUCAUSE Review, 43*(6), 36–37.

Lambert, H. D. (2004, October 19). *Collaborative Open Source software: Panacea or pipe dream for higher education?* Paper presented at the 2004 EDUCAUSE Conference, Denver, CO.

Lane, L. (2008). Toolbox or trap? Course management systems and pedagogy. *EDUCAUSE Quarterly, 31*(3), 4–6.

Martin-Blas, T., & Serrano-Fernandez, A. (2009). The role of new technologies in the learning process: Moodle as a teaching tool in physics. *Computers & Education, 52*(1), 35–44. doi:10.1016/j.compedu.2008.06.005

Mayer, R. E. (2003). Elements of a science of e-learning. *Journal of Educational Computing Research, 29*(3), 297–313. doi:10.2190/YJLG-09F9-XKAX-753D

Molina, P., & EDUCAUSE Evolving Technologies Committee. (2006). Pioneering new territory and technologies. *EDUCAUSE Review, 41*(5), 112–135.

Moore, A. H. (2002). Lens on the future: Open source learning. *EDUCAUSE Review, 37*(5), 43–51.

Moore, M. G. (2003). This book in brief: Overview. In Moore, M. G., & Anderson, W. (Eds.), *Handbook of distance education* (pp. xiii–xxiii). Mahwah, NJ: Lawrence Erlbaum Associates, Inc.

Morgan, G. (2003). *Faculty use of course management systems.* Boulder, CO: EDUCAUSE Center for Applied Research (ECAR).

National Center for Education Statistics. (2009). *Fast Facts.* Retrieved May 28, 2009, from http://nces.ed.gov/fastfacts/index.asp?faq=FFOption6#faqFFOption6

Navica. (2008). *Choosing the right open source product: Don't leave it to chance.* Retrieved June 5, 2009, from http://www.navicasoft.com/pages/osmm.htm

O'Laughlin, N., & Borkowski, E. (2008, October 29). *Transitioning learning management systems: Making the move at the enterprise level.* Retrieved June 5, 2009, from http://www.educause.edu/Resources/Browse/OpenSource/17546

Obendhain, A., & Johnson, W. (2004). Product and process innovation in service organizations: The influence of organizational culture in higher education institutions. *Journal of Applied Management and Entrepreneurship, 9*(3), 91–113.

Open Source Initiative. (2006, July 7). *The open source definition.* Retrieved May 1, 2009, from http://www.opensource.org/docs/osd

Palfrey, J., & Gasser, U. (2008). *Born digital: Understanding the first generation of digital natives.* New York: Basic Books.

Papastergiou, M. (2006). Course management systems as tools for the creation of online learning environments: Evaluation from a social constructivist perspective and implications for their design. *International Journal on E-Learning, 54*(4), 593–622.

Parker, M. (2000). *Organisational culture and identity: Unity and division at work.* London: Sage Publications, Ltd.

Priest, G. (1999). *Learn fast. Go fast.* Retrieved May 18, 2009, from http://internettime.com/Learning/articles/LearnfastGofast2.pdf

Raymond, E. S. (2001). *The cathedral and the bazaar: Musings on Linux and open source by an accidental revolutionary.* Cambridge, MA: O'Reilly.

Reschke, W., & Aldag, R. (2000, August). *The business case for culture change.* Retrieved May 20, 2009, from http://www.greatorganizations.com/culturestudy.htm

Resta, P., & Laferriere, T. (2007). Technology in support of collaborative learning. *Educational Psychology Review, 19*(1), 65–83. doi:10.1007/s10648-007-9042-7

Rogers, E. (1995). *Diffusion of innovations* (4th ed.). New York: The Free Press.

Schein, E. (1985). *Organizational culture and leadership.* San Francisco: Jossey-Bass.

Sclater, N. (2008). *Large-scale open source e-learning systems at the Open University UK.* Boulder: EDUCAUSE Center for Applied Research (ECAR).

Sen, R. (2007). A strategic analysis of competition between open source and proprietary software. *Journal of Information Management Systems, 24*(1), 233–257. doi:10.2753/MIS0742-1222240107

Smart, J., & St. John, E. (1996). Organizational culture and effectiveness in higher education: A test of the "culture type" and "strong culture" hypothesis. *Educational Evaluation and Policy Analysis, 18*(3), 219–241.

Smith, K. (2006). Case study III - Higher education culture and the diffusion of technology in classroom instruction . In Metcalfe, A. (Ed.), *Knowledge management and higher education* (pp. 222–241). Hershey, PA: Idea Group, Inc.

Suthers, D. (2006). Technology affordances for intersubjective meaning making: A research agenda for CSCL. *International Journal of Computer-Supported Collaborative Learning, 1*(3), 315–337. doi:10.1007/s11412-006-9660-y

Thomas, J., & Mullaly, M. (2008). Implementation . In *Researching the value of project management* (pp. 145–186). Newton Square, PA: Project Management Institute, Inc.

Tierney, W. (1988). Organizational culture in higher education: Defining the essentials. *The Journal of Higher Education, 59*(1), 2–21. doi:10.2307/1981868

Trice, H., & Beyer, J. (1993). *The cultures of work organizations.* Upper Saddle River, NJ: Prentice Hall.

Umbach, P. D. (2007). Faculty cultures and college teaching . In Perry, R., & Smart, J. (Eds.), *The scholarship of teaching and learning in higher education: An evidence-based perspective* (pp. 263–317). New York: Springer. doi:10.1007/1-4020-5742-3_8

Uys, P., & Morton-Allen, M. (2007). *A suggested methodological framework for evaluating and selecting an open source LMS*. Retrieved June 5, 2009, from http://www.csu.edu.au/division/landt/interact/documents/2007%2006%2007%20Sakai%20Amsterdam%20Presentation%20FINAL.ppt

Villano, M. (2006). Open source vision. *Campus Technology, 19*(11), 26–36.

Von Meier, A. (1999). Occupational cultures as a challenge to technological innovation. *IEEE Transactions on Engineering Management, 46*(1), 101–114. doi:10.1109/17.740041

Wallace, L., Keil, M., & Rai, A. (2004). How software project risk affects project performance: An investigation of the dimensions of risk and an exporatory model. *Decision Sciences, 35*(2), 289–321. doi:10.1111/j.00117315.2004.02059.x

Wentling, T. L., Waight, C., Gallaher, J., La Fleur, J., Wang, C., & Kanfer, A. (2000). *e-Learning - A review of the literature*. Retrieved May 18, 2009, from http://learning.ncsa.uiuc.edu/papers/elearnlit.pdf

Wheeler, B., & DeStefano, J. (2007, July-August). *Mitigating the risks of big systems*. Retrieved June 5, 2009, from http://www.nacubo.org/Business_Officer_Magazine/Magazine_Archives/July-August_2007/Mitigating_the_Risks_of_Big_Systems.html

Wiley, D. A. (2000). *Connecting learning objects to instructional design theory: A definition, A metaphor, and A taxonomy*. Retrieved May 27, 2009, from http://reusability.org/read/chapters/wiley

Williams van Rooij, S. (2007a). Open source software in higher education: Reality or illusion? *Education and Information Technologies, 12*(4), 191–209. doi:10.1007/s10639-007-9044-6

Williams van Rooij, S. (2007b). Perceptions of open source versus commercial software: Is higher education still on the fence? *Journal of Research on Technology in Education, 39*(4), 433–453.

Wilson, B. (1996). What is a constructivist learning environment? In Wilson, B. (Ed.), *Constructivist learning environments: Case studies in instructional design* (pp. 3–10). Englewood Cliffs, NJ: Educational Technology Publications.

Woolsey, K. (2008). Where is the new learning? In Katz, R. (Ed.), *The tower and the cloud: Higher education in the age of cloud computing* (pp. 212–218). Boulder, CO: EDUCAUSE.

Zastrocky, M., Harris, M., & Lowendahl, J. (2008). *E-learning for higher education: Are we reaching maturity?* Stamford, CT: Gartner Group.

Zhang, D., & Nunamaker, J. (2003). Powering e-learning in the new millenium: An overview of e-learning and enabling technology. *Information Systems Frontiers, 5*(2), 207–218. doi:10.1023/A:1022609809036

ADDITIONAL READING

Beatty, B. & Ulasewicz, c. (2006). Faculty perspectives on moving from Blackboard to the Moodle learning management system. *TechTrends, 50*(4), 36–45. doi:10.1007/s11528-006-0036-y

Belloni, M., Christian, W., & Mason, B. (2009). Open source and open access resources for quantum physics education. *Journal of Chemical Education, 86*(1), 125–126. doi:10.1021/ed086p125

Chao, L. (2009). *Utilizing open source tools for online teaching and learning*. Hershey, PA: IGI Publishing.

Czerniewicz, l. & Brown, C. (2009). A study of the relationship between institutional policy, organisational culture and e-learning use in four South African universities. *Computers & Education*, 53(1), 121-131.

Dewever, F. (2006). Opportunities for open source e-learning. *International Journal of Web-Based Learning and Teaching Technologies*, 1(2), 50–61.

Eckel, P. D. (2006). *The shifting frontiers of academic decision making: New pathways, new priorities.* Westport, CT: Praeger.

Ellaway, R., & Martin, R. D. (2008). What's mine is yours: Open source as a new paradigm for sustainable healthcare education. *Medical Teacher, 30*(2), 175–179. doi:10.1080/01421590701874058

Flournoy, D., LeBrasseur, R., & Albert, S. (2009). The case for open access networks. [IJTHI]. *International Journal of Technology and Human Interaction, 5*(1), 1–12.

Hewson, C. (2007). Web-MCQ: A set of methods and freely available *open source* code for administering online multiple choice question assessments. *Behavior Research Methods, 39*(3), 471–481.

Huang, C. J., Chen, C. H., Luo, Y. C., Chen, H. X., & Chuang, Y. T. (2008). Developing an intelligent diagnosis and assessment e-learning tool for introductory programming. *Journal of Educational Technology & Society, 11*(4), 139–157.

Jameson, J., Davies, S., & de Freitas, S. (2006). Collaborative innovation in the Joint Information Systems Committee distributed e-learning programme. *British Journal of Educational Technology, 37*(6), 969–972. doi:10.1111/j.1467-8535.2006.00664.x

Jara, C. A., Candelas, F. A., Torres, F., Dormido, S., Esquembre, F., & Reinoso, O. (2009). Real-time collaboration of virtual laboratories through the Internet. *Computers & Education, 52*(1), 126–140. doi:10.1016/j.compedu.2008.07.007

Kezar, A., & Eckel, P. D. (2002). The effect of institutional culture on change strategies in higher education. *The Journal of Higher Education, 70*(2), 113–133.

Leidner, D. E., & Kayworth, T. (2006). A review of culture in information systems research: Toward a theory of information technology culture conflict. *Management Information Systems Quarterly, 30*(2), 357–399.

Lencioni, P. (2006). *Silos, politics and turf wars: A Leadership fable about destroying the barriers that turn colleagues into competitors.* San Francisco, CA: Jossey Bass.

Lin, W. Y., & Zini, E. (2008). Free/libre open source software implementation in schools: Evidence from the field and implications for the future. *Computers & Education, 50*(3), 1092–1102. doi:10.1016/j.compedu.2006.11.001

Little, J. K., Page, C., Betts, K., Boone, S., Faverty, P., & Joosten, T. (2009). Charting the course and tapping the community: The EDUCAUSE top teaching and learning challenges 2009. *EDUCAUSE Review, 44*(3), 30–45.

Martin-Blas, T., & Serrano-Fernandez, A. (2009). The role of new technologies in the learning process: Moodle as a teaching tool in physics. *Computers & Education, 52*(1), 35–44. doi:10.1016/j.compedu.2008.06.005

Pfaffman, J. (2007). It's time to consider open source software. *TechTrends, 51*(3), 38–43. doi:10.1007/s11528-007-0040-x

Reeves, P. M., & Reeves, T. C. (2008). Design considerations for online learning in health and social work education. *Learning in Health and Social Care, 7*(1), 46–58. doi:10.1111/j.1473-6861.2008.00170.x

Stephenson, D. (2006). Futures in e-learning. *Campus-Wide Information Systems, 23*(2), 102–104.

Toma, J. D., Dubrow, G., & Hartley, M. (2005). *The uses of institutional culture: Strengthening identification and building brand equity in higher education.* San Francisco, CA: Jossey-Bass.

Vandamme, F., & Kaczmarski, P. (2006). E-learning perspectives and challenges. *Communication & Cognition, 39*(3-4), 117–124.

Weller, M. (2007). *Virtual learning environments: Using, choosing and developing your VLE.* New York: Routledge.

Whitehurst, J. (2009). Open source: Narrowing the divide between education, business, and community. *EDUCAUSE Review, 44*(1), 70–71.

Wyles, R. (2009). Freedom, innovation, and equity with open source software . In Marshall, S., Kinuthia, W., & Taylor, W. (Eds.), *Bridging the knowledge divide: Educational technology for development* (pp. 183–198). Charlotte, NC: Information Age Publishing.

KEY TERMS AND DEFINITIONS

Academic Sub-Culture: Faculty, non-technical instructional and research support staff, and other non-technical staff under the Chief Academic Officer (CAO) focused on teaching, learning, and research.

E-Learning: Instruction, including at least 30% of the content, delivered via electronic, network-based means using a variety of channels and technologies (e.g., wireless, satellite, mobile).

Enterprise-Wide Adoption: Identification, maintenance, and support of a single standard for one or more technologies across all campus locations.

Learning Management System (LMS): Instructional software systems that combine multimedia and social software tools with administrative tools for classroom management.

Occupational Sub-Cultures: Shared cultural forms and practices centered on defined, interrelated tasks that create self-definitions and self-perceptions as well as perceptions of relationships with other sub-cultures.

Organizational Culture: Shared values, symbols, beliefs, stories, heroes, rites and assumptions that have special meaning for an organization's employees.

Organizational Sub-Cultures: Discrete clusters of ideologies, cultural forms, and practices that compose the larger organizational culture.

Technologist Sub-Culture: Information technology (IT) staff, including academic computing and administrative computing, and the technical instructional and research support staff under the Chief Information Officer (CIO) focused on maintaining an institution's cyber-infrastructure on the one hand, and providing innovative technology platforms to support teaching, learning, and research, on the other hand.

Technology Adoption: Acceptance and integration of new technologies into the existing inventory of technologies used by an organization. The process of adoption over time is normally illustrated using Rogers' (1995) bell curve based on the psychographic profiles of five adoption groups (innovators, early adopters, early majority, late majority, and laggards).

This work was previously published in International Journal of Open Source Software and Processes Volume 2, Issue 1, edited by Stefan Koch, pp. 15-31, copyright 2010 by IGI Publishing (an imprint of IGI Global).

Chapter 5
Open and Shared Educational Resources – A Collaborative Strategy for Advancing E-Learning Communities:
A Case Exemplified by Curriki

Barbara Kurshan
Educorp Consultants Corporation, USA

Anne Schreiber
Common Sense Media, USA

Peter Levy
Levy Associates, USA

ABSTRACT

Advances in information technologies have created unique opportunities for the free exchange of ideas on a global scale. To this end, a growing number of education stakeholders are finding that applying an open source approach to content development provides an extraordinary opportunity to change the curricula paradigm. Access to quality learning materials and the free exchange of knowledge is increasing. The authors explore the increased adoption of open and shared educational resources (OSER), with such examples as Curriki. Curriki extends the model by providing an integrated learning environment and resource repository centered on a culture of collective participation.

INTRODUCTION

The UN Millennium Declaration in 2000 laid out Millennium Development Goals, stating that by 2015, all children, everywhere, would have equal access to education (UN General Assembly Resolution A/55/2). Improving educational opportunities directly improves a nation's economy and the lives of its people. The challenge of making quality education universally available is steep, and yet of crucial important. The global socioeconomic crisis of recent years is having a significant impact on the allocation of funds for educational

DOI: 10.4018/978-1-61520-917-0.ch005

purposes at both local and international levels. Many developing nations are not making adequate progress in meeting their goals.

In some cases, a lack of resources and advances in technology can work together to foster innovation, where educators collaborate to create and distribute high-quality curricula. The proliferation of technology, the high cost of traditional textbooks, and the focus on engaging students in 21st century skills are compelling many stakeholders to address the growing demand for digital content, and to evolve their business and distribution models to adapt to the new learning environment. These stakeholders include publishers, secondary and post-secondary schools, NGOs, and government organizations.

BACKGROUND

In the early 1990s, the Internet emerged as a platform for the free exchange of Open Education Resources (OER) on a global scale. More recently, Web 2.0, second-generation browsers, better graphics and simulations, and interactive systems have sparked collaboration among networked communities (Atkins et al., 2007). With the additional overlay of collaboration, OER is giving way to an Open and Shared Educational Resources (OSER) ecosystem, driven by the simple and powerful idea that new technologies provide an extraordinary opportunity to change the curricula paradigm, and thereby to dramatically expand access to quality learning and the free exchange of knowledge (Casserly & Smith, 2006).

Open Source: The Solution

The major driver in lowering barriers to access is the "free and open source" movement. Open source software generally refers to software whose source code is readily available and can

be modified by users for their own purposes. The basic principle behind open source software is simple: when developers can read, modify and redistribute the source code for a piece of software, the software evolves and improves. The GNU/Linux operating system, the Apache Web server, and the OpenOffice desktop application have all proven to be world-class software applications that are released under an open source license. (Guhlin, 2007).

These examples have also provided an instructive model for how online communities can organize and govern themselves, evaluate and improve their products, and grow in size and influence. The success of open source software demonstrates that a committed community of people can effectively modify, improve or adapt a project at an astonishing pace.

What is it that makes the efforts of a volunteer community so effective? Virtually every successful open source project has several common elements (OECD, 2007):

- An infrastructure and a process that supports collaboration between disparate individuals.
- A community that is energized and motivated to complete, publish, and support their work.
- A critical mass of content that can be used as a base from which a specific community of practice can create an enhanced or customized version exactly suited to their specific needs.

The open source framework is especially conducive to the way people interact online today in the new "Participation Age" (Schwartz, 2005). The Participation Age is about access and sharing, where networks of engaged participants work collaboratively to meet a shared objective. In the process, these networks create meaningful content, connections and relationships never before possible. As an outgrowth of this participation age, a growing number of education organizations and foundations are finding that an open source approach can bring free, high quality educational resources to those that need them.

Early examples of educators exchanging and building on learning resources in the manner or programmers exchanging and building on software programs was documented in the World Bank report that first identified Open Educational Resources (OER). The report described open source courseware as generating greater awareness and interest in all parts of the world with the United States in the lead (Materu, 2004).

Open Education for the 21st Century

The open education movement is a driving force shaping education in the 21st century. It provides opportunities to participate in the creation and sharing of educational content, curriculum, and tools to address local needs and interests of educators and learners. The model provides a bottom-up, participatory platform for creating educational environments and experiences. A further level of openness is an ability to modify, repackage and add value to a resource. This kind of openness transforms the traditional role of the consumer and the producer, to one of user-producer (Tuomi, 2006).

These innovative and transformative forces— network structures, self-organization, and cooperative strategies — are having direct impact on teaching and learning. They are driving the availability and access to open resources, self-paced learning communities, and shared education commons. These innovations contribute to the democratization of teaching and learning tools and resources, making quality education possible for more children (Delivering Success to Ohio's High Schools, 2009)

OPEN AND SHARED EDUCATIONAL RESOURCES (OSER): A NEW LEVEL OF OER

There are varying views about the term "open" as used to describe educational resources. Open Educational Resources (OER) are most commonly referred to as "digitized materials offered freely and openly for educators, students and self-learners to use and reuse for teaching, learning and research" (OECD, 2007). In an Open and Shared model, communities of teachers, parents and students can work together to modify lesson plans, textbooks, or full courses and then share them with other learners and teachers, at no cost.

Open and Shared Educational Resources (OSER) provides an added element of collaboration by engaging the community to continuously improve the resources. OSER and the Free/Libre Open Source Software (F/OSS) movement share common principles of 'free' and 'open'. Both initiatives encourage contributors to become more active "resource" creators by providing the platform, the licensing framework, and the features and tools that allow for resources to be freely re-used and maintained. The OSER model is a more collaborative approach than the OER model, which focuses on a more structured way of resource creation and participant roles.

Applied to education, the OSER process invites feedback and participation from developers, educators, government officials, students and parents. It empowers these parties to exchange ideas, improve best practices and create world-class curricula. These ad-hoc "development communities" which are common in both OER and OSER communities (Wikipedia, 2008) possess characteristics, including:

1. Open, free and inclusive participation
2. Up to date content that everyone can add, edit and update
3. Resources that are usually the product of many contributors

4. Frequent releases and updates within a continuous development cycle
5. Support for a variety of editing and workflow structures
6. A large support network provided voluntarily by the community
7. Groups that are created around a common subject area, project, pedagogical need, etc.

The OSER movement can help educators around the world share appropriate educational tools, resources, and best practices that advance their learning and teaching experiences. Ideally, this model must allow educators and learners to contribute back to an ever-growing global knowledge repository of open and shared educational resources. This agile and collaborative format engages teachers in the content development process by providing access to better resources. It also connects teachers to other teachers who can evaluate and measure the impact on an individual or project basis, as illustrated in Figure 1.

This active process of building and sharing educational resources by educators supports a deeper level of involvement and understanding of the material. This in turn builds support for creating pedagogical knowledge beyond just an isolated instance, but towards a complete curricular solution (Petrides, 2006).

A Strategy for Building Open and Shared Educational Resources

Building and supporting a community that cultivates the Open and Shared Educational Resources movement requires the kind of collaborative culture of learning, creating and sharing that is paramount to a networked learning environment.

An OSER environment should be supported by a Web site strategy that:

- *Provides a user experience that encourages teacher involvement*
- *Aggregates a comprehensive collection of open and shared educational resources*
- *Spurs growth of the community through social networking*
- *Develops scalable methods to validate the quality and efficacy of all curricula and resources*

Figure 1. Open and shared educational resources (OSER) process cycle

Provide a User Experience that Encourages Teacher Involvement

In a dynamic environment, it is vital to continuously improve and adapt a Web-based learning environment to meet the changing needs of teachers, as well as to take full advantage of innovations in education and technology.

In order to accommodate these needs, the following must be done:

- Refine the individual user experience so that it is more immediately helpful, keeps visitors at the site longer, provides bridges for teachers to move toward more engaged activities, and contextualizes each visitor's experience with state-of-the-art Web 2.0 functionality.
- Augment that individual experience with community tools to make the experience more compelling, as well as highlight classroom-proven resources.
- Create a system to incorporate user feedback from multiple sources into the development and refinement of the site.

Aggregate a Comprehensive Collection of OSER

Building an open content library that provides valuable resources for teachers, and serves as a platform for innovation among teachers and developers, can be driven by:

- The development of a vetted core collection of content fully aligned to state standards that will enable teachers to work easily with the repository.
- Partner contributions of core curricula, as well as community submissions that adhere to the site's need for high quality, standards alignment and compliance with the Creative Commons.

Grow the Community through Social Networking

In order to enrich the community's engagement and both expand the network and shape future development, it is important to:

- Increase usage and viral uptake of the site among active teachers through ongoing improvements to user experience and targeted outreach.
- Partner with innovative communities of teachers (schools, districts, charter networks, teacher associations) that will actively share guidance to inform future development and ensure the project continues to meet community and individual needs.
- Expand the role of individual volunteers as contributor, reviewers of content, active advisors on platform improvements, and evangelists for OSER.

Develop Scalable Methods to Validate Quality and Efficacy

High quality content is paramount to improving teacher effectiveness, and ultimately student achievement. In an Open and Shared environment, classroom content must be validated in multiple ways, including through longitudinal data from actual usage in classrooms. By employing a fundamentally new approach to curriculum evaluation, one that shifts the model from a reliance on expert reviewers to an emphasis on empirical results and the collective "wisdom of the crowd" of teachers, you can begin to develop a scalable method to validate quality and efficacy. Moving to a community-driven review process includes:

- Development and use of robust user rating and review tools that generate data from teachers about the usefulness of content.
- Using classroom data in rigorous evaluations of core resources.

- Maintaining strong partner and affiliate relationships with data-analytics experts to build capability for validating content quality using a diverse set of data-testing sources.

DEVELOPING A COMMUNITY OF OPEN EDUCATORS

A central aspect of the Open and Shared Educational Resource (OSER) movement is the development of a professional community. Members of this community help each other around the world to find, share and adapt educational resources that advance their local learning objectives. Ideally, this will enable educators to contribute back to a developing global repository of open education resources. A learning environment centered on a culture of collaboration is exemplified in the Curriki[1] model, which is built on the principles of collaboration; assessment and evaluation; and the promotion of participation.

Collaboration

A growing body of evidence suggests that when teachers collaborate to pose and answer questions informed by data from their own students, their knowledge grows and their practice changes (Borko, 2004). The idea of collaboration is essential, both proximately within the same school building as well as non-proximately, enabled by technology tools that allow educators to work together at their convenience.

In a study of teacher performance at nine US high schools, teachers were more likely to collect and use data systematically when working as a group. Collaboration seems to add both motivation and value. Conversely, when working by themselves, teachers tend to rely on anecdotes and intuition (Ingram et al., 2004).

Internationally, some of the best school systems have found ways to enable teachers to learn from each other. In a number of top systems, particularly those in Japan and Finland, teachers work together, plan lessons jointly, observe one another's lessons, and one another improve. These systems create a school culture in which collaborative planning, reflection on instruction, and peer coaching are part of the school environment. This enables teachers to develop continuously (Barber & Mourshed, 2007).

Curriki supports an online collaborative environment for educators, learners, and committed educational experts to work together to share and create educational materials. Collections of material can be drawn from a wide range of contributors to target a particular learning objective. Facilitated by online collaboration tools and publishing templates, groups and individuals can also modify learning materials and adapt or improve them to further differentiate instruction, and better meet the needs of an individual learning community. Additionally, Curriki provides hosting and support for development and localization efforts, including the support of curricula in multiple languages.

Assessment and Evaluation

Through its open source community, Curriki supports, aggregates and leverages the work of other organizations and individual curriculum developers. Content is provided by members of the community and by content partners. To assure quality, member created content is reviewed and validated by subject matter experts through a robust Curriki Review System (CRS).

To ensure continued improvement of resources, Curriki evaluates the impact and usefulness of the site through independent studies. These have shown evidence of the impact and the value of the open education resources model. A case study conducted by the Institute for the Study of Knowledge Management in Education (ISKME) (Petrides, 2008) on how Curriki is engaging the online community found that more than 70% of users surveyed plan to return to Curriki in the future and that finding materials that help to inform their own lessons was the most cited reason for visiting the site. In addition, users indicated that they are taking advantage of what Curriki offers by:

- Sharing Curriki resources with others (38%)
- Contributing resources to Curriki (33%)
- Remixing resources (27%)
- Editing resources (27%)
- Supplementing their own content with Curriki resources (20%)
- Connecting to other teachers and learners (25%)

In another research study, conducted by West Chester University in Pennsylvania, USA (August 2008), pre-service teachers used Curriki to create online curriculum. The research project included an assessment of the usability of the Curriki site and the quality of the training materials. The qualitative data analysis revealed that Curriki is an excellent resource for teachers, students and parents to access open and free educational materials as well as for posting and sharing curriculum ideas. Of the pre-service teachers that used Curriki, the following statements represent their responses to the assessment survey questionnaire:

- 40% agreed that they would use Curriki frequently as a teacher.
- 73% agreed that the Curriki site was easy to use.
- 72% agreed that it was easy to create a new resource on Curriki.
- 57% agreed that they felt very confident with using the Curriki site.
- 41% agreed that as a teacher they would recommend the Curriki site to other teachers.

Promoting Participation

A growing body of research suggests that educators who participate in curriculum development have a deeper understanding of the subject matter (Langer, 2001), are more engaged (Wenglinsky, 2002), and are more likely to remain in the teaching profession (Darling-Hammond et al., 2005). By engaging a community of educators in the development, review, monitoring, and refinement of curricular materials, the open curriculum movement may prove to be a powerful force in teacher professional development. Open-source materials can support student learning, and the process by which those materials are developed and refined may support teacher learning.

The Curriki model of promoting collaboration and participation is supported by studies that link teacher engagement and student achievement, among nations with top rankings in international education. For instance, Finland is the world's number one performer in math and science. It boasts some of the narrowest achievement gaps in the world. Finland has a largely local curriculum and virtually no standardized testing. Highly qualified teachers create curriculum together for their local students and dedicate almost half their time to curriculum development and planning as a group (Gruver, 2009). Singapore urges its educators to "Teach Less, Learn More" and mandates that all teachers must have at least 10 percent of their time free to come up with independent lessons designed to enhance student motivation and creativity. Japan's approach to promoting participation among teachers is the lesson study process, which is an affirmation of reflective practice and builds strength of fellowship (Jalongo, 2003). Researchers report that one of the important components of these successful countries is a "lively learning community in which teachers learn and improve together in cultures of collaboration, trust, and responsibility" (Hargreaves et al., 2008).

Figure 2. Curriki homepage

The Curriki Website

Facilitated by the website (www.curriki.org), a web-based platform that provides users with the tools to develop, aggregate, evaluate and support open and shared educational resources (OSER), Curriki offers three core sets of functionality that address the principles of collaboration, assessment and evaluation and promoting of participation (see Figure 2):

- **FIND** – allows users to locate individual learning resources and build collections of resources from the Curriki repository of open educational resources. The content cover a full range of subject areas for primary and secondary students in areas such as mathematics, science, social studies, language arts, and technology.
- **CONTRIBUTE** – empowers teachers across the globe to share their best lessons

or units of study. When teachers contribute to the Curriki repository, the global community can find the free and open resources they need, when they need them.

- **CONNECT** – invites teachers to work together to create curricular materials using the site's easy-to-use collaboration tools. Whether down the hall or across an ocean from each other, teachers can build connections around highly targeted communities of interest to create a broad array of new instructional materials.

In order to provide quality assurance and efficacy, users have access to high quality educational resources that have been validated by a team of experienced subject matter experts, through the Curriki Review System. In addition, members have the ability to post ratings and comments, which further enhance Curriki's ability to remain an open site, yet make it easy for users to find content of consistently high quality.

OPEN AND SHARED EDUCATION RESOURCES (OSER) IN ACTION

The Open and Shared Education Resources (OSER) movement has shown much promise in transforming the conditions for teaching and learning worldwide. OSER projects expand access to learning for everyone by bridging the gap between non-formal, informal and formal learning and increasing participation among learners. The rapidly growing number of learning materials and repositories has made a significant impact on schools worldwide. Through greater collaboration around the world and enhanced reuse of learning materials (in their original form or translated or otherwise adapted) the phenomenon of OSER contributes to the globalization of education.

Curriki is just one example of a "disruptive change" (Christenson et al., 2000) that is transforming the traditional model of how content is developed, published, distributed and evaluated. Other examples of OSER (and OER) ventures that have been successful, include:

CK-12[2], developed by the CK-12 Foundation, to provide an open-content, Web-based collaborative model termed the "FlexBook," as an alternative model to the traditional textbook. The content generated by CK-12 and their community serves both as educational resources for a student's learning and provides an adaptive environment that scaffolds the learner's journey as he or she masters a standards-based body of knowledge, while allowing for self-paced learning.

Connexions[3], a project that originated at Rice University, organizes content in small modules, open to use and re-use in creative ways consistent with modern pedagogy. Most modules are in English, but there are also modules written in Chinese, Italian, Japanese, Portuguese, Spanish, and Thai. Connexions provides an environment for collaboratively developing, freely sharing, and rapidly publishing scholarly content on the Web. Connexions is organized around a "content commons," an online repository that contains thousands of scholarly modules—manuscripts roughly equivalent to two or three pages of a textbook. Connexions provides free software that allows anyone to reuse, revise, and recombine the modules to suit their needs. This feature gives people the option of creating customized courses, custom textbooks, and personalized study guides.

OERCommons[4] created by the Institute for the Study of Knowledge Management in Education (ISKME) supports the development of a knowledge base around the use and reuse of open educational resources. As a network for teaching and learning materials, the site offers engagement with resources in the form of social bookmarking, tagging, rating, and reviewing. OERCommons has forged alliances with over 120 major content partners to provide a single point of access through which educators and learners can search across collections to access over 24,000 items, find and provide descriptive information about

each resource, and retrieve the ones they need. By being "open," these resources are publicly available for all to use, and principally through Creative Commons licensing, many thousands are legally available for repurposing, modifying and improving.

OpenCourseWare[5], a large-scale, web-based electronic publishing initiative that provides free, searchable access to virtually all Massachusetts Institute of Technology (MIT) course materials. This initiative enables the open sharing of the MIT faculty's teaching materials with educators, enrolled students, and self-learners around the world. The resources are available without registration. MIT OCW provides users with open access to the syllabi, lecture notes, course calendars, problem sets and solutions, exams, reading lists, and a selection of video lectures. As on October 2009, MIT OCW had published over 1,900 courses representing 35 departments and all five of MIT's schools.

OpenLearn[6] developed by the Open University in the United Kingdom, to provide learners with access to pedagogically structured open educational resources as well as less-structured materials that can be remixed and reused by the community to suit their learning needs. OpenLearn is a Web 2.0 development in that it is a participatory and collaborative site. This reflects a wider trend in social networking sites that allow users to upload and share their own content, and influence greater control over their online experience. The site contains two main areas: the *LearningSpace* with educational resources from 11 subject areas, which range from 3–15 hours study time each and range in difficulty from access level through to post-graduate, and; the *LabSpace*, an area that encourages a community of practice to develop around the sharing and re-using of the resources.

MERLOT[7], the Multimedia Educational Resource for Learning and Online Teaching is a user-centered, searchable collection of peer reviewed and selected higher education, online learning materials, catalogued by registered members and a set of faculty development support services. MERLOT is an online community where faculty, staff, and students from around the world share their learning materials and pedagogy. MERLOT's strategic goal is to improve the effectiveness of teaching and learning by increasing the quantity and quality of peer reviewed online learning materials that can be easily incorporated into faculty-designed courses.

These initiatives promote the kind of cooperation and knowledge sharing that will propel open education to the next level. These examples and many others that are yet to be developed are dedicated to a common vision of making high-quality learning materials freely available to educators around the world.

Impact of OSER

Open educational resources have significant impacts on many levels, including benefits to society and national economies. Through greater collaboration between teachers and educators around the world and enhanced reuse of educational materials, both in their original form or when translated or otherwise adapted, OSER is contributing to the globalization of education. OSER initiatives have become learning agents for outreach to students, widening participation, and providing learning opportunities for those unable to access traditional textbook offerings. Such initiatives can bridge the gap between those with access to high quality education and those without. This helps to advance a nations' human capital. At the same time open educational resources can provide social benefits to adult learners for in-service training and home study, opening new lifelong learning strategies as a means of tackling the challenges of aging societies (OECD, 2007).

Curriki and other open content models provide significant educational cost savings. These savings can be realized at the local as well as national systems of education through increased workflow efficiencies including requisition, procurement

and distribution activities. Moreover, while some resources are necessary for training and ongoing teacher support, the open and shared educational resource alternative offers significant return on investment for school systems, without sacrificing quality. The content will be just as, and in some cases more robust, in terms of variety, quality, and flexibility because they can include stimulating interactive activities such as games, simulations, virtual laboratories, and multiple representations of complex concepts.

The economic value and return on invest that open educational resources provide can be illustrated in the Curriki Educator model. This supposes an ever-expanding global community of teachers that continually hones best practices, as well as the resources they use to help students reach high achievement. With 3.1 million teachers in the U.S. and an average instructional materials expenditure of $4,500 per year, the total annual budget exceeds $14 billion (NCES, 2006). If only 10% of classrooms convert from proprietary, static and expensive curricula to open, dynamic and free content, the estimated savings for US school systems can exceed US $700 million annually, (see Figure 3.) Extending this model to other countries and the impact becomes not just transformational but miraculous.

In a financially restrictive environment, the Curriki model and other OER and OSER initiatives are valuable alternatives to traditional instructional materials. Faced with budget shortfalls, some school systems in the US have embraced the open content model by enacting education reform that puts them on a path to being better prepared to provide their students with open source learning resources. Driving the movement towards more open and free access to educational resources are state education reforms that include:

California launched an initiative to offer schools free digital textbooks for high school students. The initiative involves the development of a state approved list of standards-aligned, open-source digital textbooks for high school math

Figure 3. Financial benefits of OSER: The Curriki educator model

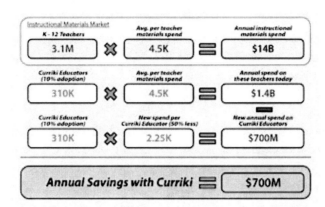

and science. The proposal attracted more than 20 submissions, which included content developers from nonprofits such as Curriki, to textbook publisher Pearson and a contribution from a university professor (Governor Schwarzenegger, 2009).

Virginia is the first state to have an organized compilation of open educational resources with the recent release of the Physics "Flexbook" using CK-12, a collaborative effort of volunteer high school physics teachers, university faculty and industry experts. It is available online for teachers to use, and other teachers are able to post updates, corrections, and suggestions. There will be periodic reviews of the Flexbook to ensure that the most relevant and appropriate information is included. This will not replace existing physics textbooks, but is a bold endeavor by a state to encourage the use of free, online, open instructional materials by schools (Virginia State Government, 2009).

The **Indiana State Board of Education** issued a referendum allowing for greater flexibility for schools to request a waiver from traditional textbook adoption requirements for specific subject areas. They have also allowed the school system "to use computers and other data devices, instructional software, Internet resources, interactive, magnetic and other media, and other systematically organized material." As technology evolves, Indiana's inclusive definition of textbook will enable schools to use open and shared educational

materials, whether packaged for them or by them (Fletcher, 2009).

Florida provided more flexibility for school districts by loosening restrictions on categorical funding, including the funds that were restricted to textbooks. Beginning in the 2008-2009 academic year, schools were permitted to use instructional materials funds for textbooks or anything they want, including digital resources to provide instructional curriculum (Fletcher, 2009).

The **Texas** State legislature enacted a law that allows for the use of textbook funds to purchase technology equipment necessary to support the use of electronic textbooks or instructional material as part of the foundation curriculum for science in elementary education. Included in the legislation is a computer lending pilot program to provide educationally disadvantaged schools with computers for students to access the electronic resources (Fletcher, 2009a).

In **Arizona,** a local school system replaced traditional textbooks for all classes with a combination of computer-based, teacher-generated materials; online subscriptions; and links to free information and activities on the web (Schachter, 2009).

The bold initiatives taken by the states noted above clearly indicate that there is a growing demand for a learning ecosystem that includes Web 2.0 technologies, wiki services, and OSER.

As momentum builds for affordable solutions that incorporate the best of the traditional textbook with the added benefit of user engagement, community collaboration, and the ability to readily update and customize, publishers will need to re-tool their models to include the new demand for online and open and shared resources.

Beyond the benefit of accessibility and cost-efficiency, open and shared educational resources represent a fundamental shift in the relationship between the creator of the content and the user of the content, which may ultimately result in better student achievement. Open and Shared Educational Resources provide a unique opportunity for teachers and students to be creators of their own knowledge. Teacher and student engagement with open online textbooks that incorporates continuous feedback provides a greater understanding of the content and context that will ultimately maximize learning. Traditional hardcover textbooks may never cease to exist, but as digital natives are more proficient with search engines than card catalogues, they will inevitably accelerate the vastly growing ecosystem of open and shared educational resources.

Sustainability and Scalability of OSER

Most open education resource projects originated with some initial funding from either institutional resources, from governmental funds or private foundations. Sustainability of OER initiatives requires a departure from the traditional revenue model – a model that focuses solely on the product. It requires a deeper acceptance and understanding of what the user community wants and improving the value provided to them with open educational resources (Dholakia, 2006). By focusing on the issue of increasing the aggregate value of the site to its constituents, the OSER model offers a significant advantage over existing content creation and distribution methods, as it has no profit motive, and can change and adapt quickly. How-

ever, these projects are not without costs. These include the production, reuse and distribution of open educational resources. Producing OSER requires human resources, workflow processes and supporting technology; the effective reuse of OER requires tools and training for resource localization; and distribution of digital media to the end users requires bandwidth and media inventory (Wiley, 2006).

The real costs associated with OSER can be met with resources other than money. To ensure longevity and support scalability, Curriki is experimenting with a number of options that include a community-based model, as well as a funding model. While it is important to support and maintain operational and technological costs with financial resources, it is just as important to build collaborative and voluntary development of open source software and content production.

As Web technologies continue to advance, as we have seen in the previous two decades with Web 1.0 and 2.0, a third, Web 3.0, is emerging that will provide even greater promise and opportunities for OSER to advance.

CONCLUSION

The advancement of the open educational movement represents a paradigm shift to a participatory culture of learning. At the center of this movement is the powerful idea that access to knowledge and tools for learning is a basic right for every child. To realize this "big idea," Curriki and others in the open education movement are completely rethinking the traditional model of how content is developed, published, distributed and evaluated. By leveraging the power of open source communities, Open and Shared Educational Resources support collaboration and participation through a global community of educators and learners that create, use, edit, extend, and share resources with one another.

As the OSER model continues to evolve and expand, Curriki and other initiatives will have to address many challenges that this innovative approach to educational content generates. These questions include:

- *How open is open for education?* Education is driven by standards and specific national and state frameworks. These frameworks inherently impose limitations on openness. Finding a balance between the need to align to standards and a desire to customize content will be a fundamental challenge to the OSER movement.
- *Can you build high-quality curriculum collaboratively?* New models of instructional design are now defined by collaboration and participation, whereas institutional governance led older models. Given the fundamental shift this change represents, will educators and teachers participate in this new process? How should membership in online resource communities be defined?
- *Can you trust the community?* Experts in the form of publishers and administrators have historically been the source of curricular material. If the community is now the expert, a whole new definition of validation and review is required.
- *How can you convert Consumers to Contributors?* As innovation will inevitably provide for newer and better ways of creating and sharing resources, what will be the motivator for users to become active contributors and collaborators in the content development process?
- *How is the open education model sustainable?* In an open economy, user participation creates the wealth and value. How can sustainable cost/benefit models be developed while maintaining free and open access?

Through a scaffolded model of support, Curriki and others in the movement are seeking to provide the infrastructure to let the community collaboratively answer these questions.

Around the globe, technology has enabled us to democratize the development and distribution of learning materials like never before. The opportunity exists to empower every teacher that wants to teach and every student that wants to learn with high-quality educational resources at no cost.

REFERENCES

Atkins, D., Brown, J., & Hammond, A., (2007, February). *A Review of the Open Educational Resources (OER) Movement: Achievements, Challenges, and New Opportunities.* Report to The William and Flora Hewlett Foundation, Menlo Park, CA.

Barber, M., & Mourshed, M. (2007). *How the world's Best Performing School Systems Come Out on Top.* Washington, DC: McKinsey & Company.

Borko, H. (2004). Professional development and teacher learning: Mapping the terrain. *Educational Researcher, 33*(8), 3–15. doi:10.3102/0013189X033008003

Casserly, C., & Smith, M. (2006). The Promise of Open Educational Resources. *Change Magazine, 38*(5), 8–17. doi:10.3200/CHNG.38.5.8-17

Christenson, C., & Overdorf, M. (2000). Meeting the Challenge of Disruptive Change. *Harvard Business Review,* (March-April): CK-12. Retrieved from http://www.ck12.org.

Commonwealth of Virginia. Governor Kaine Launches Virginia Physics Flexbook: Open content web tool to provide supplemental 21st century physics materials for Virginia teachers. Office of the Governor. Released: March 16, 2009. Retrieved October 20, 2009 from http://www.governor.virginia.gov/MediaRelations/NewsReleases/viewRelease.cfm?id=897

Connexions Project at Rice University. Retrieved from http://cnx.org

Darling-Hammond, L., Holtzman, D., Gatlin, S. J., & Heilig, J. V. (2005). Does teacher preparation matter? Evidence about teacher certification, Teach for America, and teacher effectiveness. *Education Policy Analysis Archives, 13*(42).

Delivering Success to Ohio's High Schools (2009), The KnowledgeWorks School Improvement Efforts, Building High-Performing High Schools, and Impact on Student Achievement. *The KnowledgeWorks Foundation*, January 2009.

Dholakia, U. M. (2006). *What Makes an OE Program Sustainable?* OECD papers on CERI—Open Educational Resources Program. Paris, France

Fletcher, G. (2009). Signs of a Significant Disruption in the Traditional Textbook Model. *T.H.E. Journal*, February 2009 News. Retrieved September 29, 2009, from http://thejournal.com/articles/2009/02/25/signs-of-a-significant-disruption-in-the-traditional-textbook-model.aspx

Fletcher, G. (2009a). The Disruption of the Traditional Textbook Model Continues. *T.H.E. Journal*. Retrieved September 29, 2009, from http://thejournal.com/Articles/2009/06/24/The-Disruption-of-the-Traditional-Textbook-Model-Continues.aspx

Gov. Schwarzenegger Announces One of Nation's Largest Textbook Publishers Among Those Participating in Free Digital Textbook Initiative (June 16, 2009) [Press Release] *Office of the Governor Arnold Schwarzenegger*. Retrieved, October 22, 2009 from http://gov.ca.gov/press-release/12542/

Gruver, M. (2009). Time well spent? Teacher learning debated in Wyoming, *The Associated Press.* March 11, 2009.

Guhlin, M. (2007). The Case for Open Source. *techLearning*. February 15, 2007

Hargreaves, A., & Shirley, D. (2008, October). The Fourth Way of Change. *Educational Leadership, 66*(2).

Ingram, D., Louis, K. S., & Schroeder, R. G. (2004). Accountability policies and teacher decision-making: Barriers to the use of data to improve practice. *Teachers College Record, 106*(6), 1258–1287. doi:10.1111/j.1467-9620.2004.00379.x

Jalongo, M. R. (2003). Editorial: On behalf of children: Lessons from Japan: Reflective, collaborative planning for instruction. [PD.]. *Early Childhood Education Journal, 31*, 81–84. doi:10.1023/B:ECEJ.0000005431.20794.52

Langer, J. (2001). Succeeding against the odds in English. *English Journal, 91*(1), 37–42. doi:10.2307/821652

Materu, P. (2004). Open Source Courseware: A Baseline Study. *The World Bank*, Washington, DC. MIT's OpenCourseWare. Retrieved from http://ocw.mit.edu

Multimedia Educational Resources for Learning and Online Teaching (Merlot). http://www.merlot.org

NCES. (2006). Revenues and Expenditures for Public Elementary and Secondary Education 2005-2006. *National Center for Education Statistics*. Retrieved October 11, 2009, from http://nces.ed.gov/pubs2008/expenditures/index.asp

OECD. (2007) Giving Knowledge for Free: The emergence of Open Educational Resources. *Center for Educational Research and Innovation*. Retrieved September 22, 2009, from http://www.sourceoecd.org/education/9789264031746

OERCommons. Retrieved from http://www.oercommons.org

Open Educational Resources. (2008). *Wikipedia*. Retrieved September 22, 2009 from http://en.wikipedia.org/wiki/Open_educational_resources

OpenLearn. Retrieved from http://openlearn. open.ac.uk

Petrides, L. (2006). Creating Knowledge Building and Sharing Capacity through Case Study Development. *The Institute for the Study of Knowledge Management in Education.* October 3, 2006.

Petrides, L. (2008). OER Case Study Framework. *The Institute for the Study of Knowledge Management in Education.* Retrieved September 20, 2009, from http://wiki.oercommons.org/mediawiki/index.php/OER_Case_Study_Framework

Schachter, R. (2009). Digital Classrooms Take Flight. District Administration. *The Magazine for School District Management.* October 2009.

Schwartz, J. (2005). The Participation Age. *IT Conversations Legacy Programs.* Recorded April 4, 2005.

Tuomi, I. (2006), Open Educational Resources: What they are and why do they matter. Retrieved October 10, 2009, from http://www.meaning-processing.com/personalPages/tuomi/articles/OpenEducationalResources_OECDreport.pdf

United Nations General Assembly Resolution. (A/55/2) September 8, 2000. *United Nations Millennium Declaration.* Retrieved June 2, 2009, from http://www.un.org/millennium/declaration/ares552e.pdf

Wenglinsky, H. (2002). The Link between Teacher Classroom Practices and Student Academic Performance. *The entity from which ERIC acquires the content, including journal, organization, and conference names, or by means of online submission from the author.Education Policy Analysis Archives,* v10 n12 Feb 2002.

Wiley, D. (2006), On the Sustainability of Open Educational Resource Initiatives in Higher Education, *OECD Centre for Educational Research and Innovation (CERI).* Retrieved October 20, 2009, from http://www.oecd.org/edu/oer

KEY TERMS AND DEFINITIONS

21st Century Skills: The knowledge and skills required to be competitive in an increasingly global, knowledge-based economy. These skills include using information and communications technology (ICT) to gather and assess information, collaborate, innovate, think critically, and solve problems.

Disruptive Change: Characterized by a shift in the underlying forces of an industry sector. Disruptive technology and disruptive innovation are terms used in business and technology to describe innovations that improve a product or service in ways that are non-traditional.

Education Divide: An observed disparity or gap to the accessibility access to high quality education and learning materials among groups of learners.

Open and Shared Educational Resources (OSER): Open educational resources with an added element of collaboration that engages the community to continuously improve the resources.

Open Education Resources (OER): Digitized materials offered freely and openly for educators, students and self-learners to use and reuse for teaching, learning and research.

Open Source: A method and philosophy for software licensing and distribution designed to encourage use and improvement of software written by volunteer developers ensuring that anyone can copy the source code and modify it freely.

Social Networking: The use of a website to connect with people who share personal or professional interests, place of origin, education at a particular school, etc.

Web 2.0: The second generation of the World Wide Web in which content is user-generated and dynamic, increased social interaction, naturally formed communities of practice and social networking.

Web 3.0: The predicted third generation of the World Wide Web, understood to include a rich collaborative environment that transcends time and space with increased social uses of online virtual spaces and the continuing rapid development and diffusion of new technologies.

ENDNOTES

[1]   Curriki is a nonprofit social entrepreneurship organization dedicated to improving education by empowering teachers, students and parents with universal access to free and Open and Shared Educational Resources (OSER). Curriki provides a virtual space for educators to share curricula, best practices, and other teaching resources and work collaboratively to develop new instructional materials. Curriki was founded by Sun Microsystems in March 2004 and became an independent 501 (C)(3) organization in 2006 to accelerate and focus on the OSER repository effort.

[2]   http://www.ck12.org

[3]   http://www.cnx.org

[4]   http://www.oercommons.org

[5]   http://ocw.mit.edu

[6]   http://openlearn.open.ac.uk

[7]   http://www.merlot.org

Section 3
Implementation Examples

Chapter 6
Developing a Dynamic and Responsive Online Learning Environment:
A Case Study of a Large Australian University

Janet Buchan
Charles Sturt University, Australia

ABSTRACT

Charles Stuart University adopted the open source software, Sakai, as the foundation for the university's new, integrated Online Learning Environment. This study explores whether a pedagogical advantage exists in adopting such an open source learning management system. Research suggests that the community source approach to development of open source software has many inherent pedagogical advantages, but this paper examines whether this is due to the choice of open source software or simply having access to appropriate technology for learning and teaching in the 21st century. The author also addresses the challenges of the project management methodology and processes in the large-scale implementation of an open-source courseware management solution at the institutional level. Consequently, this study outlines strategies that an institution can use to harness the potential of a community source approach to software development to meet the institutional and individual user needs into the future.

INTRODUCTION

Charles Sturt University (New South Wales, Australia) adopted the open source software, Sakai, as the foundation for the University's new, integrated Online Learning Environment called *CSU Interact*. Sakai was implemented in 2006 as a platform for research and project collaboration by selected schools, divisions, and research centers, and then subsequently at the end of 2007 across the entire University for learning and teaching. No major distinction is made here between 'e-learning' and 'learning and teaching' because the university supports blended and flexible learning and 'e-learning' is an integral part of the design of learning experiences that can include multiple modes of delivery. The move to Sakai underpins the future of learning and teaching at the university and

DOI: 10.4018/978-1-61520-917-0.ch006

represents a significant investment of resources, human and financial. This study outlines some of the challenges and successes of the project management methodology and processes which oversaw the successful large-scale implementation of an open-source courseware management solution at the institutional level.

The implementation of an open source system is only the beginning. In today's climate of rapidly changing educational technology, users demand that the online learning environment is indeed dynamic and responsive to their needs. Having entered the Web 2.0 technology era relatively late, it appears that that there is indeed transformation taking place in learning and teaching across the university. Is this due to the choice of open source software, or simply having access to appropriate technology for learning and teaching in the 21st century? This study explores the question; 'Is there in fact a pedagogical advantage to adopting an open source learning management system?'

The views expressed in this paper are primarily those of the author. The views are the result of consistent reflection on the changing educational technology environment and evolving processes and university structures over the last few years (Buchan, 2008a, 2008b; Buchan, 2009a; Buchan & Swann, 2007; Buchan & Buchan, 2003). The aim is to tease out some of the pedagogical affordances of open source software and to draw as accurate a picture as possible from the point of view of a learning/educational technologist and manager who has a strategic role within project implementation teams on Sakai software and supports the instructional designers who have a hands-on role in assisting academic staff with the application of the educational technology in their teaching. The viewpoint is from the learning and teaching support perspective. However, it is acknowledged here that there are numerous key players from a number of Divisions who have been or are still involved with the evolution of CSU's online learning environment and it is the early strategic vision of key players within the

Division of Information Technology (Rebecchi, 2004b) that has set us on our current path.

For further reading, the change and innovation strategies used during the implementation of Sakai at CSU have been well documented (Uys, 2009). The official guide to Sakai Courseware Management (Berg & Korcuska, 2009) and the SakaiProject website (available from http://sakaiproject.org/portal) are also valuable and comprehensive resources for Sakai users.

BACKGROUND TO SAKAI

"Sakai is an open source, web-based, collaboration learning environment (CLE) that is focused primarily on higher education. It supports the activities of students, teachers, researchers, and Sakai administrators. Sakai is flexible and enables users to configure it for their own specialized audiences. Sakai is mainly a courseware management platform that provides users with learning, portfolio, library, and project tools…" (Berg & Korcuska, 2009. p.5)

Sakai is a Collaborative Learning Environment (CLE), which extends the concepts of similar systems such as Learning Management Systems (LMS), Content (courseware) Management Systems (CMS) and Virtual Learning Environments (VLE). Sakai is distributed as free and open source software under an Educational Community Licence (Berg & Korcuska, 2009). The Sakai Project is based on a community source model. The understanding here is that 'open source' software is developed by a community of individuals while 'community source' software is developed by a community of organizations or institutions. The community source model is potentially extremely powerful when it is well coordinated and there is full institutional commitment.

There are many potential benefits of open source software in higher education (Joint Information Systems Committee, 2008; Whitehurst,

2009). However, supporting an open source software solution to promote high-quality learning, teaching and research in a sustainable fashion is not without its problems and challenges (Joint Information Systems Committee, 2006; Ozkan, 2008; Stunden, 2003). It calls for the institution to embrace a holistic view that goes beyond the installation and maintenance of hardware and software by information technology (IT) staff. To make a real difference the technology, systems, and processes must be solidly underpinned by an integrated management approach that focuses on the essential goal - that of student learning - with the emphasis on user needs (Buchan, 2009b; Joint Information Systems Committee, 2006). Moreover, adoption of open source entails commitment to a spirit of openness and sharing at all levels of the institution (Tan, 2007).

PEDAGOGICAL ADVANTAGES OF AN OPEN SOURCE COLLABORATIVE LEARNING ENVIRONMENT FOR E-LEARNING

This study begins with an examination of the potential pedagogical advantages of an open source CLE for e-learning. The latter part of this article, the case study, focuses on documenting details around what is seen to be a successful implementation of Sakai as a CLE for a large institution. It was the stated goal of some of those spearheading the project that the introduction of *CSU Interact* (CSU's instance of Sakai) should transform learning and teaching. By investing in a new LMS, an institution should be looking at transforming, or at least gaining significant improvements in, learning and teaching. Much has been written about the implementation of such systems and pedagogical advantages (Benson & Palaskas, 2006; Weaver, Spratt, & Nair, 2008; Zhou & Xu, 2007). It is acknowledged here that sound pedagogy is not the unique domain of open source systems, and that many commercial LMS's

will provide similar advantages. However, it is proposed here that there are in fact some unique pedagogical advantages of an open source CLE. Based largely on the literature and experience from this case study, the following pedagogical advantages are outlined. How far these advantages are realized will depend on the individual institution and its willingness to invest resources to make customizations, the models of hosting and the engagement with the open source community.

Engagement of the Institution with Learning and Teaching

Perhaps the most important factor in determining the pedagogical advantages of an open source CLE is engagement of the institution with learning and teaching *per se*. If there is a strategic approach to the selection of the CLE that fully engages the users, those who administer and support the system, those who support the users and a recognition of future directions in learning and teaching at the institution then whatever system (proprietary or open source) is chosen should provide a pedagogical advantage. When a pedagogical need that requires new educational technology and software arises, an institution must be able to be responsive to this. The institution that can respond quickly to user needs will possess the strategic advantage in supporting learning and teaching needs.

Access to Adequate Technology for User Needs

Simply having access to a CLE at an affordable price is important. No system is free and all systems require a degree of support and maintenance. For many, especially smaller institutions, the price of commercial systems might be out of reach. The annual costs of licensing a commercial LMS may rise above inflation and an institution will have little control over these. Although the costs of open source are not in licensing but are elsewhere, institutions will have more control over the unforeseen costs (Nederlof, 2009) as well as other costs. Some open source systems lend themselves more to use by small institutions, schools etc. than others. Sakai is in use at over 160 colleges and universities throughout the world (information accessed from http://sakaiproject. org/portal/site/sakai-home/page/29186420-3b36-4381-9d53-bba4d17b6f1f on 14 August 2009) with users numbering between 200 to over 200,000 in the individual institutions. There are several commercial partners specializing in supporting Sakai which helps to increase access (Berg & Korcuska, 2009).

Collaborative Learning Environment

The development of Sakai as a CLE acknowledges that having a system that can support research and collaboration is just as important as teaching applications (Available from http://sakaiproject. org/portal/site/sakai-home/page/41344e39-89f5-40cd-a153-2370382419d9, accessed on 8 August 2009). At CSU our instance of Sakai, *CSU Interact*, is actively used by researchers to collaborate with one another and to share resources in a common workspace. Individual university research institutes use *CSU Interact* project sites to enable teams of researchers to engage with one another and to share progress and information about their research.

Using the same technology for collaboration in research as well as for learning and teaching has advantages in efficiency with people only having to become familiar with a single system. It grounds research firmly in the learning and teaching realm. *CSU Interact* is also used by Divisions and administrative groups as a collaborative work environment. This is an important practical step in a multi-campus, dispersed organization with international links, where online communication becomes the norm. The uptake of a CLE to ground work practices (administrative and academic) is a significant step towards creating a learning organization. It encourages all staff, academic

and general (professional) to move into a Web 2.0 based mode of communication. Web 2.0 is defined here in the instructional design sense. "The Web 2.0 label applies to a range of technologies that wrap interactive capabilities around digital information." (Milne, 2007); and, "Web 2.0 is web-based technologies that allows [sic] a 'read/write' approach to the web and enables the learner to be both a consumer and producer of content and services. Learners are co-learners and co-authors in this type of environment. It enhances the opportunities for learners to collaborate and generate new knowledge or build expert domains by a community of practice. This is the real promise of Web 2.0!" (Putland, 2006). This supports O'Reilly's 2004 original description of Web 2.0 (O'Reilly, 2009). The use of a *CSU Interact* site for a particular work group gives members ownership of the outcomes of that group through the collaborative process and encourages the sharing of information and ideas amongst staff.

Developing the Learning Organization

A learning organization has been defined as "an organization that facilitates the learning of all its members and consciously transforms itself and its context' (Pedler, Burgoyne, & Boydell, 1997). Being a learning organization is not simply a matter of picking up the 'buzzwords'.I It can be seen as an essential strategy in adapting to the constant change in our higher education area (Buchan, 2008a, 2008b). It is suggested here that by adopting the open source Sakai solution for its online learning environment, CSU has provided the context for facilitating learning by its staff. Those programmers, testers and other IT staff who are working on Sakai are continually being presented with new challenges and learning experiences. They are also being given the opportunity to work with other developers world-wide and the university is thus investing in training and upskilling its IT staff.

Instructional (educational) designers and educational technologists played important roles in supporting academic staff through the move to *CSU Interact* and had to undertake significant professional development around the use and application of the technology. While this would have been the same if a commercial platform had been chosen, because of the dynamic nature of *CSU Interact* and the ongoing addition of new tools and other systems at the university, these staff are beginning to accept (though do not necessarily like!) learning how to use a new educational technology as a normal part of the job. Becoming an expert quickly is important in being able to then help faculty to design effective learning experiences using the technology. As professionals our roles as instructional designers and educational technologists have been completely transformed and will continue to change as the effects of technology and changes in the higher education environment are felt. As a result of the major changes, and through transforming our practise and personal knowledge, our adaptability has increased which is important in adapting to ongoing change in the higher education environment.

Developing Communities of Practice

"Communities of practice are groups of people who share a concern or a passion for something they do and learn how to do it better as they interact regularly." (Wenger, 2009). The key aspect of communities of practice here is "learning". This can be the prime focus of the CoP or an incidental outcome of members' interactions (Wenger, 2009). The Sakai community is an excellent example of a community of practice (CoP) in action. Communities of practice are formed by people who engage in a process of collective learning in a shared domain of human endeavour. In this case study those involved in the implementation and use of Sakai will attest to have undertaken most of the key activities that are associated with an effective community of practice. These activities

are: problem solving, requests for information, seeking experience, reusing assets, coordination and synergy, discussing developments, documentation of projects, visits, mapping knowledge and identifying gaps (Wenger, 2009). The use of CoPs are an important part of creating a learning organization (Senge, 1990) by getting people to take some ownership around collaborating and sharing information in their roles.

"The community includes the Sakai Foundation, individuals, teams within universities, commercial affiliates, consortiums, and diverse interest groups. The community interacts at conferences, via distribution lists, a central Wiki, conference calls, via Google docs, and directly through the addition to and modification of the Sakai source code. It is driven by the central overwhelming motivation to deploy and improve an online environment for communication and learning, and the exploration of new functional needs. It is not only about bashing code, but also consensus building about best practices and the evolution of functionality as the high education market for learning changes." (Berg & Korcuska 2009, p. 385)

Those involved in the support and implementation of Sakai at CSU report active engagement with the Sakai community at a variety of levels. At the grass roots level programmers (developers), instructional designers and educational technologists report the positive learning experience from engaging with the Sakai community and learning from people with whom they would otherwise never have contact. Because CSU is relatively isolated in Australia, attending Sakai conferences has been an important learning experience for management, those in liaison roles, developers and instructional designers. It is essential to create those opportunities to meet face to face with key members of the Sakai community.

It should be noted here that many commercial LMS products have an active community for question and answer and sharing practice, including hosting conferences and presenting awards for encouraging good practice in teaching with the technology.

Responsive to Users' Pedagogical Needs

Figure 1 illustrates the feedback pathways that are being developed in order to inform the improvement of the online learning environment. (This aspect of responsiveness is discussed in more detail later on). The use of a community source CLE potentially allows educational technology and systems to be responsive to user needs, thus providing a dynamic, and hopefully timely, way of meeting the pedagogical needs of users. In this case study the challenges for organizational management in making the most of an open source solution are firstly to understand the pedagogical needs of the institution, secondly to interpret the roadmap of Sakai development, and finally to

actively engage with the Sakai community in order to influence, where possible, the Sakai roadmap towards supporting local needs. In the rapidly changing educational technology environment it is acknowledged that a system such as Sakai may not service all the needs of an institution at a particular time and users may need to look to other solutions for particular application needs. At last count the following free software applications were in use in pockets across the university: Twitter, Facebook, Yammer, Edublogs, Slideshare, YouTube, Flickr and Second Life amongst others.

Designing a Curriculum around Open Source Software to Provide Authentic and Situated Learning Experiences

Many institutions offer courses in writing open source software. There could be significant pedagogical benefits for students and staff if some of the IT discipline courses included hands-on

Figure 1. The feedback pathways to inform improvements to CSU's online learning environment (CSU's instance of Sakai). (Source: Buchan, 2009. In press)

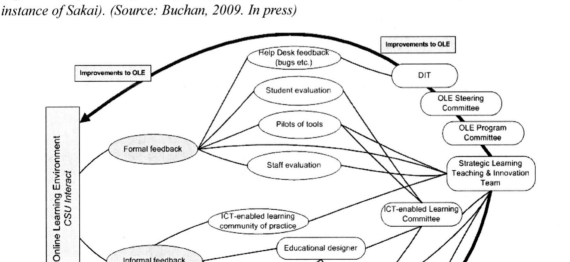

experience with Sakai as part of the curriculum. This would provide the ultimate 'situated' and authentic learning experience. (Lave & Wenger, 1990). With the availability of distance education (DE) options for study, already many IT staff get employment at CSU part way through their degree and complete their studies 'on the job'. Part of these studies include major projects which, in many cases, are directly related to the daily work of the individuals. This opens up possibilities for useful contribution to the development of Sakai tools.

Worldwide, Sakai has supported the Google Summer of Code (GSOC) project and has had a number of students working on Sakai development. This has become a prestigious and valued opportunity for young programmers.

On a more general note about the pedagogical affordances of open source software Tan (2004) suggests that teaching basic IT literacy through the use of FOSS software can have its advantages because students do not then assume that computing is based on a single platform but that exposing students to a variety of applications encourages an understanding of the basic principles of the applications so that individuals are then more adaptable to changing applications within and between institutions. It is suggested that computer literacy curricula should not be dependent on specific proprietary software but wherever possible FOSS is incorporated (ibid). This has the advantage of ensuring that students who require particular software can have access to it without the temptation to copy software illegally.

LARGE SCALE IMPLEMENTATION OF AN OPEN SOURCE CLE: A CASE STUDY

This study will now use the case study of CSU to look at some of the details around what is seen to be a successful implementation of Sakai as a CLE for a large institution. Although there will be many aspects of such an implementation that are not unique to open source software *per se*, the case study attempts to focus on those aspects are perhaps more challenging in an open source implementation.

Background

Charles Sturt University (CSU) is a regional, multi-campus Australian university that serves some 32,000 students, of whom two-thirds are enrolled through distance education (DE). It is Australia's eighth largest university, and the country's biggest provider of DE.

CSU has delivered online supported subjects through its own VLE (virtual learning environment) since 1994 (VLE here in the CSU context does not equate to the VLE = LMS but is an in-house term). At that time there were only a limited number of commercial products available. CSU adopted a best-of-breed strategy (Rebecchi, 2004a) towards creating its own VLE using a collection of tools that best suited its environment. Many of these were in-house developed. These tools included an electronic assignment submission system, a forums (discussion board) application, an online multiple choice quiz tool, a chat server, a series of flexible publishing tools and a university-wide portal known as *my.csu* (OLE Programme Committee, 2006). The CSU VLE remained primarily Web 1.0 based.

In 2006, the University made the decision to adopt the open source Sakai collaborative learning environment (The Sakai Foundation, 2009). Sakai forms the foundation of the University's new, integrated online learning environment (OLE) called *CSU Interact* which was implemented in 2007 as a platform for research and project collaboration by selected schools, divisions, and research centers, and then subsequently in 2008 across the entire University for learning and teaching. This extends to some 1000 on-campus course offerings and 2000 DE course offerings. This means every course (subject/unit) taught at the university (both on campus and DE) now has its own *Interact* site with an attendant expectation that there will be appropriate use of the online learning environment to enhance student learning.

Consistent with the original philosophy of Sakai (The Sakai Foundation, 2009) the University's vision for the new online learning environment goes beyond learning and teaching to support research, collaboration and professional development as well as learning and teaching.

"The Sakai Project began in 2004 when Stanford, Michigan, Indiana, MIT and Berkeley began building a common Courseware Management System rather than continuing their homegrown systems or licensing software from a commercial vendor. The Mellon Foundation provided initial funding for the project.

These universities recognized that research collaboration would be as important as teaching applications and developed a Collaboration and Learning Environment (CLE) that scales across many kinds of academic uses." (Available from http://sakaiproject.org/portal/site/sakai-home/page/41344e39-89f5-40cd-a153-2370382419d9, accessed on 8 August 2009).

The University funded a major project, the OLE Program, to coordinate the choice of software and implementation of the new OLE. This project was coordinated by the Project Service Centre (PSC). The PSC was established within the Division of Information Technology in 2005 in order to make best use of resources and to streamline ICT developments (Project Service Centre, 2009). The University undertook a thorough selection process in its choice of Sakai as the platform for its new OLE. The strategic decision was made that CSU would, at least initially, retain some of its existing learning and teaching ICT systems to ensure continuity. An integrated system was thus a likely choice.

The University examined ten systems initially, both commercial and open source, and the final selection at CSU was narrowed down to a very close contest between Moodle and Sakai. The final decision came down to a qualitative analysis and

while Moodle measured strongly in its framework and pedagogical aspects, the broader scope of use planned for CSU's new OLE i.e. research and administration use, favored Sakai. Also, some of the overarching concerns in the final selection process included Sakai's strength in its established processes within the Sakai community, the choice of a framework that was more representative of higher education processes, and importantly, that Sakai favored the technical community and our in-house expertise. The roadmap for Sakai favored certain aspects important to CSU.

CSU has a history of in-house developed IT systems and thus a strong capability to develop and support open source. This is an important factor in maximizing the affordances of open source software such as Sakai at an institutional level. Some of the affordances of Sakai relevant to CSU are: the ability to integrate with existing systems; the dynamic nature of the tools available in the CLE; the potential to influence the development of specific tools/applications development in the Sakai community; the ability to customize tools for in-house use and the overall responsiveness of the CLE to current pedagogical and technological trends in higher education as a result of feedback from the broad community member base. The choice of open source has enabled CSU to retain some existing applications and through *CSU Interact* users get a seamless integration of existing CSU applications (forums, an assignment submission system and a course/unit outline tool) with Sakai.

Since 2004 the university has had a strong strategic focus on technology in learning and teaching with the formation of an Information Learning Systems Committee (ILSC) with representatives from all divisions and learning and support services (Rebecchi, 2004b). Learning and teaching continues to be supported at a high level in the University with the formation in 2009 of a new Division of Learning and Teaching Services. This was an amalgamation of the existing Centre for Enhancing Learning and Teaching and the Learning Materials Centre (Figure 2). The strategists are making the most of this ongoing evolution of the institutional structure to ensure that in the long term the university is in a good position to be able to support the changing modes of teaching and technological requirements for e-learning.

Institutional Support for Open Source Systems

For an open source solution to be successful at an institutional level, it is important that an organization has sufficient IT services and resourcing dedicated to supporting learning and teaching, and that learning and teaching related projects do not have to compete for a common pool of funding. How much 'sufficient' resources are, will probably never be enough for everyone's needs. Funding for IT services has been identified as one of the Top Ten IT Issues for the past ten years (Brancheau, Janz, & Wetherbe, 1995; Camp, 2007; Dewey, DeBlois, & EDUCAUSE Current Issues Committee, 2006). However, with judicial strategic planning, institutions should be able to optimize their IT capabilities for a maximum return on investment. Higher education institutions will each have their own organizational structure, funding and resourcing models for IT services. A distinction is made here between *educational IT*

Figure 2. Institutional funding options for educational technology (Source: Buchan 2009, in press)

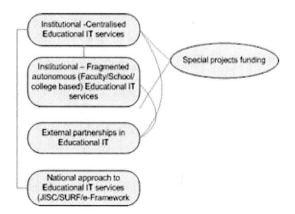

services i.e. dedicated to supporting learning and teaching related activities, and *general IT services* that support the more administrative functions of an organization.

A review of the recent literature was done on IT management and funding and IT services models for educational technology (Buchan, 2009b). The following five educational IT services resourcing options were identified (Figure 2): (1) Institutional - centralised services; (2) Institutional – fragmented autonomous (faculty/ school/ college based; (3) External partnerships; (4) A national approach to educational IT services (e.g. JISC, SURF, eFramework); and (5) Project based special funding which operates at a variety of levels. Institutions may use a mix of different resourcing options.

CSU has centralised IT services for all institutional and faculty IT needs. This includes administrative services as well as educational technology. There is occasional special project funding for learning and teaching related projects such as the OLE Program. Building on previous structures and support of learning and teaching systems, in order to support the new OLE better, CSU has provided a degree of autonomy in its educational IT management with resourcing dedicated to educational IT initiatives. Several IT programmers (developers) now work within a Virtual Team under the Systems Manager of the new Division of Learning and Teaching Services (LTS) and work exclusively on Sakai and applications associated with the OLE (see Figure 3). This 'virtual team' retains close reporting and operational links with DIT.

An important aspect of introducing open source software, especially where special funding is associated with the project, is ongoing maintenance and mainstreaming of the systems. To avoid using its valuable educational IT programmers from the LTS Systems team for day to day maintenance and bug resolution, the Division of IT Services (DIT) at CSU has retained the responsibility of general maintenance of the Sakai tools (*ibid*).

Figure 3. The changing structure of CSU's divisions and units that support learning and teaching. Focusing on those relating to dedicated support for educational technology projects (Source: Buchan, 2009, in press)

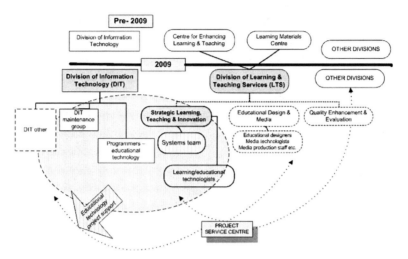

Challenges and Successes in the Large Scale Implementation of Sakai

The challenges associated with implementing an open source LMS at an institutional level will be similar to those faced when implementing any other (commercial) solution. CSU's change and innovation strategies used in the implementation of Sakai have been well documented (Uys, 2009) so are not covered here. Nor are the technical aspects of implementation addressed. As this book focuses specifically on open source software the author does not feel it necessary to burden the reader with the finer details of project management in e-learning as there is an increasing body of literature around this (2009 Journal of Distance Education, special edition. Project Management for e-Learning, in press). There are, however, some unique aspects and examples of good practice project management in this case study that it is believed will contribute to others' understanding of successfully implementing an open source system in a large, geographically dispersed institution.

Getting institutional Buy-In

For the large-scale implementation of any learning and teaching system to be successful there needs to be support from the highest level in the institution (Nederlof, 2009) including adequate funding. The Information Learning Systems Committee provides high level strategic direction in this area. High level support for the OLE Program came from the Vice-Chancellor, Deputy Vice-chancellor (Academic), Deputy Vice-chancellor (Administration) and the Executive Director of the Division of Information Technology Services with an OLE Steering Committee containing high-level representatives from the faculties and divisions. The initial OLE Program had central funding. The presence of champions for transformational change as a driving force behind the program was essential (Kotter & Cohen, 2002). The primary driving force behind the implementation of Sakai was at a middle management level. This has been well documented and we can learn from successes as well as our inadequacies (Uys, 2009).

Dealing with a Large-Scale Project

It was a challenge to introduce a CLE to over 32,000 students and to reach some 600 academic staff as well as professional (general) staff. This was done by establishing a program, known locally as the OLE Program, under a formal project management structure with a steering committee. This program was coordinated under the central Project Service Centre to maximize the use of the dedicated funding.

CSU adopted a staged implementation. In 2007 (for the start of 2008) there were some 18 individual projects and four pilots (trials) of new Sakai tools. In the ongoing implementation there were eight individual projects along with four pilots. As users identify the need for new tools in the OLE (see Figure 1) pilots and projects are set up as required to assist in the introduction of new tools. Lack of adequate resourcing to complete the staged work is still a critical issue and will continue to limit the speed at which the OLE can evolve.

As described above, once the main project was over there were significant structural changes within the divisions at the university which provided a way to mainstream the ongoing growth and support for users of the new OLE. However, together with this high level support and associated structural changes (potentially) comes increased accountability and a requirement to demonstrate 'return for investment'. Currently this is a tacit understanding but with moves in the Australian Higher Education sector towards a standards based mode of operation the OLE will be critical to CSU's long-term success in learning and teaching.

Requirement for Technical Expertise

Maintenance and development of open source software requires specialist knowledge and a high degree of input from developers, solutions coordinators, testers and other specialist staff. These were funded in the initial rollout through the main project. A significant and ongoing issue is the difficulty in obtaining the services of enough skilled IT staff (particularly programmers) - a common trend in this professional field at present.

These members of staff, however, are not working alone. The benefits of adopting Sakai with its community source base means that there is an extensive community of expertise on which to draw and at peak periods of development work - with the current shortage of skilled staff - there is a need for CSU to outsource some of the required customization of certain tools. Our programmers report their collaboration and active use of expertise in the Sakai community for solving problems.

Communication

Lack of adequate communication during the implementation of an LMS has been identified as a major factor contributing to a perceived lack of success in the uptake of the LMS by users (Benson & Palaskas, 2006; Buchan & Swann, 2007). While this is not unique to open source systems, it is fundamental to the success of any such project so has been included here. A communication project was set up in the OLE Programme as part of the change management strategy to provide consistency around the messages being disseminated to all sectors of the university. A communication plan drawn up for the OLE project itself helped streamline formal communications and set the boundaries for informal communications. There was a wide variety of communication strategies used to inform staff and students about the introduction of *CSU Interact* and a comprehensive professional development program was used to familiarize staff with the new system. This program was coordinated by the (then) Centre for Enhancing Learning and Teaching and delivered by the educational designers and educational technologists in partnership with the Faculties.

Did our communication strategies work? In our diverse and geographically dispersed structure there are, not surprisingly, differing opinions on this. What we have learned is to consider all the stories in order to improve our practice.

STRATEGIES TOWARDS DEVELOPING A DYNAMIC AND RESPONSIVE INSTITUTIONAL ONLINE LEARNING ENVIRONMENT

One of the major benefits of community source software for an institution is the potential to identify and respond rapidly to new trends in the education sector by developing and acquiring new tools and applications. The community source model provides valuable 'agility' in software development with community source that supports the desired responsiveness of the online learning environment. The Sakai Foundation has formed a new Product Council to coordinate the release of new versions of the Sakai product with the vision of the Product council being "…to ensure exceptional quality and cohesiveness of Sakai product releases in support of varied teaching, research and collaboration needs" (Korcuska, 2009).

Responding to the Individual User's Needs

On an institutional scale it is often difficult for the individual user to 'have a voice' in the choice and use of technology. Despite the best efforts at consultation when choosing and implementing new systems it will not always be possible to cater for individual needs. If a commercial LMS solution is adopted it might be easier to justify the lack of responsiveness to individual needs. However, the decision to adopt an open source solution challenges the decision makers and managers of the system to maximize the affordances of open source and to be responsive to individual needs. When adopted at an institutional scale there is considerable investment on the personnel side. A member of one of the leading UK institutions

in the Sakai community has expressed the view that their institution invested heavily in open source to ensure the agility and responsiveness to user needs. There is thus an expectation from management that their systems will continually evolve and change, and hopefully an acceptance by users that things will not remain the same. The challenge will be to ensure that all changes are positive and that students and staff have time to consolidate the use of the system before new versions and tools are introduced.

Liaison with the Sakai Community

"The community is what drives the software and what many people do not realize is that you do not have to be a developer to contribute. Your input on a particular use case, thoughts about governance, time spent testing, or design skills can really make a difference. It is your chance to help drive the direction of the community and/or ensure quality in the product that you are ultimately delivering to your users. This is an opportunity unique in community source software. Not only are there direct benefits, but there is the opportunity to develop really meaningful relationships with colleagues." (Berg & Korcuska, 2009. P.246)

The Sakai Foundation, a member supported non-profit organization, coordinates the activities of the Sakai open source community and provides shared resources to support the Sakai community activities. The Sakai Foundation also helps connect community members with similar interests and needs (http://sakaiproject.org/portal). Sakai has developed a community driven model for building the CLE. There are well developed mechanisms for feedback around the Sakai CLE in the Sakai community. These include discussion forums that connect people on areas such as development and pedagogy. Sakai Confluence is used to support a variety of community activities. The Sakai Dashboard (http://confluence.sakaiproject.org/confluence/dashboard.action) provides information on all the projects. Sakai uses Jira software for software issue management. It is used to track a variety of issues including bug reports, suggestions for new functionality, tasked work, and community contributions. The Foundation has developed guidelines around the access and use of Jira and there is open registration available to enable interested parties to comment on and contribute to Jira. (http://confluence.sakaiproject.org/confluence/display/MGT/Sakai+Jira+Guidelines). Sakai also has a well developed hierarchy of tools.

"Sakai's strength stems from the community support. If you have a common problem that others have already partially addressed, then it is worth contacting the original authors and suggesting collaboration. This approach builds up the central value rather than diffusing and repeating effort… Developers place their prototypes and proofs of concept in Contrib and sometimes these seeds grow into fully-fledged and welcomed functionality or die. The process supports a quick and agile change. The software lifecycle does not strangle innovation—rather it gives space to the community for exploration." (Berg & Korcuska, 2009, p.120)

IT staff at CSU; lead programmers, testers etc. have an active involvement in the community. For instance, CSU has provided the services of staff to contribute to community projects. They also draw on the community knowledge to fix local problems, and in some cases have identified bugs and suitable fixes that can be shared with the community.

Although the ideal is that institutions developing their own tools or doing significant work on existing tools then contribute these to the Sakai community, there can be limitations within licensing agreements and issues of intellectual property or what work done by developers constitutes institutional property. Individual institutions will need to understand and possibly amend their policies if the institution is to be able to contribute their work back into the Sakai community.

Monitoring Sakai Tool Development

In the growing Sakai community there are many different development projects. The members of the community work together to develop applications for specific needs.. To make the most of this rich source of potential solutions an institution needs to monitor developments in the Sakai community and to match these to identified needs amongst the local users.

At CSU there are a number of mechanisms being employed to enable users to have a voice in the ongoing evolution of the OLE (see Figure 1). These include an initiatives' handling process whereby any user can propose an IT initiative. There is extensive liaison between members of DIT and the rest of the university, with key roles being the DIT Learning and Liaison officer and the Director Strategic Learning, Teaching & Innovation (Learning and Teaching Services). The Sakai community-based environment is monitored for the purposes of informing academic staff of upcoming releases of tools, and in order to be able to ascertain local needs. A centralised data collection system on individual tools has been set up on an internal Sakai project site and monitoring of specific tools is shared amongst a number of areas. Educational technologists and systems administrators share the bulk of the tool monitoring with specialist tools being monitored by Library and Evaluation services representatives. Information from this monitoring of tools is used by an internal (Learning and Teaching Services) committee to inform future pathways in the OLE. Monitoring of the tools is done by following the List Serves, Sakai Confluence project site and Jira entries and also by contacting the 'owners' (developers) of the specific tools to find out about the future developments and then recording and sharing this information.

In these days of rapidly changing educational technology and the entry into cloud computing it is acknowledged that Sakai may not provide all the solutions for the institutional needs. The pathways developed at CSU for dynamic feedback into improving the online learning environment allow for investigating other software solutions. CSU has drawn up a Dashboard of its Learning and Teaching systems (Available from http://www.csu.edu.au/division/lts/docs/role/ltsystemsdashboard.pdf). This provides a snapshot of current and future work. As user needs are identified and actioned these are added to the Dashboard.

Responding to the Users: Informing Improvements to the Online Learning Environment

In order to develop a dynamic and responsive online learning environment an institution needs to listen to the users and have in place pathways that ensure that what is heard can actually be acted upon. At the 'upper' strategic levels, key liaison members of the Division of Information Technology work with other groups within the University and with the Sakai foundation to scan the Sakai horizon to plan future pathways and to meet current educational technology needs. Where there is a particular technological need, there are mechanisms in place for staff to work directly with DIT on solutions. Figure 1 attempts to outline some of the ways in which user feedback is monitored and captured by Learning and Teaching Services and the processes by which this feedback can be fed back to those making decisions about enhancements to the OLE, and those who actually make the technical changes. The primary interface between the users of educational technology (staff) and those supporting and developing the systems are various groups and individuals within the Division of Learning and Teaching Services. These individuals include the educational technologists and educational designers at the grassroots level. The sections involved in collecting feedback include Evaluation Services and Strategic Learning, Teaching and Innovation.

Firstly, a distinction is made here between formal and informal feedback. Rigorous research and robust evaluation of processes and outcomes is important, especially in an academic setting. In today's environment where accountability to management is important, one needs to be able to demonstrate that resources have been used well, that outcomes have been achieved and that areas for continual improvement have been identified. Thus a recognised mechanism for formal feedback is essential.

The formal feedback mechanisms contribute to improvements in the OLE in a number of ways. Firstly there are formal evaluation surveys of staff and students. These inform us how *CSU Interact* is being used in learning and teaching and highlight any areas of concern with specific tools or support processes. Specific feedback can also inform future directions of new tool acquisition. The results from these surveys filter all the way through from higher levels of the OLE Program and Strategic Learning Teaching and Innovation group throughout the relevant support areas so that the variety of issues raised can be appropriately addressed.

Secondly, all tools are put through a pilot phase prior to full implementation. This involves a full user test of the tool in the live production environment culminating in a formal evaluation. This ensures that technical 'bugs' are ironed out, the need for any customization of the tool is identified, and any issues associated with support, such as professional development, development of user help guides etc. are dealt with.

Finally, the IT Services Help Desk fields a variety of queries of a technical and user related nature. There are clear pathways for directing user enquiries associated with *CSU Interact* to the right area for action and feedback.

However, formal evaluations and pilots only allow for sporadic and specific types of feedback. In order to monitor the state of the online environment one needs a way to harness and respond to the *ad hoc* feedback that is constantly coming through. This is termed 'informal' feedback here and can be thought of as 'corridor' or 'tearoom' monitoring. These are the casual conversations or occasional emails about a particular issue or idea that ring alarm bells, trigger new ideas or identify a particular need. At CSU this informal feedback can be picked up by DIT, educational designers, educational technologists or others involved in the day to day support of learning and teaching, and fed back into relevant groups. The Division of Learning and Teaching Services has a team of educational (instructional) designers in each of the four faculties as well as three educational technologists supporting across campuses. Amongst other services, these staff provide hands-on support for *CSU Interact*. Educational designers working closely with staff in the individual schools around learning and teaching needs are in a good position to identify issues, future needs and trends.

What is important here is that if a user identifies a bug in the system, a new tool they have heard of, or a particular technological need, this can be passed on quickly to the right people for consideration. While a solution may be slower in coming forth it is important that individuals see firsthand that their interests are being addressed and that our OLE is indeed responsive to user requirements.

An effective way of informally monitoring what people are doing with Sakai and what needs there are for improvements is through a community of practice. CSU has established a community of practice (CoP) around what it calls ICT-enabled learning. Members of this group include the 'champions', educational technologists, with an open invitation to other interested academics. The social networking software Yammer is currently being used as one communication channel for sharing ideas and practice around ICT-enabled learning. In 2009 there have been four successful ICT-enabled Learning CoP Showcase events with staff sharing snapshots of their work with technology in teaching. In our dispersed campus mode these were conducted via videoconference across up to 13 sites with over 50 attendees at some events.

Some faculties and schools have established their own groups to explore teaching technologies specific to their own needs. As support for the technology is necessarily centralized it is important that these groups have an avenue of communication around these needs.

There is probably still more work that can be done at the university level to make the formal avenues of communication and response to educational technology needs more transparent.

CONCLUSION

"It's not about information. Or technology. It's what we do with IT that counts." (Educause website, 2009, Accessed from http://www.educause. edu/ on 20 August 2009).

In exploring some of the pedagogical advantages in e-learning of Sakai as a collaborative learning environment it is hoped that people will see beyond just the application and affordances of individual tools in a Web 2.0 environment. The community source approach to development of open source software has many inherent pedagogical advantages.

While the reasons for choosing open source software will vary, the primary reason for adopting new educational technology *per se* should be to enhance learning and teaching. This chapter has perhaps been a bit heavy on the in-house organizational and inter-divisional detail but, as a large organization, CSU will not be unique in its complexities and a strategic, integrated and collaborative approach to large-scale, open source educational technology solutions is essential to the success of the venture. Given its international, regional, multi-campus and strong distance education focus there are unique complexities in technological solutions facing Charles Sturt University. However, if the challenges associated with open source software and management can be solved in our environment at this level, then it should be able to be done elsewhere. For smaller installations of Sakai, management solutions do not have to be so complex to be effective!

Can an open source collaborative learning environment achieve an online learning environment that is indeed dynamic and responsive to user needs? I believe that it can and that we are making good progress towards this end - but it is still early days in our Sakai history. However, technology on its own can do nothing without the people. Thus there need to be clear pathways of communication, feedback loops for action and above all, a commitment to the community of practice that belonging to an open source community demands.

ACKNOWLEDGMENT

The assistance of Matt Morton-Allen (DIT) is acknowledged in providing access to historical documents and valuable feedback on the chapter content. Although a solid attempt has been made to draw an accurate picture of the ever-changing organizational structures and interactions at CSU, the views expressed remain those of the author.

REFERENCES

Benson, R., & Palaskas, T. (2006). Introducing a new learning management system: An institutional case study. *Australasian Journal of Educational Technology, 22*(4), 548–567.

Berg, A., & Korcuska, M. (2009). *Sakai Courseware Management*. The Official Guide.

Brancheau, J. C., Janz, B. D., & Wetherbe, J. C. (1995). *Key Issues in Information Systems Management:A Shift Toward Technology Infrastructure*. Boulder, CO: University of Colorado Graduate School of Business.

Buchan, J. (2008a, September 9-11). *Rethinking management strategies for the online learning environment*. Paper presented at the ALT-C Rethinking the Digital Divide Conference, Leeds, UK. Retrieved from http://csusap.csu.edu.au/~jbuchan/html/publications.htm

Buchan, J. (2008b, December 2008). Tools for survival in a changing educational technology environment. In *Where are you now in the landscape of educational technology? Proceedings ASCILITE Melbourne 2008 Conference,* Melbourne, Australia.

Buchan, J. (2009a). Putting ourselves in the big picture: a sustainable approach to project management for e-learning. *Journal of Distance Education.*

Buchan, J. (2009b). Putting ourselves in the big picture: a sustainable approach to project management for e-learning. *Journal of Distance Education.*

Buchan, J., & Swann, M. (2007). A Bridge too Far or a Bridge to the Future? A case study in online assessment at Charles Sturt University. *Australasian Journal of Educational Technology, 23*(3), 408–434.

Buchan, J. F., & Buchan, A. J. (2003). Lessons from nature: developing an adaptive management model for sustaining quality learning environments. In *Proceedings of the 16th Biennial Forum Conference on Open and Distance Learning*. Retrieved August 8, 2007, from http://odlaa.une.edu.au/publications/2003Proceedings/pdfs/buchan.pdf

Camp, J. S. (2007, May/June). Top 10 IT Issues. *EDUCAUSE Review, 42,* 12–32.

Dewey, B. I., & DeBlois, P. B., & EDUCAUSE Current Issues Committee. (2006, May/June). Top-10 IT Issues 2006. *EDUCAUSE Review, 41,* 58–79.

Joint Information Systems Committee. (2006). *Open source software: briefing paper.*

Joint Information Systems Committee. (2008). *Open source software: briefing paper.*

Korcuska, M. (2009). Sakai Product Council announcement: Sakaiproject.

Kotter, J. P., & Cohen, D. S. (Eds.). (2002). *The heart of change.* Boston: Harvard Business School Press.

Lave, J., & Wenger, E. (1990). *Situated Learning: Legitimate Periperal Participation.* Cambridge, UK: Cambridge University Press.

Milne, A. J. (2007). Entering the Interaction Age: Implementing a Future Vision for Campus Learning Spaces. *EDUCAUSE Review, 42*(1), 12–31.

Nederlof, H. (2009). A crib sheet for selling Sakai to traditional management . In Lumsden, J., Mangarole, S., & Shanker, A. (Eds.), *Sakai Courseware management. The official guide* (pp. 369–384). Birmingham, UK: Packt Publishing.

O'Reilly, T. (2009). *What is Web 2.0? Design patterns and business models for the next generation of software.* Retrieved September 23, 2009, from http://oreilly.com/web2/archive/what-is-web-20.html

Ozkan, B. (2008). *How to effectively use free and open source software in education.* Paper presented at the World Conference on E-Learning in Corporate, Government, Healthcare, and Higher Education 2008 Chesapeake VA.

Pedler, M., Burgoyne, J., & Boydell, T. (1997). *The Learning Company: A strategy for sustainable development* (2nd ed.). London: McGraw-Hill.

Project Service Centre. (2009). *Roles and responsibilities.* Retrieved February 16, 2009, from http://www.csu.edu.au/division/psc/roles-and-responsibilities/

Putland, G. (2006). *Blogs, Wikis, RSS and there's more? Web 2.0 on the march. Education.au Limited.* Retrieved May 21, 2007, from http://www.educationau.edu.au/jahia/Jahia/home/pid/337

Rebecchi, M. (2004a). *Implementation of a Commercial Virtual Learning Environment at Charles Sturt University.*

Rebecchi, M. (2004b). *Strategic Approaches to e-Learning: Delivering Quality.* The Charles Sturt University Experience.

Senge, P. (1990). *The Fifth Discipline.* London: Century Business.

Stunden, A. (2003). The muscles, aches, and pains of open source. *EDUCAUSE Review, 38*(6), 100–101.

Tan, W. T. (2007). *Free/open source software: education.* Retrieved August 20, 2009, from http://www.iosn.net/education/foss-education-primer/fossPrimer-Education.pdf

The Sakai Foundation. (2009). *Sakai.* Retrieved August10, 2009, 2009, from http://sakaiproject.org/portal

Uys, P. (2009). *Change and innovation strategies during the implementation of an open source LMS: an Australian case study. Research, Reflections and Innovations in Integrating ICT in Education.* Paper presented at the V International Conference on Multimedia and ICT in Education (m-ICTE2009), Lisbon, Portugal.

Weaver, D., Spratt, C., & Nair, C. (2008). Academic and student use of a learning management system: Implications for quality *Australasian Journal of Educational Technology, 24*(1), 30-41.

Wenger, E. (2009). *Communities of practice.* Retrieved August 13, 2009, from http://www.ewenger.com/theory/index.htm

Whitehurst, J. (2009). Open source: narrowing the divide between education, business and community. *EDUCAUSE Review, 44*(1), 70–71.

Zhou, G., & Xu, J. (2007). Adoption of educational technology ten years after setting strategic goals: A Canadian university case. *Australasian Journal of Educational Technology, 23*(4), 508–528.

This work was previously published in International Journal of Open Source Software and Processes Volume 2, Issue 1, edited by Stefan Koch, pp. 32-48, copyright 2010 by IGI Publishing (an imprint of IGI Global).

Chapter 7
Building Open Learning Environment for Software Engineering Students

Alexey Khoroshilov
Institute for System Programming of the Russian Academy of Sciences (ISPRAS), Russia

Victor Kuliamin
Institute for System Programming of the Russian Academy of Sciences (ISPRAS), Russia

Alexander Petrenko
Institute for System Programming of the Russian Academy of Sciences (ISPRAS), Russia

Olga Petrenko
Moscow Institute for Open Education, Russia

Vladimir Rubanov
Institute for System Programming of the Russian Academy of Sciences (ISPRAS), Russia

ABSTRACT

The chapter discusses principles of open education and possibilities of implementing these principles for software engineering education on the base of open source software development projects. A framework of practical courses for software engineering students built on these ideas is presented. Experience of building courses on the base of this framework is discussed on the example of "Software Engineering" course provided to students of the System Programming departments of the two Russian top-ranked universities, Moscow State University and Moscow Institute of Physics and Technology.

INTRODUCTION

Educational system should match the needs and tendencies of continuously developing society to sustain its evolution. That is the reason of evergrowing demand for innovation education programs, methods, and supporting infrastructure across all over the world. A conceptual base for innovation education in Russia was formed by academician M. A. Lavrentev (Computer Museum, 2006) who states a principle of "sciences— personnel — industry" (triangle of Lavrentev

DOI: 10.4018/978-1-61520-917-0.ch007

(Khristianovich, Lavrentev & Lebedev, 1956 and Dobretsov, 2001)). Most of currently applied approaches of innovation education implement this idea in modern conditions – education happens during generation of new knowledge as a result of integration of fundamental science, educational process, and industry.

Traditional system of professional education is mainly based on transition to students of fundamental knowledge helping them to feel themselves with confidence in some area and skills that can be applied in some practical work at once. However, under the conditions of intensive technological evolution, such an approach to education becomes irrelevant because students slowly become able to transform fundamental knowledge to practically applicable one as well as concrete practical knowledge quickly becomes outdated and unclaimed. The main abilities demanded in these circumstances become adaptability, constant knowledge update, decision making unbiased from established patterns, dynamic activity planning, etc.

All these issues are applicable to the area of software engineering, which evolves very quickly. Schematically, the main fields of skills and knowledge of information technology professionals can be presented as in Figure 1 (A.K. Petrenko, O.L. Petrenko & Kuliamin, 2008). So,

just subject knowledge is not enough for successful work of a good specialist in the modern society. The Memorandum of European Commission on lifelong learning (2000) emphasizes the need in such social skills as acting with confidence, result-oriented focus of personal activities, right balancing of risks and responsibility in decision making, as well as such cognitive skills as ability to learn continuously, adaptability to changing environment, skills in finding right information in various areas, and ability to filter necessary information in the huge informational flow that each active individual in the modern society is subject to.

In general some specific arrangements are required to make high school graduates more compliant with labor market requirements. In some high schools teaching Information Technologies undergraduates have few possibilities to work with real-life examples in their domain, so starting their career they immediately face with the issues not covered in the traditional university courses. Such courses are usually focused on scientific and technical aspects of the domain and contain (if any) only rather shallow presentation of organizational and social issues. Potential of many undergraduates is inhibited by lack of knowledge and skills at these areas. One more

Figure 1. Main skills of modern IT-professionals

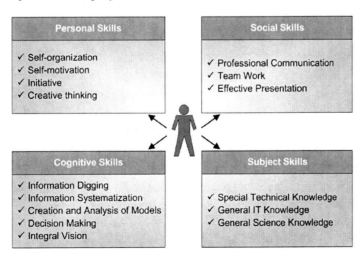

impediment to their growth is lack of comprehension of relations between theoretical matter they get in university and their practical work, so many of them think sincerely that most of that theory has no real use. This usually demonstrates lack of (and bad training in) an important skill — systematic analysis of routine technical issues, which force to use scientifically approved methods presented in theoretical courses.

The first step to change this situation may comprise in introduction of courses targeted to development of social skills necessary for professional work in the related technical domain. An objective of such a course is nurturing these social skills that help to realize technical skills and knowledge obtained and to resolve non-technical problems met in real professional life.

The necessary skills to develop in these courses are:

- writing technical and scientific texts;
- preparation of presentations and performing them in public;
- organization of technical or scientific presentation, in particular, fitting in time and attracting the audience;
- various techniques of information classification and systematic analysis;
- professional argumentation based on scientific methods and knowledge;
- adequate answering on questions;
- posing adequate questions.

A course block intended to develop text creation skills may consider the following topics.

1. Professional communication as a significant component of profession. Specifics of professional communication.
2. Determine the personal communication style (with the help of a test). Using personal communication style in developing professional relations.
3. Verbal and written communications.
4. Characteristics of written communications. How to prepare a written report.
5. Styles of writing. Characteristics of different styles. Practice in preparation of texts written in different styles.
6. Presentations and talks. Time management during talks. Presentation content change techniques.
7. Specifics and requirements for scientific communication and texts. Structure of scientific text.
8. Work with information sources during scientific text preparation.
9. Argumentation and reasoning. How to use arguments in texts and what arguments to use.
10. Practice in scientific text preparation.
11. Scientific presentation. Characteristics and structure of scientific talk. How to answer questions during a talk.
12. How to choose a talk style. Feedback types. Talk evaluation.

However, introduction of courses focused on social skills necessary in technical domains is not sufficient. The entire existing education environment should be modernized in accordance with needs of social development. It is necessary to create such an environment that helps to prepare graduates adapted to the needs of modern industry and markets.

Acknowledging these principles of continuous lifelong learning stimulates transition of educational systems towards so called open educational system. This system is mainly oriented on upbringing independent self-motivated individuals that are able to effectively collaborate with the quickly changing world individuals that can and want to effectively learn constantly rather than just apply known and established practical skills in some steady work.

In such open educational systems, educational opportunities are open to students - they can see paths of possible education and evolution and thus it becomes possible to discuss with its mentor the means and specific actions for achieving individual goals in the broad space of these opportunities. One of the main characteristics of open education is responsible decision making by the student about the needed educational goals and means to meet them. Students have to realize and take full responsibility in this.

The main principles of open education are (Wedemeyer, 1974):

- individualization of education;
- responsibility for own success;
- collaboration;
- continuous learning.

Transition to the open education may be based on the following principles:

- It is necessary to teach students to be self-dependent in education. Being active is a key thing for this.
- Students must be involved in the mutual personal communication.
- The starting and the target points of each particular part of the educational path should be individual.

- Explicit stage of reflection should be introduced in the education process.

The important general step towards open education is creation of special open learning environment that stimulates students to be actively involved in leading professional societies in the studied field and to actively communicate and collaborate within them. Such societies provide various opportunities in implementing educational goals and students can freely and independently choose whatever fits them best individually.

In this chapter we discuss possibilities of building such open learning environment for software engineering students on the base of open source software development projects. We present a framework of practical courses for software engineering students built on these ideas. Experience of using of the framework is discussed by the example of "Software Engineering" course.

SOFTWARE ENGINEERING EDUCATION AND OPEN SOURCE SOFTWARE DEVELOPMENT PROJECTS

M. A. Lavrentev (1971) once wrote: "There are many ways by which scientific ideas come to industry. The forms of cooperation between science and industry themselves also require scien-

Figure 2. Open education principles

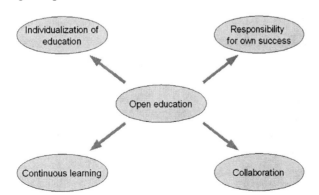

tific approach, creativity, and choice of optimal solutions in each particular case". Open source software has recently become such a way in the area of software engineering. Benefits of using open source software in high education institutes and especially in the area of software engineering are discussed a lot. Just a few examples are Allen, Cartwright & Reis (2003), Carrington & Kim (2003), Fuhrman (2006), O'Hara & Kay (2003), M.Pedroni, Bay, Oriol & A.Pedroni (2007). Traditionally, a possibility to investigate internal software structure is mentioned at the first place as a consequence of source code availability. But it is also important that open source software development projects are also open, i.e. their development process is public and all discussions regarding design and coding decisions, software architecture evolution, and project documentation development are available for investigation too. Thus, open source software development projects provide good material and rich infrastructure for education of software engineering students.

Moreover open source software development projects can be a good basis for building participatory learning environment in the area of software engineering. Such projects can effectively and easily enable the following tools and educational means for almost any specific technical subject.

- Rich educational materials: feature requests from users and ideas of developers, requirement documents, the executable software itself, specifications of its architecture, implementation source code, lists of already fixed and still standing issues and features elaborated at the development and maturity phases of the product lifecycle, detailed argumentation in favor of or against some particular solutions and approaches in the context of real system.
- Ready infrastructure for practical classes: configured information systems for version control and project collaboration with

possibility to communicate with real developers of the product.
- Possibility to create strong motivation for students by involving them in the practical activities in real life development projects, especially if such projects have high social importance and prestige.
- Help to students in creation of personal portfolio and finding a job in future by possibility to demonstrate results of their work evaluated by expert community to potential employers.

Documents and source code of one or several projects can be used as a ready-to-use education material. But more important is the diversity of open-source software projects that provides students a wide variety of choice options for thinking and finding individual learning paths within the general software engineering educational plan. Also, open source projects provide wide variety of choices of technical aspects such as programming languages, development technologies and methodologies, even within a specific topic, because there are usually a number of different competing projects that use different technical approaches for implementing the same functionality or a product of the same kind. This variety and freedom of choice demonstrate real life complexity to students and improve their motivation and responsibility.

At the same time, using open source software development projects for education is not a trivial task. Members of open source software projects are not always happy to be a training ground for a crowd of students. They would like to see future colleagues (even beginners) but not short term students. This fact has to be given proper weight in organizing learning environments on the base of open source software projects. For example, communications between students and open source developers should not be a mandatory element of an educational process. It may be an optional element available for most motivated students. In this case some introduction into professional communications and open source development culture should be provided for students.

Another conclusion is that solely open source projects are not enough to build an effective learning environment. Work with open source projects should be supplemented by a substantial set of activities provided by an educational organization. These activities should help students to dive into open source development environment by:

- explaining general models of open software development and hidden details of open source development culture;
- answering any kind of questions related to the project chosen;
- helping to start communication with open source community;
- advising useful informational sources and transferring patterns and best practices of work with them.

It is also important to stimulate discussions between students on their experience in investigation of open source projects and to provide general theoretical materials constituting a background of practical world of open source projects.

PRACTICAL SOFTWARE ENGINEERING COURSES FRAMEWORK

ISP RAS developed a framework of practical courses for software engineering students based on open source software development projects and principles of open education. The key elements of the framework are as follows:

- participation in individual open source project;
- personal mentors;
- theoretical lectures;
- colloquiums devoted to joint discussion of students results.

Instead of classic practical classes based on pre-selected model examples and tasks we introduced a requirement for students to participate in at least one public open source project that they can choose by their own decision. A possibility to choose the project on their own is very important to improve students' motivation as it was discussed above. Some courses may impose limitations on the projects so that the project can be used to cover required material in the domain under learning. For example, learning basic software engineering principles or methods of analysis and development of huge and complex systems can be supported well by projects of rather big size. Learning architecture styles and design patterns requires projects explicitly and adequately using such styles and patterns, while a majority of open source software cannot be considered as satisfying to this requirement. Learning algorithms may require spending some time in search for open projects and libraries that actually use some sophisticated algorithms.

We assign to each student a personal mentor who keeps in close touch with the student, answers his/her personal questions, monitors student activities, evaluate their effectiveness for learning the chosen domain, and advises useful informational sources and rules of work with them. One mentor can serve no more than 4 students.

In parallel to a practical course a corresponding theoretical course should be provided. It is recommended to keep small time interval between providing theoretical material and using the material in practice. But it is also possible (and usually helpful) to have anticipatory practical tasks, theoretical material for which is provided between a start of the task and the colloquium, where results of the task are presented. Theoretical lectures can be conducted in classic style, but also may incorporate elements of active learning and participatory education.

Colloquiums devoted to joint discussion of students results are the main form of students work control. Students make presentations of their results to the classmates and mentors and are asked any questions by the audience. Mentors ensure that the students can make correspondence between the theoretical information taken from the course with specific practical aspects of their projects by proper questions. Such organization of learning helps to overcome a gap between pure theory and practice and in that way to increase efficiency of the lectures. In addition, the joint colloquiums help to enable inter student experience sharing.

The main stages of a practical course include the following.

- Choice of an open-source development project. The project must have a public infrastructure and be active, that is it should have on-going developments or active maintenance. Students may also join any open-source project, which is performed in ISP RAS itself. Students evaluate various projects by themselves, mentors just check if the final choice meets all the necessary requirements from the domain learning viewpoint.
- Acquaintance with the project. Students study their selected projects on their own with the focus on those aspects important for their personal educational path and for the specific courses at the faculty. At the end of this phase, students make presentations of their projects to the classmates and mentors where they can be asked any questions by the audience to demonstrate mastering of the project information and understanding of design solutions made in it. Additionally, students are asked to prepare written reports with a predefined structure.
- Practical tasks. Mentors prepare a number of tasks for students with some weight points assigned to each task. Such tasks may include analysis, refinement, including formal modeling and specification, and documenting of requirements, extracting design patterns used, modeling and analy-

sis of anticipated software characteristics after possible change of design decisions, preparation of design documentation or user/administrator documentation, implementing new modules, code refactoring, resolving bugs in existing modules, design and executing of tests with reporting of issues found and providing possible solutions for them, providing test documentation, porting the project or its part on some unsupported platform, implementing automated installation, and so on.

Students may choose a number of tasks to perform to reach a defined target in terms of these points. Students provide regular presentations of their work similarly to the presentations at the acquaintance phase. Mentors ensure that the students can relate adequately the theoretical information from the course with specific practical aspects of their projects, thus increasing the efficiency of lectures.

In preparation of the practical tasks it is important to consider the additional opportunities provided by open source software development projects that can be useful for educational process, such as communication with project team and domain experts on professional topics, providing clear argumentation for requirements, design and test decisions.

Mentors encourage students to directly collaborate with the real project team and use feedback of the team as indicators of successful direction of their work. If it is possible, feedback of open source project community should be used to evaluate results of students' work. This improves students' motivation as the feedback from external parties is perceived by students as more objective than the one provided by teachers and group-mates. But feedback of community should not be a primary tool of evaluation, in particular, because of existing discrepancies, first, between specific project objectives and goals of learning process and, second, between open source community discussion and communication culture and students' expectations and habits.

Freedom of task choice also improves significantly students' motivation and attitude to his/her education (Carrington & Kim, 2003 and M. Pedroni, Bay, Oriol & A. Pedroni, 2007). It enables individual choice of depth of education and allows forming knowledge and skills at his/her own depending on his/her preferences and needs.

A CASE STUDY

An example of a practical course built on base of the framework presented is the course "Software Engineering". The course is provided to students of the System Programming departments of the two leading Russian universities — Moscow State University and Moscow Institute of Physics and Technology. In parallel to the first two stages of the practice the theoretical course "Software Engineering — Component Approach" (Kuliamin, 2007) is conducted. In addition, before start of the practice an extra lecture "Open Source Software" is provided to introduce students with basic principles of open source software development and open projects organization.

Initially the only limit on choice of open source project was the requirement to choose a project with an open development process. After analysis of the first experience we decided to limit choice by mature and big enough (25000-30000 lines of source code) projects only. General software engineering education requires that the project chosen has issues specific for complex software development, which usually correlate with project code size.

Students have two months to choose a project and to acquaint themselves with it — to read and analyze project documents, to comprehend the main decisions made, and to understand code-related issues. After that we organize the first colloquium, where students present their projects and answer questions from some predefined list.

The key idea of the list is to encourage students to find in the project instances of ideas, techniques, patterns, and approaches discussed in the theoretical course. The questionnaire used currently consists of the following 5 main areas:

- project as a whole;
- requirements;
- architecture and design;
- quality assurance;
- personal participation.

In addition, during acquaintance with the project students are asked to prepare one of project documents (project concept description, requirements sketch, architecture and design outline, test plan, etc.) according to the given template.

The next stage is actual practical work. For this course we have prepared about 30 practical tasks covering various areas of software engineering:

- modeling of business domain;
- requirements management;
- software architecture;
- software quality assurance and control;
- debugging and bug fixing;
- feature planning;
- user documentation;
- user support;
- complex tasks.

The practical work takes about 4 months. Results of the tasks are evaluated by mentors and discussed on joint colloquiums. If the results are good enough, we encourage students to publish them for review by open source project team. And as a result the students get constructive critique as well as positive feedback that are used to finalize the tasks.

To date, we have provided the practical course for two years as an optional element complementing the theoretical course "Software Engineering – Component Approach". The total number of students completed the practical course is about

20. At the first presentations, students are usually in almost complete confusion because at the first years at their universities they get used to the traditional system of fixed information to learn with subsequent exams so that they are always directed what to do. Only after a while, after working in the more flexible and open environment, they start realizing the real diversity of the problems in projects and the importance of proactive position of participants to solve them. Eventually this helps to understand and learn all the principles of software engineering at the significantly higher level.

Our experience confirms that possibility to choose domain of open source project really improve students' motivation in performing consequent tasks. Also an interesting conclusion is that open source projects can be used for demonstration both best practices of software development and common mistakes and decisions that should be avoided.

The experience of this case study demonstrates that many learning objectives can actually be reached in learning process based on open software development projects. Information digging and systematization, integral vision, effective presentation skills are improved. On the other side noticeable improvements in social skills, decision making, dynamic activity planning require introduction of additional patterns into organization of learning process. This is issue for further development of the approach presented. Perhaps, learning all the necessary skills in single practical course is an idealistic goal, and more realistic method is to build a sequence of 3-4 courses developing those skills gradually.

CONCLUSION

Open source software development projects provide a good basis for building open learning environments. They give both a rich set of education materials and examples of implementation of abstract principles and methods, and possibility to take part in a real-life activity, communicating with recognized experts in the domain of learning. However, it is not a simple task to build an adequate and productive collaboration between students and open source community.

We presented a framework for building practical courses for software engineering students on the base of open source projects. And our experience demonstrates positive effects on all the main fields of skills and knowledge of information technology professionals mentioned in Fig. 1. In particular, feedback of students shows improvement of motivation and independence in decision making.

REFERENCES

A Memorandum on Lifelong Learning. (2000, October 30). Commission of the European Communities. *A Memorandum on Lifelong Learning*. Brussels, 2000. Retrieved June 4, 2010 from www.bologna-berlin2003.de/pdf/MemorandumEng.pdf.

Allen, E., Cartwright, R., & Reis, C. (2003). Production programming in the classroom. *Proc. of the 34-th SIGCSE technical symposium on Computer science education* (pp. 89-93)Reno, Nevada, USA, 2003.

Carrington, D., & Kim, S.-K. (2003). Teaching software design with open source software. *Proc. of 33-rd ASEE/IEEE Frontiers in Education Conf.*,(pp. 9-14). November 2003.

Computer Museum. (2006). *Russian Virtual Computer Museum*, M. A. Lavrentev. Retrieved June 4, 2010 from http://computer-museum.ru/english/galglory_en/Lavrentev.htm

Dobretsov, N. L. (2001). "Triangle of Lavrentev": the principles of science organization in Siberia. *Bulletin of the Russian Academy of Sciences*, *71*(5), 428–436.

Fuhrman, C. P. (2006, July). Appreciation of software design concerns via open-source tools and projects. *Proc. of 10-th Workshop on Pedagogies and Tools for the Teaching and Learning of Object Oriented Concepts,*(at ECOOP 2006). Nantes, France, July 2006.

Khristianovich, S.A., Lavrentev, M.A. & Lebedev, S.A. (1956, February 14). Actual tasks of scientific work organization. Pravda, 14.02.1956.

Kuliamin, V. V. (2007). *Software Engineering. Component-based Approach.* Moscow: INTUIT-Binom.

Lavrentev, M.A. (1971, February 13) Highways of Siberian science. Izvestia, 13.02.1971.

O'Hara, K. J., & Kay, J. S. (2003). Open source software and computer science education. *J. Comput. Small Coll., 18*(3), 1–7.

Pedroni, M., Bay, T., Oriol, M., & Pedroni, A. (2007, March). Open source projects in programming courses. *ACM SIGCSE Bulletin, 39*(1), 454–458. doi:10.1145/1227504.1227465

Petrenko, A. K., Petrenko, O. L., & Kuliamin, V. V. (2008). Research Organizations in IT Education. *ISP RAS Proceedings, 15*, 41–50.

Wedemeyer, C. (1974). Characteristics of open learning systems . In *Open Learning Systems.* Washington: National Association of Educational Broadcasters.

Chapter 8
Data Mining User Activity in Free and Open Source Software (FOSS)/ Open Learning Management Systems

Owen McGrath
University of California, Berkeley, USA

ABSTRACT

Free and Open Source Software (FOSS)/Open Educational Systems development projects abound in higher education today. Many universities worldwide have adopted open source software like ATutor and Moodle as an alternative to commercial or homegrown systems. The move to open source learning management systems entails many special considerations, including usage analysis facilities. The tracking of users and their activities poses major technical and analytical challenges within web-based systems. This chapter examines how user activity tracking challenges are met with data mining techniques, particularly web usage mining methods, in four different open learning management systems: ATutor, LON-CAPA, Moodle, and Sakai. As examples of data mining technologies adapted within widely used systems, they represent important first steps for moving educational data mining outside the research laboratory. Moreover, as examples of different open source development contexts, exemplify the potential for programmatic integration of data mining technology processes in the future. As open systems mature in the use of educational data mining, they move closer to the long-sought goal of achieving more interactive, personalized, adaptive learning environments online on a broad scale.

INTRODUCTION

At a basic level, collegial sharing of source code has been around as long as computing itself in academia (Roof & Frazier, 1962). What has varied over the years and across contexts is how these code sharing efforts are organized. The history of open source in academic research and instruction has received prominence in recent analyses of how the open source phenomena got started. The success of open source, it is argued, has as much to do with the various open source processes and organizational arrangements as with the code itself (Weber, 2004). The four open source learning

DOI: 10.4018/978-1-61520-917-0.ch008

management systems that serve as backdrops for the data mining projects described in this chapter represent a spectrum of higher education open source undertakings. As projects and products, ATutor, LON-CAPA, Moodle, and Sakai differ in terms of technology, design, size, target audiences, organizational structures, funding models, software licensing choices, extendibility, and their pace of development. In no small way, analyzing why and how educational data mining techniques are being employed in these four open source contexts also involves understanding the underlying organizations and processes, not just the technologies and system designs.

Data mining of web-based educational systems is also not particularly new. For more than a decade, exciting and visionary applications of educational data mining in web-based learning systems have been conceived, prototyped, and tested (Johnson, 1998). As Romero and Ventura show, much of the work to date has been carried out mainly within the lifecycle and setting of individual research and development projects with small populations of research subjects (Romero & Ventura, 2007). In contrast, the projects described in this chapter involve data mining technologies and techniques being adapted to widely available open source learning management systems. For many reasons, traditional techniques for studying online users have proven inadequate when applied in systems of the scale and complexity seen in these widely adopted, open technology and open learning management systems (McGrath, 2008b). As an alternative for studying usage, educational data mining techniques are being embraced because the techniques excel at uncovering usage structure and access patterns within the enormous volume and variety of loosely structured user data generated in large systems. And while exploratory in nature, the four projects described here are not only for research and development. They lean more towards developing practical approaches to building and managing distributed capture and analysis systems for large web-based production deployments in

production at many universities and colleges. The four projects involve fairly simple applications of data mining, from external usage analytics to association-rule based feedback, that only begin to tap the fuller potential educational data mining has shown in pure research prototype systems. Two are grant funded research experiments, but in all four cases practical needs have motivated the turn towards applying the algorithms of data mining and machine learning as a way of understanding users and usage.

BACKGROUND

As more teaching, research, and administrative processes are moved online, there arise both needs and opportunities for tracking, analyzing, and improving the online institutional systems involved. Important to the success of these online environments, for instance, is meeting increasing demands to document educational outcomes. Even as the distance between students, faculty, and administrators decreases online, demands for more detailed and rigorous accounting of teaching activities, curricular progress, and learning outcomes are increasing. Before the advent of large cross-institutional open source projects, e-learning tracking and reporting functionality was typically provided by software vendors. An educational technology group at a college or university could confine its efforts to meeting the mandates and needs of the local institution by using the reporting features of the commercial systems. In the case of open source applications, are often left to consider how information should be captured and managed, how to ensure that these requirements are ever included in the development process, or how to address these needs in other ways (e.g., data mining) when they're not.

Behind open and community source projects such as ATutor, LON-CAPA, Moodle, and Sakai are organizations still experimenting with management structures that might allow them better to coordinate distributed software development (Wheeler, 2007). Many of the same principles (e.g., simple services, loose-coupling, lightweight data standards), that make these open source projects possible present challenges to building out full-featured web analytic tools customarily found in commercial systems. In particular, the distributed design can make it more difficult to develop elaborate features in areas such as user event logging and analysis. In order to facilitate the development of new tools by a loose-knit community of developers, these consortia aim at minimal requirements and overhead for applications to plug into the framework. Attempts at building in core usage analysis functionality have often not met with much success. As an alternative, collecting, transforming, and analyzing disparate log information through external data mining processes is hard work, but it opens up the possibility for finding patterns, clusters, associations and commonalities that would otherwise be missed. When it succeeds, this approach can result in surprising insights about near and long-term usage patterns, thereby giving support personnel, usability researchers, instructional designers, and many other decision makers a handle on what is really going on in learning management systems that has been deployed.

FOSS/Open Learning Management Systems

Academic institutions are increasingly involved in collaborative efforts to develop open source alternatives to commercial applications such as repositories, portals, and collaboration environments. This shift in the locus of software development away from commercial companies and into loosely organized consortia of higher education institutions, however, ends up with noticeably different processes and results. More recent approaches to open source software development reflect accelerated development cycles in so called extreme or agile programming techniques. As implied by

the names, these approaches quicken the pace of development by avoiding a long preliminary analysis phase before the start of development. Coding begins much earlier and requirements can even change during the development process in agile approaches. Crucial to making this fast flexibility work, however, is an even more intensive focus on the core needs of product's customers and key stakeholders. The time between capturing customer needs and programming usable code is necessarily shortened, requiring earlier customer input and a development cycle that changes flexibly in response. Rather than wait for software to proceed through development and quality assurance testing before unveiling it to users, these new approaches bring user needs in as early as possible by characterizing them in usage scenarios and dividing the project into smaller functional modules that can be completed and refined around those scenarios. By enabling and even inviting changes to the original requirements as development proceeds, the goal is to eliminate surprises. Rather than discover a mismatch in requirements specifications and user expectations after the fact, the extreme and agile approaches try to flush out these differences early on. Obviously, for the approaches to succeed, core usage scenarios get the most attention. They are supposed to be at center stage throughout the project lifecycle. This sort of disciplined focus on user experience, however, can have a side effect of allowing secondary functionality (e.g., behind-the-scenes administrative tools) to be neglected in some distributed open source projects (McGrath, 2006).

Mining Usage Data in Web-Based Educational Systems

Research into data mining usage of web educational systems goes back nearly to the advent of the web itself (Castro, 2007). As a newer sub-field of data mining, educational data mining in the web-based learning management systems context encompasses a wider range of research questions and approaches. Romero & Venture provide an excellent literature review of the field (Romero & Ventura, 2007). A fair generalization can be made that much of the inquiry and practical wisdom developed center on applying computational techniques to large data sets, typically those pulled together from disparate sources in online learning application. Educational data mining projects have examined similarities across thousands of online sessions to reveal useful characteristic aspects of students' interaction with e-learning content. These analyses have identified common conceptual error sequences that can then inform pedagogical design issues, such as whether subgroups of students share similar difficulties, or how the content and sequencing might be re-ordered. Only recently within the educational data mining field has the user analytics of open source learning management systems become a topic growing of interest, as practitioners seek to understand better the activities carried out in systems like ATutor, LON-CAPA, and Sakai.

Mining Usage in ATutor

In contrast to some of the cross-institutional projects described later in this chapter, development management of the ATutor system is based within one main institution, the University of Toronto, at its Adaptive Technology Resource Centre (ATRC). While often filling the role of learning management system at many universities and colleges, ATutor also sees broader use in online training and professional development settings. Technically, it is considered a learning content management system (LCMS). The ATRC application development group benefits from having central control over managing the development of ATutor while still allowing for external participation by those who wish to propose new features or contribute code. As an open source application developed and managed by a single institution, ATutor's design reflects this unusual level of overall control. Where products developed by distributed

open source consortia tend by necessity to favor modular extensible design, ATutor more closely resembles traditional monolithic core approaches to systems design (Cocea, 2006). For Vajirasak Vanijja, Montri Supattathum in the School of Information Technology (SIT) at King Mongkut's University of Technology Thonburi in Thailand, this monolithic design offered an advantage in that ATutor serves as a central distribution point at their institution not only for traditional course materials but also for digitized video lectures. As the use of learning management systems to augment traditional course activities is a major focus of open source development in higher education, the creation and distribution of digitized video and audio recording of lectures has become a focus of the higher education open content movement. Coursecasting, the video and audio recording of lectures and events for live or on-demand playback, has become another significant service at many institutions of higher education like SIT. By making available on the web collections of full-length digitized recordings of lectures, college and university information technology groups find themselves supporting student learning activities across increased spans of time and distance. Managing the up-to-date production and on-demand delivery of this kind of open content requires a technical infrastructure for capturing, publishing, and archiving that can adapt quickly to changing workload demands (Almeida et al., 2001).

For Vanijja and Supattathum, the tracking of users and their round-the-clock interaction with learning materials and video files at SIT posed special technical and analytical challenges. In particular, knowing not just how the kinds of material and media are being used in the ATutor system but also how groupings of users might be understood as different audiences was an important objective (Vanijja & Supattathum, 2006). In addition to low-level capture of web log traffic, the ATutor system provides some basic content usage and student tracking that allow instructors to monitor student progress and pathways through the content. There are also facilities for exporting tracking data for external analysis. Analyzing how users' interactions with course and video content vary in terms of network access quality was also crucial. Tools for answering these kinds of questions with the ATutor system depend in part on the underlying web technology. The monitoring features available to administrators of the system rely heavily on the underlying web server logs as a record of the visitor's access locations. Automatically generated web logs remain a low-level but vital source of data in most data mining efforts in web-based learning management systems. In some systems, a higher level of logging by the system can provide more information that, for instance, encapsulates each user's individual session in the system, records what content they access, or what tools they use. In ATutor, these higher-level system generated tracking logs are available as a valuable complement to the low-level web log data. Vanijja and Supattathum also supplemented the logging information with student registration information data to answer their questions about patterns among different degree program audiences, for instance.

Mining Usage in LON-CAPA

Where the ATutor data mining project sought answers about general correlations among a small sets of gross characteristics (e.g., media access quantity and audience enrollment attributes), another kind of data mining technique called affinity analysis enables the line of questioning to extend simultaneously to varying units of analysis across a large number variables. Using affinity analysis to explore highly dimensional data sets from learning management system activities can lead to the discovery of so called association rules. Association rules offer a measure of support and confidence about the co-occurrence of multiple variables. Unlike traditional user–tailored approaches to instruction that require a good deal of assessment and face-to-face observations, the association

mining techniques in web-based educational systems can provide insights and automated tailored response within very short time spans. In the case of the Michigan State University's LON-CAPA web-based educational system, Behrouz Minaei-Bigdoli and colleagues were interested in mining across several online courses using data sets that record students' interaction with course materials and their performance on assessments. Using affinity analysis, they were particularly interested in finding association rules about learning activities and learner characteristics that distinguish less successful students from their peers in terms of study habits, difficulty of the material, and student background. The discovery of such associations can generate models of student interaction with the learning management system that allow, in turn, for intervention or even responsive tailoring to individual needs in the online environment.

Minaei-Bigdoli and her colleagues were able to mine a particularly rich collection of data due in part to the extensive integration and successful adoption of LON-CAPA within the curriculum at their institution. Moreover, like ATutor, LON-CAPA development falls under the purview of a single institution. Michigan State University, where LON-CAPA originated, continues to manage the semi-annual releases of the software. LON-CAPA's design emphasizes measuring and tracking individual student progress through online material with frequent assessment and feedback, a model particularly well-suited to math and science instruction. Over the years, LON-CAPA has received extramural funding support from and the Sloan Foundation, Mellon Foundation, and the National Science Foundation that have cultivated a network of like-minded instructors at other institutions who share the instructional content they've developed for it. While LON-CAPA offers a standard set of learning management system tools (e.g., assessment, synchronous and asynchronous communication), its architecture is also uniquely well suited to fostering a web-based learning community. Underlying LON-CAPA installations are specialized content repositories that serve as hubs for the other services and for networking with other institutions. In addition to capturing detailed, high-level logs of student interaction with content and assessment tools, the system also holds user characteristics derived from the local student information system. The success of Minaei-Bigdoli's project rests in part on affordances LON-CAPA provides for easily pulling these disparate data sources together for use in data mining exploration.

Mining Usage in Moodle

The cross-institutional sharing of both open code and open content within the LON-CAPA network points toward another trend in higher education open source: the organizational and project management issues these consortia face when working with and for each other. A globe-spanning open source community like Moodle's, for instance, consists of scores of developers around the world using and contributing to a shared code base. To facilitate distributed development, the Moodle framework design places minimal requirements on those who might want to create or integrate a new tool. By minimizing the overhead of tool creation and re-writes, however, the Moodle framework offers as a side effect very little out-of-the-box administrative functionality in areas such as usage reporting, as Romero points out in his data mining study of Moodle use at the University of Cordoba (Romero, Ventura, & Garcia, 2008). Although Moodle maintains extensive high-level logs of user interactions with tools and content, it provides very little functionality for viewing or analyzing this data.

Mining Usage in Sakai

As mentioned, Moodle's database of logged activity is extensive but its reporting tools are not. A similar situation exists in the Sakai Project. Sakai like Moodle provides very little functionality for

analyzing the user activity data it captures internally. Whether configured for use as a learning management system or more generic collaboration environment, the Sakai platform offers a basic set of tools along with the capacity to easily add or adapt new tools. The code base can be downloaded by anyone anywhere for free. And many pre-existing web applications have been adapted to work within Sakai in a loosely-coupled fashion. Yet, while the Sakai end-user sees a harmonious arrangement of tools that interoperate and share a common interface style, the behind-the-scenes view of Sakai in operation reveals a piecemeal and heterogeneous affair. In particular, responsibility for logging of information about users' interaction within a running instance of Sakai varies across tools, as event logging implementation is largely left up to individual tool developers. Moreover, the actual logging of this data is spread across several locations in a typical production installation.

Each user in Sakai is assigned to membership in system-wide roles (e.g., instructor, teaching assistant, and student) and every time they log in, they see a personal workspace and collection of course sites to which they belong. Moving within a particular course site, the user has access to content and tools (e.g., calendar, group discussion, email archive, chat, quizzing, and a gradebook). After logging into the Sakai framework and using tools and accessing content, the user either logs out or their session lapses automatically. In a typical production installation, the user's contact and interactions are logged in a web server's various logs, application container log, and in many tables of a relational database. Because Sakai provides no core tools for collecting and analyzing this information, the usage data must be gathered and studied externally in order to yield even the simplest basic usage information, as McGrath notes in his data mining study of Sakai use at UC Berkeley (McGrath, 2007).

DATA MINING ISSUES IN FOSS/OPEN SYSTEMS

Practices, Techniques, and Processes

Despite the difference across the four data mining projects in the learning management contexts described above, the data mining methodologies they employ follow a similar iterative process. Although formalized methods are not widely adopted in the kinds of nascent higher education data mining efforts surveyed in this chapter, there is sensible emphasis on good initial planning followed by data pre-processing, pattern discovery, and reporting steps. As detailed in the case studies in this chapter, the specific benefits that data mining yields in answering usage questions about these large institutional production system are influenced, though not wholly determined, by the set of initial objectives, scope, and strategy.

Preparation Phase: Gathering & Pre-Processing

Process-wise, data mining of user activity requires that educational technologists integrate several key steps into the larger workflow of their analysis projects: capturing, aggregating, pre-preprocessing, and exploring usage data. While basic reports and summary statistics can be generated from a few sources, a more complete picture requires aggregating and preprocessing the data first. In the ATutor and LON-CAPA contexts, this step involved harvesting and coding the various data from the internal tracking and web log file sources. In the cases of Moodle and Sakai, the preparation phase also involved gathering varied data, file and log formats but also analyzing the differences in the information models within the relational database. For example, merging semi-structured common log format files from web servers, the status messages generated by code in application servers, and the structured relational data captured in a relational database can require a range of transformations such as de-normalization and dimensionality reduction. At this stage differences in logging approaches across the distributed systems involved in most online system also becomes a key issue. Not all of the systems log activity in the database, and among those that do so, decision about what qualifies as a user session or action and when to log them can be difficult to decipher.

Once the various data sources are merged, an exploratory data analysis phase can help chart a course for choosing among data mining approaches (e.g., clustering, classification, and association). In the case of Vanijja and Supattathum who were interested in video lecture and course content usage, summary statistics served as first steps towards getting to know the general relations between media access and audience type: the kinds of resources they access, access levels, where they came from and what they did. The sheer size of the user activity data generated by any web-based production system might require carving the initial dataset with an initial set of coding categories. In the case of the LON-CAPA, for instance, Minaei-Bidgoli and colleagues used a long exploratory process to devise a four attribute (student, problem set, problem set interaction, course interaction) scheme by which to organize three combined semester-long data sets for courses in Physics, Biology, and Chemistry. In the context of the Moodle study, Romero's university setting also involved thousands of students accessing material in nearly 200 course sites. Likewise, in the Sakai example, the various forms of user activity data captured could easily grow by megabytes per day. In most contexts, questions that arise from finding initial connections within and across the dataset might then point to access time and content location patterns as starting points for further investigation. Summarizing the data in an exploratory fashion is a first step towards organizing and prioritizing questions to pose next (Larose, 2006).

Analysis Phase: Finding Patterns

Data mining algorithms look for inherent patterns and similarities in large data sets and can discover groupings and relations that might otherwise prove hard to detect. Clustering analysis makes a good first step in data mining, as the various techniques available can be tuned across a range of variables in processing huge datasets (Markov & Larose, 2007). In the area of clustering algorithms, the data mining software usually offers a choice of algorithms that work particularly well with huge multi-dimensional data sets. Selecting a semester's worth of session instance data from the flat file as input to the clustering algorithm, one can choose a seed value for the number of clusters desired or use the default. Romero performed a clustering analysis of student Moodle users' variables covering mean session time and the percentage on assignments. Three main clusters emerged around groupings that revealed quick, medium, and extended visits.

One might also wonder about patterns within sessions, such as common activity sequences. As an aid in answering such questions, the data mining software usually provides functions for applying association rules as a method of revealing co-occurrence relations among and across item sets. The goal of an association analysis is to discover affinity patterns in sequences of data (i.e. things that tend to go together). Unlike in clustering where items are grouped based on their inherent similarity, an association rule discovery can often find surprising pairings of sequences within large data sets. Sometimes referred to as market basket analysis, association analysis can give results that resemble correlations. In the case of Sakai usage data, McGrath's participants' activities, as revealed by event messages logged during each session, were mined for associations. Looking at cross-classified counts of tool activity events initially revealed cases where the session activities that co-occur were unsurprising: content reads go together with content reads, login events go together with announcement reads.

But further analysis revealed some less obvious co-occurrences: document editing events often co-occurred with discussion forum reading events within sessions, for example.

Since the significance of any association is very easy to overstate, their true usefulness comes into play mainly when they are followed up in another fashion. Sakai tool activity associations in their own right mean very little until combined with some further empirical investigation of, say, the course sites in which they occur. For example, a major challenge to cultivating institutional best practices for using a system like Moodle or Sakai is knowing what students and instructor are really doing. With hundreds of instructors, thousands of sites, and tens of thousands of students, it can be very difficult to know how tools are actually being taken up and used. The clusters and associations offered up through data mining analyses essentially become a launch pad for collecting, analyzing, and inquiring further about how features and content are being accessed. Though not to be relied upon solely for documenting activity, the data mining results can offer quick and focused access to the usage patterns that, if confirmed, ultimately help inform planning and support decisions.

As a summary of the data mining process discussion, the table below provides a synopsis across the four project contexts mentioned and how each project's particular questions influence the selection of data sources and methods of analysis. Data sources and methods were both varied. This in understandable given the range of contexts and systems involved, but the processes have much in common.

Prospects: FOSS/Open Future Development Data Mining Usage

As mentioned, the goals of the data mining analyses described in this chapter include discovery of inherent groupings and co-occurrence within across the large usage data sets with many variables. These goals are fairly modest in comparison to what has been achieved over the past decade

Table 1. Selective overview of web usage mining approaches in the four contexts

Questions	Data Sources	Methods of Mining Analysis	References
Atutor 1. How are the different materials and media in the system being used? 2. How do access location, network access quality and media access volume relate? 3. What access patterns characterize different audiences (e.g. different curricula or degree program enrollments)?	• ATutor tracking logs • web log files • student information system data	• correlation, multinomial modeling	(Vanijja & Supattathum, 2006)
LON-CAPA 4. What association rules exist that can distinguish high and low performing students based on their background, their interaction with the system, the difficulty of the content material?	• activity log database • student characteristic database • content material	• Affinity Analysis looking for contrastive associations	(Minaei-Bidgoli et al., 2006) (Minaei-Bidgoli, 2005) (Minaei-Bidgoli et al., 2004)
Moodle 5. How should student users of Moodle be grouped in terms of their Moodle activities and their performance in the course? 6. How can Moodle activity be used as a gauge to identify users who would benefit from intervention during the course?	• Moodle database tables • Student information system data	• Clustering analysis of student sessions • Classification analysis student grades • Affinity analysis of tool events	(Romero, Ventura, & Garcia, 2008) (Garcia et al., 2006)
Sakai 7. How do Sakai users (i.e., students and instructors) access sessions change over time? 8. How can users of the Sakai environment be grouped and how are the Sakai tools used together within the system?	• Sakai database tables • web log files	• Clustering analysis of student sessions • Affinity analysis of tool events	(McGrath, 2007) (McGrath, 2008a)

in research proof-of concept systems involving educational data mining. The particular open source contexts of these four projects also differ from each other in terms of design, technology, and organizational management. To look ahead and try to anticipate how more sophisticated data mining efforts might develop in these same four contexts is, in part, to wonder about the way any new functionality finds its way into open source projects. Traditional practices in software development tend to assume that a product's intended stakeholders (i.e., users, customers, and clients) are fairly well known and generally accessible. As mentioned, the projects in this chapter reveal difficult issues faced by those who would undertake feature development in the context of open source projects in which the loose-knit user communities are widely distributed.

In their own ways, the four examples described are drawn from varied experiences of managing data mining process development largely outside and alongside the particular learning management systems. These higher education efforts to build and share course management frameworks for supporting online collaboration in academic courses and projects tend to address the most pressing and commonly agreed upon features and functionality requirements centered on user experience. With a far-flung community of users and developers, these projects require new approaches to eliciting, analyzing, and prioritizing institutional administrative needs for adding data mining technology in more integrated ways. The issues outlined in the data mining projects in this chapter were met by a preliminary, piecemeal set of practice-oriented processes. Collecting requirements, feature requests, and suggestions in any open source project is often all about finding commonalities, negotiating priorities, and previewing design solutions before committing to development. At its best, this approach can result in open debate and fair negotiation of near and long-term development plans, thereby giving community representatives and decision makers a handle on what they can expect as they implement the learning management system at their local institutions.

CONCLUSION

This chapter has been intended mainly as an overview of how four higher education institutions have made efforts to address the particular usage reporting needs of online open learning management systems and how they are using basic techniques and tools of web usage mining. Even with these mining techniques in hand, gathering and comprehending usage activity obviously remains a very time consuming challenge. Here the combination of data mining approaches and project management disciplines have enabled a basic set of exploratory approaches to pattern discovery in the enormous amounts of data involved. As this field matures, the next arena of analysis to be explored is building in the techniques of data mining as functionality within the open source content management system. If successful, the results could lead towards near real-time processes that truly leverage the potential and promise of data mining for personalization and responsiveness. Internally or externally, data mining in the learning management system context offers potential benefits for assisting those in higher education who are responsible for implementing and deploying online open environments in support of research, teaching and learning. For internet-based projects in higher education to keep up with the increasing expectations and demands that the Internet era has brought to teaching and learning, the analytical tools and processes we employ will need ever greater power and flexibility.

REFERENCES

Almeida, J., Krueger, J., Eager, D., & Vernon, M. (2001, June). Analysis of Educational Media Server Workloads. In *Proceedings of the 11th International Workshop on Network and Operating System Support for Digital Audio and Video (NOSSDAV 2001)*.

Castro, F., Vellido, A., Nebot, A., & Mugica, F. (2007). Applying Data Mining Techniques to e-Learning Problems. In Jain, L., Tedman, R., & Tedman, D. (Eds.), *Evolution of Teaching and Learning Paradigms in Intelligent Environment*. New York: Springer. doi:10.1007/978-3-540-71974-8_8

Chen, C., Hsieh, Y., & Hsu, S. (2007). Mining learner profile utilizing association rule for web-based learning diagnosis. *Expert Systems with Applications, 33*(1). doi:10.1016/j.eswa.2006.04.025

Cocea, M. (2006). Extendibility of educational systems to include a learner-adaptive motivational module. In R. Vasile, R. Kimari, & D. Andone (Eds.), *Proceedings of the 12th NETTIES (Networking Entities) International Conference: The Future of E:Advanced Educational Technologies for a Future e-Europe* (pp. 195-198). Timisoara, Romania: Orizonturi Universitare.

García, E., Romero, C., Ventura, S., & Castro, C. (2006). Using rules discovery for the continuous improvement of e-learning courses. In *Proceedings of the International Conference Intelligent Data Engineering and Automated Learning,* (pp. 887-895). Burgos, Spain.

Gaudioso, E., & Talavera, L. (2006). Data mining to support tutoring in virtual learning communities: Experiences and challenges. In Romero, C., & Ventura, S. (Eds.), *Data mining in e-learning, Advances in Management Information Series* (*Vol. 4*, pp. 207–226). Southampton, UK: WitPress. doi:10.2495/1-84564-152-3/12

Johnson, W. (2003). Using agent technology to improve the quality of web-based education. In Zhong, N., & Liu, J. (Eds.), *Web Intelligence.* New York: Springer.

Larose, D. T. (2006). *Data mining methods and models.* Hoboken, NJ: Wiley-Interscience.

Markov, Z., & Larose, D. T. (2007). *Data mining the web: Uncovering patterns in web content, Structure, and Usage.* Hoboken, NJ: Wiley-Interscience.

McGrath, O. (2005, November 6-9). Gauging adoptability: a case study of e-portfolio template development. In *Proceedings of the 33rd Annual ACM SIGUCCS Conference on User Services,* Monterey, CA (pp. 214-217). New York: ACM.

McGrath, O. (2006, November 5-8). Balancing act: community and local requirements in an open source development process. In *Proceedings of the 34th Annual ACM SIGUCCS Conference on User Services,* Edmonton, Alberta, Canada (pp. 240-244). New York: ACM.

McGrath, O. (2007, October 7-10,). Seeking activity: on the trail of users in open and community source frameworks. In *Proceedings of the 35th Annual ACM SIGUCCS Conference on User Services,* Orlando, Florida (pp. 234-239). New York: ACM.

McGrath, O. (2008a, October 19-22). Insights and surprises from usage patterns: some benefits of data mining in academic online systems. In *Proceedings of the 36th Annual ACM SIGUCCS Conference on User Services Conference,* Portland, OR (pp. 59-64). New York: ACM.

McGrath, O. (2008b). Open Educational Technology: Tempered Aspirations. In Iiyoshi, T., & Kumar, M. S. V. (Eds.), *Opening Up Education: The Collective Advancement of Education through Open Technology, Open Content, and Open Knowledge* (pp. 13–26). Cambridge, MA: MIT Press.

Minaei-Bidgoli, B. (2005). *Data Mining for a Web-Based Educational System.* Unpublished doctoral dissertation, Michigan State University.

Minaei-Bidgoli, B., Kashy, A., Kortemeyer, G., & Punch, W. (2004). Optimizing classification ensembles via a genetic algorithm for a web-based educational system. In *Proceedings of the Joint International Association For Pattern Recognition (IAPR) Workshops on Syntactical and Structural Pattern Recognition (SSPR 2004) and Statistical Pattern Recognition (SPR 2004),* Lisbon, Portugal.

Minaei-Bigdoli, B., & Tan, P. Kortemeyer, G., & Punch, W.F. (2006) Association analysis for a web-based educational system. In C. Romero & S. Ventura (Eds.), *Data mining in e-learning* (pp. 139-156). Southampton, UK: Wit Press.

Romero, C., & Ventura, S. (2007). Educational data mining: A survey from 1995 to 2005. *Expert Systems with Applications, 33*(1). doi:10.1016/j.eswa.2006.04.005

Romero, C., Ventura, S., & Garcia, E. (2008). Data mining in learning management systems: Moodle case study and tutorial. *Computers & Education, 51.*

Roof, S., & Frazier, G. (1962). Note: An IBM 704 computer program for computing bartlett's test of homogeneiety of variance. *Biometrics, 18*(2), 251–252. doi:10.2307/2527464

Sen, A., Dacin, P. A., & Pattichis, C. (2006). Current trends in web data analysis. *Communications of the ACM, 49*(11), 85–91. doi:10.1145/1167838.1167842

Vanijja, V., & Supattathum, M. (2006). *Statistical analysis of e-learning usage in a university.* Paper presented at the Third International Conference on eLearning for Knowledge-based Society (eLearningAP 2006), Bangkok, Thailand.

Wang, W., & Zaiane, O. R. (2002, September 2-6). Clustering web sessions by sequence alignment. In *Proceedings of the 13th International Workshop on Database and Expert Systems Applications DEXA* (pp. 394-398). Washington, DC: IEEE Computer Society.

Weber, S. (2004). *The success of open source.* Cambridge, MA: Harvard University Press.

Wheeler, B. C. (2007). Open source 2007: How did this happen? *EDUCAUSE Review, 39*(4), 12–27.

KEY TERMS AND DEFINITIONS

Affinity Analysis: Affinity analysis is one kind of data mining investigation. In this approach, the goal is to see what association rules if any exist, i.e., what actions co-occur. In the context of web usage, an affinity analysis might yield a rule such as 'if page A is visited, then page D is visited' which might indicate a previously unknown navigational path popular among users. Affinity analysis is also sometime referred to as market basket analysis, as it can provide retailers with information about products that consumers purchase together.

Clustering Analysis: Clustering analysis is another common kind of data mining investigation. Often performed as part of an initial exploration of data, the goal is to see what natural groupings if any exist, i.e., what items in the data are alike. In the context of web usage, a clustering analysis might reveal that the site's users fall into two distinct groupings: those who use the site's menu and those who go directly to specific pages within the site.

Data Mining: In common parlance, data mining often refers generally to the idea of probing deeply into some mountain of data. This informal use of the term usually says little about the techniques used to do the probing. In contrast, the more formal use of the term refers specifically to using computational techniques to uncover patterns in huge data sets. Here the techniques range widely from statistics to artificial intelligence. The range of data mining investigations is also varied and ever increasing, but some of the better-known approaches include clustering, classification, and affinity analysis.

Learning Management System: The familiar online learning management systems can be found at most colleges and universities today. Called by different names (e.g. virtual learning environment, learning content management system) around the world, the products in this category are either home-grown, commercially licensed, or open source software. Regardless of their provenance, these systems all tended to pull together in one package the same sorts of tools and functions (e.g., mailing list, bulletin board, and chat programs). While annual licenses for commercial systems range into the hundreds of thousands of dollars, a user would see very little difference in functionality between commercial and open source products. However, unlike the commercial counterparts, open source learning management systems often lack full-featured usage tracking tools.

Web Usage Mining: As a sub-field of data mining, web usage mining focuses specifically on finding patterns relating to users of a web based system: who they are, what they tend to do, etc. In contrast, other types of web data mining (e.g., web text mining) might focus on finding patterns in the content itself. Web usage mining relies on data captured behind the scene in server logs and databases.

This work was previously published in International Journal of Open Source Software and Processes Volume 2, Issue 1, edited by Stefan Koch, pp. 65-75, copyright 2010 by IGI Publishing (an imprint of IGI Global).

Chapter 9

Implementing an Open Source ePortfolio in Higher Education:
Lessons Learned Along the Way

Stein Brunvard
University of Michigan-Dearborn, USA

Gail R. Luera
University of Michigan-Dearborn, USA

Tiffany Marra
University of Michigan, USA

Melissa Peet
University of Michigan, USA

ABSTRACT

This article describes the identification of goals, selection of an Open Source Platform and the initial implementation stages of an Integrative Knowledge ePortfolio Process (which has both pedagogy and tools) at a midwestern University School of Education. Faculty and students are using the Integrative ePortfolio approach to reflect on, connect, and document their learning and accomplishments over time, and to create an Integrated Professional Teaching Portfolio that showcases their knowledge, skills and contributions to others. Lessons learned during the preliminary phase include the importance of garnering support of adopters, providing sufficient support in order for faculty and students to gain the skills necessary to produce meaningful and dynamic portfolios and transitioning from multiple ePortfolios to a uniform platform that works across programs. The insights gained from the experience will be helpful to other institutions that are interested in adopting Open Source Platform ePortfolios.

INTRODUCTION

Portfolios, in particular ePortfolios, have the potential to be powerful generative and trans-formative pedagogical tools for students, faculty and institutions (Inoue, 2009; Lorenzo & Ittelson, 2005a). Students can use ePortfolios to represent their learning and reflect on the different artifacts they create and experiences they share throughout their coursework (Young, 2002). Faculty can use

DOI: 10.4018/978-1-61520-917-0.ch009

ePortfolios to evaluate the effectiveness of specific courses or entire programs of study in order to determine if standards are being taught or if changes to the curriculum need to be implemented (Lorenzo & Ittelson, 2005b) and institutions can use ePortfolios to facilitate the accreditation process. Free and open source software represents a promising opportunity for a large number of higher education institutions looking for an effective way to integrate ePortfolios into their learning experiences (Wheeler, 2004).

Since 2007 the School of Education (SOE) at the University of Michigan-Dearborn (UM-D) has been implementing an open-source ePortfolio system (OSP) that is unique in its reflective and integrative stance. Undergraduate students as well as university faculty have used the ePortfolio to uncover their tacit knowledge and create representations of their learning and professional growth as educators. The following chapter chronicles that process, shares insights and provides guidance to help inform other institutions that may be looking to adopt similar ePortfolio systems.

BACKGROUND

The University of Michigan-Dearborn is one of two regional campuses connected with the University of Michigan system. The Dearborn campus is in southeast Michigan and offers a wide range of degrees and academic programs to a population of nearly 9,000 graduate and undergraduate students. Of that population, roughly 2,200 undergraduates are working on teacher certification within the School of Education and another 1,000 graduate students are enrolled in various education related Masters and certification programs. In 2001, the SOE started to explore the use of ePortfolios with its students as a way to help them reflect on their learning and create representations of their knowledge that the school could use to demonstrate how the different state mandated standards were being met across the curriculum. This process of

exploration and implementation are described in greater detail later in the chapter but it is important to articulate the rationale for using ePortfolios before moving forward.

Review of Literature

ePortfolios facilitate reflective learning (Richardson & Ward, 2005) and provide an electronic forum with which reflections, experiences and artifacts can be shared with a wider audience as a way to demonstrate mastery of relevant concepts and strategies. However, throughout the literature, the term "ePortfolio" is ambiguous and often characterized as having multiple purposes and definitions. The following typology (adapted from Wolf & Dietz, 1998) is widely used to describe these purposes: (1) assessment management portfolios capture evidence of students' learning for institutions; (2) learning development portfolios prompt students to reflect on and connect learning within courses and over time; and (3) self-expressive professional portfolios support learners in creatively documenting their knowledge, skills, identities and accomplishments for others. However useful, this typology is also problematic as most institutions use ePortfolios for several of these purposes (Barrett, 2000).

The diverse purposes of ePortfolios actually reflect fundamentally different approaches to learning and present clear challenges for institutions wishing to adopt these tools (Barrett, 2000; Jafari, 2004). For instance, the self-expressive portfolios reflect a learner-centered "constructivist" view of knowledge and identity development wherein, ideally, students select, reflect on, synthesize and creatively present a series of artifacts that demonstrate both formal and informal knowledge, skills and values (Cambridge, 2001; Peet, in press). This type of ePortfolio is commonly referred to as a "learning portfolio" (Annis & Jones, 1995) because of its use by students to track their growth and development through a specific course of study. A key element of this kind of portfolio is that the learner, rather than the institution, is in control of the artifacts and knowledge presented making it a more accurate representation of his/her thinking (Siemens, 2004). In contrast, the assessment management portfolios support an institution-centered need to document more formal, content-based knowledge gained from academic settings. With this type of portfolio students identify and reflect on learning artifacts in order to show evidence of institutionally-defined learning goals (Jafari, 2004). This is helpful to institutions of higher education that need to demonstrate student outcomes and make connections between those outcomes and relevant standards of proficiency (Lorenzo & Ittelson, 2005b).

Another category of ePortfolio gaining popularity in higher education is the "teaching portfolio" (Lorenzo & Ittelson, 2005a). Faculty use this type of portfolio to demonstrate their efficacy with teaching and scholarship both to students and to tenure and promotion committees, replacing the need to assemble three-ring binders with hard copies of course evaluations, syllabi and publications. Using a digitized environment to showcase professional development makes it possible for faculty to share representations of their work that extend beyond the limitations of paper-based artifacts and could include podcasts of lectures, videotaped observations and collaborative work with Web 2.0 technologies such as Wikis and blogs.

Although the literature widely touts ePortfolios as student-centered tools that support life-long learning and professional identity development (Cambridge, 2001; Clark & Eynon, 2009; Jafari, 2004), most schools adopt these tools in order to gather and aggregate data for accountability purposes (Barrett, 2000). Thus, in most cases, the institution, not the student, "owns" the eportfolios and accompanying artifacts. Currently, most commercial ePortfolio systems support learners to reflect on academic learning and identify artifacts for assessment purposes. Yet, these same systems do not support the kinds of pedagogy

students need in order to truly "own" their learning and use the tools beyond the academic environment for professional development and lifelong learning (e.g. prompts for meta-reflection that can help students connect and integrate learning from all areas of life, and design templates to help students creatively demonstrate learning to others). The tension between "student-centered" and "institution-centered" portfolios has prompted a concerted effort by leading scholars as well as several policy and professional organizations in US higher education to take action to bridge this gap.

Research comparing the influence of different types of ePortfolios (assessment, development and self-expressive) on student learning and development is lacking. Similarly, although several informal studies have been conducted, there is no research to date that systematically compares commercial and open-source systems. A review of the literature in 2004 by Crowley identified very little empirical evidence related to ePortfolios and improvements to learning. Since then, a handful of studies have shown that highly structured reflective and assessment portfolios can increase students' reflective and critical thinking capacities in academic settings (Diller & Phelps, 2008). When students are prompted to connect learning artifacts to specific outcomes or goals, most learn to identify progress and value in their learning (Diller & Phelps, 2008). However, there is no evidence to date indicating that students can apply these critical thinking skills outside the classroom or develop a sense of ownership regarding their eportfolios. In terms of self-expressive (student-owned) ePortfolios, only one institution, LaGuardia Community College, has shown that this type of ePortfolio can contribute positively to students' retention, reflective ability, identity development and levels of aspiration when supported by, and integrated into, courses that encourage students to reflect on and integrate their learning (Eynon, 2009).

Even though many institutions have spent several years piloting ePortfolios, there are very few successful campus-wide implementations in the United States to date. Although no studies have yet explored why institution-wide implementations are so difficult, a summary of the current literature provides the following insights:

- The term ePortfolio appears to be a moving target; in order to be meaningful, "ePortfolio" needs to be locally defined by multiple stakeholders at a given institution.
- The agendas, needs and purposes articulated by multiple stakeholders can be fundamentally and philosophically at odds with one another, thus causing confusion.
- There is not yet any agreed-upon set of practices, tools or conceptual framework that can act as a shared reference point for addressing both assessment and self-expressive ePortfolios.

This existing body of literature informed the creation of the conceptual model that guided the ePortfolio initiative at UM-D. That model is explained in greater detail next.

Conceptual Model: The Integrative Knowledge Portfolio Process

The Integrative Knowledge ePortfolio Process™ (IKPP) (Peet, in press) adopted by the UM Dearborn School of Education is an integrative learning pedagogy and an accompanying set of open-source portfolio tools that were developed through several years of action research at the University of Michigan. This pilot process, which evolved from a previous action research effort in the UM School of Social Work, involved more than a dozen academic and co-curriculr units on several UM campuses. The pilot addresses the needs for both a student-centered "self-expressive" ePortfolio, and tools that can help gather and ag-

gregate data for assessment purposes. In the IKPP, students learn to:

- Develop meta-cognitive skills by learning to ask, "Who am I becoming? What and how am I learning? What are my strengths, values and capacities? How do I intend to make a difference?"
- Understand, retrieve, and articulate different types of knowledge
- Identify, reflect on, and synthesize learning that has occurred both within and beyond the classroom (e.g. in clinical contexts, internships and paid work)
- Develop the kinds of knowledge, skills and awareness needed for professional competence and leadership
- Connect learning with personal values, a sense of purpose and goals for the future

Students engage in analysis, reflection, feedback and dialogue in order to help them understand the different types of knowledge and insights they've gained from academic coursework and other related experiences. They are guided to make connections between the tacit knowledge (i.e. how to negotiate competing interests and agendas) gained from life experiences, and the explicit knowledge (i.e. formal theories and concepts) accumulated in academic courses and field-based learning experiences. Students then document their learning through the creation of web pages that become part of their completed ePortfolios. The most important section of these ePortfolios is the "Work Showcase", which links to a number of "Examples of Work" pages that are organized according to knowledge and skill areas. The other pages include "Philosophy Statement", "Welcome", "Goals" and "Supporting Links". The end result is a web-based ePortfolio that illustrates, through text, images and supporting materials, a student's knowledge and skills, as well as the values, goals and commitments that underlie his/her work.

Each of the four phases of the IKPP has both a process (e.g. reflection and dialogue activities) and product (content for ePortfolio pages) dimension. By engaging students in specific types of integrative pedagogy, the process is designed to help students retrieve and document different types of knowledge over time, which in turn provides the insights and content they need to create a coherent and compelling ePortfolio. Engaging in the process and creating the product enhances students' meta-cognitive capacities by fostering a deep sense of what they have learned and how they can use their knowledge. Students who have participated in this process have found it very beneficial. Some have argued that it should become an integral part of the UM learning environment, while others have described it as a deeply transformative and empowering experience (Peet, 2008). Research on integrative portfolio-based learning has demonstrated that students:

- become more effective and engaged learners
- gain essential leadership capacities
- develop integrative approaches and ways of thinking
- identify gaps in their learning
- express a sense of curiosity or inquiry, rather than fear, when faced with difficult challenges (Peet, 2008)

The initiative to bring ePortfolios to UM-D was motivated by a desire to take advantage of what they had to offer to the individual student as well as the faculty member and institution. The specific rationale behind that initiative is more clearly defined in the following section.

Rationale for Implementing an ePortfolio System

The process of determining the goals of the ePortfolio and the selection of the technology to develop the portfolio took several years. This deliberate articulation of rationale and subsequent focus of the ePortfolio is typical of most institutions (Lorenzo & Ittelson, 2005b). Initially, the primary goal for the SOE ePortfolio was "to align the standards and the courses and then identify artifacts that might be included in the portfolio for the purposes of accreditation..." (unpublished memo, "Portfolio Alignment Committee final report", 2003). Over time, and as a result of numerous discussions at faculty meetings, SOE faculty identified a much wider array of reasons for implementing an ePortfolio system. These reasons included rationale that took into consideration the perspective of UM-D as an institution, the SOE as a center of teacher preparation and the individual faculty and students who would be using the ePortfolio.

Institutional Rationale

The UM-D accreditation review by the Higher Learning Commission (HLC), a Commission of the North Central Association of Colleges and Schools, requires that the university show what students can do by providing artifacts, called examples of evidence, that represent achievement of the institution's goals (Higher Learning Commission, 2003). The ePortfolio was viewed as an effective way to provide the HLC with the required evidence. Another institutional reason for implementing the ePortfolio in the SOE resulted from the initial discussions among the university schools and colleges to have support for a portfolio on a campus-wide scale. SOE faculty were motivated to select and pilot ePortfolios in order to model best practices in documenting and assessing program effectiveness and student learning to the rest of the University.

SOE Rationale

The SOE's rationale was similar to the goals described by Lorenzo and Ittelson (2005a) whereby the School shares information with others (i.e. other schools and colleges within the University, teacher preparation institutions, accrediting agencies, prospective students and parents, etc.) about the SOE's mission, goals, accomplishments and challenges. An additional reason to implement the ePortfolio was to provide the SOE with a tool they could use to facilitate the accreditation process through the Teacher Education Accreditation Council (TEAC). Similar to the HLC example of evidence that must be provided by the University, TEAC requires that teacher education agencies show what students can do by providing access to artifacts (2009). This process involves many different steps and requires institutions to provide the accrediting agency with various forms of data and evidence to support claims of student learning and growth. ePortfolios are an effective way to collect and showcase this kind of evidence to a broad audience. Finally, ePortfolios were viewed as an interactive and authentic way to market the program to prospective students and employers.

Individual Faculty/Student Rationale

Perhaps the primary reason individuals, whether they were students or faculty, wanted to create their own ePortfolio was to document their learning and accomplishments. Faculty viewed student ePortfolios as an important instructional tool to help students build conceptual connections across the program. The ePortfolio would provide an environment for students to demonstrate their learning over time at the university, through extra-curricular activities, and into their careers as professional educators. It was envisioned that the ePortfolio environment would be a place where students could practice meta-cognitive reflection on a wide range of learning experiences and also be able to share various artifacts such as lesson plans, images, presentations, videos and other multimedia elements that would help demonstrate their growth and represent who they are as educators. Therefore, the ePortfolio was viewed as a process and a tool to initiate reflective practice,

which faculty hoped would be continued into student's professional career.

Another goal of the ePortfolio was to provide SOE faculty with a dynamic electronic medium to demonstrate and reflect on their own learning and professional growth. SOE administrators viewed the ePortfolio as a more efficient and effective way for faculty to submit materials for the tenure and promotion process by allowing them to select, share and synthesize different representations of their teaching, scholarship and service. It was also reasoned that by having faculty develop their own portfolios they would be better able to provide support and guidance to their students.

DEVELOPING AN EPORTFOLIO SYSTEM

Since 2001, the University of Michigan-Dearborn, School of Education (UM-D, SOE) has been preparing for a school-wide implementation of ePortfolios by considering and researching the best fit of methods and tools for the school. In order to provide a context for the selection of Open Source Portfolio (OSP) as the school-wide ePortfolio tool, this section outlines the work that has been completed and how that work has informed the functional requirements for a campus-wide deployment of ePortfolios at the SOE.

Aligning Courses, Standards, and Artifacts

In 2003, the then Dean, John Poster, formed a faculty committee to align the Michigan State Standards for beginning teachers with courses offered at the SOE. By aligning standards and courses, assignments could be identified from specific courses to serve as artifacts for students to submit to their portfolio in order to demonstrate their attainment of specific standards. In the process of aligning standards and courses, the committee identified several issues that would need to be addressed by governing faculty before proceeding with the integration of portfolios at the SOE. Many of the issues that were raised by the committee were primarily policy questions, including how do state standards align with UM-D, SOE's goals; what is the meaning of basic proficiency; does requiring faculty to incorporate specific assignments impinge on academic freedom; and will portfolios be used as a means of program assessment and course alignment. Other issues would drive the functional requirements for tool adoption, including who would own student portfolios; how to manage access between students and faculty/administrators; how can portfolios demonstrate individual development over time; by what process should faculty assess student portfolios; and how to add materials into the portfolio.

The technological requirements for implementing school-wide ePortfolios were further refined from 2003-2005. Documented in ePortfolio Committee meeting notes from September 23, 2005, the minimum requirements included enabling students, faculty, and administrators to:

- Create a customized portfolio structure that clearly identifies the requirements that teaching candidate must satisfy.
- Track students' progress as they submit artifacts to their portfolios; review and comment on individual artifacts or a student's entire body of work.
- Evaluate individual artifacts or the entire portfolio to assess competency with respect to certification requirements.
- Generate progress reports documenting individual submissions and scores, as well as the progress of the entire program.
- Organize, aggregate, and disaggregate data required for the accreditation process.
- Create a system that would be compatible with other ePortfolios used by some disciplines within the SOE, such as the Science Ed program.

- Allow students access to their individual portfolios.
- Allow faculty access to student portfolios.
- Provide initial training and on-going support for faculty, staff, and students.
- Provide online tools that will interface with links relevant to ePortfolio development, such as the Michigan Department of Education's Curriculum Framework.

Selecting an ePortfolio System

In order to meet these requirements, the ePortfolio Committee explored a variety of options and tools for creating a viable ePortfolio system. This included reviewing commercial applications as well as utilizing UM-D's Information Technology Services (ITS) department for building a customized, local application. At this point in the process the use of an open source portfolio was not considered, as committee members were not aware of the existence of this option.

Commercial Applications

Two commercial applications, LiveText and TaskStream, were identified as best matches for the SOE's needs. Both of these applications could offer hosted solutions for students and faculty to create ePortfolios to be shared with others for review. They would also allow faculty to assess student learning and administrators to aggregate data for reporting purposes. Despite each system's potential, neither was implemented because each application lacked the flexibility to modify competencies to be school specific and the required scaffolding to help students tailor their individual ePortfolios. Additionally, once the recommendations of the committee were presented to the Provost's Office, both were determined to be cost prohibitive for the school and for students. Both TaskStream and LiveText had administration costs that would be charged to the university as well as individual costs that would be assessed to students.

In-House/Local Resources

It was quickly determined that the ITS department at UM-D lacked the resources and capacity to develop, host and maintain a reliable ePortfolio system. However, in order to move forward with ePortfolios, many SOE professors utilized local resources (i.e. WYSIWIG HTML editors, UM-D server space, and internal personnel for trainings, etc.) to create ePortfolios for students to use in individual classes. This approach was implemented by faculty members from Science Education, Language Arts, Educational Technology and in the Michigan Teachers' Technology Education Network (MITTEN) learning community. These initiatives evolved independent of one another and resulted in the creation of several discrete ePortfolio systems rather than a school-wide system designed to meet the needs of *all* departments, faculty and students. This meant that students had to learn several different systems in order to meet the requirements of their individual classes. In addition, these ePortfolios were largely used to showcase a student's work for a specific class and lacked meaningful reflection on learning. In essence, the portfolios represented what the students did (i.e. the artifacts they created) in the class but not what they learned or how their thinking about the profession of teaching had evolved.

Another problem with this system of ePortfolios was that while the use of local resources provided great flexibility for faculty to define the requirements and structure of student portfolios, there were limitations in how finished ePortfolios could be used for administrative purposes. Because students were creating their ePortfolios as standalone websites, data was not systematically being collected that could be aggregated for accreditation or that could result in progress reports for students or faculty. There were also limitations in how faculty could provide feedback to portfolio pages and how student work on portfolios for different disciplines (i.e. Science Education and MITTEN) could be intertwined. Students ended up with several different, and somewhat disconnected, portfolios each representing work completed in a specific course rather than a single comprehensive portfolio that represented growth and learning across the entire curriculum. This was clearly a disjointed and inadequate way to implement ePortfolios across the school.

The Open Source Option

As the SOE explored different ePortfolio models, a parallel initiative was underway at the main U of M campus in Ann Arbor (UM-AA). In January 2004, UM-AA, in collaboration with Indiana University, MIT, and Stanford, joined together to consolidate their educational software tools into an open source collection of tools known as the Sakai Project (http://sakaiproject.org/portal/site/sakai-home) (Unicon, 2009). The Sakai community is made up of several educational institutions working together to develop a range of open source applications around a collaboration and learning environment (CLE). These applications include online course management tools as well as ePortfolio and administrative tools that can be used to help facilitate different types of teaching and learning. One of the tools developed by the Sakai community is a course management environment, which is used throughout the University of Michigan system and known as CTools. CTools provides users with multiple ways to communicate and collaborate through the use of chat, discussion boards, forums, blogs, internal e-mail and Wikis. In addition, professors can create lesson plans, learning modules and assignments within CTools to support students in face-to-face, hybrid or fully online courses.

While the UM-AA was joining forces with other members of the Sakai project, a separate open source community initiative decided to build its new release of Open Source Portfolio (OSP) using the Sakai framework. This merger allowed OSP to leverage "the common software infrastructure and services of the Sakai framework and the growing Sakai community (Coppola, 2005)". This was of interest to UM-AA, since the campus was already committed to using Sakai as their primary course management system and OSP would provide additional functionality for the integration of portfolios into courses and programs.

Benefits of Adopting OSP

The adoption of OSP for school-wide deployment offered many benefits, both financially and technologically that neither the in-house models nor commercial applications could provide. In addition, the OSP system could be tailored to address both the institution centered need for assessment and the student-centered need for integrative learning, self-expression, and professional identity development. The OSP system also provided a customizable solution that was a cost-effective way to make ePortfolios available to the entire SOE.

Cost-Effectiveness of OSP

Given that faculty members were already familiar with the Sakai interface, using another tool within the same environment minimized the amount of training required for faculty, which reduced the start-up costs for implementing OSP. As stated by Wheeler, "minimizing change is one tactic for achieving sustainable economics through lower IT costs (2004, p. 12)". Additionally, because UM is interested in deploying OSP across the entire university system, the cost of customization and ongoing development is shared among several departments and programs. This approach allows for development to be controlled locally, even if not at the school or program level, without requiring each program to have development support on staff.

Costs are further distributed since the Sakai-OSP community, consisting of over 10 institutions, maintains the OSP open source code, and therefore shares in the cost. The Sakai Foundation oversees the ongoing development of the system, which ensures that the code will be kept current and that the interests of multiple institutions are addressed.

Customization of OSP

The ability to customize the core functions and scaffolding within OSP offered many benefits to the SOE. This flexibility allowed for the development of a portfolio structure that included requirements of earning a teaching credential, while also allowing objects submitted to the portfolio to be attached to program defined competencies and certification requirements. For example, faculty at the SOE have created question prompts and rubrics specific to their teacher certification program that are incorporated into the tool to help guide students as they create their portfolios.

The core functions of OSP integrate common features needed by many institutions, including accreditation collection and reporting of data. Features included within OSP allow the SOE to review individual student artifacts or to review the entire portfolio and to aggregate student data for accreditation. Currently, reporting tools for organizing data and generating progress reports are not available within OSP, but are under development.

Authentication to access Sakai is managed centrally on the main campus in Ann Arbor, allowing access controls to portfolios to be easily maintained within OSP. Students and programs can control who has access to student portfolios. A program can assign faculty, staff, or administrators mentor status that will allow them to see the work of students and students can share their portfolios with individuals both in and outside the university. Mentors and students can also be grouped so that mentors can only see their group of students. Additionally, because OSP is being adopted as a school-wide tool, portfolios that are developed across programs will be compatible and easy for students to consolidate to create a portfolio that represents their growth and learning across the entire certification program rather than just a single course. To provide a better sense of how OSP is actually being used at the SOE, the following section describes the process of implementing the ePortfolio system within the school.

Process of Implementation

Once OSP was selected, a presentation was given to the entire SOE faculty in order to familiarize them with the ePortfolio tool and provide them with an opportunity to be a part of the ePortfolio implementation process. Considering that the SOE faculty would be asked to implement the use of the OSP system, and support students in developing integrative ePortfolios in their courses, it was vital to have their buy-in. This initial presentation included an overview of the integrative pedagogy faculty would need to adopt in their courses and provided insight into the important role ePortfolios could play within the SOE. The end result was that a large portion of the faculty became invested in the idea of using the ePortfolio system with students, making the incorporation of ePortfolios into the teacher education program more faculty driven and not administratively dictated.

Following this presentation, faculty approved the adoption of OSP and a series of planning meetings were held to revisit and revise previous decisions about the specific layout, functionality and features that would be available in the ePortfolio. Attendees at these planning sessions included administrators, faculty and technology support personnel from the SOE. Each member of the planning group brought a different perspective to the implementation process and this helped to ensure that the needs of all stakeholders were represented. Administrators expressed their need to have a portfolio system that would be robust enough to support a growing student population while at the same time providing access to the data and information required to meet national accreditation standards. Faculty members indicated the need to have a system that was intuitive

to learn and could accommodate a wide range of representations of student learning. Technology support personnel stressed the need to have a system that could operate within the existing technological infrastructure of the SOE.

Piloting the ePortfolio

Since many of the features requested by the SOE faculty and administration had already been developed and were in use by other departments, the design and development of the SOE ePortfolio was accomplished with minimal iterations. The next step in the implementation process was to pilot the ePortfolio with a small group of students. This pilot was conducted across multiple terms with a variety of different classes as indicated by the schedule below.

- Summer 2008
  ○ EDD 486/586: Environmental Interpretation
- Fall 2008 Semester
  ○ EXPS 420: Science Capstone
  ○ EDC 412: Seminar in Early Childhood Education
- Winter 2009 Semester
  ○ EXPS 420: Science Capstone
- Fall 2009 Semester
  ○ EDC 300: Educational Psychology
  ○ EDT 211/511: Technology in Secondary Education
  ○ EXPS 420: Science Capstone
  ○ EDC 412: Seminar in Early Childhood Education

In each class where the ePortfolio was introduced, students were provided with two different types of training that included technical training as well as instruction on content creation (meta-reflection) for the ePortfolio. During the technical training, students were shown how to edit their own portfolios, add samples of work, upload different types of files and publish their finished portfolios.

During content creation training, students learned more about the kinds of work samples and artifacts they might want to include in their portfolios and how to write compelling meta-reflections, which would become a Work Showcase page, that described the value of a particular learning experience, including the knowledge and skills they gained, and how they were going to apply their learning to other situations. The UM ePortfolio Team provided both the technical and content creation training with support from SOE faculty. This arrangement modeled the training for faculty and helped them become more confident about leading the training on their own. Students were provided technical support via e-mail, phone and one-on-one training for the duration of the term to ensure their success in the project. Several impressive portfolios were created during the pilot process and Figure 1 is a screenshot that shows a Work Showcase page from one of those samples.

Students were asked for their feedback and suggestions throughout the pilot process and one common message echoed by many students was the need for more training and support in the development of their ePortfolios. As a way to provide that additional training, the SOE developed an Introduction to Education course intended to be taken by incoming students in their first term. This new course will be devoted, in part, to introducing students to the ePortfolio and will provide them with multiple opportunities to learn the technical aspects of the system as well as how to create different content elements for their portfolios. Ideally, students will leave this introduction course with a solid foundation in the ePortfolio and they will be able to build on that knowledge with each subsequent class they take in the certification program.

Development of Faculty Portfolios

In addition to piloting the ePortfolio in the courses listed above, all faculty members were invited to learn more about the OSP system and the integrative learning approach by attending two optional training sessions. The focus of these sessions was similar to the training provided to the students who participated in the pilot. During the first session, UM ePortfolio team members walked faculty through the process of selecting relevant learning

Figure 1. Work showcase from student ePortfolio

experiences, reflecting on those experiences and developing representations of their learning to be included in their portfolios. The second session was devoted to learning about the technical aspects of the ePortfolio. Faculty members who attended the second session were given the chance to start building their own portfolios. Several individuals, including all untenured faculty, took advantage of these sessions. To further promote the development of faculty portfolios, the Dean of the SOE gave faculty the choice to submit their tenure and promotion materials as an ePortfolio rather than as a traditional paper-based portfolio. Two non-tenured professors took advantage of this option and submitted their tenure and promotion materials for their four-year review.

Lessons Learned

Even though the process of implementing OSP at the SOE is still ongoing, there have been a variety of lessons learned up to this point that are worth noting. First of all, as with any decision of this magnitude, it is vital to have buy-in from faculty and staff when looking to implement a new technological system such as an ePortfolio. Different individuals have different opinions and apprehensions about technology and in order for everyone to feel comfortable it is important that they have the chance to experiment with new systems and get a sense of what they are going to be expected to do. Part of getting people to support the use of a new technology involves providing adequate training and support so that they can become proficient in the use of the tools without feeling overburdened.

In addition to providing training on the use of the technology it has also been necessary to provide extensive training on the use and purpose of ePortfolios as well. Participating in thoughtful reflection on one's own learning does not come naturally and helping individuals see an ePortfolio as more than just a repository of artifacts requires time and training. For example, specific training

sessions were held for faculty that focused on how to conduct generative interviews and how to identify emergent themes from the interviews in one's ePortfolio. As SOE students and faculty gain skill in uncovering and representing their tacit knowledge in ePortfolios, the value of the experience becomes apparent to portfolio creators and viewers alike.

The pedagogical shift needed to implement the IKPP required significant changes to student and faculty assumptions and approaches to teaching and learning. Faculty members needed to rethink the notion that they were teaching individual classes and envision a more integrative and holistic view of preparing students to learn for life. Likewise, students needed to learn to view their ePortfolios as vehicles to support lifelong learning within and beyond SOE. This included realizing that the contents of a given portfolio should focus on the development of a professional identity rather than specific assignments from an individual class. Many of the SOE faculty expressed an interest in personally experiencing IKPP for their own development and to better facilitate the process with students. This was viewed as a key component in helping all faculty and students make the necessary shift in pedagogical approach.

In addition to shifting the approach of faculty and students, it became clear early on that there was a need for work to be done within individual departments before the ePortfolio implementation could be successful. This included needing to re-think the goals of specific programs, creating portfolio "touchpoints" across the curriculum that could be used to demonstrate student learning, altering current systems of academic credit and modifying existing courses, assignments and feedback mechanisms. Even though it would require this additional work, adoption of the Integrative Knowledge portfolio was seen as a curricular and educational change process that would help the SOE to prepare more integrative, adaptive and reflective lifelong learners and leaders.

Another challenge faced by the SOE was the fact that faculty in their respective courses were already using many different ePortfolio systems. Therefore, it was important to make sure that the new school-wide ePortfolio contained the functionality and capability of all the disparate systems that were already in use. Many individuals had invested time, energy and resources into the content specific ePortfolio systems they were using so making the switch to a new tool was not always easy. However, adopting a school-wide system enabled faculty to rethink the role of ePortfolios as a means to reflect the growth of the student across the entire program of study rather than just an individual class, content area, or program. It also meant that students only had to learn one ePortfolio system, which allowed them to become proficient more quickly with the tool.

FUTURE RESEARCH DIRECTIONS

The implementation of ePortfolios at the UM-Dearborn, SOE is still a work in progress, which makes it an area that is rich with research possibilities. One area of interest is investigating the effectiveness of the Introduction to Education course as a way to train students about the ePortfolio. Since this course is intended to build a foundation for the students it is imperative to learn how to provide the most effective instruction so that students leave the class feeling competent and confident in adding to their ePortfolios.

Before ePortfolios can be fully implemented at the SOE the faculty will need to make decisions about what artifacts of work students should include from the various classes they take in order to create a comprehensive and accurate representation of their learning and competencies. The process of selecting these artifacts will no doubt take a great deal of time and effort and chronicling this process will provide valuable insight into the types of work and experiences we value and the ways in which we structure our courses to insure

that students complete the teacher education program prepared to enter the classroom.

As has been mentioned previously in this chapter, ePortfolios make it possible to include multimedia based artifacts that are not easily incorporated in traditional hardcopy portfolios. In addition, an ePortfolio is a dynamic representation of learning that can be easily edited and updated at anytime by the author. This, of course, is not the case with a paper-based portfolio submitted for review in a three-ringed binder, which will only reflect changes when new copies are printed and distributed. As the use of ePortfolios becomes more prevalent by both students and faculty it will be revealing to see how the digital nature of ePortfolios changes the way people choose to represent their learning and growth. How will multimedia elements such as videos, podcasts and interactive images be used to demonstrate knowledge? What process will be used to judge the value of these elements such that individuals with less technological ability are not adversely impacted? These questions will need to be explored in order to learn more about ePortfolios and how they can be used to assess professional growth and learning.

In addition to tracking how people represent themselves digitally, it will also be important to better understand how others interpret ePortfolios. Over this past year, there has been anecdotal evidence that through ePortfolios, faculty have learned about facets of students lives that were previously inaccessible to them (i.e. their life beyond the classroom and ways of thinking). In turn, faculty members have been able to use this additional insight to modify their curriculum to better address student needs. Moving forward, data should be collected to address the following questions: How do student representations of self in ePortfolios affect faculty perceptions of students? How does faculty modify their curriculum as a result of new knowledge about students gained through ePortfolios?

One of the many outcomes of the explosion of Web 2.0 tools over the past several years is the availability of social networks and media that allow web users to connect, collaborate and communicate. These social tools provide numerous opportunities for users to share information about themselves by posting comments, images, videos and tagging elements with metadata that can be searched and re-purposed by other users. The end result is a vast network of users that are connected through relationships, experiences and the content they have shared online. ePortfolios stand in contrast to this idea of socially mediated content since they are intended to be created by a single author and represent the thinking and learning of that individual. It will be interesting to observe the evolution of ePortfolios to see if they adapt any of the collaborative aspects of social networks. OSP would seem particularly prone to this kind of adaptation since it is built on an open source platform, which relies on collaborative work and the open sharing of innovation. Determining an effective way to reconcile the notion of the social creation of digital content with the individualistic aspects of an ePortfolio will be an important area to explore and research going forward.

CONCLUSION

The process of implementing ePortfolios at UM-Dearborn has provided the faculty and staff involved with the project multiple opportunities for reflection both on individual learning and growth and reflection on the teacher education program as a whole. While much of the work remains to be done, several important steps have been taken including gathering input and feedback from the various stakeholders and making sure to incorporate that information into the design of the ePortfolio to be used by the SOE faculty and students. It is quite evident that this will continue to be a learning experience for all participants.

REFERENCES

Annis, L., & Jones, C. (1995). Student portfolios: Their objectives, development, and use . In Associates, P. S. (Ed.), *Improving College Teaching* (pp. 181–190). Bolton: Anker.

Barrett, H. C. (2000). Create your own electronic portfolio. *Learning and Leading with Technology, 27*, 14–21.

Cambridge, B. L. (2001). *Electronic portfolios as knowledge builders*. Washington, D.C.: American Association for Higher Education.

Clark, E. J., & Eynon, B. (2009). E-portfolios at 2.0--Surveying the field. *Peer Review, 11*(1), 18–23.

Coppola, C. (2005). Understanding the open source portfolio Retrieved June 10, 2009, from http://www.rsmart.com/assets/understandingOSP_Dec2005.pdf

Diller, K., & Phelps, S. (2008). Learning outcomes, portfolios and rubrics, oh my! Authentic assessment of an information literacy program. *Libraries and the Academy, 8*(1), 75–88.

Eynon, B. (2009). It helped me see a new me: ePortfolio, learning and change at LaGuardia Community College Retrieved June 12, 2009, from http://www.academiccommons.org/commons/essay/eportfolio-learning-and-change

Higher Learning Commission. (2003). Handbook of accreditation 3rd. Retrieved June 8, 2009, from http://www.ncahlc.org/download/Handbook03.pdf

Inoue, Y. (2009). Linking self-directed lifeline learning and e-learning: Priorities for institutions of higher education . In Stansfield, M., & Connolly, T. (Eds.), *Institutional Transformation Through Best Practices in Virtual Campus Development: Advancing E-learning Policies* (pp. 22–37). Hershey, PA: IGI Global.

Jafari, A. (2004). The sticky ePortfolio system: Tackling challenges and identifying attributes. *EDUCAUSE Review, 39*(4), 38–49.

Lorenzo, G., & Ittelson, J. (2005a). *An Overview of E-Portfolios*: Educause Learning Initiative.

Lorenzo, G., & Ittelson, J. (2005b). *Demonstrating and Assessing Student Learning with E-Portfolios*. Educause Learning Initiative.

Peet, M. (2008). *Creating Institutional Pathways for Transformation and Change: Educating for Leadership and Social Innovation*. Paper presented at the Annual Meeting for the Association for the Study of Higher Education.

Peet, M. (in press). The integrative knowledge portfolio process: A program guide for educating reflective practitioners and lifelong learners, from http://services.aamc.org/30/mededportal/servlet/segment/mededportal/information/

Richardson, H., & Ward, R. (2005). *Developing and Implementing a Methodology for Reviewing E-portfolio Products*. The Centre for Recording Achievement.

Siemens, G. (2004). ePortfolios Retrieved June, 11, 2009, from http://www.elearnspace.org/Articles/eportfolios.htm

Teacher Education Accreditation Council. (2009). Quality principles for teacher education programs Retrieved June 8, 2009, from http://www.teac.org/?page_id=170

Unicon (2009). Sakai Collaboration and Learning Environment. Retrieved June 10, 2009, from http://www.unicon.net/opensource/sakai

Wheeler, B. (2004). Open Source 2007: How did this happen? *EDUCAUSE Review*, (July/August): 13–27.

Wolf, K., & Dietz, M. E. (1998). Teaching portfolios: Purposes and possibilities. *Teacher Education Quarterly, 25*(1), 9–22.

Young, J. (2002). 'E-Portfolios' Could Give Students a New Sense of Their Accomplishments. *The Chronicle of Higher Education, 48*(26).

KEY TERMS AND DEFINITIONS

Accreditation: The process of gaining official approval of a program of study by demonstrating how required standards are being met.

Assessment Management Portfolios: Portfolios designed to capture evidence of students' learning for institutions often to help make a case for accreditation.

Integrative Knowledge Portfolio: Portfolios designed to represent both the tacit and explicit knowledge of the learner through the presentation of artifacts, experiences and reflections on learning.

Metacognition: Thinking about one's own thinking and being aware of one's mental processes.

Sakai: A community of open-source developers made up of several educational institutions working together to develop a range of open source applications around a collaboration and learning environment (CLE).

Tacit Knowledge: Knowledge that is implied but not expressed.

Chapter 10
LeMill:
A Case for User–Centered Design and Simplicity in OER Repositories

Tarmo Toikkanen
Aalto University School of Art and Design, Finland

Jukka Purma
Aalto University School of Art and Design, Finland

Teemu Leinonen
Aalto University School of Art and Design, Finland

ABSTRACT

LeMill is an open source OER repository where the emphasis has been placed on designing a service to meet the actual needs of teachers preparing for classes. The development of LeMill has utilized open, collaborative, and iterative design methods and many features have been refined or redesigned during the process. Emphasis on design work has helped LeMill avoid and fix problems that generally pester OER repositories because of their origins as learning object repositories. The authors recognize that LeMill, as an open source project, has had the rare benefit of a long, structured dissemination phase incorporating actual teacher training. Even when developers and designers try to keep teachers in mind, actual behavioral patterns and needs appear only after the service has been in use. Therefore systems should initially be flexible enough to allow changes resulting from new findings.

INTRODUCTION

This chapter starts with a short history of open educational resources (OERs) and the repositories supporting them. The authors will show how current OER repositories are still based on earlier models of disseminating learning objects through learning object repositories. The shift from learn-

ing objects to OERs, however, has created new challenges that OER repositories have not yet fully tackled. They will briefly describe these challenges. Then they will explain the design process of LeMill and give a short overview of its features. Finally, the authors will return to the general challenges in fostering collaborative OER creation and show how some of these have been met in the development of LeMill.

DOI: 10.4018/978-1-61520-917-0.ch010

The Library Model of a Learning Object Repository

Between 1997 and 2001, various projects involved in digital educational resources created a common standard for Learning Objects (LOs). In this standard, a LO was vaguely defined as "Any entity, digital or non-digital, which can be used, re-used and referenced during technology-supported learning" (IEEE, 2002). Standardization enabled the moving of LO metadata across repositories. Along with the general optimism related to the Internet, there was a proliferation of Learning Object Repositories (LORs) and related projects. LORs were seen as having potential for providing a cost-effective way to share reusable learning resources with a wide audience (e.g. Downes, 2001).

Because of the initial vagueness of the LO definition, there was room to rethink and redefine learning objects and how they should be used. Wiley (2000) linked them with instructional design and instructional theory, assuming that the creation of learning objects was a task best left to instructional designers. Bannan-Ritland et al. (2000) in turn linked them with constructionist learning. The publishing and brokering of learning objects was seen as a growing new market (Johnson, 2003). Much effort was put into various brokerage systems to ensure that publishers could control their resources (Anido et al., 2002; Van Assche & Massart, 2004).

Learning objects were understood to be discrete entities that needed to be stored and protected, and repositories were modeled after the existing workflows between the publishing industry and libraries. In the library model, learning objects are acquired from publishers and catalogued into a repository by curators. The curators write descriptive metadata if it is not already provided by the publishers. Repository users search by using metadata fields and select interesting LOs from the results. The selected LOs are then retrieved for use. Collis and Strijker (2004) separate the process into five phases: *Obtaining, Labeling, Offering, Selecting,* and *Using.*

Some of the foundational projects that were instrumental in developing the learning object standard are not repositories in the sense that they store learning objects onsite. Some, like MERLOT[1] only provide metadata and links to actual objects. The ARIADNE project provides a federated search over many 'knowledge pools' and passes the requested learning objects to the user as archived file sets (Duval et al., 2001; Forte et al., 1997). McGreal (2007) analyzed 58 repositories and categorized them into either content repositories, linking or metadata repositories, or hybrid repositories based on whether they store content inside the repository or not. This categorization displays the importance of metadata in the LOR discussion; whatever LORs are, at least they have metadata.

Although early repositories designed their infrastructures to support paid content, the majority of their content was free from the beginning, coming from schools, academia, or the public sector. In Duval et al. (2001) 88% of ARIADNE content was reported to be free, and at the end of 2003 only 1.8% of MERLOT linked resources had been marked as involving costs. Instead of joining existing repositories, commercial operators often attempted to create their own repositories and user communities around their products.

Criticism on Learning Objects and Repurposing Repositories

The labeling of just about anything as a 'learning object', in addition to the unfounded promises made about them, received criticism from learning technology theorists. Wiley (2003), McCormick (2003) and Friesen (2004) based their critique on the contextual nature of learning and the decontextual aspirations of LOs. Wide-scale personalized learning would require automation, and automation would require decontextual, machine-readable, Lego-like learning objects. The result would be a chain of decontextual objects, with no capability of meaningfulness for the learner (Wiley). Wiley, McCormick, Friesen, as well as Leinonen (2005) all suggested that since learning objects are so ineffectual at implementing pedagogy, pedagogy should be separated from learning objects. Instead of learning objects, the discussion should be about learning resources that emphasize the people using the resources (Leinonen).

Studies of the actual use of learning object repositories support this criticism. In Recker and Dorward (2004) it was found that LORs were used to find 'pretty much frills and extras' to support teaching. Uncertainty about copyright issues and nonstandard formats hindered resource modification. Studies on the ICT use of teachers in the United Kingdom have confirmed a steady increase in the use of digital resources in lesson planning, but also that most teachers use digital resources they have created themselves (Kitchen et al., 2007; Smith et al., 2008). Most of the teachers who created their own digital resources shared them within their school (86%), but only a few (17%) shared them with other schools. About a third of secondary school teachers adapted resources created by others to suit their own needs (Kitchen et al.). It does seem like the loose definition of a learning object—as any digital resource that can be used in teaching—is reflected in the actual use of LORs.

Akpinar and Simsek (2007) examined the claim that LOs should be designed by professional instructional designers (made by Wiley, 2000) and found out that K-12 teachers produced LOs of equal quality to those of instructional designers. The quality was tested both with a dedicated evaluation tool (LORI; see Akpinar, 2008) and with actual learning results. The only significant difference was that teachers used more text and less multimedia assets (Akpinar).

Margaryan and Littlejohn (2008) explored the differences between the perspectives of curators and users on LORs and emphasized how the needs of users are short-term and contextual. Learning

object repositories have answered to the perceived needs of teachers by adding community features such as recommendations, reviews, personal collections, and folksonomies. Most of these features are not part of any metadata schema, and as such they do not easily travel from one repository to other.

This development towards communities instead of federated networks cannot be separated from the larger shift towards social media and Web 2.0. An important part of this shift was the development of new, more open licensing schemas and the resources that embrace them.

Open Educational Resources

The concept of Open Educational Resources (OERs) was first introduced in 2002 at the UNESCO Forum on the Impact of Open Courseware for Higher Education in Developing Countries. There isn't an official definition of an OER, but there is a shared understanding that OERs should be free, licensed in such manner that modification is possible, and if the resource is software or other compiled type, the source code needed for modification should be available. OERs are part of the larger free culture movement, aiming to make important parts of human culture and knowledge available to everyone for free (Benkler, 2005).

Spearheaded by an ambitious investment by MIT, OpenCourseWare (OCW) has had an even larger impact on online education than OERs. MIT OCW[2] has agreed to provide MIT's courses online as free resources and has created strong institutional tools to help lecturers publish their resources. Institutions that have agreed to the same goals have formed an Open Courseware Consortium[3]. MIT OCW and OCW members usually publish full courses. In the OCW context, OERs are often used to represent a resource for an entire course. In further discussion about OERs in this chapter, OERs are understood to be resources with smaller granularity, comparable to LOs.

The OER movement requires a licensing scheme that allows modifications and the re-publishing of derived works. Creative Commons[4] (CC) has established itself as the leading licensing model for open content, both in the educational sector and in general. CC provides several different licenses from which the author can choose. Common to all licenses is the requirement to attribute the author whenever presenting their works. Most CC licenses do not restrict the use of a licensed work in any way, allowing its use in any context. This makes CC-licensed resources especially easy to work within the educational sector.

With the increasing popularity of the OER movement, existing learning object repositories have begun to revise their content to see if they are able to fit the OER definition. For example, MERLOT is now an OER repository. Just like the learning object definition helped to create new LORs, OERs have inspired projects to develop OER repositories, the most notable being OER Commons[5]. OER repositories have the benefit of ignoring the complexities of digital rights management (McGreal, 2005), but taking advantage of the freedoms to edit, modify, and republish OERs requires features that don't fit easily into the traditional library model. In the next section we review these specific features and their problems in OER repositories.

The Problem with Collaboration

Although many OER repositories are based on existing LORs, there are some key differences that make OERs unwieldy as learning objects. OER repositories need to assume that resources are mutable, as OERs and their metadata can change, be erroneous, or of poor quality. To allow editing by the repository community, OERs should reside inside the repository, not just be linked to it. If OERs are mutable, then repositories should be able to contain many drafts, stubs, or other unfinished low quality resources. Syndication of unfinished objects needs to be considered, as it

reduces the quality of search results but may offer new collaboration possibilities.

A major problem for OERs is the demand for reviewed and quality-assured resources. Some OER repositories try to create a review process by mechanical means, creating a publication workflow where a resource has to be reviewed or accepted (OER Commons), or can be sent to a review board to gain some kind of quality assurance (MERLOT). Others try softer, community-based approaches, where teachers are called upon to write reviews of resources or to rate them (MERLOT, Connexions, LRE for Schools). Having some quality control and quality assurance is deemed important by teachers (Wilson, 2008) and researchers (Akpinar, 2008; Van Assche & Vuorikari, 2006), but all statements about resource quality can be misleading if the resources are changing and collaboratively developed. In the worst case, a bad review for a resource discourages efforts to make it better, as the bad review or rating will remain even after the improvements are in place.

Having a fixed review process is also problematic for multilingual and multinational repositories. A resource's success or failure to cover some part of a curriculum may be a major factor when determining the resource's worth, but it may be an invalid review for some other curriculum, or for countries where there are no fixed requirements in a curriculum. A truly multinational repository would require multiple different review processes, each fitted to the requirements of the respective community—a formidable challenge to implement. In Wilson (2008) the same OER repository[6] was introduced to distance learning operations in both South Africa and an open university in the United Kingdom. In South Africa, the staff saw the resources as potentially fitting into their curriculum, whereas in the UK the resources were seen suitable only to non-accrediting studies.

Even now, when collaboration and teachers creating resources for other teachers have become familiar themes, spontaneous collaboration is rare. In Connexions[7], which is hailed as one of the most successful OER repositories, Petrides et al. (2008) found that 78% of resources had only one author working on them. In the OLCOS roadmap for 2012 (Geser, 2007), turning educational repositories into communities of practice was seen as a requirement for successful user-contributed content. In the JISC roadmap for 2013 (Heery, 2009) there is a call for more incentives and support for teachers sharing their materials in open repositories. Petrides and Jimes (2008) reported a successful teacher-based spontaneous collaborative OER project from South Africa, but replicating conditions for this success seems unattainable—one of the main motivators was the genuine local need for drastically cheaper science teaching resources.

Monge et al. (2008) gave six strategies to increase 'Web 2.0' features in repositories in order to improve participation in authoring OERs. Interestingly, it seems that the OER repository and teacher community 'LeMill' had already implemented them a few years prior:

1. Clear Authorship and Use License Attribution Systems
2. Rapid Content Creation Systems
3. Indexable Content for Search Engines (Permalinks)
4. Social Tagging Systems
5. Reputation Systems for Content
6. Social Recommendation Systems

The next sections describe the work made in designing the LeMill OER repository, and how we have tried to solve the problem of collaborative creation of OERs.

Designing LeMill

The OER repository and teacher community entitled 'LeMill' was developed as part of the three year CALIBRATE project (Durando, 2008) and was considered one of its most successful outcomes (Kárpáti, 2008). LeMill's development goals were both to foster grassroots activity among European teachers (including encouraging them to start authoring OERs) and to increase their use of web-based educational resources in their own teaching. LeMill was originally presented as a 'toolbox for teachers', not as an OER repository. The CALIBRATE project also contained a separate work package to develop the Learning Resource Exchange for Schools[8], a more typical LOR with federated search and paid content functions, and some community features. The initial division between 'portal' and 'toolbox' helped LeMill focus on collaborative authoring and resource creation.

Developing LeMill

An important part of the OER movement is the belief that software to be used in education should also be free and preferably open source. It was therefore obvious that LeMill would be an open source project. There was a genuine need to keep things open: LeMill needed to develop into something that no one could envision at the start of the project. The people involved in the work were located in four European countries, so issues of communication, cultural differences, language barriers, and participants' hidden agendas were very real. Distributed development where teams are not colocated has traditionally been a major challenge in software development. Dispersed development where individual team members are not colocated is an even larger challenge. An agile development methodology was needed to counter many of these problems.

The practices of the development project were based on Scrum (Schwaber & Beedle, 2001) and XP (Beck, 1999), were fine-tuned during the first year of the project, and as they were proving to be successful, were reported in the XP2006 conference (see Toikkanen & Leinonen, 2006). To summarize, this development project focused on transparency on all levels; all meeting agendas and minutes, all tasks, source code, and other logs were publicly available on the web for anyone to see. Standards on source code quality, test coverage, work reports, ticket handling, etc., were all written into the project wiki as recommended practices. These rules were not fixed, but rather were modified as needed in order to accommodate the changing nature of the project (Toikkanen and Leinonen).

Research-Based Design with Software as Hypothesis

From the designer's perspective, the chosen software development method can be seen as the machinery that allows designers to operate more freely and to iterate their design decisions. The overall design model used in LeMill development is described as 'research-based design with software as hypothesis' (Leinonen et al., 2008) and is visualized in Figure 1.

During the first iteration (typically two to five weeks), the four main phases of the model are entered one after another. Results from each phase are collected and serve as additional inputs for the following iterations. As the work progresses, design and development tasks may become differentiated, with designers working according to their own schedule, and software developers to

their own. Communication between these two factions happens continuously.

In the case of LeMill, the first phase produced potential scenarios that were used as the starting point for discussions in design workshops with teachers[9]. The first full iteration was completed in one month, resulting in the very first version of the envisioned product. This version was, of course, very rough and was not shown to teachers, but it helped the designers see some of their design ideas in concrete form and helped to refine them. During the following three years of development, a new version was released every two to five weeks. After six months of development, the prototype was shown to teachers and feedback was collected by national validators as well as the main interaction designer. The validation was done simultaneously with the other CALIBRATE product, LRE for Schools. This feedback was translated by national validators and analyzed and distilled into design ideas. The designers then worked out design solutions that were added to the next iteration's work queue. The participatory design process clearly benefited from having the main interaction designer hold most of the LeMill teacher workshops—about 50 so far—and thus

Figure 1. Research-based design with software as hypothesis-model for designing and developing software solutions for research questions (Leinonen et al., 2008).

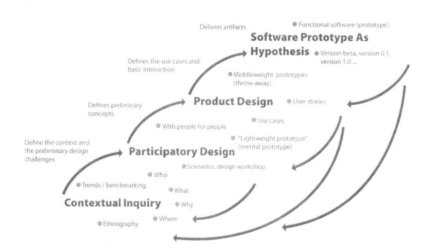

having been able to continuously receive feedback and see how people unfamiliar with LeMill interact with it. All the main developers have also participated in teacher workshops at some point.

The iterative and agile software engineering practices allowed the software developers to quickly re-factor even major portions of the prototype to accommodate the changing design solutions. Thus the designers were not confined by earlier prototypes, but were allowed to change their minds during the project without disrupting the development effort. During the project, numerous ideas were proposed by teachers, developers, and designers and some were worked into design solutions and then implemented. Several ideas were redesigned based on teacher feedback, sometimes refined several times until a good solution was found.

Overview of LeMill

LeMill is a 'web community for finding, authoring and sharing learning resources'[10]. It consists of four main sections: *content*, *methods*, *tools*, and *community*. This division is based on early participatory design meetings, where teachers voiced opinions on what kinds of things they expect to find in a 'teacher's toolbox'. In addition to content, which is what OERs usually provide, they expected to find activities, pedagogical ideas, and ideas for new devices and tools they could use in teaching. Activities and pedagogical ideas merged into methods, and tools were deemed to be so important and different from content and methods that they earned their own section. Community was based on the general need to communicate with teachers with similar subjects and interests.

All resources in LeMill are licensed under the Creative Commons Attribution-Share Alike International license, which guarantees that they can be remixed together and used freely for any purpose. The Attribution clause states that any re-published resources must give attribution to the original authors, while the Share Alike clause states that any derived works must be published using the same license. These clauses make sure that free resources stay free, and also protect the authors' rights by preventing unfair exploitation of the resources while still allowing for their commercial use. LeMill itself is licensed under the GNU Public License (GPL), and can be freely downloaded in source code format[11]. In fact, LeMill is available both as a free service at http://lemill.net, and as free/libre software for setting up your own server.

Layout

LeMill is built on top of Plone[12], a content management system (CMS) that also powers Connexions. Plone supports complex workflows and author roles, and allows for easy design of content types, templates, and other features that were thought to be necessary in the beginning of the development process. Later we had to replace many of these features, as the assumptions they made complicated the user interface of LeMill.

LeMill's four main sections each have a different color scheme, yet have a similar basic layout (Figure 2). On the left is the link to create new resources typical to that section, in the middle is the actual viewable or browsable content, and at the top are section links, links to the user's own page, and language selection links. The left section is always reserved for actions available in the current context, be it a section, a single resource, a member, or a group.

Browsing

When browsing for resources, options are limited, as can be seen in Figure 3. The only actions available are digging further by adding filters that make sense in the respective context.

The section front pages guide users by showing the most important metadata fields and the three most popular terms for each of them (Figure 2). Clicking on metadata field names leads to tag

Figure 2. Front page of LeMill's content section. The organization of the page still shares parts with Plone.

clouds that visualize the distribution of values in that category. Tag clouds give an impression of how many results can be found behind each value. These links and tag clouds also have the secondary effect of making LeMill results visible to search engines, thus implementing suggestion 3 from the list by Monge et al. (2008). The searchability of content also reduces the importance of complete metadata descriptions.

Figure 3. Browsing resources is kept simple by allowing only filters that make sense in a specific context.

It should be emphasized that the word 'metadata' is not used anywhere in LeMill. The user interface uses more natural terms, such as 'browse by language', 'browse by tags', and 'browse media pieces'. When teachers publish resources, LeMill strongly recommends them to add cover images for their works. Cover images are not useful as machine readable metadata, but for humans they can give a quick visual cue about a resource and help in recognizing resources later on.

Viewing resources

When viewing a single resource, the cues for follow-up actions are always placed on the left side of the page (Figure 4). Actions depend on the type and status of the resource. The 'methods' and 'tools' sections have only one resource type each, but the 'content' section has several types of resources. Some of these content resources are either static (media pieces, PDFs) or reference resources outside LeMill, so many options that make sense for other resource types do not work well with them. For example, media pieces cannot

be translated or be kept as drafts. They don't need cover images because they can use thumbnails of themselves.

Both library-based repositories and CMSs try to achieve maximum generality for their objects by designing a single interface and a set of options to fit all resources. We have decided to value context over generality. The CMS background of LeMill made it arduous, as the general implementations of actions and their presentations had to be replaced with specific, appropriate options for each resource type.

Another concession to comfort over generality is to make references themselves into a specific content type. Teachers want to use resources they have found, whether they are OERs or not. This makes LeMill a hybrid repository in McGreal's categories (2007). Without references it would be much more difficult to point out useful institutional resources like museums' collections or the NASA website. Like in MERLOT, the reference itself is a Creative Commons-licensed object, but the referred resource doesn't have to be.

Figure 4. Viewing a resource

For learning resources, there is an option to select the student view (Figure 5, bottom left link). This will further simplify the layout by hiding everything but the content itself and a small link bar that takes the user back to the more complex view. The student view is intended to be the page which teachers use to show resources directly from LeMill.

Creating and Editing Resources

When creating web-based learning resources in LeMill, there are a few subtypes which teachers can choose from: web page, presentation, PILOT[13], exercise, lesson plan, or learning project. These are assembled from elements including chapters of text, images, audio clips when applicable, questionnaires, and other small blocks, which again are dependent on the template. The basic editing is done with a visual editor, which is stripped from options that would encourage creation of badly designed web pages—for example, the color and font cannot be changed. Whenever the user has a form to fill out, all generic links and actions are removed to help the user to focus on the essential task (Figure 6).

Making resource editing simple is a major technical challenge for LeMill, because in many

ways it has to provide a comparable experience with other web based authoring tools. The development team did not have the necessary AJAX expertise to provide features that web-savvy teachers may expect. Also the database structure itself doesn't support the constant writing of small changes that is required for a smooth user experience. Instead, we have made a compromise and divided each resource into blocks, or chapters, that are edited one by one. A similar solution is used in Wikipedia to decrease the chance of conflicting edits.

One important part of resource editing and creation are the permissions governing who is allowed to edit what, as well as keeping the user informed about these restrictions. These features are often the backbone of CMSs. Just as library-based repositories lure developers and designers to emphasize metadata, CMS-based repositories emphasize editing rights, user roles, and document workflows. Here, after initial complications, we have overridden Plone's workflow system and substituted it with a single clear ideology: wiki-like editing. This also implements the first strategy of Monge et al. (2008): clear authorship. The person who first creates the resource is the first author; after that the order of authors is calculated by the

Figure 5. Student view of a resource

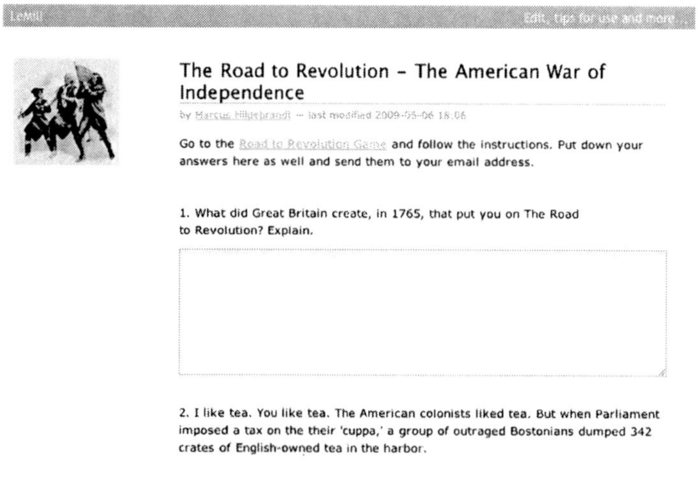

Figure 6. Editing content

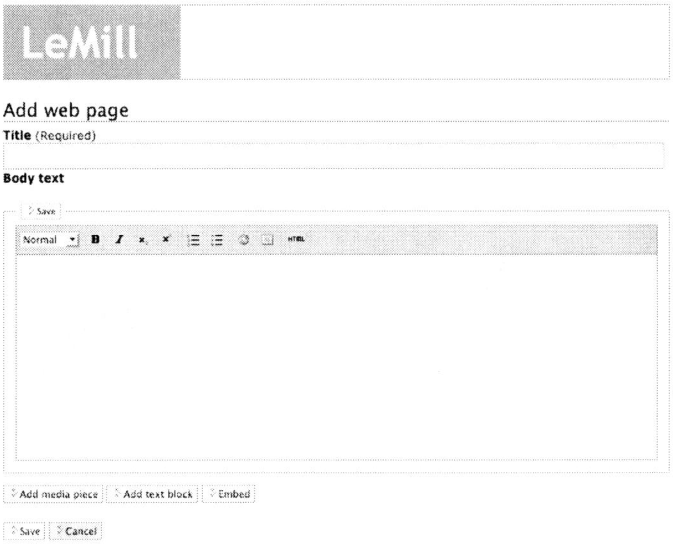

extent of changes they've made, and everyone can make changes.

Methods, tools, and simple content types are always editable by everyone. Because of teachers' expressed reservations about having unfinished work in public view, we have had to add an option to keep learning resources as either public or private drafts. Public drafts omit authors' names so teachers can start a new resource without having their name prominently displayed next to an unfinished draft. Drafts also don't have cover images, thereby providing a visual cue that they are unfinished. Private drafts are invisible until published, but once published are editable by everyone.

Collections and Community Features

A strong interest in interaction with other teachers was expressed in collaborative design sessions. The aim of the project was to encourage collaborative editing of resources with other teachers, so we have tried to tie community features into resource creation. Each user in LeMill has his or her own profile page, which displays a portfolio of resources which he or she has contributed to. When browsing people, users who have been most active in editing, especially editing works not initially theirs, are displayed more prominently.

Individuals can form open groups and invite others to join them. The main purpose of a group (Figure 7) is to take responsibility for certain resources. Any resource can be assigned to a group or several groups. Any discussion related to that resource is also visible on its group's page. When trying to edit a resource assigned to a group, LeMill asks if the user wants to join that group. Groups can also have discussions not tied to any resources, and groups provide their own RSS feeds that make it possible to follow their activities using a news feed reader.

Each individual can also add resources to collections. Collections can be used for any purpose; they can be used as bookmarks, cherry-picking like 'Top Lists' in Amazon, or course or lesson plans. There is one usage case we encourage, which is a 'teaching and learning story'. If a collection has at least one content resource, one tool, one method, and an explanatory description of how these were used together or how they are

Figure 7. Groups collaborate on resources

supposed to be used together, then the collection will be classified as a teaching and learning story. These stories are visible on LeMill's front page as well as on all the resource pages that belong to the story. Learning stories are our version of Learning Design; putting human readability and flexibility before other standards.

Collections also provide functionalities to export and download resources from LeMill, either as independent web pages, SCORM-packages or PDF booklets. A collection can also be viewed in 'student view', when all of the resources in the collection are shown as an ordered and navigable set of pages.

Lessons Learned

This section highlights some of the major insights that were discovered based on the three years of design and development of LeMill, and the continuing work of building a teacher community around LeMill.

Curricula Issues

Within the CALIBRATE project, LeMill was piloted by hundreds of teachers in seven European countries. Within these educational settings, the differences in educational policy are quite challenging. One of the goals in the project was a mapping of the curricula of any two European countries, but this proved to be nearly impossible to complete. The ontological structure of curricula varied greatly, and even the grade systems were different (e.g. in Hungary there are four parallel routes through the primary and secondary education systems, with different courses and goals for each route).

As the mapping of curricula didn't proceed to completion, LeMill had to opt for the lowest common denominators for choosing grade levels and subject areas: grade levels from 1 to 12, and a general selection of 24 subject areas and 3 special classifications (school-community relationship, educational administration, and cross-curricular education). More detailed metadata mapping would inevitably be incompatible with the educational system of some countries, and even this mapping does not fully fit into all European curricula. However, when Estonian teachers started to use Methods in a sense of "to teach curriculum issue X we do Y and Z", we added a new resource template, 'Lesson plan' that allows linking to other resources and free text description of the aims of the lesson. We expect this template to be used in countries where the linking of study materials to curricula has to be made explicit.

Critical Mass

For any OER repository, the amount of useful content needs to reach a certain threshold for a new visitor to see added value and make the effort of integrating that repository into their working routines. Many traditional repositories are pre-filled with commercially created learning objects, and usually meet this criterion. Many open repositories, however, may be challenged in acquiring the necessary amount of useful resources.

In the case of LeMill, none of the content was prefabricated or imported. Everything has been made by LeMill users. Thus the arranged pilot phase was crucial in getting motivated teachers to not only use LeMill but also to author new resources within its repository.

However, as LeMill was deployed in a pan-European setting, and as most primary level teachers aren't very fluent in English (and even if they are, their students often are not), there was a clear need for content in each user's native language. Thus the challenge of critical mass needs to be tackled repeatedly for each new language. If a Polish teacher searches LeMill for content related to her subject area (say, biology) even thousands of available high quality resources in Estonian are not going to help. So for each language area, there would need to be a pilot or other effort, which encourages a group of teachers or content authors

to come in and create resources that, together, can provide value to others of the same language area.

LeMill has one clear advantage in clearing this critical mass challenge. Most OER repositories contain only learning objects, which are resources that can be presented to students during a learning activity. To achieve critical mass, a repository would need to cover dozens of subject areas, at several levels of complexity and difficulty. The required number of good quality resources could be in the range of thousands. However, besides learning objects, LeMill is also a repository of meta-learning objects, specifically descriptions of tools and activities that are directed to the teacher. To achieve critical mass in these categories is much more feasible. Even as little as 30 good descriptions of various pedagogically sound learning activities can serve as a valuable reference to a teacher, and even one hundred descriptions of physical and online tools can do the same. These amounts are easily achievable by a small group of dedicated teachers or other experts within the space of just a few weeks.

At the time of writing this article, the Georgian community has achieved self-sufficiency and produces on average 2.2 new OERs per day. The Estonian community is supported by workshops and competitions, and the Estonian OER production is more uneven: spikes are visible near competition deadlines, and during and after workshops. There is a Finnish AVO-project, which aims to support Open Culture in Finland and which holds LeMill workshops and theme weeks with teachers. The Finnish community aims to concentrate on producing methods and tools from seeds created by the authors of this article.

Special issues of a Multi-Lingual Environment

While use of the English language is becoming increasingly common within school and other educational activities, the level of mastery varies hugely from country to country. And even if an individual teacher is fluent in English, most of her students probably aren't. In Europe, anything that is only available in English cannot become mainstream in the foreseeable future. LeMill was originally tested in seven European countries, but by August of 2009 LeMill had community members representing over 50 languages, and had content authored in over 30 languages. This multitude of languages has presented its own challenges, and for some of these, solutions have been found.

One problem was discovered when the Estonian community became very active on the site, and the amount of Estonian content kept growing. Teachers from other countries started seeing too much Estonian content, and had difficulties finding resources in their own language. For this reason, language filtering was developed. Each member of the LeMill community can specify the languages that they are fluent in on their profile page. Whenever they search or browse the site, they are shown resources in those languages and in that order. To further ease language filtering, it is also tied to the overall interface language. At the top of the LeMill page there is always a list of languages into which the LeMill interface has been translated (currently 11 languages). Selecting any of them also defines the first language of displayed search results.

Another design decision was to make English the default language. Therefore all browse and search views will first list any matching resources in the user interface language, then the languages that the user has in their profile, and finally in English. It seemed to the designers that if people know two languages, the second, more often than not, is English, so it makes sense to show English content at all times.

One of the original goals of LeMill was to allow good content to travel across language barriers. For textual content, this is a major obstacle. LeMill has tools to allow easy translation of content from one language to another. So if a bilingual teacher sees a good resource in one language,

she can simply select the translation function and author a translation in another language. All translations of a resource are linked together, so others can quickly see different language versions of a resource. However, the translations will not be strictly identical, but rather will drift as others keep improving them. This makes it possible to localize each resource further, so in addition to having a resource in one's native language, the resource can also discuss things from a national or local perspective.

The most common route by which a resource written in a minor language ends up translated into another minor language (such as from Finnish to Czech), is through English. So first a bilingual Finnish teacher translates the content to English, and then a bilingual Czech teacher translates it from English to Czech.

Another language issue which remains to be resolved is the use of tags. All resources in LeMill can be described by tags, which do not have language information in them. So the system does not know which tags are in English, or in some other language. Typically this is not a problem, as languages rarely share the same word, but on occasion this is an issue (e.g. in Estonian the word for mold or fungus is 'hallitus', which happens to mean 'government' in Finnish; and mold in Finnish is 'home', which is a common word in English). In practice multilingual tags make tag clouds quite difficult to use, as large language groups tend to dominate the clouds (Figure 8). In LeMill, tag clouds tend to feature words in Estonian and Georgian, which are the two dominant languages. Possible solutions would be to add language information to tags (which isn't easy to do in a way that still makes tag entry simple), deduce language information based on the language of the resource (which isn't very accurate), or to try to match tags to vocabularies (which would not work for identifiers that aren't words in the natural language).

Role of Teacher Training

Our experiences from the CALIBRATE project and in earlier collaborative European projects in the field (see Dean & Leinonen, 2003) show that teacher training plays a key role in the adoption of any system, be it open source or proprietary. Teachers, as a rule, are busy either teaching or preparing to teach. They have very limited time to spend on learning new tools or processes. This may be one reason why social media is being adopted so slowly in the educational sector.

In this project we quickly learned that teachers needed hands-on tutoring. A typical half-day workshop would start with presentations on social media, copyright, open content, and LeMill. This would be followed by a workshop session, where teachers would be instructed to browse LeMill, create a user account, create some simple resources, create a collection or two, find colleagues, and join suitable groups. After the workshop the teachers would have the basic skills to navigate the site and actively participate in the creation of learning resources.

In Ochoa and Duval (2009) it was found that repositories that produce full courses have a more active user base than repositories that concentrate on resources of smaller granularity. A course is a natural context for a teacher to return and work on. It appears that repositories for smaller resources need to establish these contexts, and we have found that workshops and competitions help in that.

Consequences of Open Source Development

Opting to publish project outcomes as open source has several consequences. One is that, in general, EU funders seem to favor open solutions, as these ensure the wider adoption of project results; therefore this is an advantage when submitting project proposals.

Figure 8. Multilingual tags make tag clouds difficult to use

32757 results.

In general, going open source does not create additional work for project personnel. Setting up version controls, ticket systems, documentation, and other infrastructure needs to happen anyway, and having them openly available online is merely a configuration issue. Most online open source projects never gather a vibrant developer community around them, and if that is the case, then open sourcing has not given much benefit, though it hasn't drawn on any resources either. In some cases, other parties become interested in the product and a developer community forms. When this happens, the original product developers are, of course, naturally the coordinators of the continuing development, potentially beyond any funding period that they have. This is an additional responsibility, but one that can be dropped in the hope that someone else will continue coordinating the development. However, in this case the product development gains additional free resources, as individual developers or institutions contribute to the development with their own time and brain power. The gains easily outweigh the costs.

Open sourcing also gives added visibility to the project, and can help in forming serendipitous contacts around the world. In the case of LeMill, a teacher in the USA decided to set up his own LeMill server—which would not have been possible if it had not been an open source product—and started promoting LeMill in his area. On a larger scale, the Ministry of Education in the Georgian republic decided to use LeMill as the platform for all their digital learning resource development and publication and set up their own server in Georgia. We've also received contributions in the form of additional user interface translations by volunteer individuals, who happily offered their work effort for an open source project.

Finally, it should be mentioned that in the case of funded development projects, as the funding ends the developed products too often disappear, as no-one can develop them further or give support to potential users. Only if the product has become so successful that it can support com-mercial activity can it survive. If the product is published as open source, any interested party can continue its development, offer services and support around it, or create a different variant of it for a special need.

Working with a Flexible Design

One goal of LeMill development was to make the system as easy to use as possible, with minimal training needed. In retrospect, a surprisingly large portion of the development effort went into user interface improvements, and actual creation of new features was not so central once the basic functionality had been created.

Selecting appropriate names for concepts turned out to be quite crucial. One feature of LeMill was the creation of 'learning patterns' consisting of content, methods (which also were originally named 'activities'), and tools. This name was too abstract for most teachers, and was later changed into 'tips for use'. This, while more concrete, was too general, and gave too little contextual support for teachers to understand what was needed. The final name for the feature, 'Teaching and Learning Story', at last proved to be concrete and exact enough to convey the correct meaning. As a name, it is quite a mouthful, and thus it was not an easy decision to switch to using it, but ultimately no better candidate was available.

Adaptation of existing user interaction patterns to the increasing needs of a growing repository became necessary during this project, and is something that is not usually discussed in software development literature. When LeMill was originally published, it was nearly empty. The browsing function, for example, was very simple, as it only needed to filter a relevant set of matches from a few hundred resources. But after a year or so, when the number of resources reached thousands, it became obvious that teachers needed more powerful filtering tools, at which time the current browsing user interface (see e.g. Figure 3) was designed. Similarly, many views in the community, the tag clouds, and resource authoring tools needed to be rethought as the repository and the community grew. Solutions that were optimized for a small system became inadequate in a large system. On the other hand, these later solutions would have been confusingly complex in the beginning, so we see this feature evolution as a necessary part of community and repository growth.

FUTURE DIRECTIONS

The funding from CALIBRATE ended in 2008, but the server and software development live on. The future of LeMill is open but promising. It has already attracted thousands of registered members, and is actively used by teachers in several countries. LeMill is growing at a healthy rate: there are on average 8.0 new resources created per day, excluding media pieces. In comparison, Ochoa and Duval (2009) reported that the average growth measured in November 2007 for Connexions was 1.8, for MIT OCW 1.0[14] and for MERLOT 4.6. In November 2007, LeMill's growth was 3.4 resources per day.

It is our hope that LeMill's design will inspire designers of other OER repositories to re-look at how to present resources, catalogues, and metadata to teachers in a way that teachers find comfortable and productive. Our experience is that designing for simplicity is by no means an easy task, but is well worth the effort.

This chapter has touched on some potential future steps for OER repositories in general. Additional focus on user experience design would be quite beneficial to any online service, but for OER repositories, while metadata is an important part of their functioning, teachers would appreciate a user experience that is closer to their own professional concepts, workflows, and terminology, than that of a professional librarian.

A core feature of LeMill is the expansion of OERs to cover not just learning material that is presented to the student, but also meta-resources such as pedagogical method descriptions and tool descriptions. This is something OERs in general should look at, as teachers clearly are not only interested in learning material, but also in tips and instructions on how to improve their teaching practices (see e.g. Kárpáti, 2008).

Another distinguishing feature of LeMill is its openness in terms of internal structure and limitations. While pedagogical activities have previously been worked on, for example, in the scope of IMS Learning Design, the strict workflow specifications of IMS-LD make them unsuitable for some advanced learning scenarios and thus limit the professional creativity of the teacher (Dolonen, 2006). LeMill's answer is to make resources more freeform, so teachers can express their ideas for pedagogical activities in any way they deem suitable, and other teachers can learn and adapt those activities to their own needs.

ACKNOWLEDGMENT

LeMill development was conducted as part of the CALIBRATE project, which was funded by the European Commission's 6th Framework Programme in the ICT research effort.

REFERENCES

Akpinar, Y.& Simsek, H. (2007). Should K–12 teachers develop learning objects? Evidence from the field with K–12 students. *International Journal of Instructional Technology and Distance Learning, 4*(3).31–44.

Akpinar, Y. (2008). Validation of a learning object review instrument: Relationship between ratings of learning objects and actual learning outcomes. *Interdisciplinary Journal of E-Learning and Learning Objects, 4*, 291–302.

Anido, L. E., Fernández, M. J., Caeiro, M., Santos, J. M., Rodríguez, J. S., & Llamas, M. (2002). Educational metadata and brokerage for learning resources. *Computers & Education, 38*, 351–374. doi:10.1016/S0360-1315(02)00018-0

Bannan-Ritland, B., Dabbagh, N., & Murphy, K. (2000). Learning object systems as constructivist learning environments: Related assumptions, theories and applications. In Wiley, D., (Ed.), *The Instructional Use of Learning Objects*. Agency for Instructional Technology and the Association for Educational Communications and Technology. http://reusability.org/read/

Beck, K. (1999). *Extreme Programming Explained; Embrace Change*. Addison-Wesley Longman Publishing.

Benkler, Y. (2005). *Common Wisdom: Peer Production of Educational Materials*. Retrieved from http://www.benkler.org/Common_Wisdom.pdf

Collis, B., & Strijker, A. (2004). Technology and human issues in reusing learning objects. *Journal of Interactive Media in Education, 4*, 1–32. http://www-jime.open.ac.uk/2004/4/.

Dean, P., & Leinonen, T. (2003). ITCOLE final report. Technical Report IST-2000-26249, European Commission, ITCOLE Project. Retrieved from http://www.euro-cscl.org/site/itcole/

Dolonen, J. (2006). Empirical study of learning design. Retrieved from http://calibrate.eun.org/shared/data/calibrate/deliverables/D3p1_v2.pdf

Downes, S. (2001). Learning objects: Resources for distance education worldwide. *International Review of Research in Open and Distance Learning, 2*(1). http://www.irrodl.org/index.php/irrodl/issue/view/11.

Durando, M. (2008). Project final report. CALIBRATE, IST-028025, European Commission. Retrieved from http://calibrate.eun.org/shared/data/calibrate/deliverables/CALIBRATEFinalReport.pdf

Duval, E., Forte, E., Cardinaels, K., Verhoeven, B., Durm, R. V., & Hendrikx, K. (2001). The Ariadne knowledge pool system. *Communications of the ACM, 44*(5). doi:10.1145/374308.374346

Forte, E. N., Forte, M. H. K. W., & Duval, E. (1997). The ARIADNE Project (part 1): Knowledge pools for computer-based and telematics-supported classical, open and distance education. *European Journal of Engineering Education, 22*(1), 61–74. doi:10.1080/03043799708923438

Friesen, N. (2004). Three objections to learning objects and e-learning standards . In McGreal, R. (Ed.), *Online Education Using Learning Objects* (pp. 59–70). London: Routledge.

Geser, G. (2007). Open educational practices and resources — OLCOS roadmap 2012. OLCOS. Retrieved from http://www.olcos.org/english/roadmap/

Heery, R. (2009). Digital repositories roadmap review: towards a vision for research and learning in 2013. *JISC*. Retrieved from http://www.jisc.ac.uk/media/documents/themes/infoenvironment/reproadmappreviewfinal.doc

IEEE. (2002). IEEE 1484.12.1-2002, *Learning Object Metadata standard. Final draft, IEEE Standards Department*. Retrieved from http://ltsc.ieee.org/wg12/files/LOM_1484_12_1_v1_Final_Draft.pdf

Johnson, L. F. (2003). Elusive vision: Challenges impeding the learning object economy. *New Media Consortium*. http://archive.nmc.org/pdf/Elusive_Vision.pdf

Kárpáti, A. (2008). Final evaluation report. CALIBRATE, IST-028205, European Commission. http://calibrate.eun.org/shared/data/calibrate/deliverables/D4_3_Evaluation_ReportFinal.pdf

Kitchen, S., Finch, S., & Sinclair, R. (2007). Harnessing technology schools survey 2007. National *Centre for Social Research (NatCen)*. http://partners.becta.org.uk/index.php?section=rh&rid=14110

Leinonen, T. (2005). Urinal as a learning object. http://flosse.dicole.org/?item=urinal-as-a-learning-object

Leinonen, T., Toikkanen, T., & Silfvast, K. (2008). Software as hypothesis: Research-based design methodology. In *The Proceedings of Participatory Design Conference 2008*. New York: ACM.

Margaryan, A., & Littlejohn, A. (2008). Repositories and communities at cross-purposes: issues in sharing and reuse of digital learning resources. *Journal of Computer Assisted Learning, 24*(4), 333–347. doi:10.1111/j.1365-2729.2007.00267.x

McCormick, R. (2003). Keeping the pedagogy out of learning objects. EARLI. http://celebrate.eun.org/eun.org2/eun/Include_to_content/celebrate/file/KeepingPedagogyOutOfLOs3v2.doc

McGreal, R. (2005). Copyright wars and learning objects. *Interactive Technology and Smart Education, 2*, 141–153. doi:10.1108/17415650580000039

McGreal, R. (2007). A typology of learning object repositories. *Athabasca University*. http://hdl.handle.net/2149/1078

Monge, S., Ovelar, R., & Azpeitia, I. (2008). Repository 2.0: Social dynamics to support community building in learning object repositories. *Interdisciplinary Journal of E-Learning and Learning Objects, 4*.

Ochoa, X., & Duval, E. (2009). Quantitative analysis of learning object repositories. *IEEE Transactions on Learning Technologies, 2*(3), 226–238. doi:10.1109/TLT.2009.28

Petrides, L., & Jimes, C. (2008). Building open educational resources from the ground up: South Africa's free high school science texts. *Journal of Interactive Media in Education, 7*. http://jime.open.ac.uk/2008/07/.

Petrides, L., Nguyen, L., Jimes, C., & Karaglani, A. (2008). Open educational resources: inquiring into author use and reuse. *International Journal of Technology Enhanced Learning, 1*(1), 98–117. doi:10.1504/IJTEL.2008.020233

Põldoja, H., Leinonen, T., Väljataga, T., Ellonen, A., & Priha, M. (2006). Progressive Inquiry Learning Object Templates (PILOT). *International Journal on E-Learning, 5*(1), 103–111.

Recker, M. M., & Dorward, J. (2004). Discovery and use of online learning resources: Case study findings. *Journal of Educational Technology & Society, 7*(2), 93–104.

Schwaber, K., & Beedle, M. (2001). *Agile Software Development with Scrum*. Upper Saddle River, NJ: Prentice Hall.

Smith, P., Rudd, P., & Coghlan, M. (2008). Harnessing technology: Schools survey 2008. National Foundation for Educational Research. http://partners.becta.org.uk/index.php?section=rh&rid=15952

Toikkanen, T., & Leinonen, T. (2006). Distributed design and development using agile methods and Trac. In *VTT Symposium 241. The 7th International Conference on eXtreme Programming and Agile Processes in Software Engineering*, (pp. 85–86). Espoo, Finland. VTT.

UNESCO. (2002). Forum on the impact of open courseware for higher education in developing countries. Final report, UNESCO. http://www.wcet.info/resources/publications/unescofinalreport.pdf

Van Assche, F., & Massart, D. (2004). Federation and brokerage of learning objects and their metadata. In *Fourth IEEE International Conference on Advanced Learning Technologies (ICALT'04)* (pp.316–320).

Van Assche, F., & Vuorikari, R. (2006). A framework for quality of learning resources. In Ehlers, U., & Pawlowski, J. (Eds.), *European Handbook for Quality and Standardization in E-Learning*. Berlin, Germany: Springer. doi:10.1007/3-540-32788-6_29

Wiley, D. (2000). Connecting learning objects to instructional design theory: A definition, a metaphor, and a taxonomy. In Wiley, D.,(Ed.) *The Instructional Use of Learning Objects*, chapter 1. Agency for Instructional Technology and the Association for Educational Communications and Technology. http://reusability.org/read/

Wiley, D. (2003). Learning objects: Difficulties and opportunities. http://opencontent.org/docs/lo_do.pdf

Wilson, T. (2008). New ways of mediating learning: Investigating the implications of adopting open educational resources for tertiary education at an institution in the United Kingdom as compared to one in South Africa. *International Review of Research in Open and Distance Learning, 9*(1).

KEY TERMS AND DEFINITIONS

Agile Software Development: A group of software development methodologies based on iterative development, frequent inspection and adaptation, teamwork, self-organization, and accountability.

Content Management Systems (CMS): Are usually web-based services that allow for content authoring, editing, publication, workflows, and user roles.

F/OSS, FOSS, FLOSS: Free/Libre/Open Source Software is software that is liberally licensed to grant its users the rights to study, change, and improve its design through its openly available source code.

Learning Design: An effort to provide a machine-readable language to describe various pedagogies and learning situations.

Learning Objects (LO): Are resources, usually digital and web-based, that can be used and reused to support learning. If a learning object fulfills the openness criteria, it can be considered to be an OER.

Metadata: Information that describes an object. In OERs, metadata often includes fields such as title, author, subject area, intended age group, and license. Some metadata schemes can include hundreds of such fields.

Open Educational Resources (OER): Digital online resources that are openly and freely available to anyone interested in them.

Participatory Design: Actively involves end users in the design process to help ensure that the product meets their needs and is usable.

Repository: A service that holds metadata about objects, and in some cases stores the objects themselves. Allows users to search for and browse the contents of the repository.

User Experience Design: Pertains to the creation of the architecture and interaction models that impact a user's perception of a device, system or service. It contains activities such as interaction design and user interface design.

ENDNOTES

[1] MERLOT, http://www.merlot.org/
[2] MIT OpenCourseWare, http://ocw.mit.edu/
[3] OpenCourseWare Consortium, http://www.ocwsonsortium.org/
[4] Creative Commons, http://www.creative-commons.org/
[5] OER Commons, http://oercommons.org/
[6] OpenLearn, http://openlearn.open.ac.uk/
[7] Connexions, http://cnx.org/
[8] LRE for Schools, http://lreforschools.eun.org/

9   Scenarios used can be found at http://lemill.org/trac/wiki/Scenarios and workshop results at http://lemill.org/trac/wiki/DesignSessionResults.

10   Tag line from http://lemill.net/

11   LeMill source code is available at http://lemill.org/

12   Plone, http://plone.org/

13   A special template intended for starting a Progressive Inquiry project, see Põldoja et al. (2006).

14   MIT OCW produces full courses. Ochoa and Duval (2009) estimate one course to be 20 resources.

Chapter 11
What Audacity!
Decreasing Student Anxiety while Increasing Instructional Time

Peter B. Swanson
Georgia State University, USA

Patricia N. Early
Georgia State University, USA

Quintina M. Baumann
Cobb County Schools, USA

ABSTRACT

Promoting student engagement in the second language classroom can be difficult for teachers. Multiple obstacles such as perceptions of the irrelevance of authentic language applications and the affective barriers (e.g. performance anxiety speaking before peers) tend to hinder student oral language performance. For teachers, especially for beginners, other obstacles appear such as being given the most challenging assignments with little to no professional support. Many times these educators scramble to squeeze the most out of every minute in the classroom for instructional purposes while trying to increase student achievement. Three free and open source software options are presented and findings from two studies of focusing on the use of Audacity indicate multiple benefits for both teachers and students. Afterwards, the authors demonstrate how to use Audacity for oral language assessment and discuss its implications for the world language classroom.

INTRODUCTION

Fostering student engagement in the classroom is a challenging endeavor, particularly when teachers face so many obstacles that decrease teacher instructional time in the classroom. First, and in no particular order, are the bureaucratic impediments, such as large classes, complex work schedules, unnecessary meetings, and little say in school policy, all of which complicate the daily reality of teaching (Futernick, 2007). Secondly, the testing requirements inherent in *No Child Left Behind* can seem overwhelming to teachers as they lose precious instructional time due to off-task preparation and administration of the exams (Zellmer, Frontier, & Pheifer, 2006). A third factor, which

DOI: 10.4018/978-1-61520-917-0.ch011

has remained unchanged throughout decades of education as noted by Goldman (1991), must be acknowledged as loss of classroom time and student focus due to sports and extracurricular activities.

Concurrent with struggling with these difficulties, all educators, regardless of their discipline, must also endeavor to capitalize on every minute in the classroom for instructional purposes while trying to enhance student achievement. Second language instruction faces these same challenges while adding an additional component of a multiplicity of manners in which proficiency is assessed. At its core, second language instruction in the communicative classroom is dedicated to the ideals, if not the practice, of developing second-language proficiency in the Three Modes of Communication: the Interpersonal, the Interpretive, and the Presentational (National Standards in Foreign Language Education Project, 1999). Formerly known as the four skills (reading, writing, listening, and speaking), the Three Modes of Communication are three parts of a single goal of communication rather than any one skill in isolation. While proficiency in reading, writing, and listening are measured mainly through common assessment instruments such as written exams, the assessment of students' oral language skills has continually presented numerous challenges, including the development of useful and flexible rubrics (Foster, Tonkyn, & Wigglesworth, 2000) and the time expended in individual learner assessment (Flewelling, 2002).

Additionally, unlike assessments for reading and writing, oral assessments, traditionally conducted in the classroom, do not leave an archivable assessment artifact. This lack of an artifact impedes overall performance evaluation, as an artifact could be used to measure similarities and/or differences in learner progress towards proficiency goals, can materially support assessment outcomes, and can be presented as concrete evidence of language proficiency to stakeholders and third-party program evaluators or accreditation certifiers. In an

effort to address these concerns, older language laboratories are being transformed to accommodate digital recordings that can facilitate whole-class concurrent, archival recordings (Flewelling, 2002). Presently, researchers are investigating the manifold uses of emerging technologies and their potential uses within the context of oral proficiency and assessment (Chan, 2003; Egbert, 1999; Volle, 2005).

BACKGROUND

Because younger teachers are more likely to have grown up in a technology-rich environment, their comfort and skills with technology may lead to an increased use of computers for instructional purposes (National Center for Education Statistics, 2000). Furthermore, many of these novice educators are confident using technology but perhaps lack the time and resources to develop technologically rich lessons (Pierson & Cozart, 2005). Even with an abundance of available software, hardware, free ware, and webware, Cuban (2001) finds that school systems have not been restructured fully to support the integration of technology for instruction. In an effort to balance student security and privacy with access to instructional technology, schools have restricted access to a plethora of opportunities for students and teachers, including many interactive web tools, such as blogs, *Skype*, and *YouTube*. Furthermore, it is not uncommon for teachers to lack the administrative privilege to install or configure software, even free or open-source software, on their classroom computers.

For language teachers, the inability to use cutting-edge technology for instructional and assessment purposes forces them to continue to use traditional assessment methods that were espoused decades ago. Specifically in the area of oral language assessment, teachers rely on time consuming face-to-face interactions in the classroom, which diminish precious instructional time.

For example, if a French teacher has 30 students in a class and spends approximately two minutes per student listening and evaluating performance on an assessment task, approximately an hour of instructional time is lost to the class as a whole. Of course, even more time can vanish if teachers must deal with a variety of disruptions from students who are not being assessed at the moment.

For students, traditional methods of oral language assessment can be detrimental too. Many times second language learners suffer from performance anxiety which is known to increase one's affective filter, and as a result may adversely influence their performance on the assessment. According to the Affective Filter Hypothesis (Krashen, 1981), affective variables such as anxiety and self-confidence play a role in language acquisition. When negative emotional factors are present, language acquisition is more difficult. Conversely, when students feel more relaxed and comfortable, language acquisition becomes easier. To this end, many researchers have found that this anxiety is negatively related to language performance with some researchers claiming that the presence of this affect is one of the strongest predictors of foreign language success (MacIntyre, 1999).

In a study focused on English language learners ($N = 275$) in Australia that were in their final months of studying English immediately prior to enrollment in university courses, Woodrow (2006) examined the relationship between second language anxiety and speaking performance. Both quantitative and qualitative measures were used to investigate the relationship between anxiety and oral performance in English. Findings from her research indicate that students reported the most stress for giving oral presentations and performing in front of classmates during in-class situations. Specifically, the major stressors reported by the subjects were performing in front of class and talking to native speakers. The researcher noted that it was important to consider communication both in and outside the classroom and ensure that students have the necessary skills and practice for everyday communication, which she expressly stated "could be achieved by setting out-of-class tasks utilizing the rich linguistic resources available to learners" (p. 324).

Historically, these resources have been primarily in the form of educational language laboratories that emerged in the early 1960s and 1970s using cassette players with headphones. Later, these exclusively audio language labs began to be replaced with the latest state-of-the-art digital technology, which quickly transformed into a multimedia approach to language learning. With the emergence of Computer-Assisted Language Learning (CALL), the multimedia center, combined with an appropriate methodology, allows teachers to move from a teacher-centered or textbook-centered instructional practice to a student-centered approach (Hai-Peng & Deng, 2007). Among others aspects of language learning, CALL can be used with reading (reading on-screen), writing (word-processing), listening (digital archives), and speaking (Levy & Hubbard, 2005).

From a pedagogical stance, popular teaching methodologies such as constructivism (Piaget, 1973) and socioculturalism (Vygotsky, 1978) have emerged that work well with CALL. Both constructivism and socioculturalism stress the importance of the teacher as a facilitator of individualized learning by giving students control over what they do, how fast they do it and even the ability to find and correct their own mistakes, resulting in a transformation of the learning process. Here, the role of the teacher is deemphasized and students are given active learning experiences. These approaches are designed to promote fluency over accuracy in order to allow students to take risks in more student-centered activities. Research has shown that the reduction of a strong teacher presence is related to larger quantity and better quality of communication, observable as more fluidity and more use of complex sentences (Stepp-Greany, 2002).

Research suggests that, with regards to the affective concerns addressed earlier, CALL has a number of benefits for students in the world language classroom context. Beauvois (1998) reported that students participating in a Local Area Network writing project showed positive attitudes about learning in that setting because the LAN not only represented a low-anxiety situation, they also they expressed that they felt more control than in a traditional classroom. In a study investigating English writing skills, the researchers found that the use of technology redistributes teacher and classmate attention so that less able students can become more active participants in the class (Hartman et al., 1995). While specific to the second language classroom, it may well be that these findings are generalizable to classes in other disciplines as well.

Given the obstacles all teachers face, the rapid technological advancements available to classroom teachers now, and the benefits these digital tools have for both teachers and students alike, we will present three free and open source recording tools currently available and then discuss research findings from two separate studies where students used digital technology for oral language assessments. Afterwards, we present strategies for using digital recording software in the language learning classroom and highlight the implications of using free and open source software in the classroom.

FREE OPEN SOURCE SOFTWARE RECORDING TOOLS

While there have been rapid advances in technology, especially where language labs or other technology installations are concerned, many of these new capabilities may not be available to language students in schools and universities due to either shrinking budgets or policy restrictions. The rapid advances in personal digital technology and the availability of both hardware and software resources for individual recording have the potential to allow interested language instructors to use digital technology for oral proficiency measurement. While many tools are available for these purposes, we begin by briefly outlining three free and open source software options that are free of adware, spyware, or license limitations, and that do not monopolize computer processing and storage resources. However, as noted earlier, teachers may not have the administrative rights to download and install software on their classroom computers. It is recommended that in these cases, teachers consult with their campus technology support resources to determine the best compromise between network security and pedagogical advantage.

Freecorder

The *Freecorder Toolbar*© < http://applian.com/asktoolbar/>, created by Applian Technologies, is a free audio recorder that uses state-of-the-art sound recording technology that includes a *Google*-based search menu. *Freecorder 3.0* can be used as a song recorder, an audio extractor from videos, internet radio recorder, and a sound recorder from the computer's microphone or line-in ports. Once downloaded, the software installs as a tool bar and with one mouse click users can record, stop, pause, and play audio, using easily recognizable and universally-accepted symbols for each of these functions. Once the record button is activated, the user's voice in the form of sound waves is graphically displayed. Audio can be recorded and saved in either the popular *mp3* format or as a *wmv* file. Basically, if it can be heard on the computer's speakers, *Freecorder* can record it. It uses a Sound Card Independent recording technology, which does not require users to have a special sound card driver that may cause awkward side effects.

Unlike many other sound recorder software packages, *Freecorder* supports all *Windows* systems. Additionally, *Freecorder* is able to separate sounds from individual applications and eliminate background noises. It also eliminates silence at the beginning and end of the recording. It starts to record when it first detects audio and stops when the audio stops. This unique audio recorder is easy to use and the interface is intuitive, which may be an advantage for younger users and less technologically-savvy individuals.

Skype

Skype is an exciting and extremely versatile voice-over-IP [VOIP] software tool, available for free at<< www.skype.com>>. VOIP allows for the possibility of real-time communication over the internet, using high-speed cable, LAN or DSL connections. Calls via *Skype* can fall into three categories: *Skype-to-Skype*, in which one user on a computer speaks to another user on a computer; *Skype-to-Phone*, in which the *Skype* user can utilize dialing options in the software to call a land-line phone; and *Phone-to-Skype*, in which the user establishes a *Skype* phone-number that allows outside land-lines to call into *Skype* and interact with the software as if it were a traditional telephone with a voice mail option. While the second user options require the purchase of additional *Skype* packages, minutes, and other premium options, the first option remains free to all *Skype* users. Once a user downloads and installs the software, they are prompted to create a free user account.

This ability to talk *Skype-to-Skype* is what makes this software uniquely adaptable to education, in that students in one location can speak in real-time to their instructor, their classmates, or international speaking partners in remote locations. The additional option of video chatting via *Skype* allows speakers to see each other, including gestures, expressions, and other types of meta-language, making the communication more realistic, compelling, and rich in communicative cues. Files such as documents, images, and sound files can be transferred instantly via integrated peer-to-peer file-sharing capabilities. *Skype* calls can be recorded and archived for assessment or to create multi-phase communication tasks such as interviews, transcriptions, or inclusion in student presentation or media creation. In short, the rich media capabilities of *Skype* enable a wide variety of communicative tasks to take place both inside and outside the classroom.

For an additional fee of about $30 per year, a teacher can also set up a *Skype* phone number with voice mail, which will allow students to call the *Skype* number from a regular phone and leave a voice recording as a voice mail message. In this way, a teacher could record a greeting that was, in fact, the oral assessment prompt, and the student could "leave a message" that was the response to the oral assessment prompt. The student has the option of reviewing their recording before submitting, and can re-record their response until they have achieved a recording that they feel best represents their language proficiency level. In addition, these voice mail messages are reviewable and archivable by the teacher.

Audacity

The *Audacity*® recorder (Mazzoni & Dannenberg, 2000), available at <http://audacity.sourceforge. net/>, is an open-source recorder available to the public with relaxed or non-existent intellectual property restrictions. It is free software distributed under the terms of the GNU General Public License and the registered trademark of Dominic Mazzoni. Its familiar buttons and interface, while allowing for simple operation, belies the relatively sophisticated editing capabilities built into the software. It is available for Mac OS X, Microsoft Windows, GNU/Linux, and other operating systems. *Audacity* can be used for multiple purposes such as recording live audio, converting audio files from cassette tapes and vinyl records to digital recordings or CDs, editing a variety of sound file types (e.g., *Ogg Vorbis*, .wav, .mp3), cutting, copying, and splicing sounds together, and changing the speed or pitch of a recording. Sound files are recorded by default in the *.wav* format, but if an *.mp3* recording is required because of file storage limitations, an additional *LAME™ MP3 Encoder* can be easily downloaded and installed from the web site. *Audacity* does not distribute the *LAME MP3 Encoders,* but supports linking to third-party *LAME* libraries for *mp3* encoding subject to the legal precedents for software patents in the country of use.

The most recent release of *Audacity* is the *1.3.9 Beta* version. The creators note that it is a work in progress and it is not available yet with complete documentation or translations into world languages. They recommend it for more advanced users while the version *1.2.6*, considered a stable release, is complete and fully documented. The creators mention on the website that both *Audacity 1.2.6* and *1.3.9* can be installed on the same machine. For a complete list of functions, refer to the website.

CURRENT RESEARCH

In the following sections we present the results from two distinct oral language assessment studies while integrating strategies for using free and open source software in the second language classroom. In both studies instructors chose to use *Audacity* as the digital recording tool. The first study investigated eight undergraduate students' perceptions of using digital voice recordings for assessment purposes from a qualitative perspective. The second study focused on middle school student perceptions ($N = 76$) using quantitative measures. We developed a 7-point Likert scale survey as a guide (See Appendix A) and asked students to rate their agreement on a scale from 1 (*Strongly Disagree*) to 7 (*Strongly Agree*) on 13 questions. Survey statements focused on three areas of interest: accuracy to use the target language, student anxiety, and student grades on assignments. Two additional statements were added to gauge student creativity and ease of use of *Audacity*.

Students in both studies were also asked to rank order the four skills of language learning (listening, reading, speaking, writing) in order of importance to them, if they liked using voice recordings for oral language assessment, preference to traditional or digital oral language assessments as well as giving some demographic data (e.g. age, gender, etc.). In addition to student perception, we interviewed the instructors from the two studies to understand their feelings about using *Audacity* as a resource for oral language assessment. In order to analyze the data from the interviews with the eight undergraduate Japanese students and the instructors' interviews, we used a modified version of Glasser and Strauss' (1967) constant comparative analysis to group answers and make connections to common questions. Field notes and memos were also used to help establish major themes as well as interesting observations noted during the interviews. At the end of the semester, member checks (Guba & Lincoln, 1981) took place to allow participants to identify anything they might find inaccurate, unfair, or uncomfortable for them. By doing so, member checks preserve the dignity of the participants and ensures the researcher accuracy in reporting the results. Instructors and students selected a pseudonym for reporting purposes.

Using Audacity for Oral Language Assessment

In this section, we outline strategies for first creating the digital space; that is, selection of the software, determining the frequency of digitally recorded assessments, the delivery method and the organization of incoming assignments, and the archiving system of student work. Afterwards, we then discuss best practices in creating oral language assessment tasks and evaluation tools.

The first step for individuals interested in using free and open source for oral language assessment purposes is to evaluate these software options available and discuss the selected software with the school's technology personnel. During the evaluation process, we recommend that instructors spend ample time familiarizing themselves with the program. Teachers should not only practice recording the assessment tasks but we also encourage them to practice responding, listening, and editing their recordings, and ultimately turning in the final work as students would be expected to do.

Earlier we outlined several programs and the instructors chose to use *Audacity*. During the interviews, the instructors mentioned that they had spoken with their technology officials about using it in the schools. Tina, the middle school teacher, stated that the technology director already had prior knowledge about *Audacity* and had it installed on the computers, so it was an easy decision. As for the two Japanese instructors, Kuki and Kami, the technology laboratory director researched *Audacity* prior to consenting to installing *Audacity* on the lab's computers. The instructors stated that they opted to use *Audacity* because it was fast and simple to download and install. They felt that if they did not have any difficulty downloading, installing, and using it, neither would their students. Furthermore, the instructors noted that the interface was intuitive and that they felt their students would not require intensive training to use it. Data from the student survey as well as the interviews with the teachers indicated that students and instructors alike enjoyed the range of options *Audacity* offers such as being able to set audio levels for speaking and listening. Additionally, the instructors favored the *Audacity's* flexibility because students could download and use it at home for free. Lastly, the teachers mentioned that their technology personnel particularly favored the notion of having students save files as *mp3* files because this type of audio file is compressed, thus leading to less storage space needed.

Once the software is selected and installed, the second step is to determine the frequency of assessments. For the undergraduate Japanese classes, the instructors assigned 14 oral language assessments at the beginning of the spring 2009 semester in order to assess students' oral language proficiency digitally each week beginning the second week of the semester. The students ranged in age from 18 to 22 years of age. However, Tina opted to require her 13 and 14 year-old students to use *Audacity* to record responses to her language performance tasks every other week during the eighteen week semester for a total of nine student recordings. We recommend that instructors do not assign performance tasks the first week the students are introduced to the software. It is imperative to give students time to tinker with the program so that their linguistic performance is not hindered due to unfamiliarity with the technology.

Next, teachers need to determine how students are to submit recordings for assessment purposes and how students should title the digital files. First, several options are available for digital receptacles such as having students email responses directly to the teacher or assigning students to use a computer in the school's media center to deliver digital assignments to a teacher's mailbox using a jump drive or CD. While the former is relatively easy for students with internet access away from school, the quantity of emails cluttering and possibly even overloading a teacher's email server space may become problematic. Nevertheless, such delivery would allow teachers a means for personalized feedback once evaluation has taken place.

Using the latter as an option, teachers can construct and title mailboxes such as "Week 3 Speaking Assignment". Students can be required to upload their assignments on the appropriate due dates whereby teachers can access the recordings for evaluation. With such a procedure in place, teachers would not need to sort through and open dozens of emails in order to evaluate student performance. Additionally, internet access would not be required to assess the assignments. Teachers could simply copy all of the students' files from the mailbox to a jump drive or *iPod* and evaluate students' oral language proficiency away from school at home or even during a daily commute using public transportation.

We recommend that regardless of the collection system for assignments, teachers take time to create a system for identifying student work and continue to use the system throughout the academic year. For example, a third week assignment could be titled using the assignment name and the student's name (week3john_doe). Using such nomenclature allows teachers to quickly identify not only the assignment but also the student who turned in the assignment. A useful *Audacity* feature is that once a file name is composed and saved, a supplementary tag window is displayed where users can add more information about the recording such as additional comments. For students in both studies, the instructors required students to use the assignment title immediately followed by both first and last name (e.g., myfamily_john_doe).

The purpose for such continuity, which is essential for the accurate archiving of student work, leads to our next step in the digital recording process, teachers creating folders where student performances can be saved. Using the Windows Explorer tool located in the Accessories folder (accessible via the Start Menu by clicking on *Programs > Accessories > Windows Explorer*), teachers can quickly create and label folders in which to place student work. For example, a French I instructor requires students deposit 15 weekly assignments in a folder created on the school server in the media center titled "French I Speaking Assignments". On her class computer, or even her own personal laptop, she can create one folder called "French I" on her desktop. Inside that folder she can create 15 subfolders and name each one "Week 1", "Week 2", "Week 3", and so forth. As students deposit their work weekly, the teacher can copy/move the files to her computer, place each recording in its proper location, and then assess student proficiency outside of class time.

Our research with the undergraduates found that the instructors began by having them email their work weekly to them. The voice recordings were sent as attachments with the files saved as "firstname_lastname_assignmentweek". Early in the process, Kuki and Kami found the email too difficult to manage and quickly set up weekly drop boxes on the course management system, *uLearn©*. After the third week of assessments, students were expected to deliver their weekly responses to the instructor-created oral language assessment objectives to the appropriate mailbox where the assignments were automatically marked with the date and time. Tina, on the other hand, created a series of folders for each class period and asked students to place their work in the appropriate folders. Her students performed all the assigned tasks in the school computer lab at the school administration's request, due to the fact that not all students had access to computers outside of school, and also because most of the assignments required a partner for role-plays. This allowed her to observe students while they recorded, and she was able to note how students improvised their speaking, became confident enough to the point where they did not write their scripts before speaking, and how they self-corrected themselves and /or corrected their partners. However, this function was found to be more useful in the middle school context more than with the undergraduates because the college professors stated that they did not continually check to see if students were turning in assignments or not.

As for the usefulness of having digital archives of student work, the three instructors mentioned on multiple occasions that having these files improved instructor feedback because students could listen to their recordings as the instructors made constructive comments. Additionally, all of the instructors quickly determined that the recordings had the potential to be listened to by multiple evaluators allowing for more consistency of evaluation. On several occasions, a few Japanese students questioned a grade on a particular assignment and the recording was re-evaluated by the other instructor.

In fact, Kuki noted that these recordings would work well as indicators of student progress for students. Tina reiterated the notion and added that her middle schoolers occasionally remarked that they did not feel they were making much progress using the language. By having the students listen to their previous recordings, personalized discussions between Tina and the students took place to highlight improvement and progression toward fluency. In similar fashion, she used the archived files during parent-teacher conferences to document student improvement in the target language. Tina also mentioned that another unique advantage is that the recordings can be used for student portfolios. Both Kuki and Kami added that the recordings hold the potential to serve as a body of evidence for accreditation purposes. Kami stated that all of the Japanese students' digital files were already archived on the department's server for college and university accreditation purposes. However, the three teachers were quick to inform us that while the digital voice recording had certain advantages, the traditional face-to-face oral assessment was not completely eradicated because of its advantages. They noted the importance of having in-class impromptu real-time student-teacher interactions as well as student-student communications.

Now that the preliminary work has been established for teachers and students to use digital recording technology for oral language assessment, teachers need to spend some time telling students about the process upon which they are about to embark. The instructors mentioned that they spent part of a class period introducing students to the notion of using *Audacity* for out-of-class oral/aural assignments. We favor the Present, Perform, and Practice approach. First, teachers should spend a few moments presenting *Audacity* to students. We encourage teachers to give students time to read *Audacity's* Table of Contents under the Help pull down menu. A few minutes spent reading this section may help answer many student questions without consuming a great deal of time. Next, we urge educators to perform a practice language assessment task in front of the students. Here, the teacher may show an example of a speaking assignment and the accompanying scoring guide. Then, the teacher can open *Audacity*, record a response, revise it as necessary, and then deliver it to the appropriate area for evaluation. Once completed, the teacher can give students time to work on the same assignment whereby they practice recording, editing, deleting, re-recording responses, and finally submitting final work. Afterwards, the instructor can show students his or her procedure for collecting assignments for evaluation purposes.

Now that the process has been established and organized, the next step is the development of quality and meaningful oral language assessment tasks. Met (2004) affirms that students need to carry out meaningful, motivating, purposeful tasks that allow them to use language for understanding others and for communicating their own ideas regardless if instruction is delivered by teachers or through technology. Furthermore, because learning objectives must be measurable (Kim & Kellough, 1995; Orlich, Harder, Callahan, Kauchak, & Gibson, 1994), we urge teachers to use the notion of the ABCD approach (Audience, Behavior, Conditions, and Degree). First, the audience must be clearly defined; that is, who is the learner? Secondly, what is the observable behavior or what task is to be accomplished? We suggest writing in terms of action verbs and objects. Thirdly, what are the conditions under which the behavior is to occur? And finally, what are the criteria for acceptable performance or even mastery of the task?

An example of a well-designed oral language assessment task is:

You are calling your new host family in Argentina and going to leave them a voicemail. Give them all of the following details: your name, the date and time you expect to arrive in Buenos Aires, your flight number, and what you will be wearing when you depart Customs in Buenos Aires. Once you are done recording and satisfied with your message, place your audio file in the mailbox in our school's media center.

A second type of performance task can be where the teacher poses a series of questions and leaves enough space between the questions for students to respond. For an intermediate level French class the teacher could post a picture on his or her blog and have a link below the photograph that opens an audio file that the teacher has recorded for the students. For example:

Listen to the following questions about the picture you see. Be sure to answer each question in a complete sentence. When you are finished, place your recording in my folder on the desktop.

1. What is the woman in the red hat wearing? (approximately 5 second pause)
2. Where is the couple standing? (approximately 5 second pause)
3. Why do you think they are outside? (approximately 10 second pause)

Performance tasks such as this one can be easily created in *Audacity* where the teacher cre-ates a file that students can listen to the questions and then respond to them using the same file. To do so, open *Audacity*, pull down the Edit menu, click on Preferences, click on the Audio I/O tab, and then click the box that says *Play other tracks while recording the new one*. The teacher can then record the performance task leaving adequate space for student responses and then save the file. When students open the file, they can play the file to listen to it. Then the students can se-lect the Record button and listen to the teacher's questions and record their answers as they listen to the questions. If students want to delete their responses and begin again, they can simply click the "x" next to their recording track (see Figure 1). Once completed, the students save the questions and the responses as one file.

Clearly, performance tasks can take many forms from student narration of an event to re-sponding to questions to describing a cultural scene from a photograph. For great cultural pho-tographs from throughout the world, we strongly urge world language teachers to explore the *REALIA Project* <www.realiaproject.org>, to view the collection of peer-reviewed media for the teaching and study of modern languages and

Figure 1. Two track recording. (Audacity ® 1999-2009 Audacity Team. The name Audacity ® is a reg-istered trademark of Dominic Mazzoni. Used with permission).

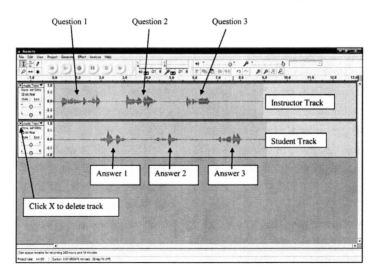

cultures. Additionally, we recommend that language teachers design performance tasks that continually strive to challenge students to use the language in a realistic manner. That is, to develop tasks that students would have to use in the target language environment.

In our studies, the instructors used the ABCD model and wrote their own language performance objectives. Kuki, the senior professor, began the study by recording the oral language assessment objectives in Japanese and then emailing them to students on Mondays with the student responses due on Fridays. Tina handed out paper copies of the objectives to the students three to four days in advance writing the objectives in both Spanish and English. Because we remain committed to the notion of teaching in the target language 95-100% of the time, we strongly urge teachers to compose oral language assessment objectives in the target language and present them to students in aural form. Here, the language learning is transformed from a speaking exercise to one of listening and responding without the use of the learner's first language.

In addition to providing students a solid language performance objective, we feel it is equally important to give students the assessment tool that the teacher will use to evaluate performance at the same time the assignment is given. By doing so, students immediately know what is expected of them. Such tools come in forms of rubrics and check lists. While check lists typically note the existence or absence of certain criteria, rubrics help identify the quality of a performance using performance levels. While there are a plethora of great resources describing best practices in rubric construction, we recommend our 10-step procedure that teachers can use to not only improve rubric integrity but also improve the accuracy of measuring student oral ability (Swanson & Early, 2008).

1. Determine and state learning outcome(s).
2. Align outcomes to national and state standards for world language education.

3. Determine assessment objective(s) and decide if an analytic or holistic rubric would best measure student achievement.
4. Work collaboratively with others from different schools to develop assessment criteria.
5. Select succinct titles for the performance levels.
6. Articulate quality definitions for each criterion.
7. Assign a numerical scale that is congruent with overall grading measures.
8. Solicit student and colleague opinion and revise as necessary.
9. Share the rubric with students before assessment is administered.
10. Following assessment, encourage students to archive rubrics as a means to document oral language development and progress.

In our research, the rubrics were given to the students at the time the language tasks were assigned. Analysis of the two datasets indicated that students in both study groups felt that student performance improved because the students were aware of the evaluation criteria. In fact, when asked if they felt that their grades were improving by using digital recordings for speaking assessments and having the scoring guide present, the majority of the middle school students expressed that they prepared more for assignments when they had the scoring guide at the time of recording. The same was found with the Japanese students.

Research Findings about Using Audacity for Oral Language Assessment

Student Perceptions

Data analysis from the undergraduate interviews and surveys administered to the middle school students revealed several interesting findings. First, the majority of the students in both contexts

Table 1. Student preference of learning the four language skills

	Middle School	**Undergraduate**
Speaking	79%	88%
Listening	47%	62%
Reading	36%	38%
Writing	37%	12%

valued learning to speak and listen in the target language over the other skills (See Table 1).

Next, from a perspective of linguistic accuracy, the majority (75%) of the undergraduates strongly agreed that their recorded responses were an accurate representation of their ability to use Japanese while the remaining 25% expressed moderate agreement. However, all of the participants strongly agreed that their digital voice recordings are more accurate than their in-class performances. When asked about using voice recordings to help improve their ability to speak Japanese, all of the participants either agreed or strongly agreed. Several students mentioned that they enjoyed the ability to listen to their recordings in order to identify errors in pronunciation and to enrich the vocabulary for the recordings. Similar findings were found among the middle school participants. The majority (89%) either agreed or strongly agreed that their recorded responses were an accurate representation of their ability to use Spanish. Only one student felt that his recorded responses did not accurately characterize his linguistic ability. When asked if the digital recordings were more accurate than in-class performance, only 16% of the students disagreed. In similar fashion, 83% of the students felt that the voice recordings helped improve their ability to speak Spanish and the same percentage perceived more self-confidence speaking in Spanish when using *Audacity*.

Turning to feelings of student anxiety, only one of the Japanese students found recording answers stressful. She mentioned that she had

difficulties managing both the linguistic tasks and the production of the voice clips. For her, a self-admitted technophobe, the learning curve was just another uncomfortable impediment to learning a language. However, once she learned how to use *Audacity*, she stated that she discovered her anxiety emerged more from having to use unfamiliar software than from the language itself. The remainder of the undergraduates expressed that the recording software was intuitive and easy to use. Overall, the students remarked that using voice recording software decreased their performance anxiety because they did not have to speak in front of classmates. The interviews helped us understand that speaking in front of peers in class was a source of stress for these students. Six of the eight strongly agreed that impromptu in-class speaking was stressful and the other two moderately agreed. When asked about the moderate agreement, several students casually mentioned that the two students were the best in the group. Nevertheless, the two, even though they felt confident to use the language, felt that speaking in front of peers does cause them some sense of language learning stress. When asked about using *Audacity* for out-of-class oral assessment, the group of students unanimously agreed that they felt less stress and more comfortable speaking in Japanese. However, 75% stated that they did not feel that their voice recordings were any more creative than responses they would give in-class or one-on-one with the Japanese professors. Again, similar results were found with the middle school students. Only one of the students found creating the recordings stressful. Similarly, only 5% of the students (3 girls, 1 boy) disliked recording their voices for assessment purposes. All (100%) expressed that *Audacity* was easy to use and 82% felt that their answers were more creative than their answers given during in-class assessments.

Next, we investigated student perception of the grading of their responses. Two of the Japanese students felt that they wanted to be graded on their face-to-face ability to listen to, interpret, and formulate a response in the language directly to the instructor. Further, the two stated that they wanted real-time feedback to their language ability and felt that personal contact with another speaker was crucial to learning to listen and speak in any language. However, one of the students who preferred recording and submitting her responses stated that she wanted every chance to turn in her best work for a grade. She, like many others, stated that they spent up to an hour recording, editing, and re-recording their responses before submitting their final version to the professors. However, none of the interviewees felt that his or her grade would improve because of the use of digital technology.

However, among the middle school students, only 14% preferred speaking in class for a grade to recording their answers. Two-thirds of the students (64%) reported that they typically recorded and re-recorded responses more than once with almost a quarter (24%) stating that they had recorded their responses at least four times or more before turning them in for grading. Fifty-eight percent of the students felt that their grade in Spanish would improve because they were recording their voices instead of speaking in class while a third of the students were uncertain (34%). Most felt that they prepared more for the assignment when using *Audacity* than for in-class oral assessments. Ninety-five percent stated that they liked using voice recording for assessing their ability to speak Spanish.

In general, students in both contexts felt that by using *Audacity* their responses were more accurate and representative of their speaking ability. Moreover, the students indicated that they perceived less stress when speaking in the target language for assessment purposes, even the ones who were seen as the best students in the class. While the undergraduates remained uncertain about the effect of the recordings on their overall grades, the middle school students reported that they felt their grades would improve since they had multiple opportunities to turn in their best work.

Instructors' Perceptions

The researchers interviewed the instructors to better understand their perceptions about using digital technology for oral language assessment. In addition to talking about the themes of student accuracy using the target language, student performance anxiety, and grades on assignments, instructors were also asked about their preference of using either traditional in-class oral language assessment practices or using digital technology, administrative flexibility for grading performances, increased reliability of assessment, and the use of students' digital recordings as an artifact of progress for students' speaking proficiency. These interviews confirmed student perceptions using *Audacity* and the conversations identified multiple advantages of digital voice recordings (See Table 2).

Overall, the three instructors noticed varying degrees of improved linguistic accuracy by students. They felt that any improvement in linguistic accuracy could be explained by several factors, one of which was the time (typically 1-2 days) students had to compose, revise, and submit responses to teacher prompts. Survey data showed that students re-recorded responses multiple times to improve the quality of their work and that some of the recordings were the product of at least an hour of practice before submitting the final recording for evaluation. Because of the opportunity to turn in their best work, Tina remarked that the students loved using *Audacity* and they said so on multiple occasions.

Yet, Tina noted that while there were positive aspects to using *Audacity*, she felt that overall the use of digital technology for assessment purposes did not improve the majority of the students' accuracy in the target language and that "perhaps middle school-age students were not mature enough to realize the benefits of improved second

Table 2. Instructors' perceptions of traditional and digital voice recording for oral language assessment

Traditional Method	Digital Voice Recording
• Decreases student likelihood of using newer vocabulary and grammatical structures. • Tends to increase student anxiety dramatically. • Increases loss of classroom time. • Is time consuming and disengages learners. • Leaves more potential for classroom management problems. • Is not replicable and does not allow for second opinion of student grade. • Fosters apprehension for students who are worried about looking foolish in front of peers. • Tends to encourage students to write, memorize, and then present.	• Improvement of linguistic accuracy remains unclear. • Increases sense of student control of the language and success using the target language. • Increases experimentation with target language. • Tends to improve completeness of language assessment tasks. • Diminishes student performance anxiety significantly. • Increases student excitement and inquiry among students. • Improvements in overall course grades remain unclear. • Decreases time required to evaluate student performance. • Increases accuracy of evaluation. • Increases instructional time in class. • Offers wider flexibility for evaluating student performances at unconventional times and locations. • Leaves a digital artifact for indication of student progress, accreditation data, and increased reliability of assessment. • Increases personalized student-teacher dialogue about language learning. • Permits multiple opportunities for student success. • Allows students to record responses at home or school. • Encourages students to practice before turning in recordings. • Makes students more aware of their errors and encourages self-correction. • Encourages more creativity. • Encourages improvisation instead of writing a script to be read or memorized. • Tends to increase costs if students do not treat school recording equipment respectfully.

language proficiency". The Japanese instructors felt that the college students were acutely aware of the benefits of improved proficiency and had set language learning goals far beyond the classroom. Nevertheless, interviews with the instructors showed that students felt like they were more in control of their answers using *Audacity*. Students using voice recordings appeared to experiment more with the language and grammar and spoke with broader vocabulary. Additionally, students' responses to language tasks were longer and for the university students, their recorded responses tended to be more complete than their in-class performances. The instructors also noted that the students chose to express themselves differently depending on the assessment procedure. All of the instructors indicated that during in-class assessments, students not only appeared less likely to use newer vocabulary and grammatical structures but were also less likely to complete the speaking

task completely and more likely to recite their task or sound unauthentic.

Turning to perceptions of the effects of *Audacity* to reduce student anxiety, all three instructors agreed vehemently that there was virtually little student performance anxiety as compared with in-class assessments. Before exploring digital recording options, Tina said that her students disliked having to speak in class. "Some students would be absent on days when oral assessment took place in an effort to avoid having to speak in front of peers. Other times, students would ask to be assessed privately." Many times, students would avoid volunteering to be assessed and she would have to resort to assessing students alphabetically to avoid any appearance of unfairness by students. However, when oral assessment tasks were given using *Audacity*, students would become excited and asked more in-depth questions about the assignment's specifics. She added that normally she could note student angst in their voices and even see physical evidence of nervousness (profuse sweating and antsy behavior). Because of such trepidation, many times student performance suffered when Tina knew that the students were able to manage the language successfully. Again, Kami reminded us that they had expected many of the students to prefer recording their responses to having to speak in class, while she noted in-class speaking assessments to be a great source of anxiety for language learners.

According to the instructors, part of student anxiety was due to the percentage of the course grade assigned for speaking. In the Japanese courses, students' grades were based primarily on speaking and listening ability (80%), whereas in the middle school Spanish course, the weight for speaking was much less, 15% of the total grade. All of the instructors agreed that the amount of influence speaking has in the classroom will ultimately determine how seriously students take the assignments. For Tina at the middle school level, this was especially true because she felt that if her department would raise the percentage of the grade for speaking her students would be increasingly more motivated to improve orally.

As it stands right now, my students know exactly how many points they need before their grades become affected. Depending on how many activities they are in and how badly they want to earn a certain grade, they make conscious decisions about how much effort to put into the speaking assignments. I'm sure if the speaking grades made up a higher percentage of their final grades, maybe 40% or so, their speaking skills would improve dramatically.

Next, the instructors talked about the traditional method of face-to-face oral language assessment and expressed concern about in-class oral assessments mostly because of the loss of instructional time. The instructors reported that in-class speaking assessments lasted approximately three to six minutes per student, which consumed almost two entire class meetings. "While a solo speak-

ing piece, or even a presented conversation may take only a minute, it takes several other minutes to fill out the rubric, give feedback, and get the next person(s) ready", remarked Tina. Kuki and Kami reported that assessing the college students took even more time in class because students requested specific feedback about a variety of linguistic details (e.g. pronunciation, intonation). Further, Tina found that her in-class assessments increased student concern about appearing foolish performing in front of classmates. All three instructors mentioned that the digital recordings were evaluated much quicker and definitely more accurately because they did not have to deal with classroom management issues of disruptive behavior (mostly loud discussions and asking to leave the room). All three instructors indicated that by using digital recordings for oral language assessment, their instructional time had increased.

In addition to having more instructional time, the instructors indicated a high degree of satisfaction with the flexibility that digital voice recording offers in terms of time and place of evaluation of student performance. The instructors mentioned that they graded student voice recordings outside of their offices or classrooms. Kuki stated that she takes public transportation frequently. While she rides the metro, she can listen on her *iPod* and assess the students' recordings using rubrics she has printed. She felt that she was evaluating student work perhaps even more carefully since she could listen to the recordings several times if needed. Kuki boldly stated that traditional in-class speaking assessments can only be reviewed once and that the digital recording can serve many purposes such as reliability of assessments. Tina concurred by adding that because of the flexibility offered by using digital recordings for assessment, she can differentiate the tasks better among students with different levels of oral proficiency.

While noted earlier, all of the instructors immediately noted that the recordings had the potential to increase the reliability of assessment because multiple evaluators could listen to and evaluate the same recording, allowing for more consistency than the traditional method of oral assessment. In fact, Kuki stated that the recordings would work well as indicators of student progress for students. Tina reiterated the notion and mentioned that her middle schoolers occasionally remarked that they did not feel they were making much progress using the language. By having the students listen to archived files, personalized discussions between Tina and the student took place to highlight improvement and progression toward fluency. Additionally, as touched on earlier, the two university professors noted that the recordings hold the potential to serve as a body of evidence for accreditation purposes. Kami stated that she saved students' digital files on the department's server for an upcoming college accreditation review.

Compared with the traditional face-to-face method, the instructors noted that by using a digital recording system, students can have multiple opportunities for success on the language tasks because they can revise their recordings as much as they see fit at locations other than school if they so choose. Using *Audacity* helped students monitor any linguistic or pronunciation errors while the teachers encouraged students to make corrections as necessary. All three instructors also mentioned that digital recordings encouraged students to express themselves with more linguistic creativity and improvisation instead of relying on a written or memorized script. According to the three instructors, the traditional method decreased the likelihood that students would use newly introduced vocabulary and grammar because they felt the students did not want to risk using the unfamiliar word and constructions. Also, assigning in-class oral language tasks fostered an environment of students writing, memorizing, and presenting their work, which is nothing more than the oral presentation of a writing activity. Nevertheless, findings from these studies indicate that there are serious considerations for continuing to use traditional methods of oral language assessment.

FUTURE RESEARCH DIRECTIONS

While we have presented strategies to use *Audacity* in the second language classroom at both the public school and undergraduate levels, we call for further research in the area. With increased attention focused on urban and high needs schools, it would be interesting to explore *Audacity's* use in these educational contexts. Perhaps even including other venues for students to use *Audacity* (e.g. public libraries) where students could access technology would provide valuable insight because many of these students may not have access to computers and the internet at home. Moreover, it would be intriguing to know elementary and high school students' perceptions on using digital technologies for oral language assessment purposes. Additionally, studies conducted in international contexts would provide a more expanded perception of *Audacity's* abilities from a global perspective.

Results from our two studies may also have implications for other content areas. Perhaps speech, debate, and English as Second Language teachers may find curricular applications for using one of the free and open source software options described earlier. For example, debate coaches could require students to record persuasive monologues on various topics, have students upload these audio files to student-created blogs, and require students to evaluate peer performances. Regardless of the class or even the assignment, we encourage educators to review the current literature in their content areas, design a strategy that aligns well with the technology tool selected, and even collaborate with colleagues in the field to improve current practices. Clearly, the technology available to teachers has improved dramatically over the past several decades and we encourage readers to discover and learn more about provocative uses of free and open source software in the future.

CONCLUSION

Teaching, regardless of content area, is a challenging profession to say the least. Specifically for world language teachers who are charged with teaching students to communicate in a second language, impediments to language learning surface when assessing student oral ability and competency. Findings from the two studies presented here document multiple benefits for both teachers and their students when using a digital recording method to assesses student oral language proficiency. The research indicates that student performance anxiety decreased when implementing recording software as opposed to using traditional face-to-face assessment. However, as with any implementation of technology in the curriculum, potential barriers to both technology use and technology access are inherent.

We have discussed the policy and administrative barriers that are often encountered in education, such as security concerns, the inability of an individual instructor to download and install software under restricted administrative privileges, and the difficulty in balancing student privacy and welfare against the pedagogical affordances offered by interactive multimedia software. With all of the benefits of using digital technology for oral language assessment, we feel it is important to note a hidden limitation to using digital technology for such purposes that neither study revealed. This process requires the use of somewhat expensive hardware and irresponsible users may misuse or even harm the computers, which in turn increases costs to deliver such a program. What has not been addressed, but continues to be of concern in student technology use, is the imperative to insure that all students have equal access to the technology required. Teachers must be vigilant against potentially harmful assumptions that all students have access to high-speed connectivity at home, and build in safeguards that allow for either on-campus opportunities to complete work or alternative paths for assessment.

We outlined three technology tools for oral language assessment purposes. While each has its advantages, the teacher needs to spend quality time selecting the appropriate tool for the pedagogical task. *Audacity* is one of several free and open source software options that is simple to use free and available to anyone. The time it takes to download, install, and use is relatively minimal. Its interface is intuitive and a few moments spent reading the Contents page will aid users immensely and even shorten the time it might normally take to become acquainted with this versatile digital tool.

Clearly the educational landscape has changed dramatically over the past several decades. Teachers are faced with more obstacles on a daily basis and many times teachers must choose to sacrifice precious instructional time in order to conduct oral language assessments in the classroom. Noting the heightened affective filter of students and the time required to assess each student, state-of-the-art technology in the form of free and open source software has the potential to be beneficial to both students and teachers. The three free and open source recording tools available to world language teachers presented here serve as basic examples of the technology for oral language assessment available today, with many more in development continuously. Findings from our research suggest that using digital technology for oral language assessment is a preferable option. While we presented a few strategies for implementing *Audacity* in the world language classroom, the creative and imaginative instructor will surely devise even more.

NOTE

Audacity(R) software is copyright (c) 1999-2009 Audacity Team. Web site: http://audacity.source-forge.net/. The name Audacity(R) is a registered trademark of Dominic Mazzoni.

REFERENCES

Beauvois, M. (1998). Conversations in slow motion: Computer-mediated communication in the foreign language classroom. *Canadian Modern Language Review, 54*(2), 198–217. doi:10.3138/cmlr.54.2.198

Chan, M. (2003). Technology and the teaching of oral skills. *CATESOL Journal, 15*, 51–57.

Cuban, L. (2001). *Oversold & underused: Computers in the classroom*. Cambridge, MA: Harvard University Press.

Egbert, J. (1999). Classroom practice: Practical assessments in the CALL classroom . In Egbert, J., & Hanson-Smith, E. (Eds.), *CALL environments: Research, practice, and critical issues* (pp. 257–271). Alexandria, VA: TESOL.

Flewelling, J. (2002). From language lab to multimedia lab: Oral language assessment in the new millennium. In C. M. Cherry (Ed.), *Dimension: Proceedings of the Southern Conference on Language Teaching,* (pp. 33-42). Valdosta, GA: SCOLT Publications.

Foster, P., Tonkyn, A., & Wigglesworth, G. (2000). Measuring spoken language: A unit for all reasons. *Applied Linguistics, 21*, 354–375. doi:10.1093/applin/21.3.354

Futernick, K. (2007, October). Study Examines Why Teachers Quit and What Can Be Done. *District Administration, 43*(10), 16.

Glasser, B. G., & Strauss, A. L. (1967). *The discovery of grounded theory*. Chicago: Aldine.

Goldman, J. P. (1991, April). Balancing School Sports and Academics. *Education Digest, 56*(8), 67–70.

Guba, E. G., & Lincoln, Y. S. (1981). *Effective evaluation*. San Francisco: Jossey-Bass.

Hai-Peng, H., & Deng, L. (2007). Vocabulary acquisition in multimedia environment. *US-China Foreign Language, 5*(8), 55–59.

Hartman, K., Neuwirth, C., Kiesler, S., Sproull, L., Cochran, C., Palmquist, M., & Zabrow, D. (1995). Patterns of social interaction and learning to write: Some effects of network technologies . In Berge, Z., & Collins, M. (Eds.), *Computer-mediated communication and the online classroom* (pp. 47–78). Creskill, NJ: Hampton Press, Inc.

Krashen, S. (1981). *Second Language Acquisition and Second Language Learning*. New York: Pergamon Press.

Levy, M., & Hubbard, P. (2005). Why call CALL "CALL"? *Computer Assisted Language Learning, 18*(3), 143–149. doi:10.1080/09588220500208884

MacIntyre, P. D. (1999). Language Anxiety: A Review of the Research for Language Teachers . In Young, D. J. (Ed.), *Affect in Foreign Language and Second Language Learning. 4 Practical Guide to Creating a Low-anxiety-Classroom Atmosphere* (pp. 24–45). Boston: McGraw-Hill College.

Mazzoni, D., & Dannenberg, R. (2000). *Audacity* [software]. Pittsburg, PA: Carnegie Mellon University.

National Center for Education Statistics. (2000). *Teachers' tools for the 21st century. A report on teachers' use of technology*. Washington, DC: Author.

National Standards in Foreign Language Education Project. (1999). *Standards for foreign language learning in the 21st century*. Yonkers, NY: Author.

Piaget, J. (1973). *To Understand is to Invent*. New York: Grossman.

Pierson, M., & Cozart, A. (2005). Novice Teacher Case Studies: A Changing Perspective on Technology during Induction Years. In C. Crawford et al. (Eds.), *Proceedings of Society for Information Technology and Teacher Education International Conference 2005* (pp. 3332-3337). Chesapeake, VA: AACE.

Stepp-Greany, J. (2002). Student perceptions on language learning in a technological environment: Implications for the new millennium. *Language Learning & Technology, 6*(1), 165–180.

Volle, L. (2005). Analyzing oral skills in voice e-mail and online interviews. *Language Learning and Technology, 9*(3), 146-163. Retrieved June 2, 2009, from http://llt.msu.edu/vol9num3/volle/

Vygotsky, L. S. (1978). *Mind in Society.* Cambridge, MA: Harvard University Press.

Woodrow, L. (2006). Anxiety and speaking English as a second language. *RELC Journal, 37*(3), 308–328. doi:10.1177/0033688206071315

Zellmer, M. B., Frontier, A., & Pheifer, D. (2006, November). What Are NCLB's Instructional Costs? *Educational Leadership, 64*(3), 43–46.

KEY TERMS AND DEFINITIONS

Affective Filter: The Affective filter is a perceived screen between learners of a second language and the input needed to learn and acquire a second language. If the filter is high, the learner is blocking out input. Conversely, if the filter is lower, more input is received. Learning environments with low levels of anxiety are deemed better for language learning.

Instructional Time: The amount of time teachers have once the class has begun.

MP3 Files: A digital audio recording file format that compresses the size of the file for storage purposes.

Oral Language Assessment: The manner in which individuals or groups of language learners are evaluated in terms of their speaking ability.

Performance Anxiety: Also known as stage fright, it is the fear an individual has when requested to perform in front of an audience.

Three Modes of Communication: Developed for the American Council on the Teaching of Foreign Languages, the three modes describe the Interpretive domain (the appropriate cultural interpretation of meanings that occur in written and spoken forms), the Interpersonal domain (active negotiation of meaning among people), and the Presentational (the creation of oral or written messages).

Traditional Method of Oral Language Assessment: Teachers listening to and evaluating student oral language performance in-class.

World Languages: Also known as foreign languages, these languages can include modern and classical languages, American Sign Language, and even computer programming languages.

Chapter 12

Open for Social:
How Open Source Software for E-Learning can Take a Turn to the Social

James Laffey
University of Missouri, USA

Matthew Schmidt
University of Missouri, USA

Christopher Amelung
Yale University, USA

ABSTRACT

Online learning in K-12 and higher education has been growing rapidly, and open source software has the potential to improve the quality of e-learning. This paper describes how FOSS enables turning e-learning from a potentially restrictive and narrow framing of the education experience to an emergent and social experience. The authors identify several key elements of the FOSS model that position open source initiatives to contribute to the emergent and social nature of experience in e-learning. The authors also describe several challenges to developing FOSS in a community of educators for e-learning. These elements and challenges are illustrated in a brief case report about the development of an open source software system called Context-aware Activity Notification System (CANS). CANS (http://cansaware.com) is a notification system that integrates with collaborative work and learning systems and is designed around the importance of awareness of user activity, a user's social context and personal notification preferences.

INTRODUCTION

Nearly 4 million students were enrolled in at least one online higher education course in 2007 (Allen & Seaman, 2008). This number represents a 12% increase over the previous year. In addition to on-line courses, web-facilitated courses and blended courses (courses that meet face-to-face but have portions of content delivered online) are spreading across campuses (van Rooij, 2009). As an example, at the University of Missouri-Columbia (MU), thousands of courses—representing tens of thousands of student enrollments—use online course management tools each academic year. In

DOI: 10.4018/978-1-61520-917-0.ch012

the Fall 2005 semester, 83% of all MU students enrolled in at least one course that blended face-to-face instruction with online learning through the use of a course management system (CMS).

While lagging somewhat behind the growth in higher education, online education in K-12 is also growing rapidly. Based on a national survey of school district administrators, the Sloan Consortium estimates that over one million K-12 students were engaged in online learning in the 2007-8 school year (Picciano & Seaman, 2008). This number represents a 47% increase from the 2005-6 school year. The report recognizes a special value of online courses for small rural districts in that online courses can provide access to courses that cannot be made available because of teacher shortages or other limiting factors. However, the range of students opting for online learning spans those seeking Advanced Placement courses, those with special needs, those choosing home schooling, those needing credit recovery and those who for some reason do not fit well in traditional school settings. Clayton Christensen, author of "Disrupting Class" (Christensen, Horn & Johnson, 2008), predicts that by 2013 10% of all K-12 school enrollments (with approximately 53 million K-12 students in the US) will be online and that by 2018 the number will be 50% of all enrollments. As another indicator of growth, the fifth annual "Keeping Pace Report" (Watson, Gemin & Ryan, 2008) notes that, as of Fall 2008, 44 states offer significant online learning opportunities for students with 34 states providing state-led programs.

Online courses have great potential to improve access to education. Positive reports of online learning success show its impact and potential, such as relative equivalence in test-result outcomes with face-to-face learning courses (Talent-Runnels, Thomas, Lan, Cooper, Ahem, Shaw & Xiaoming, 2006). However, while online learning is far advanced from traditional correspondence courses, concerns remain about a diminished social experience in online courses that may

be detrimental to both the student-to-instructor and student-to-student relationships needed for sufficient engagement and retention of online students. (e.g., Yang & Cornelius, 2005; Berge, 2001; Bower, 2001; Hara & Kling, 2000). Indeed, this lack of social interaction was found to be a factor that depresses student satisfaction in online learning (Arbaugh, 2000). Consequently, dissatisfaction with online learning may be seen in high rates of attrition of online students. Chyung (2001) found that online learners who dropped out perceived that their online learning environment was not engaging, had low levels of confidence while learning at a distance and had low satisfaction levels for the instructional processes used in the online learning environment.

Today's approach to online learning is implemented through CMSs, of which proprietary systems, such as Blackboard and Desire2Learn, and open source systems, such as Moodle (http://moodle.org/) and Sakai (http://sakaiproject.org/), represent popular applications. These CMSs implement ways for instructors to give and control access to information about a course (syllabus, assignments, grades) and about the subject matter (instructional resources). They also provide some facilities for direct interaction through discussion boards and chat rooms. Such approaches help manage the course and the information of the course but are very limited in how they support the interaction, coordination and cooperation needed to do course activity. Students today use Twitter, YouTube, Facebook and many other social networking applications (Dunlap & Lowenthal, 2009) and are accustomed to their online experience being a social experience (Caruso & Salaway, 2007). Given that a large portion of students use social networking sites daily (Caruso & Salaway, 2007), it is easy to envision many of these students multitasking with Skype and Facebook and other applications while working in their CMS. Indeed, a qualitative study (Goggins, Laffey & Tsai, 2007) of how members of small groups cooperate in online courses found that multitasking while doing online coursework was a key theme. Multitasking occurred in settings where the student was using mobile devices to engage in coursework and when the user was physically present with non-class others while doing the online coursework. We argue that this adaptation by the student leads to unequal resources for students and to unmanaged and unsupported experiences for students. In an era where the need to understand and design for "human computer interaction" is being replaced by the need to understand and design for "human-to-human interaction via the computer" and where e-learning needs to fully mediate teaching and learning, not simply support face-to-face instruction, current CMSs represent tired and limited ways of working (Vrasidas, 2004; Marra & Jonassen, 2002).

So what does it mean to have CMSs take a turn to the social? One key aspect of being social is to have a sense of community. Sense of community is an attribute of being social that represents a feeling of belonging and having others to ask for support (Blanchard, 2000; Wellman & Gulia, 1999). Having a high sense of community indicates a greater flow of information among members, availability of supports, commitment to group goals and higher collaboration among members (Wellman, 1999; Dede, 1996; Scott, 2004). Sense of community and the ability to interact effectively with others have been identified as two critical factors influencing students' level of online participation and social interaction (Rovai, 2002; Putnam, 2000; Lin, Lin, Liu, Huang, et al., 2006; Picciano, 2002). Students in their non-academic online experience are finding this sense of community through Facebook, Twitter, blogging and other forms of social computing, but these social networking capabilities are not found in current CMSs.

A second key aspect of being social is activity awareness. By activity awareness we mean being aware of what significant others are doing around you and knowing that these others are also aware of what you are doing. Dourish and Bellotti (1992) defined this form of awareness

as "an understanding of the activities of others, which provides a context for your own activity" (p. 107). Carroll and colleagues (2003) identified three different types of awareness information for productive synchronous and asynchronous collaboration: social awareness (who is around?), action awareness (what is happening to objects?) and activity awareness (how are things going on?). They noted that a core problem of the educational site was the complexity involved in maintaining awareness for long-term activities. Traditional classroom-based learning includes natural forms of awareness because members can watch their teacher, fellow students and changes to classroom objects during and across class periods. There is usually little reason for activity awareness outside of the classroom because homework assignments are typically crafted to be individual tasks and instructors do not presume that students work together on their homework. Online learning throws this model on its head as natural forms of activity awareness are no longer available for teaching, and learning activity and non-instructor led collaboration or at least connectivity is usually built into the online learning tools. The opportunity for collaboration and learning with and from others online can be supported by activity awareness, but to make activity awareness effective we need to understand what knowledge about the activity of others is valued, how members relate to each other and use activity information in forming and shaping those relationships and how CMS can represent the needed activity information in ways that resonate with how people work and learn. Carroll and his colleagues (2003) concluded that to coordinate and effectively work in the online cooperative world of educational settings, users (instructors and students) need sets of tools for managing objects in the learning process, knowing when someone does something to an object and keeping track of objects over a span of time and work practice. Their work suggests the need for notification systems that not only convey information, but also put that information into the context of work practices and social roles.

The current CMSs have a large installed base in education, and educational institutions are notoriously slow to adopt new technology. Thus, those working with CMS systems need ways to incorporate new, open and social approaches to supporting teaching and learning. We believe that access to code, an ethos of users working collectively to meet their own needs and community support for innovation make FOSS in education a key approach for helping e-learning take a turn to the social. In the following sections we forward a justification for these claims using a brief case report of our experience participating in FOSS development with the CANS project to illustrate our progress and key lessons learned.

FOSS AND POTENTIAL FOR E-LEARNING

It is probably a mistake to think of FOSS as a single idea or approach. FOSS is dynamic and evolving in who, what, how and to what impact. FOSS is an approach to software development and distribution that includes source code and forms of licensing which permits ready customization and evolution while preserving the software as a common good. FOSS is also a system of development with demonstrated advantages for reliability, security and adaptability over closed source or proprietary software. FOSS represents an ethos as well as sets of communities with common goals and a commitment to collective invention. The FOSS approach started with early time-sharing systems at MIT and with the development of the ARPANET in the 1960s. In those days FOSS was simply a smart way of working that supported systems improvement, the work of integrating new systems with existing systems and learning how to harness the power of computing systems. In the 1980s, in response to the growing presence and dominance of proprietary software, a "free

software" movement began in order to create special licensing approaches to ensure open access to software. For 20 years or so this movement was a vibrant but, for most practical educational purposes, a fringe approach to software development. However, in the last 10 years open source has captured an increasing share of software development because users see it as an attractive alternative approach to the dependence on a single vendor created by proprietary software.

We view the value of open source software for the improvement of CMSs as hearkening back to the roots of the FOSS movement when "freedom" meant flexibility and empowering the union of developer and user, and when "community" did not just mean customer, it meant an environment and network in which your own practices took place. FOSS provides opportunities for stakeholders, from users to developers, to participate in the community development effort which simultaneously contributes to meeting local needs (Lin & Zini, 2008; Carmichael & Honour, 2002). However, it is important to note that participation in and coordination of FOSS community development requires dedicated resources and expertise. While there is little doubt that many universities employ tremendously talented software developers, many of them are students who move on to work in industry and other jobs upon matriculation. At the same time, applying limited development resources to work within the greater FOSS development ecosystem allows universities to leverage the resources of the larger community to their individual needs and the needs of their users (Coppola & Neelley, 2004).

Our vision for how open source software can improve the quality of e-learning is to reassert a more direct relationship between development communities and users so that developers are members of the user community, not simply providers, and where innovation is driven by the integration of the practices of teaching and learning with the flexibility and freedom to develop. To date, this vision has not been systematically approached in the literature. While the impact of FOSS on building pedagogically valid learning environments has yet to be assessed (van Rooij, 2007), educational institutions are looking to FOSS as a way to balance pedagogy and administrative efficiency. A starting point for addressing this gap in the literature is to systematically investigate lessons learned from FOSS e-learning communities like those which have emerged around the open source CMSs Sakai and Moodle (van Rooij, 2009). We view our own story (Laffey & Musser, 1996; Musser, Laffey & Lawrence, 2000; Remidez, Laffey & Musser, 2001; Laffey et al., 2003; Laffey & Musser, 2006) of working in higher education over the last 15 years to build open source software to improve education as a case that illustrates both the potential and the challenges inherent in using FOSS to improve the quality of e-learning and especially the social nature of the e-learning experience. We use a case report about the development of CANS, an activity notification system for Sakai, to share a part of that story and the perspective we have developed through those 15 years of work.

CASE REPORT: CANS

CANS is licensed under the Educational Community License (version 1.0) open-source license, and was designed to provide activity awareness, that is, awareness of what is going on in the CMS, for instructors and students. CANS captures activity information by establishing a vocabulary of tools and action events, maintains a history of activity, makes notifications available based on the context of use and allows users to configure their notification preferences. CANS works by observing activity in Sakai, such as when a member logs in, reads a discussion board item, uploads a document, or enters a chat message. The records of all these observations are stored and matched with profiles for access to awareness information set by the members. Matches lead CANS to send

information to members who want the information in a form they have selected. For example, a student in a group may want to know when the instructor has posted an assignment and have that information immediately emailed or delivered via a desktop widget (a small application that can always be visible on one's desktop). The student may want to see who has posted new messages or read existing messages, but only want that information when they enter the course website. An instructor may want the same information but want it organized in a table to see who has contributed and how much to a discussion. Thus, the awareness information is a resource for instructors and students in knowing and understanding what is happening in the course, for making decisions about when and how to act and also as a tool for an instructor to identify to what extent his or her expectations for student behavior are being met. Given this brief introduction, we direct readers who want more information about CANS to http://cansaware.com or to a chapter directly about the system (Laffey & Amelung, in press). The remainder of the case report is provided to illustrate the benefits and challenges of developing a system like CANS with a FOSS approach.

First Phase

In the late 1990s a project team at MU developed an open source licensed intranet system for schools called Shadow netWorkspace™ (SNS), intended to help poor and rural schools use network services such as file sharing, discussion boards and email, and do so within a secure environment. We were inspired by seeing how our own work and teaching was changing with Internet services and how slowly many schools were moving to put these services into place. For example, at that time the service provider to schools in Missouri was allocating 2 email addresses to school districts which then had to share those among administrators, teachers and students. As SNS became operative as an online information system we started to use it in our own teaching and project work. We complained amongst ourselves that it took too long to go into a course and look around to see if students had posted in the discussion board or uploaded documents, etc., so we decided to build a monitor that would show what had been recently done. Fortuitously we created the Activity Monitor (see Figure 1) with links to the objects they referenced. In our own behavior and in those we observed in usage studies we saw members using prior students' activity as a menu for linking to the objects. In short, the monitor transformed the interface from one based on system structures to one based on user activity and changed our perspective from developing an information system to developing a social system.

These insights led us to focus on the social nature of the online learning experience and develop a construct and instrumentation for assessing social ability in online learning (Laffey, Lin & Lin, 2006; Yang et al., 2006; Lin & Laffey, 2006). By social ability we mean the person's capacity to associate with fellows and to use the members, resources and tools of the social context to achieve something of value. However, the implementation of the activity monitor in SNS proved to be problematic. As the semester progressed and there were more and more activities to examine, the activity monitor substantially

slowed down SNS' overall performance. The architecture and mechanisms of the monitor needed to be reconsidered and redeveloped. Chris Amelung, one of the doctoral students on our SNS team, took on the redevelopment for his dissertation work and the result was the first implementation of CANS (Amelung, 2005). In 2005 our academic unit also made the decision to retire SNS as our CMS and implement Sakai. Sakai is a collaboration and learning environment used by around 100 institutes of higher education as a CMS. Sakai is a free and open source product that uses a community source development model. CANS was readily re-implemented in Sakai and was being used at MU as early as 2006.

This preliminary work and early phase of the CANS project illustrates several advantages of FOSS in e-learning. First we identified several key insights about information systems through a "continuous improvement" process that put our own ideas into action. Educational researchers also use the term "design research" as a methodology for continuous and simultaneous efforts to improve both systems and theory (Laffey, Amelung & Goggins, 2009; DBRC, 2002). Secondly, access to code and the ability to create a local modification of a system allowed Amelung to first develop CANS for SNS and then port it to Sakai. And, thirdly, we were quickly able to continue our implementation

Figure 1. Illustration of how the Activity Monitor was integrated into the personal desktop of SNS.

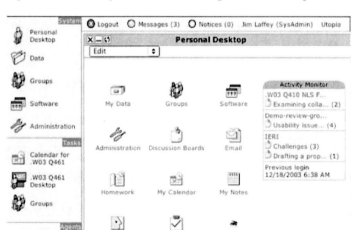

and research into the social nature of learning because members of the Sakai community provided expertise and consultation for making the move to Sakai. However, FOSS also has some downsides and one illustrated in our report is the shuttering of the SNS project. Because the K-12 schools for whom it was intended, primarily rural and poor, did not have many resources to put to its implementation and not any to put to its continuous improvement, the weight of advancing SNS, even to upgrade for new versions of browsers, fell to a small team of developers and eventually the system could not be sustained. FOSS projects need to develop communities of supporters and contributors in order to thrive and survive.

Second Phase

Shortly after the move from SNS to Sakai we were granted an award from the Fund for the Improvement of Postsecondary Education, U.S. Department of Education (Project # P116B060045). The grant allowed us to continue the development of CANS to include a listener for Sakai and new forms of notification. The listener works within Sakai to report events (discussion posts, downloading a file, opening an assignment document, etc.) to the CANS server. One challenge we encountered was the diversity of ways that events were represented across various functions of Sakai. Because Sakai is a collection of programs from various universities integrated by some core services, it offers a great breadth of e-learning functionality but also much diversity in how each application is programmed. We also developed three ways of reporting events back to the members: an email digest, an interactive web page and widgets. The digest provides a reporting mechanism that is outside of Sakai so we do not have to depend on students logging in to Sakai to be informed. The interactive webpage allows the user in Sakai to directly link to a web page with capabilities for dynamically (using FLEX technology) representing social information allowing for when members are engaged in

the learning activities and have a question about the levels and types of activity underway in the class. The widgets provide flexibility to deliver information directly to a member's desktop or can be embedded in the homepage of the course. Figure 2 shows an example of a widget providing social comparison information so a student knows how their activity in certain aspects of the course compares with that of the most active student and the average for all students. The social comparison widget may have less detail about what has been done than a digest, but in this example the widget frames the information so as to make it personally relevant to the question of, "How does my level of activity relate to that of others in the class?"

As part of our work in developing the new notification features we undertook a case study of a group working on a collaborative project within a class. Findings from this study showed some of the challenges of being an active member of a social learning unit when computers are used to fully mediate learning. Two core themes came from the analysis of how the group worked. One theme was an emphasis on managing *social identity* so as to maintain a cordial environment and not risk social capital. Members stated that they did not disagree with people online because it is too easy to have things misunderstood or result in bad feelings and, after all, they did have to work with these people over an extended period of time and a large number of activities. Such findings provide evidence that the available tools of current CMSs do not provide appropriate mechanisms and structure for argumentation and fail to provide the contextual cues for managing those types of exchanges. In fact "thin communication" such as that which we try to achieve with activity awareness may be viewed suspiciously by participants. By thin communication we mean the abstracting of certain attributes of an activity (such as it happened) and providing that in a list or other de-contextualized form. What makes this type of communication somewhat problematic is that instead of a person making the

193

Figure 2. A sample social comparison widget

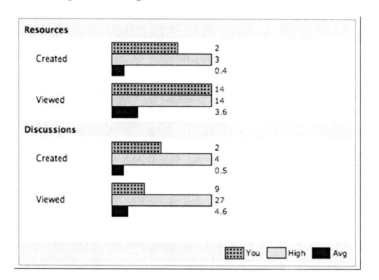

observation that someone just looked at their report, they may wonder "why" someone looked at their report. In our theoretical world of social navigation we might predict that seeing someone look at a report might cause others to look at a report. However, in the real world it might create suspicions of copying ideas, or feelings that others were checking up on you, etc. The other theme is one of *multitasking*. Students are doing their coursework as a part of their other activities. For example respondents told us, "I've actually been driving down (the highway), talking to my husband and posting to my team," and "Sometimes I get distracted when my boyfriend blows something up in Gears of War while I'm chatting with my team online."

Awareness as a support for participants in an environment where they are likely to be multitasking and with many possible distractions from the online learning tasks became an important attribute of the users' design personas. As we considered our design in the context of multi-tasking learners, one approach was to consider how to focus attention on the learning tasks and mitigate distractions. Further analysis drew us to the belief that we needed to embrace the idea that students were multitasking and support how they man-

aged the learning tasks within their multitasking context. They were multitasking across course tasks, across courses and outside course tasks. For some students it appears that multitasking is a natural way to work and learn, for some it is necessary given timelines and responsibilities and for others the stimulation of multiple activities or distractions seems to be an alternative to falling asleep at the keyboard.

To address the issue of multitasking we conceptualized two dimensions that seem to be in play for awareness information in multitasking situations. One dimension is *salience*. Awareness reports may be too meek to draw attention given other factors being considered, such as in the examples mentioned above of driving and observing a game being played. The opposite end of the salience spectrum may be overbearing intrusions that, especially in a multitasking situation, could lead to awareness overload. A second dimension is *meaningfulness*. How will users make sense of the new information? If the information is too disconnected from the users' mental models it will be interpreted as noise and disregarded. If the information is tightly coupled to a specific event or process, it may be represented in a way that is inefficient. For example, if a user is developing a response to a discussion board message, it may be helpful to know that the author is currently online and working in the discussion board tool, but overwhelming to also know details about the new thread the author is in and activity surrounding that thread. This nuance seems similar to the construct of social translucence (Erickson & Kellogg, 2003). Social translucence refers to the goal of providing appropriate information and representations so that human-computer interaction (HCI) can be gracefully undertaken. A physical example is when two people approach a door and one may open the door into the face of the other. Having a glass door allows for seeing the other, but the needed action does not actually require knowing who the other person is or distinct attributes about them. Thus the door can have a filmed glass so that all that is known is that another person is approaching. Another aspect of social translucence is accountability. It may be excusable to open a door into someone's face if a wooden door made it impossible to know the other person was on the other side, but once cues are available for "knowing," then you are accountable for your actions. This objective of providing activity awareness information as needed and in appropriate representations seems a good fit for helping members derive meaning in a multitasking situation and creating online learning environments where users are more accountable for their actions.

This recognition of the importance of social identity and multitasking and the complexity of providing salience and meaningfulness led us to design a notification manager application in Sakai that would allow instructors or students to set up what, when and how they wanted notifications. The manager application allowed us to not only provide activity and social information in multiple forms, but also to allow those forms to be customized by local knowledge of the learning tasks and how members related to each other. For example, a course that used team project work could set up digests or widgets for the team members and exclude other members of the course from being

able to access this information. This might allow members to be more comfortable with what type of information was shared and to have it be more meaningful to the decisions they were making about how to work. However, the step of building a notification manager that could be accessed as a Sakai tool required a programmer with experience developing for Sakai to ensure that the interface and the way data were handled conformed to best practices in Sakai programming.

The work we undertook in phase 2 of developing functionality for CANS to work within Sakai showed the power of integrating our work with a larger community, in that Sakai had many more functions for e-learning than did SNS. Clearly, our work also benefited by our ability to add functionality to CANS, such as the notification manager, as we developed new insights about how activity and social information is used in e-learning. This ability for local adaptation as a means to test approaches to supporting the social nature of online leaning and to investigate the impact of the approaches, and then to repeat the process based on newly informed ideas, is needed for continuous improvement and knowledge building. This ability for design research and continuous improvement of software and testing in large systems deployed at educational institutions is uniquely supported by the FOSS model. Just imagine what it would be like to try and talk your campus administrators and the executives of a proprietary system to do a trial of your new idea! However, this ability to try innovative approaches may not be easy to execute. We found substantial complexity and overhead in trying to integrate CANS within Sakai. The need for a programmer with capabilities specific to implementation in Sakai could not be readily filled by our team, but fortunately was available within the larger community.

Third Phase

In the third phase of the CANS project we are attempting to support other universities in the use of CANS. At present we are focusing on efforts to test the viability and usefulness of CANS at the University of Michigan, Rice University and East China Normal University (ECNU) in Shanghai, China. All three of the universities are performing some form of testing with a plan for a pilot implementation. This step beyond MU shows some key benefits of working with FOSS and some key challenges. On the benefit side, it is an exciting part of the design and development process to find collaborators who share your vision and are willing to invest time and staff to try the software as well as make contributions that extend your own work. These other universities bring experience and expertise that go beyond what our team at MU can provide. For example, the University of Michigan operates a large network to meet the needs of its very large Sakai user base. Heretofore in our development we had not addressed the need for load balancing and other concerns to support system performance under high load conditions. Their leaders and staff address these concerns as a common part of how they work and are able to both identify issues and help us address them. The leaders at Rice University have particular interests in using data for institutional research as part of their academic computing decision-making. Their concerns and insights are both pushing us and helping us see new approaches to extend the value of CANS beyond notification in the learning context. Similarly, at ECNU they need a version of CANS that can report in Chinese and are developing solutions to make language a variable within the system. All of this collaboration extends our small team and pushes and pulls CANS to be a better system.

A motto of the Sakai community is "Designed by Educators, for Educators." This motto implies that there may be special insights that those who practice education can understand and bring to the design work that may be hard to identify and articulate in a product development cycle that includes educators as customers and not as a community of practitioners. This is not to say that FOSS is the only or even best way to develop software for education, but just that it is a different way than developers of proprietary systems apply and it has some unique benefits. We characterize a key difference in development approaches as proprietary companies have a great focus on locking in the value of their accomplishments, by adding to their customer base and by seeking patents on their inventions. In contrast we see the focus in the small CANS and larger Sakai community as unlocking the potential of the technology to meet felt needs. In part, this unlocking comes from the daily experience of applying the technology, confronting its limitations and seeing its possibilities. Of course, for long-term success one must be able to both lock in value and unlock potential. Our view, that was expressed in the introduction about the limitations of CMSs, is that at this point in time the need to unlock potential is great. Working with partners and being a part of a community is both inspiring and productive for extending CANS, undertaking design research and seeing potential with new eyes.

While earlier we pointed out that diversity of programming creates a challenge for integrating CANS into Sakai, diversity of thought is a key asset of working in a community. In the case of Sakai and the goal of making it a more social place for learning, we are developing CANS to impact access to and the use of social information. Other researchers, also having the goal of making Sakai a more social place for teaching and learning, are developing other approaches. A key initiative in the development of the next generation of Sakai is to include social networking functionality. The addition of social networking in Sakai will use Apache Shindig (an application intended to support social networking developed by the Apache open source project). The addition of social networking to Sakai is intended to support collaboration within sites and possibly across sites. Additionally it is hoped that this work will help define the purpose and role for social networking in an academic context.

Phase 3 has also shown us additional challenges for FOSS in e-learning. Working with other universities shows not only the breadth of their needs and interests, but also the diversity of their technology infrastructures. A key attraction to the universities that have adopted Sakai is the ability to customize it to their own local requirements. Perhaps this leads to more diffusion in types of infrastructures found at Sakai campuses than would be found at campuses adopting a proprietary system. We speculate that the decision to purchase a proprietary system starts a process of coordinating all systems to work with the chosen system, whereas a decision to adopt a FOSS starts a process of customizing the FOSS to work with other existing systems. Of course it is also likely to be true that the company selling a proprietary system invests heavily in making sure the system fits with the most popular configurations found on campuses.

The lessons learned through the three phases of CANS development illustrate both the benefits and challenges of the FOSS approach for making online learning more social. Access to source code and support from a community of peers, the fundamental aspects of FOSS, enable local perspectives and expertise to shape new software. In the field of e-learning much of this local experience pushes the software to address the social and emergent nature of learning which is not well supported by current CMS. Progress in this area is further supported by the ability to learn from field tests of new systems capabilities, such as CANS, and improve both the conceptual framework for what you are trying to accomplish and the software systems in use. The challenges of developing software are substantial and while Universities have ready pools of student programmers and resident faculty expertise, this combination is not well suited to the sustained and systematic effort needed to develop software. This challenge is further complicated by the work efforts needed to move from software that works as a prototype to a product that can be distributed to a broader

community. Aligned with the challenge of moving from prototype to product is the need to integrate the software with that of the broader community, in our case integrating CANS into Sakai. While our local team had the capabilities to develop CANS we struggled to understand the complexities of integration with Sakai which indeed was a moving target as Sakai is under continuous development to meet other pedagogical needs and administrative needs of the broader community. In many ways it is best for innovation to exist at the margins of a community where new ideas can be tried in a rapid fashion and where failure is appreciated as a learning experience. At some point or points those innovations must be harvested by the broader community to spur advances and meet needs. This transition has many challenges as the innovation must be ready for product status and the community must embrace change and some level of risk. As van Rooij (2007 & 2009) illustrates in her review of open source implementation case reports, efforts such as ours offer potential for building new knowledge about how open source software can enable improvements to pedagogy and find a balance of sound pedagogy and technical efficiency.

DISCUSSION

Starting from a perspective that online learning, a key form of e-learning in higher education and K-12 education, is rapidly growing and increasingly important in education, this chapter has described a need for improved CMSs to support e-learning with a particular focus on enhancing the social nature of the online experience. We have also characterized the processes needed for supporting the emerging needs of viewing CMS as a social place for learning as requiring innovation, building systems from insights gained from practice and continuous improvement. The chapter has also used our experience of developing CANS to illustrate some of the key benefits and challenges of the FOSS approach and how they fit the new requirements of e-learning. We have identified and illustrated two key themes of how FOSS supports the types of innovation and improvement needed for having CMS take a turn to the social. The first theme is the freedom of development made possible by access to code and licensing forms that allow local modifications. This freedom of development couples with a commingling of developers and practitioners to move from insights for improvement to trials of new code and functions. The second theme is that of having community support for innovation and collective invention. There is a form of natural selection that forms a community around the use and extension of an open source system that encourages and invites innovation and improvement. Having a community means that there are physical, social and intellectual resources that can be brought to bear on challenges.

The theme of freedom to develop was shown in the ability of the CANS developer to have direct access to the code and system representations that stand for activity in a system, such as event messages. This access is enhanced by collegiality among developers in a community and the valuing of innovation. Discussions with other developers led to improved models and approaches to how to utilize events messages. FOSS provides an unprecedented level of software freedom in comparison with proprietary counterparts, which can be both advantageous and challenging. Such freedom allows for profound flexibility in software design and implementation, but it is this flexibility that can result in difficulties like non-standardized event messages. Issues like this are not necessarily problems, but rather the logical outcomes of software freedom. Just as freedom of speech results in wildly diverse opinions, software freedom results in diverse designs and implementations. We argue that diversity is a necessity for influencing and realizing innovation and is core to the nature and success of the FOSS model. However, the freedom

that allows for such diversity is not without its own unique set of challenges.

The theme of having community support for innovation is also critical to the work of innovation and improvement in e-learning. For example, the Sakai community has an annual worldwide meeting and various local meetings as well as fostering lively discussions about systems implementations and improvements via listservs. Of course, proprietary systems develop communities of users who meet to discuss practices and lobby for improvements, but lobbying for improvements as a request to a corporate entity is different than being engaged in the discussion about how the improvement will work with the members working to make it happen, or being one of the members making it happen. As mentioned earlier, one can argue the efficacy of a proprietary or FOSS approach to development for large complex systems. However, we argue that the FOSS approach is uniquely well suited to drive innovation and lead to more social places for learning.

While software freedom and working in a community that support innovation grants flexibility for innovation, this flexibility comes at a price. In the case of open source CMSs, universities and other educational institutions that wish to modify or change the software require resources to do so. Yet, these institutions are often under-resourced. Finding expert developers and programmers to develop open source CMSs is difficult, as these experts are in high-demand in the job market and receive high salaries. And while many brilliant programmers do work with universities, most are students who move to higher-paying jobs after graduation. Hence, significant time and resources are spent continuously training new developers; yet the return on the investment for time and resources spent training these developers is short and unsustainable. This continuing turnover makes it difficult to build strong and efficient development teams. In addition, because many institutions are under-resourced, they must focus on their own specific needs. Consequently, the development done at these institutions may be so specialized that there is limited generalization to the broader needs of the community. And while it is understandable that institutions want to invest their resources to meet their own specific needs, attention to matching these specific needs to the broader needs of the greater community is a challenge for the leadership in any FOSS project. However, it has been our observation that even when the specific code developed at one institution may be limited in its application across the community, the community advances by seeing the efforts and understanding the context of the new development. In this way the community develops both social and intellectual capital from innovative practices and the sharing of ideas and results. A key illustration of this in the Sakai community is the sharing of best pedagogical practices using Sakai across institutions. An awards program highlights faculty members who are recognized for innovative and effective use of Sakai in their teaching. No one expects a faculty member from another institution to simply implement the same course on their campus, but the sharing of information within a community that values innovation is a great asset. This last point is also supported related to software development by our own CANS Phase 3 development story and underscores the importance of community and working with others in FOSS to account for diversity of needs and interests.

Our story of CANS development also illustrates the need for a community of contributors, not just users, in order to sustain a project and the challenge of integrating contributions in complex development environments such as that encountered in Sakai. For example, in Sakai there are many developments and developers. One result of this is that event messages from one application in the system (e.g., a forum tool) may have different expressions than event messages from another tool (e.g., a wiki tool).

To be sure, working within a community and expanding the scope of CANS to encompass the needs of other institutions has helped us to make advances and improvements in the project. From a development perspective, the project has attracted more development input from other institutions, which is helping to grow CANS in scope and impact. Considerations of incorporating CANS in heavy-load environments, using CANS for decision-making and even incorporating multilingual support are improvements that result in a more mature product which is better suited to meet the needs of the greater community. In addition, by expanding the scope of CANS we are effectively introducing more use cases to be considered for further design and development work. By incorporating into our design processes the needs of a diversified user base that goes beyond the original constituency of the CANS team, we are able to innovate and push our ideas and theories further. And, by including the user base in the design and development process, we create a sustained feedback channel, allowing for continuing improvements to design and development work. These factors compounded make it possible for us and others to create software that better aligns with the social needs of online learners and better supports the social nature of online learning.

NOTE

The work reported in this chapter was partially developed under a grant from the U.S. Department of Education. However, those contents do not necessarily represent the policy of the U.S. Department of Education, and you should not assume endorsement by the Federal Government.

REFERENCES

Amelung, C. (2005). *A Context-based Activity Notification Framework for Developers of Computer Supported Collaborative Environments.* Unpublished doctoral dissertation. University of Missouri-Columbia.

Arbaugh, J. B. (2000). Virtual classroom characteristics and student satisfaction with internet-based MBA courses. *Journal of Management Education, 24*(1), 32–54. doi:10.1177/105256290002400104

Berge, Z. (2001). *Concerns of Online Teachers in Higher Education.* Retrieved from http://www.emoderators.com/zberge/iste98.html

Blanchard, A. L. (2000). *Virtual behavior settings: A framework for understanding virtual communities.* Unpublished doctoral dissertation, Claremont Graduate University, Claremont, CA.

Bower, B. (2001). Distance education: Facing the faculty challenge. *Online Journal of Distance Learning Administration, 4*(2). Retrieved June 21, 2009, from http://www.westga.edu/~distance/ojdla/summer42/bower42.html

Carmichael, P., & Honour, L. (2002). Open source as appropriate technology for global education. *International Journal of Educational Development, 22*(1), 47–53. doi:10.1016/S0738-0593(00)00077-8

Carroll, J. M., Neale, D. C., Isenhour, P. L., Rosson, M. B., & McCrickard, D. S. (2003). Notification and awareness: Synchronizing task-oriented collaborative activity. *International Journal of Human-Computer Studies, 58*, 313–322. doi:10.1016/S1071-5819(03)00024-7

Caruso, J. B., & Salaway, G. (2007). *The ECAR study of undergraduate students and information technology, 2007.* Retrieved December 8, 2007 from http://www.csplacement.com/downloads/ECAR-ITSkliisstudy.pdf

Christensen, C. M., Horn, M. B., & Johnson, C. W. (2008). *Disrupting Class: How Disruptive Innovation Will Change the Way the World Learns.* New York: McGraw-Hill.

Chyung, S. Y. (2001). Systematic and systemic approaches to reducing attrition rates in online higher education. *American Journal of Distance Education, 15*(3), 36–49. doi:10.1080/08923640109527092

Coppola, C., & Neelley, E. (2004). *Open source-opens learning: Why open source makes sense for education.* Retrieved from http://www.rsmart.com/assets/OpenSourceOpensLearningJuly2004.pdf

Dede, C. (1996). The evolution of distance education: Emerging technologies and distributed learning. *American Journal of Distance Education, 10*(2), 4–36. doi:10.1080/08923649609526919

Design-Based Research Collective. (2002). Design-based research: An emerging paradigm for educational inquiry. *Educational Researcher, 32*(1), 5–8. doi:10.3102/0013189X032001005

Dourish, P., & Bellotti, V. (1992). Awareness and coordination in shared workspaces. In *Proceedings of the Conference on Computer-Supported Cooperative Work,* Toronto, Canada.

Dunlap, J., & Lowenthal, P. (2009). Tweeting the night away: Using Twitter to enhance social presence. *Journal of Information Systems Education, 20*(2).

Erickson, T., & Kellogg, W. A. (2003). Social Translucence: Using Minimalist Visualizations of Social Activity to Support Collective Interaction . In Höök, K., Benyon, D., & Munro, A. (Eds.), *Designing Information Spaces: The Social Navigation Approach* (pp. 17–42). New York: Springer.

Goggins, S., Laffey, J., & Tsai, I.-C. (2007). *Cooperation and groupness: Community formation in small online collaborative groups.* Paper presented at the ACM Group Conference.

Hara, N., & Kling, R. (2000). Student distress in web-based distance education course. *Information Communication and Society, 4*(3), 557–579. doi:10.1080/13691180010002297

Laffey, J., & Amelung, C. (in press). Using notification systems to create social places for online learning . In Dumova, T., & Fiordo, R. (Eds.), *Handbook of Research on Social Interaction Technologies and Collaboration Software: Concepts and Trends.* Hershey, PA: IGI Global.

Laffey, J., Amelung, C., & Goggins, S. (2009). A context awareness system for online learning: Design based research. *International Journal on E-Learning, 8*(3), 313–330.

Laffey, J., Lin, G., & Lin, Y. (2006). Assessing social ability in online learning environments. *Journal of Interactive Learning Research, 17*(2), 163–177.

Laffey, J., & Musser, D. (1996). Designing a journal system for learning from field experience in teacher education. *Technology and Teacher Education Annual*, 649-653.

Laffey, J., & Musser, D. (2006). Shadow net-Workspace: An open source intranet for learning communities. *Canadian Journal of Learning and Technology, 32*(1).

Laffey, J., Musser, D., Remidez, H., & Gottden-ker, J. (2003). Networked systems for schools that learn. *Communications of the Association of Computer Machinery, 46*(9), 192–200.

Lin, Y., & Laffey, J. (2006). Exploring the relationship between mediating tools and student perception of interdependence in a CSCL environment. *Journal of Interactive Learning Research, 17*(4), 385–400.

Lin, Y., Lin, G., Liu, P., Huang, X., Shen, D., & Laffey, J. (2006). *Building a social and motivational framework for understanding satisfaction in online learning.* Paper presented at the Annual Conference of American Educational Research Association, San Francisco.

Lin, Y. W., & Zini, E. (2008). Free/libre open source software implementation in schools: Evidence from the field and implications for the future. *Computers & Education, 50*(3), 1092–1102. doi:10.1016/j.compedu.2006.11.001

Marra, R. M., & Jonassen, D. H. (2001). Limitations of online courses for supporting constructive learning. *Quarterly Review of Distance Education, 2*(4), 303–317.

Musser, D., Laffey, J., & Lawrence, B. (2000). Center for echnology Innovation in Education, University of Missouri-Columbia. In Branch, R., & Fitzgerald, M. A. (Eds.), *Educational Media and Technology Yearbook* (*Vol. 25*, pp. 89–95). Engelwood, CO: Libraries Unlimited, Inc.

Picciano, A. (2002). Beyond student perceptions: Issues of interaction, presence, and performance in an online course. *Journal of Asynchronous Learning Networks, 6*(1), 21–40.

Picciano, A. G., & Seaman, J. (2008). *K-12 online learning: A 2008 follow-up of the survey of U.S. school district administrators.* The Sloan Consortium.

Putnam, R. (2000). *Bowling alone.* New York: Simon & Schuster.

Remidez, H., Laffey, J., & Musser, D. (2001). Open Source and the diffusion of teacher education software. *Technology and Teacher Education Annual, 3*, 2774–2778.

Rovai, A. P. (2002). Development of an instrument to measure classroom community. *The Internet and Higher Education, 5*(3), 197–211. doi:10.1016/S1096-7516(02)00102-1

Scott, J. L. (2004) *Graduate students'perceptions of online classroom community: A quantitative research study.* Unpublished doctoral dissertation, Capella University, Columbia.

Tallent-Runnels, M. K., Thomas, J. A., Lan, W. Y., Cooper, S., Ahern, T. C., & Shaw, S. M. (2006). Teaching courses online: A review of the research. *Review of Educational Research, 76*(1), 93–135. doi:10.3102/00346543076001093

van Rooij, S. W. (2007). Open Source software in US higher education: Reality or illusion? *Education and Information Technologies, 12*(4), 191–209. doi:10.1007/s10639-007-9044-6 van Rooij, S. W. (2009). Adopting Open-Source Software Applications in US Higher Education: A Cross-Disciplinary Review of the Literature. *Review of Educational Research, 79*(2), 682. doi:10.3102/0034654308325691

Vrasidas, C. (2004). Issues of pedagogy and design in e-learning systems. In *Proceedings of the 2004 ACM Symposium on Applied Computing* (pp. 911-915).

Watson, J., Gemin, B., & Ryan, J. (2008). Keeping [*Online Learning: A Review of State-Level Policy and Practice*. Evergreen, CO: Evergreen Consulting Associates.]. *Pacing and Clinical Electrophysiology*, K-12.

Wellman, B. (1999). The network community: An introduction to networks in the global village . In Wellman, B. (Ed.), *Networks in the global village* (pp. 1–48). Boulder, CO: Westview Press.

Wellman, B., & Gulia, M. (1999). Virtual communities as communities: Net surfers don't ride alone . In Smith, M., & Kollock, P. (Eds.), *Communities in cyberspace* (pp. 163–190). Berkeley, CA: Routledge.

Chapter 13
Computer Assisted Active Learning System Development for History of Civilization E-Learning Courses by Using Free Open Source Software Platforms

Dilek Karahoca
Bahcesehir University, Turkey

Adem Karahoca
Bahcesehir University, Turkey

Ilker Yengin
University of Nebraska-Lincoln, USA

Huseyin Uzunboylu
Near East University, Northern Cyprus

ABSTRACT

This chapter explains the developmental reasons and design to implementation cycles of the Computer Assisted Active Learning System (CALS) for History of Civilization (HOC) courses at Engineering Faculty of Bahcesehir University. Implementation purpose of CALS is to develop set of tools in a systematic way to enhance students' critical thinking abilities for HOC courses. Dynamic meta-cognitive maps, movies, flash cards and quiz tools were developed. In order to reduce implementation costs of CALS, open Free and Open Source Software (FOSS) standards and platforms were utilized in the development and implementation cycles. This study also investigates the importance of the e-learning platform usage in HOC courses in Engineering Faculty of Bahcesehir University to improve the level of students. Results indicate that the concept based meta-cognitive tool improves learning instead of students just memorizing the class material. Also, engineering students improved their positive attitude towards who wants to

DOI: 10.4018/978-1-61520-917-0.ch013

learn the history of civilization by using CALS. This study shows that software helps to change human behavior in the learning cycle. This chapter highlights the implications of successful development of FOSS for the CALS.

1. INTRODUCTION

Nowadays, information is increasing in an uncontrolled manner. Based on this cycle, information learning and teaching approaches should be supported with information communication technologies (ICT) and web based educational technologies. In this mean, information dissemination and sharing processes can be supported by Free Open Source Software (FOSS) components for online education. This phenomenon has been supported in different perspectives extensively. As stated in "gnu.org", free software is a matter of the users' freedom to run, copy, distribute study, change and improve the software. More precisely, it refers to four kinds of freedoms, for the users of the software (http://www.gnu.org/):

1. The freedom to run the program, for any purpose (freedom 0).
2. The freedom to study how the program works, and adapt it to your needs (freedom 1). Access to the source code is a precondition for this.
3. The freedom to redistribute copies so you can help your neighbor (freedom 2).
4. The freedom to improve the program, and release your improvements to the public, so that the whole community benefits (freedom 3). Access to the source code is a precondition for this.

The FOSS practice also can be carried out in web based education supporting tools such as learning management systems (LMS) or course management systems (CMS). LMS manages learners, but CMS is related with learning contents. From this view point, Massachusetts Institute of Technology (MIT) started the OpenCourseWare project (http://web.mit.edu/ocw) in 2001 and share on the Internet in 2002 (Richards, 2001). This open source project served as an inspiration to other web based course management projects for supporting university teaching. Online course management platforms supported with FOSS based systems such as the Moodle (Modular Object-Oriented Dynamic Learning Environment) project (http://docs.moodle.org/en/Online_Learning_History) for 2001. Moodle is a software package for producing Internet-based courses and web sites. It is a global development project designed to support a social constructionist framework of education. Moodle is provided freely as Open Source software (under the GNU Public License). Basically this means Moodle is copyrighted, but that you have additional freedoms. You are allowed to copy, use and modify Moodle provided that you agree to provide the source to others; not modify or remove the original license and copyrights, and apply this same license to any derivative work. Moodle can be installed on any computer that can run PHP, and can support an SQL type database (for example MySQL). It can be run on Windows and Mac operating systems and many flavors of Linux (for example Red Hat or Debian GNU) (http://docs.moodle.org/en/About_Moodle).

Kanuka, Rourke and Laflamme (2007) highlight the importance of engaging students into learning by introducing the deeper level of thinking. They argued the importance of active learning strategies where students are involved in debates and challenged to think critically. Computer tools are very effective to engage students actively into learning and make them to think critically (Aher & Repman, 1994). In Bahesehir University, a system of online computer tools were developed that engage students actively into their learning for the history of civilization lessons. In the design and development of these tools also FOSS phenomena was followed. For this purpose, these learning tools using free open technologies were designed and developed and were embedded as learning modules in Moodle.

The purpose of this chapter is to describe the design to development cycles of CALS and its implications in education. In the background section, reasons of developing CALS for HOC is presented by introducing literature review. In the software design section, requirements analysis of CALS will be presented and design scenarios of software tools will be detailed. Finally, the conclusion section will summarize the results of using CALS for HOC in Engineering Faculty of Bahcesehir University.

2. BACKGROUND

Many history lectures following traditional lecturing are reputedly dull; they are repeatedly cited as a root cause of student's somnolence and unrest. These traditional lectures dominating classrooms for much of the 20th century (Winn & Snyder, 1996) used mostly teacher centered approaches (McKeachie, 1954) where the teacher set the goals, little verbal participation by the group took place, and most of the interaction came from the teacher. In traditional lectures, individual work and teacher evaluation are promoted, and the teacher made most of the decisions. This could be the reason students to withdraw from the courses (Yang, 2007). These kinds of lectures are mostly based on rote learning rather than critical thinking. To make the lessons more interesting and enjoyable, lecturers prefer to use electronic presentations. Also studies show that students prefer electronic presentations to overhead transparencies (Harknett & Cobane, 1997; Blokzijl & Naeff, 2004). However, students' performance doesn't increase with presentation based lectures. There was no significance according to the relevant studies (Lowry, 1999; Bartsch & Cobern, 2003; Szabo & Hastings, 2000;

Amare, 2006). In the classroom, the effectiveness of technology usage depends on the lecturers' attitude towards technology and teaching style. The use of presentations does not ensure success (Hacifazlioglu, Sacli & Yengin, 2006). The misuse of presentations, however, can cause the loss of student understanding in lectures. For example, a rigidly structured presentation with slides filled with too much text and presented in dark room can be poorly received (Gareis, 2007). Due to not getting the message across, the use of presentations in history classes can have very little or no impact on lessons. These facts showed that in order to get students in deeper understanding without losing attention to the lesson, higher thinking abilities of students such as critical thinking and analysis must also be infused in history lessons (Reed, 1998).

In contrast to dull lecturing and electronic presentations; cinema, sound, and television are more visually exciting and have come a long way toward filling our daily lives with striking images (Raack, Smith, & Raack, 1973). Hence, the usage of films in history lessons can be more colorful and stimulating for the students only if we can create learning that involve higher level learning skills such as critical thinking within the classroom context. For example, according to Sexias (1993), teachers can discuss popular films in class to engage critical thinking for students. Rather than just showing the film in the lessons this type of critical thinking based discussions are very important and the beneficial for the students, because discussions can solve many problems in the learning. One of these problems in history lesson is that the historical characters often fail to "come to life" during lectures (Sexias, 1993). Most of the times students watch movies without critical thinking and they are likely to be taken into the "historical" world as presented film, but unlikely to exercise their critical judgments of the filmic depiction of the past. Another problem is to invite the student (imaginatively) into the circumstances of the past and to get the student to step out of the filmic depiction of the past

(Sexias, 1993). Many students' understandings of the history are war and peace, gender relations, intercultural relations, and national development which are affected by presentations in the popular media (Matthew, Levstik, & Levstik, 1991). Therefore, the study of popular films in the classroom is crucial for the students to understand history correctly within its context. Studying films and analyzing their topics according to real historical facts can enhance critical thinking.

Furthermore, students also should be an active participator of the lecture by joining to discussions and taking their own responsibility of learning. Students must engage in higher order thinking tasks such as analysis, synthesis and evaluation. Use of these techniques in the classroom is vital because of their powerful impact upon students' learning. For example several studies have shown that students prefer strategies promoting active learning to traditional lectures. However, while evaluating students' achievement many strategies have demonstrated that promoting active learning are comparable to lectures in promoting the mastery of content but superior to lectures in promoting the development of students' skills in thinking and writing (Bonwell & Eison, 1991). Several strategies promoting active learning have similarly been shown to favorably influence students' attitudes and achievement. An active learning approach is more likely a teaching methodology and instructional activities involving students in doing things and thinking about what they are doing. This kind of instruction attempts to engage students in activities that support knowledge construction through media use, but which is not designed to control learning. In this model, learners use media to investigate and to think. This type of learning activity can lead to it being described as active learning (Bonwell & Eison, 1991). Some of the strategies promoting active learning in the classroom are as follows:

- Students are involved in more than listening.

- Less emphasis is placed on transmitting information and more on developing students' skills.
- Students are engaged in activities (e.g., reading, discussing, and writing).
- Greater emphasis is placed on students' exploration of their own attitudes and values (Ragains, 1995).

The key principles of active learning suggested by (Barnes, 1989) are as follows:

- **Purposive:** the task is seen by the learner as relevant to his/her concerns;
- **Reflective:** the learner reflects on the meaning of what is being learnt;
- **Negotiated:** the teacher and learner negotiate the goals and methods of learning;
- **Critical:** the learner appreciates different ways of interpreting learning;
- **Complex:** the learning tasks reflect real life complexity;
- **Situation-driven:** the learning tasks arise out of the needs of the situation;
- **Engaged:** the learning activities reflect real life tasks.

One of instructional strategy to promote active learning is to use computer assisted learning (CAL) environment which is heavily based on multimedia and hypermedia usage. CAL involves different activities such as interactivity, entertainment, exploration, communication, knowledge and active learning. In those environments, students feel interactivity, involvement, and motivation in their learning (Chen, Wigand & Nilan 1999; Clark, 1994). In CAL similar systems, several studies have shown that there are some factors and conditions such as enjoyment, tele-presence, focused attention, engagement and time distortion associated with the concept of flow (Chen, Wigand & Nilan 1999; Shin, 2006; Novak, Hoffman, & Yung, 2000) that is a psychological state in which an individual feels cognitively efficient, motivated, and happy. Also CAL technology can trigger the interest of both students and teachers by creating many new opportunities and educational teaching experiences and learning methods. The use of computers in the classroom changes the concept of a history course from textbook reading to authentic interpretation of historical material (Kozna & Johnston, 1991). There are numerous examples of studies discussing several technology usages in history classes (Stephens, 2005; Kornblith, 2003; Yang, 2003; Trentin, 2000; Dollinger, 2000). Technology, such as the internet can be used merely as a source of information for the history lessons (Stang & Street, 2007). In addition, technological tools can be used as part of the curriculum in history lessons. For example the use of technology can help students gaining a sense of history as a process shaped by individuals and communities in an online format (Thorp, 2005) or can be used as a communication tool such as weblogs where teachers can be interactive by posing questions and asking students to respond (Risinger, 2006). Also web-based tools can be used in history, to allow students to take their own responsibilities for their learning (Ferster, Hammond, & Bull, 2006). Educational technology makes it possible to provide students with innovative ways of understanding complex problems in history (Stephens, 2005). In specific occasions using the computer in history lessons or social studies helps teachers better to meet the diverse learning styles of students (Dils, 1999).

In the end, the use of technology merely in history classes is not a magic tool by itself (Cuban, 1986). The preference of the lecturer to use of technology and their beliefs about using it in lessons play an important role (Doppen, 2004). For example, historians teach larger courses than other disciplines and make less use of technology in their classes (Townsend, 2006). Furthermore, the right use of technology is an important issue (Kelly, 2001) because technology can help enhance teaching and learning only if they are used properly. Proper use of technology in his-

tory lessons can be achieved through the proper identification of the best way the technology can be applied (Stephens, 2005; Lyons, 2004).

The literature highlights the importance of using movie discussion methods to enhance critical learning in history lessons and the importance of using active learning strategies. Also studies showed that the use of right technology in class can be very sufficient. Although studies show several strategies to benefit from technology in history learning no studies showed how to create such an active leaning system. Additionally, no studies showed the importance of using movie discussion in the learning to create active learning environment. With this understanding, a CALS were designed and developed to improve students' critical thinking skills. CALS let students to engage their own learning by actively using online and in class web tools. Dynamic meta-cognitive maps, movies, flash cards and quiz tools were developed for this purpose to support in class movie discussion and active learning for students. In the following sections, processes of design, development and implementation of CALS in history of civilization lectures are introduced.

3. REQUIRMENTS FOR ANALYSIS

The problems presented in the background section of this study form the main conditions and needs of students in history learning. Also before designing CALS, requirements analysis was run to determine the other needs or conditions of students to meet. In the CALS, authors focused on students considering them main and frequent users. In the analysis phase, the stakeholder identified that engineering students have terribly low concentration levels. To learn socially related course such as the History of Civilization is a challenge for them. Mandatory technical courses have heavy contents to learn in every semester. They have to expend much more time in the technical laboratory courses to focus on engineering area. From this viewpoint, history teaching to engineering students is a very difficult thing. To solve this paradigm, the lecturer should use a blended learning approach to help students both learning in class and outside the class by using active learning components. In order to create such a blended learning opportunity, students are introduced self study application (online tools) and in class application in the CALS. The assignment applications also ensured the evaluation processes in the CALS. Self study application tools cover the meta-cognitive tool, flash cards, and a quiz for flash cards. In class activities include movie presentations, movie discussions, cognitive map and keyword matching quizzes. Assignment application is examining students on the online platform. Student centered CALS helps both teacher and students to follow blended learning models both in class and outside the class (see Figure 1).

Another issue in design requirement analysis is to understand students' preferred learning style. In order to understand students learning styles Index of Learning Styles instrument by Felder (1994) was employed. Felder (1994) states that active learners retain and understand information best by doing something active with it discussing or applying it or explaining it to others. *Reflective learners* prefer to think about it quietly first; sensing learners like learning facts; intuitive learners often prefer discovering possibilities and relationships; *visual learners* remember best what they see—pictures, diagrams, flow charts, time lines, films, and demonstrations and *sequential learners*

tend to gain understanding in linear steps, with each step following logically from the previous one. *Global learners* tend to learn in large jumps, absorbing material almost randomly without seeing connections, and then suddenly. As Felder (1990) claims that in most of the college classes, very little visual information is presented and most of the students do not get nearly as much as they would if more visual presentation was used in class. In the design phase of the CALS only the visual/verbal and sequential/global dimensions were analyzed since CALS tools are designed according to these dimensions of learning styles.

4. DESIGNING THE SELF STUDY TOOLS

The results of requirement analysis directed the design cycles of course and indicated that the learning styles of engineering students should be taken into account to support them for teaching the history of civilization courses in an active learning environment. From this viewpoint, self study tools are designed to execute Meta Cognitive and Flash Card Tools for the online computer based environment to learn historical concepts sequentially or conceptually by themselves. Meta cognitive maps and flash cards are designed based on the weekly syllabus. Every week, new content was designed to present to students for using self study tools.

Figure 1. The Main Components of CALS

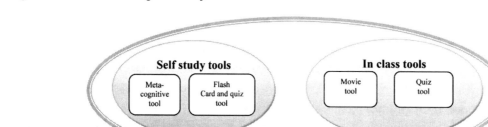

4.1. The Meta Cognitive Tool

The requirement analysis showed that sequential presentations are boring for analytical thinking learners. For this reason, a meta-cognitive tool was designed to help verbal and sequential learners who have a learning style similar to classical methods. Meta-cognitive maps include a hierarchical concept sequence, rather than historical chronology. Concept sequences are related with reasons and results of specific conceptual keywords. As it is known, the cognitive capacities of learners vary. Thus, meta-cognitive maps help learners to increase their cognitive capacity and learning success. As shown in Figure 2, instructors can create meta-cognitive maps and students can follow them to enhance their learning. By using this tool, global learners who have non-linear logical thought patterns can learn concepts by studying non-linear maps and thinking about the relationships of concepts within the cognitive maps. The meta cognitive tool help students visually to enhance better understanding of the concepts. The meta-cognitive map application attracts students to the history course.

Figure 2. Use case diagram for online learning system

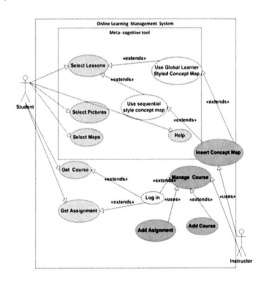

4.2. The Flash Card Tool

According to the specifications in the requirement analysis, flash card tools were designed to support conceptual learning of the students by requiring them to link keywords and concepts for the related topics. Thus flash card is a useful tool to help students remember terms and definitions related to the history class (see Figure 3). Flash card is not a new concept; these cards are strips of cardboard on which are printed various words, phrases or numbers. They are used for rapid drill on topics that have been thoroughly studied (Gianella, 1916). In CALS, flash card software organizes key concepts by their meaning, definition and image or map. It was designed to help linear thinking models rather than rote learning. In the design phase authors aimed to have at least 25 flash cards for each weekly chapter which have to be learned consecutively. The flash card software leads students to a short quiz that provides at least 25 multiple questions. Students can complete the quizzes when they want to do so. Finally, the design of flash card software aims to create positive learning environment for students to enjoy with as game – like usage to challenges students.

Flash cards may be listed by using related chapter from selected list. Terms and definition buttons can be used to close definitions or terms. Students may be zooming to the pictures or images. After then, when they study and learn the card, they have to click the learned card button to pass the next term-definition couples. When all flash cards learned, a dynamical quiz generator shows the multiple choice questions to examine the learning level of the students. This application uses a XML file for collecting the terms, definitions, and image paths.

5. DESIGNING IN-CLASS TOOLS

As stated in the background section of this chapter, the problems may be solved by using films

Figure 3. Flash card tool main screen

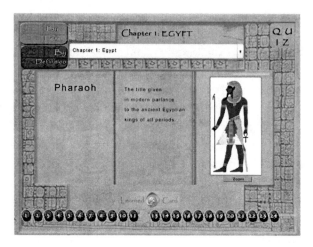

with discussions in history courses. In order to stimulate critical thinking and active learning in-class activities in-class tools were designed to address these problems. In-class activities may be supported with applications such as a movie player that covers some fragments of the popular Hollywood movies which are included in the weekly syllabus. Also in class, different quizzes are given to students to direct them to movie and the hot topic of that week. The quiz tool is used to facilitate critical thinking within class discussions. The main purpose of quiz tool is to provide ideas, structures, information, and in some cases motivate students to learn the course content. The system provides students with an opportunity to advance their knowledge as a result of participating and creatively thinking as they use computer applications.

5.1 In Class-Activities: Move and Quiz Tool

The movie tool has been designed in the open source flash application as designed and coded in OSflash. The main purpose of this tool is to support to class presentations. The sequences of the in class presentations are as follows:

1. The goals of the current topics are presented,
2. The quick overview of the lesson is presented,
3. The fragments of the movies are presented,
4. The key concepts and scenes of the movie are presented for feedback,
5. The quiz organized based on keyword matching (5a), concept maps from previous week (5b) and standard questions (5c) are presented.

According to the sequences listed above, the flow for in-class activities starts with an opening where goals and current topics should be presented. **(1)** In the presentations a specific picture presented to students. This picture is used in other materials such as in the meta-cognitive tool and flash card tool as a reminder of the lessons. In the beginning of each class, the topic and goals were presented by the lecturer. The introduction is placed in the opening section. The lecturer states the important points where students will need to pay attention during the class. **(2)** After the opening a quick review and the objective lists were presented to students. **(3)** Following the overview, the objectives are presented and the rest of the lesson continues with the aid of the movie selected before. In the movie presentation the lecturer can control the movie flow by using the play head and the navigational controls of the movie application. **(4)** When the movie is studied or between the scenes, the lecturer can proceed into the key scene and the concept slides. In those slides students are reminded of the key historical concepts by the help of the scenes in the presentation. For example in the middle of the movie, the application stops between the scene and present a question to start a classroom discussion. **(5)** After the lessons are complete, the drill part of the lecture begins. **(5a)** In the keyword matching section students are required to match the presented keyword group with the correct item. The keywords are grouped according to their occurrence in the movie or presentation and their relationships. All the key-words come from a previous week. The students are supposed to study this keyword both in class and during the previous week and by themselves using the online system; in this case the flash card tools. **(5b)** In the concept map quiz section students are instructed to find the correct item for the missing branch indicated in the presentation. The students are supposed to study these maps both in class during the previous week and/or by themselves using the online system in this case meta-cognitive tool. **(5c)** In the standard question part, students are presented which classical quiz questions that cover the current topic learned on that day. The questions are based on the movie and the important points discussed in the class during movie.

6. TOOL DEVELOPMENT AND IMPLEMENTATION PHASE

In the development phase concept maps was used to be sure they are matching the thought process of the subject matter expert (SME) and to be sure tools are producing correct content structure to present according to students' different learning styles. The idea of concept maps was borrowed to use as a meta-cognitive tool that helps to organize ideas. The concept maps also are useful to improve students' achievements in history courses. The use of the concept map approach can help the users to understand the thought process of the SME who design these maps. The branching hierarchy of the concept maps was limited with the three levels for the youngsters because the information that must be learned at working memory has a capacity of about four chunks in young adults (Cowan, 2001). In fact there is no single correct way of creating concept maps on specific content (Cañas et. al). Authors created the concept maps by using a graph format for presenting knowledge (Safayeni, Derbentseva, & Cañas.2007).

Concept maps also organize concepts so that they are accessible to learners having different learning styles. The concept maps are used in a meta cognitive learning which supports different learning styles as stated in Figure 4.

Concept map based software interacts with users and allows them to choose from different interfaces according to users-preferred learning styles. Sub objectives in creating such a tool can be listed as follows: the design of a multi-modal interface for the learning tool, testing the usability problems in the developed prototypes, and the integration of the concept map based meta-cognitive tool into the online learning management system.

6.1. The Prototyping Phase of the Interfaces

The development stages of the first interfaces were started by analyzing and designing the course content with SMEs. The content was then transformed into the concept maps and links were created between each node in the concept maps and the visual materials. There are many types of tools used to create concept maps. The commercial tools are available at the market. A recent study of the development of a software tool called LEO, an approach to the creation of a course depiction from a Concept Map which was announced by (Coffey, 2005). In this study, FOSS, FreeMind

Figure 4. Cognitive map instance

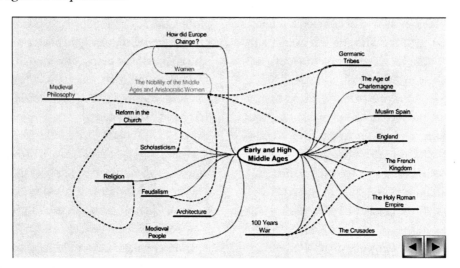

(http://freemind.sourceforge.net/) was used to create the visual presentation of the concept maps. The authors selected this software because it is user-friendly, especially for the instructors, and FreeMind was developed in Java platform. For the developer, the ability to export the FreeMind visual presentation to XML format is crucial.

Once the content design was finished, the learning tool was developed to fit the contents into concept maps. Complex concept maps must be presented in both sequential/global forms and verbal/visual forms. The developed software just loads XML and presents concept maps in either sequential or global layouts. The software interfaces were designed according to the students' learning styles which are sequential and verbal domains (Felder, 1990). In sequential forms, the learner interacts with the software using a step by step approach to study concept maps. In global forms, users are presented a global view of the concept maps and they interact with the software in a holistic way. All the concept map

Figure 5. Beta version of the meta-cognitive map interface

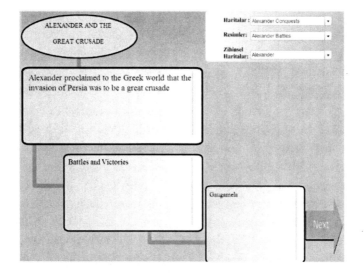

Figure 6. The user interface of meta cognitive tool after interface study

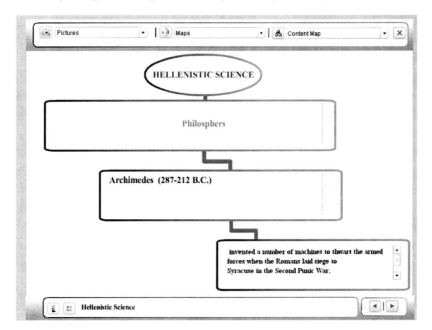

presentations are in verbal layouts and supported with visual aids.

After the development stage of the meta-cognitive tool, it was integrated into an online course management system that had been previously used within an e–learning system which was based on Java based Apache and Tomcat platforms. An extra module was added to the online course management system (See Figure 2). The module provides an interface which enables the instructor to add XML files of the concept maps and visual aids into the system. Then, the meta–cognitive tool can be associated with an online assignment module. The most important factors in the user interface development are the transfer of the exact information displayed in the concept maps into the software and the support of different learner requirements depending on their learning styles. The software distributes the contents into the nodes specified in the XML. Then, it presents the concept-mapped information either as a whole or in sequential steps. In addition, the software presents the information both verbally (the depiction of the content maps) and visually (pictures and maps related to the content).

As depicted in Figure 5, the first prototype of concept map tool was tested using usability engineering methodologies to see the problems within system and interface. After the problems of the interfaces determined, the meta-cognitive map interface was re-designed (See Figure 6) according to the findings of usability tests.

Navigational interactions include the "Next" labeled button in the bottom right corner of the screen and the three lists that are placed at the right top corner of the screen labeled respectively as "Pictures", "Maps", and "Content Maps". In this new prototype, sequential learners can follow a one-way navigation that always goes forward. In this way, the learner has to click only the "Next" button. Here, the nodes of the content maps are displayed in three leveled boxes connected by orange color lines. This display is a hierarchal flow that is from left to right to match the natural eye movement of the readers. The users just need to read the hierarchical texts from the left top of the corner and follow red lines.

Then the users click the "Next" button to proceed further. Also the global learners can reach the whole concept map using the concept maps list control to see the information at a glance.

Other tools were implemented as extra modules to the flash card software. The Flash cards is for the self study for online access via the e-learning system where students are presented with three sets of cards as displayed in Figure 3. On one of the three cards is a keyword or a concept from a related topic, on another is the description of the keyword or concept, and the last one is a representative picture of this keyword and description. The additional picture is either an iconic representation or a picture or a scene from the movies. All the visual images for the picture cards are used in the learning materials that are a meta-cognitive tool, presentation, movie or quiz. By providing a picture card, the authors tried to create strong statements in students' visual memory. In the opening of the program, all of the cards are closed. Students reviewed all the cards in the deck by opening each closed card set. If a student believes she has learned the card she marks the card as a learned one by

clicking "Learned Card Button". Also, she can increase the challenge by locking one of the cards if she likes; if she clicks on one of the definition or term button (keyword or concept). After a student completes all the cards in the deck, she can take a quiz by clicking the "QUIZ" button at the top corner of the screen. The different quiz questions are provided randomly each time the quiz starts. In the quiz, students are required to match terms with definitions. According to selection of student, the quiz question may be a term or a definition. Students also select items that are provided form the cards in the deck. This means that all the items are different for each student and related to the topic in the deck. This self study quiz question comes from the cards and was prepared by the SMEs. After questions were entered into system they were transformed into the XML file so this information can be used both in this software and in online exams.

The meta cognitive map tool and flash card tool was designed using Flash and action script 2.0 (http://osflash.org). OSFlash is a watering hole for open source Flash developers and users

Figure 7. Quiz screen of flash card tool

to meet and talk about and contribute to new and existing open source projects for the Flash Platform. The Open Source Pattern-Based Rich Internet Application (RIA) Framework for the Flash Platform; ARP currently supports Macromedia® Flash® and Flex™-based RIA Development in ActionScript 2 and ActionScript 3.

7. LEARNING SYSTEM EFFICIENCY AND INVESTIGATING STUDENTS' ATTITUDES

In this study, CALS was designed and investigated by trying to create an active learning environment for students with the help of computer tools to enhance students' critical thinking. Specifically, the learning system implemented to change the atmosphere of teacher centered passive learning with the linear logical power point presentation based lectures. With the help of developed computer tools, intended to support active learning with non-linear dynamic cognitive mappings, to provide an environment for discussion on films, to enhance critical thinking by grouping structures within keyword learning in flash cards and several quiz applications at student learning in history improved.

In this study students' attitudes towards to the learning system and their performances within this system have been investigated in detail. According to the results, CALS can support active participation by main properties of the system rather than dull slide presentations:

1. Implemented system supports active learning and critical thinking via;
    a. Movie application where class room discussions held,
    b. Quiz application,
2. Implemented system uses computer tools to help students to create links and relations in the content and supports different learning styles of the students (online) via;

a. Meta cognitive learning tool: The metacognitive tool displays concept maps in different interfaces according to the different learning styles of students.
b. Flash cards and quiz for flash cards: Flash card application provides a game like experience that accommodates keywords and concepts for the related topics.
3. Implemented system motivate students in class more than traditional lectures: Film and Quiz application (Multimedia Tool; Active Presentations)

The CALS suggests students take more active control in the learning process. The following CALS model was implemented to enhance active learning as stated in Figure 1. Active participation of students was essential for the success of the model. The role of the instructor is a facilitator. The computer tools cannot be considered alone independently from the learning environment in the system. Therefore, the success of the computer applications depends on the students' attitudes towards to the proposed learning environment.

8. FUTURE RESEARCH DIRECTIONS

In this chapter the authors discussed that how they have been created a collaborative environment by developing a CALS to help students in history of civilization learning in class and outside the class. Distance learning initiatives can be started after this stage to support engineering students by using project and collaborative learning approaches. Developed tools are based on FOSS platforms to minimize software development costs. However, the software development cycle was time consuming for the encountered technical difficulties in dealing with the free software platforms. When open source software community share with you, contents and tools are already prepared, FOSS approach is suitable to use. Such as Moodle and

OpenCourseWare software tool and contents are good enough for creating an e-learning platform and engineering course contents. When your content is not ready to put on the LMS or CMS, the designer needs to develop the course content with supportive tools and interactive course materials. For these reasons, FOSS is good approach to develop new e-learning contents and tools, but you have to be good enough to create and execute online tools and contents. You have to collaborate with SMEs and good developers to achieve successful running of e-learning courses.

9. CONCLUSION

This chapter has introduced computer assisted active learning software which depends on open source software platforms for history of civilization courses. Developed tools have supportive components for the in and out of class activities. Java is used as a main programming environment to run tools which is one of the environment for object oriented and web based programming platform. Flash interfaces developed for creating interactive e-learning environment and FreeMind tool is used to create cognitive maps, and the XML conversion is made to generate dynamic cognitive maps.

Note that the meta-cognitive map tool was an online self-study tool to help students prepare for the class in their own time. The improvement in the scores was mainly observed within the group of students whose scores were above the class average in the first test as well. This suggests that these students already know how to prepare for the class on their own; they are likely to be hardworking students who are also attentive in the class.

The student who uses the software must be alert and pay careful attention for learning the material. This type of study effort causes students to learn significantly more. As the results of the study show, "hardworking and attentive" students (the ones

who achieved significantly higher scores than the class average) made improvements in their scores when they studied with this software. These are the students who were likely to spend time and energy to study in a systematic way which the software requires and enables. The authors believe the software improves the learning for those students who ran it. On the other hand, students who received low grades on exams did significantly worse when they used the software. This suggests that these students did not spend the required time to learn the concept maps. One reason may be that these students are likely to memorize the material presented in the presentation slides instead of really understanding and learning it. When they are asked to study the material in interactive software they proceeded to memorize it. The results of the study indicate the concept based meta-cognitive tool improves learning instead of just memorizing the class material. The meta-cognitive tool can help students to control their learning process by taking advantage of the learning opportunities that technology offers.

This chapter tries to explain, in a blended learning approach, active technology usage helps students who have motivation and are able to concentrate in the courses. If students are unmotivated and they do not try to learn, neither software tools nor genius teachers can help them. In class activities and the tools goal is to increase motivation, and create positive learning attitudes for students.

Free and open source software (FOSS) components, platforms and standards are not ready enough to stand in front of the giant companies of the software sector. In the e-learning field, there are a lot of good samples which highlight our road to reach our academic goals in online teaching activities. Therefore, academic researchers and software developers have to share their e-learning contents with academic communities such as MIT to help and improve developing countries by using online education systems.

REFERENCES

Aher, T. C., & Repman, J. (1994). The effects of technology on online education. *Journal of Research on Computing in Education, 26*(4), 537–546.

Amare, N. (2006). To Slideware Or Not To Slideware: Students' Experiences With PowerPoint Vs. Lecture. *Journal of Technical Writing And Communication, 36*(3), 297–308. doi:10.2190/03GX-F1HW-VW5M-7DAR

Barnes, D. (1989). *Active Learning.* Leeds: University of Leeds TVEI Support Project.

Bartsch, R. A., & Cobern, K. M. (2003). Effectiveness of PowerPoint Presentations in Lectures. *Computers & Education, 41*(1), 77–87. doi:10.1016/S0360-1315(03)00027-7

Blokzijl, W., & Naeff, R. (2004). The Instructor as Stagehand: Dutch Student Responses to PowerPoint. *Business Communication Quarterly, 67*(1), 70–78. doi:10.1177/1080569903262046

Bonwell, C., & Eison, J. (1991). *Active Learning: Creating Excitement in the Classroom.* Washington, D.C.: Jossey-Bass.

Cañas, A. J., Carff, R., Hill, G., Carvalho, M., Arguedas, M., Eskridge, T. C., et al. Concept Maps: Integrating Knowledge and Information Visualization. Retrieved April 8, 2007 from http://cmap.ihmc.us/Publications/ResearchPapers/ConceptMapsIntegratingKnowInfVisual.pdf.

Chen, H., Wigand, R. T., & Nilan, M. (1999). Flow activities on the Web. *Computers in Human Behavior, 15*(5), 585–608. doi:10.1016/S0747-5632(99)00038-2

Clark, R. E. (1994). Media will never influence learning. *Educational Technology Research and Development, 42*(2), 21–29. doi:10.1007/BF02299088

Coffey, J. W. (2005). A meta-cognitive tool for courseware development, maintenance, and reuse. *Computers & Education, 48*(4), 548–566. doi:10.1016/j.compedu.2005.03.008

Cowan, N. (2001). The magical number 4 in short-term memory: A reconsideration of mental storage Capacity. *The Behavioral and Brain Sciences, 24*(1), 87–113. doi:10.1017/S0140525X01003922

Cuban, L. (1986). *Teachers and machines: Classroom use of technology,* New York: Teachers College Press. Dils, K. (1999). The use of technology to reach the various learning styles of middle school history and social studies students. *Journal of the Association for History & Computing, 2*(3). Retrieved June 1, 2008, from http://mcel.pacificu.edu/jahc/jahcII3/index.htmlhttp://mcel.pacificu.edu/jahc/jahcII3/index.html

Dollinger, M. (2000). Materials engineering and the challenge of teaching history in the community college. *The History Teacher, 34*(1), 9–20. doi:10.2307/3054370

Doppen, F. H. (2004). Beginning Social Studies Teachers' Integration of Technology in the History Classroom. *Theory and Research in Social Education, 32*(2), 248–279.

Felder, R. M. (1988). Learning and teaching styles in engineering education. Retrieved April 8, 2007 from http://www.ncsu.edu/felder-public/Papers/LS-1988.pdfhttp://www.ncsu.edu/felder-public/Papers/LS-1988.pdf

Felder, R. M. (1990). Meet Your Students: 2. Susan and Glenda. *Chemical Engineering Education, 24*(1), 7–8.

Felder, R. M. (1994). Meet Your Students: 5. Edward and Irving. *Chemical Engineering Education, 28*(1), 36–37.

Ferster, B., Hammond, T., & Bull, G. (2006). Primary Access: Creating Digital Documentaries in the Social Studies Classroom. *Social Education, 70*(3), 147–150.

Freemind. (n.d.). Retrieved from http://freemind. sourceforge.net/http://freemind.sourceforge.net

Gareis, E. (2007). Active Learning: A Power point Tutorial. *Business Communication Quarterly, 70*(4), 462–466. doi:10.1177/10805699070700 040304

Gianella, A. F. (1916). The Use of Flash Cards for Drill in French. *Modern Language Journal, 1*(3), 96–99. doi:10.2307/313582

Harknett, R. J., & Cobane, C. T. (1997). Introducing Instructional Technology to International Relations. *Political Science and Politics, 30*, 496–500. doi:10.2307/420130

Kanuka, H., Rouke, L., & Laflamme, E. (2007). The influence of instructional methods on the quality of online discussions. *British Journal of Educational Technology, 38*, 260–271. doi:10.1111/j.1467-8535.2006.00620.x

Kelly, M. (2001). Using new media to teach East European history. *Nationalities Papers, 29*(3), 499–507. doi:10.1080/00905990120073735

Kornblith, G. J. (2003). Textbooks and Teaching - Editors' Introduction: More than Bells and Whistles? Using Digital Technology to Teach American History. *The Journal of American History, 89*(4), 1456–1457.

Kozna, R. B., & Johnston, J. (1991). The Technological Revolution Comes to the Classroom. *Change, 23*(1), 10–22.

Lowry, R. B. (1999). Electronic Presentation of Lectures—Effect Upon Student Performance. *University Chemistry Education, 3*(1), 18–21.

Lyons, J. F. (2004). Teaching U.S. History Online: Problems and Prospects. *The History Teacher, 37*(4), 447–456. doi:10.2307/1555549

Matthew, T., Levstik, D., & Levstik, L. S. (1991). *Teaching and Learning History. Handbook of Research on Social Studies Teaching and Learning.* New York: Macmillan.

McKeachie, W. J. (1954). Student-Centered versus Instructor-Centered Instruction. *Journal of Educational Psychology, 45*, 43–50. doi:10.1037/h0060215

Moodle. Retrieved June 15, 2009 from http://docs.moodle.org/en/About_Moodlehttp://docs.moodle.org/en/About_Moodle

Moodle. Retrieved June 15, 2009 from http://docs.moodle.org/en/Online_Learning_Historyhttp://docs.moodle.org/en/Online_Learning_History

Novak, T. P., Hoffman, D. L., & Yung, Y. F. (2000). Measuring the Customer Experience in Online Environments: A Structural Modeling Approach. *Marketing Science, 19*(1), 22–42. doi:10.1287/mksc.19.1.22.15184

OpenCourseWare. Retrived June 15, 2009 from http://web.mit.edu/ocwhttp://web.mit.edu/ocw

OsFlash. Retrieved June 15, 2009 from http://osflash.orghttp://osflash.org

Raack, R. C., Smith, A. M., & Raack, M. L. (1973). The Documentary Film in History Teaching: An Experimental Course. *The History Teacher, 6*(2), 281–294. doi:10.2307/491726

Ragains, P. (1995). Four variations on Drueke's active learning paradigm. *Research Strategies, 13*(1), 40–50.

Reed, J. H. (1998). *Effect of a model for critical thinking on student achievement in primary source document analysis and interpretation, argumentative reasoning, critical thinking dispositions, and history content in a community college history course.* Unpublished doctoral dissertation, University of South Florida, Florida.

Retrieved June, G. N. U. 15, 2009 from http://www.gnu.org/http://www.gnu.org/, Hacifazlioglu, O., Sacli, O. A., & Yengin, I. (2007, May). *Lecturers' Attitudes Towards The Use Of Technology: Alternative Strategies For Faculty Administrators.* Paper Presented at International Computer Education Conference, North Cyprus.

Richards, P. (2001). MIT to make nearly all course materials available free on the World Wide Web, Retrieved June 15, 2009, from http://web.mit.edu/newsoffice/nr/2001/ocw.htmlhttp://web.mit.edu/newsoffice/nr/2001/ocw.html.

Risinger, C. F. (2006). Using Blogs in the Classroom: A New Approach to Teaching Social Studies with the Internet. *Social Education, 70*(3), 130–132.

Safayeni, F., Derbentseva, N., Cañas, J., & Concept Maps, A. A Theoretical Note on Concepts and the Need for Cyclic Concept Maps. Retrieved April 8, 2007, from http://cmap.ihmc.us/Publications/ResearchPapers/Cyclic%20Concept%20Maps.pdfhttp://cmap.ihmc.us/Publications/Research-Papers/Cyclic%20Concept%20Maps.pdf

Seixas, P. (1993). Popular Film and Young People's Understanding of the History of Native American-White Relations. *The History Teacher, 26*(3). doi:10.2307/494666

Seixas, P. (1993). Popular Film and Young People's Understanding of the History of Native American-White Relations. *The History Teacher, 26*(3), 351–370. doi:10.2307/494666

Shin, N. (2006). Online learner's flow experience: an empirical study. *British Journal of Educational Technology, 37*(5), 705–720. doi:10.1111/j.1467-8535.2006.00641.x

Stang, K., & Street, C. (2007). Tech Talk for Social Studies Teachers: The Jamestown Colony: Access and Technology. *Social Studies, 98*(3), 88–89. doi:10.3200/TSSS.98.3.88-89

Stephens, R. P. (2005). Using Technology to Teach Historical Understanding. *Social Education, 69*(3), 151–154.

Szabo, A., & Hastings, N. (2000). Using IT in the Undergraduate Classroom: Should We Replace the Blackboard with Power Point. *Computers & Education, 35*(3), 175–188. doi:10.1016/S0360-1315(00)00030-0

Thorp, D. B. (2005). Using Technology to Teach Historical Understanding. *Social Education, 69*(3), 151–154.

Townsend, R. B. (2006). Historians Teach More And Larger Classes, But Make Less Use of Technology. *Perspectives: American Historical Association Newsletter, 44*(4), 18–23.

Trentin, G. (2000). The apprentice historian: studying modern history with the help of computers and telemetric. *International Journal of Educational Telecommunications, 6*(3), 213–225.

Winn, W., & Snyder, D. (1996). Cognitive perspectives in psychology. In Jonassen, D. H. (Ed.), *Handbook of research in educational communications and technology* (pp. 112–142). New York: Macmillan.

Yang, S. C. (2003). Learner-generated oral history: spanning three centuries project. *Computers in Human Behavior, 19*(3), 299–318. doi:10.1016/S0747-5632(02)00060-2

Yang, S. C. (2007). E-critical/thematic doing history project: Integrating the critical thinking approach with computer-mediated history learning. *Computers in Human Behavior, 23*(5), 2095–2112. doi:10.1016/j.chb.2006.02.012

Yengin, I. (2006). *Role of computer assisted active learning system in history of civilization teaching,* Unpublished master thesis, University of Bahcesehir, Istanbul.

ADDITIONAL READING

Amant, S. A., & Still, B. (2007). *Handbook of Research on Open Source Software Technological, Economic, and Social Perspectives*. IRS.

Badre, A., Levialdi, S., Foley, J., Thomas, J., Strohecker, C., De Angeli, A., et al. (2007). Human Centric E-Learning and the Challenge of Cultural Localization, (*Lecture Notes in Computer Science*, pp. 690-691). Berlin, Germany: Springer.

Baldi, S., Heier, H., & Stanzick, F. (2002, June). Open courseware vs. Open source software – A critical comparison. Paper presented at ECIS 2002 Gdansk, Poland.

Bouras, C., & Tsiatsos, T. (2006). Educational virtual environments: design rationale and architecture. *Multimedia Tools and Applications, 29,* 153–173. doi:10.1007/s11042-006-0005-7

Chao, L. (2009). *Utilizing Open Source Tools for Online Teaching and Learning: Applying Linux Technologies.* IGI Pub.

Chen, C.-M. (2009). Personalized E-learning system with self-regulated learning assisted mechanisms for promoting learning performance. *Expert Systems with Applications, 36,* 8816–8829. doi:10.1016/j.eswa.2008.11.026

Dalzial, J. (2003). Open Standards Versus Open Source in E-learning. *Educase Quarterly, 4,* 4–7.

Donnelly, R., & McSweeney, F. (2009). *Applied E-Learning and E-Teaching in Higher Education, ISR.* InIn.

Feller, J., & Fitzgerald, B. (Eds.). (2001). *Understanding Open Source Software Development.* Reading, MA: Addison-Wesley Professional.

Holmes, B., & Gardner, R. (2006). *E-Learning: Concepts and Practice.* Thousand Oaks, CA: Sage.

Howard, C., Boettcher, J. V., Justice, L., Schenk, K., Rogers, P., & Berg, G. A. (2005). *Encyclopedia of Distance Learning* (*Vol. 4*). Hershey, PA: Idea Group.

Johnson, S., & Aragon, S. (2002). An Instructional Strategy Framework for Online Learning Environments. In *Proceedings of World Conference on E-Learning in Corporate, Government, Healthcare & Higher Education,* (pp.529-536).

Kaderali, F., & Ehlert, O. Experience with Open Source for e-learning. Retrieved from http://www.campussource.de/events/docs/e-Bologna_conference_Kaderali.pdf.

Kaoa, C.-P., & Tsai, C.-C. (2009). Teachers' attitudes toward web-based professional development, with relation to Internet self-efficacy and beliefs about web-based learning. *Computers & Education, 53*(1), 66–73. doi:10.1016/j.compedu.2008.12.019

Littlejohn, A., & Pegler, C. (2007). *Preparing for Blended E-Learning: Understanding Blended and Online Learning, Routeledge.* New York: Taylor & Francis.

Lytras, M. D., & Naeve, A. (2007). *Open Source for Knowledge and Learning Management: Strategies Beyond Tools.* Hershey, PA: IGI Pub.

Narciss, S., Proske, A., & Koerndle, H. (2007). Promoting self-regulated learning in web-based learning environments. *Computers in Human Behavior, 23,* 1126–1144. doi:10.1016/j.chb.2006.10.006

Oyria, K., & Murray, P. J. (2005). Using free/libre/open source software to build a virtual international community for open source nursing informatics. *International Journal of Medical Informatics, 74,* 937–945. doi:10.1016/j.ijmedinf.2005.07.023

Pahl, C. (Ed.). (2008). *Architecture Solutions for E-Learning Systems.* ISR.

Yong, J. (2005). Internet-Based e-Learning Workflow Process, (*Lecture Notes in Computer Science,* pp.516-524). Berlin, Germany: Springer.

Yudko, E., Hirokawa, R., & Chi, R. (2008). Attitudes, beliefs, and attendance in a hybrid course. *Computers & Education, 50*(4), 1217–1227. doi:10.1016/j.compedu.2006.11.005

Zaharias, P., & Poulymenakou, A. (2003). Identifying training needs for ICT skills enhancement in South-Eastern Europe: Implications for designing web-based training courses. *Journal of Educational Technology & Society, 6*(1). Available at http://ifets.ieee.org.

Zaharias, P., & Poulymenakou, A. (2005). Implementing the Learner-Centered Design Paradigm for Web-Based Training Curricula. *IFIP International Federation for Information Processing Springer Boston, 167/2005*, 1571–5736.

KEY TERMS AND DEFINITIONS

Active History Teaching: The set of well designed learning activities constructed to present - impart history related concepts to students.

Cognitive Maps: A mental model of students which presents information in a visualized schema where the related concepts are linked to support learning or ease of recall of these concepts.

Cognitive Styles: A term used to call the variety of thinking ways or thinking behaviors of students in particular situations.

Computer Assisted Active Learning: Use of computers to support the student learning process with student centered active learning strategies.

Critical Thinking: Thinking and learning strategy where students are constructing a meaning and understanding of given cases by analyzing, or discussing their accuracy.

Flash Cards: A set of cards which are used to support students to learn the specific concepts, terms, definitions in a subject by repetition of the sets of cards in question – answer based drill practices.

Free and Open-Source Software (FOSS): Indicating the software is licensed to free use, distribute or study where the modification to the original software is possible by changing the source code.

Chapter 14
Web 2.0 as Potential E-Learning Tools for K-12 English Language Learners

Lucy Green
Texas Tech University, USA

Fethi Inan
Texas Tech University, USA

ABSTRACT

Federal legislation demands academic success of all students as well as instructional modifications for special needs students. Even so, school districts struggle with funding educational programs and products that would greatly benefit students grappling with language and content acquisition. Free and open source Web 2.0 tools present exciting opportunities for the creation of educational material that reflects best teaching practices for English Language Learners. The chapter conducts an analysis of second language acquisition research that identifies the most common components of effective second language teaching practice. With these determined, the attention is focused on the characteristics of Web 2.0 technologies that might be used to promote educational activities and opportunities that embody these effective SLA pedagogical practices while meeting the unique instructional needs of ELL students. Although the chapter focuses on ELL students, many of the instructional methods and technology tool characteristics will benefit other students in all content areas.

INTRODUCTION

The population of English language learners (ELL) in the American public school system has increased dramatically in the last ten years. Of the 49 million students enrolled in pre-kindergarten through 12th grade, five million are English language learners, reflecting a growth of 57.17% since 1995 (Department of Education, 2006). Along with the exponential growth in immigrant populations, ELL education reform has moved from a state-level issue to an important component of national policy. No Child Left Behind, the landmark 2001 legislation, now holds schools to a much higher level of accountability for ensuring the academic success of ELL students (Department of Education, 2004). The mandates of the Title III NCLB section push for a more rapid acquisition

DOI: 10.4018/978-1-61520-917-0.ch014

of English language skills and the assessment of ELL students on the same content and level as other student groups. In addition, all students are expected to be linguistically ready to read, write and communicate within electronic environments by the 8th grade (Capps, Fix, Murray, Ost, Passel & Herwantoro, 2005).

The continual growth and change of technology tools have created a new technological literacy, literacy that will continue to progress with the development of technology. Not only does the technologically literate person need a variety of technical skills, but must also be able to apply these skills across multiple contexts (Barton, Hamilton, & Ivanic, 2000; Gee, 2000; Street, 1984). The combination of legislative and technological development in education presents teachers with new challenges within the struggle to meet the myriad of instructional requirements and unique needs of ELL students. To complicate matters, funding for professional development, technology products and tools, and even personnel is a continued concern for school districts. In a deteriorating economy, over thirty-seven states face crippling budget deficits, cutting over $15 billion from their 2008-2009 annual budgets (National Governors Association, 2008).

Free and open source Web 2.0 tools (e.g., podcasting, vodcasting, blogs, and wikis) present exciting opportunities for the creation of educational experiences and material that reflect best teaching practices for ELL students as identified in Second Language Acquisition (SLA) research (Rose-Aguillar, 2007; Lacina, 2004; Brown & Green, 2008). Articles that focus on describing specific Web 2.0 tools serve as a strong starting point (Rose-Aguillar, 2007). However, the rapid pace of technological change and the abundance of freely available Web 2.0 tools can make the search for appropriate tools overwhelming. Therefore, it would seem more beneficial to focus on the particular characteristics Web 2.0 tools possess that would directly impact ELL instruction, and how these characteristics are favored in SLA research.

Hence, we begin with a comprehensive analysis of SLA theories and the effectiveness of Web 2.0 tools as they apply to sound second language teaching practices. Subsequent sections examine the unique instructional needs of ELL students and contemporary ELL teaching strategies. The final section explores how Web 2.0 tools might contribute to the performance of English language learners in acquiring a second language as well as a brief overview of recommended free and open-source Web 2.0 technologies. The authors would like to remind the reader that while the focus of this chapter is on English Language Learning, the pedagogical issues and use of the tools to be discussed are applicable to a number of other fields such as language arts and social studies. Cross-curricular applications to math and science can also be made.

SECOND LANGUAGE THEORY

Second languages encompass any languages beyond a learner's original language or 'mother tongue' referring to the learning of any language at a point in time after the acquisition of a learner's first language (Mitchell & Myles, 1998). Second language acquisition is considered a relatively new and developing field, and separate from its major contributor, Linguistics. Linguists focus on primary languages whereas SLA researchers study the issues and questions revolving secondary languages (Eckman, 1995). Perhaps because of its newness, SLA is not readily identified with any one specific theory. In fact, Eckman (1995) and Long (1993) consider the term 'SLA theory' to be misleading since consensus on a formal SLA theory has yet to be achieved. Even so, recent research has helped to focus the field's attention on language learning through social activities. This line of research suggests that collaborative interactions help learners acquire language, strongly questioning the idea of language learning as an individual mental activity contextually separate from culture and society (Gibbons, 2006; Hall 1995; Kramsch, 1993; Toohey, 2000). As the detailed study of all SLA theories is beyond the scope of this chapter, this paper will only review the landmark theories in SLA that emphasize social interaction.

Processing Perspective

The processing perspective looks at how second language learners' ability to process language grows throughout acquisition (Lee & Benati, 2007). One of the most influential processing theories is Krashen's Five Hypotheses: Acquisition-Learning, Monitor, Natural Order, Affective-Filter and Input (Krashen, 1982). The acquisition-learning hypothesis differentiates between 'learning' and 'acquiring'. Whereas learning refers to the structured study of language, its grammar, its usage; acquired language is language that can be used in a natural almost 'native'-like conversation. The monitor hypothesis claims that language teaching should concern itself with communication and not repetition so that the learner is able to consciously monitor form and syntax; while the natural order hypothesis simply states that the rules and structure of a language are acquired in a typical and invariable order (Peregoy & Boyle, 1997). The affective-filter hypothesis concerns itself with the social and emotional factors involved in language learning, and identifies three of these types of variables that can impact language acquisition: level of anxiety in the learning environment, level of student motivation and level of self-confidence and self-esteem (Krashen, 1985). The input hypothesis frames acquisition within communicative exchange as opposed to grammar and syntax. It shares a similar scaffolding approach to Vygotsky's Zone of Proximal Development (Vygotsky, 1978). The popularity of Krashen's theory is due to his willingness to look at how second language learning occurs in the classroom environment (Peregoy & Boyle, 1997).

Interactionist Perspective

Interactionists believe that the most important contributor to the language acquisition process is natural communication between second language learners and native speakers. Interactionist research preoccupies itself with negotiation of meaning, an exchange in communication where the language learner and the native speaker engage in gesturing, paraphrasing and gentle correction to arrive at a mutual understanding (Long & Porter, 1985). Long (1985) proposed his Interaction hypothesis as an extension to Krashen's Input hypothesis (Krashen, 1982). The interaction hypothesis views input as a cyclical process where the negotiation of meaning forces input to become more comprehensible so that it can be acquired by the language learner (Long, 1981). Long noted that in the struggle to communicate, native and non-native speaker pairs used many conversational scaffolds or feedback, such as repetitions, confirmation checks, comprehension checks, or clarification checks (Mitchell & Myles, 1998). Researchers have identified several types of feedback offered in the course of meaning negotiation. These recasts are verbal cues provided by native speakers that model the correct usage of the target language (Mackey, Oliver, & Leeman, 2003). Recasts can either occur as negative evidence, a stated correction or rephrasing of an incorrectly formatted statement, or as positive evidence, any modeling of correct target language utterances (Gibbons, 2006). Swain (1995) further developed the Interactionist perspective with the Ouput hypothesis, claiming that only the production or output of language helps the brain to process grammatical structures and that input is insufficient for well rounded language acquisition. Studies have shown that when provided with feedback such as recasts, language learners will, to a certain extent, incorporate the feedback and output the corrections in their own speech (Oliver, 1995; Towell & Hawkins, 1994).

Naturalistic Perspective

The naturalistic approach to SLA is best exemplified by Schumann's Acculturation Theory, which was developed based on a study that observed nonnative speakers using language utterances similar to pidgin, basic language exchanges that are not associated with any native speaker (Schumann, 1978). The more complex the pidgin utterances, the more 'acculturated' the language learners seemed to be. Acculturation theory believes that the more integrated a language learner feels in his or her adopted community, the more he or she will acculturate and acquire the target language (Mitchell & Myles, 1998). Acculturation depends on eight factors which together comprise the amount of social distance a language learner feels from his or her target language community. The first, social dominance refers to the relationship of power between the two groups involved in language exchange (or in the case of a classroom, peer-teacher and peer-peer). Another is the pattern of integration, whether the language learner is part of a group that assimilates or preserves its culture. These are followed by enclosure (how self-sufficient the language learner perceives him or herself to be in the native language community), cultural similarities, community size, attitude and how long the language learner will be staying in the native language community (Long, 2007; Schumann, 1978).

Although second language acquisition theories vary in perspective and focus, taken together, they help classroom teachers consider the multitude of factors that impact English language learners and the native speakers present in their classrooms. As clarified by Long (2007): "The theories themselves may not say anything to teachers about how to teach, but perhaps something about who and what it is they are trying to teach..." (p. 19). With the role of SLA theories in teaching thus established, the next section of this chapter will discuss the unique characteristics and instructional needs of English language learners.

INSTRUCTIONAL NEEDS OF ELL STUDENTS

English language learners come to American K-12 classrooms with a wide range of background characteristics, making the task of defining the typical ELL student almost impossible as the variability in ELL characteristics ranges from socio-economic to the level of education (Gibbons, 2006). Some ELL students are at a relative grade level, some have experienced sporadic schooling; a few are severely traumatized due to war conditions in their home countries and others are American by birth but live with non-English speaking caregivers. For this kaleidoscopic population, studies have found that, compared to native speakers, ELLs need a large amount of time to acquire language skills needed for academic success (Collier, 1989; Cummins, 1996). In order to help ELLs develop into strong language learners, teachers must take into consideration the unique characteristics and instructional needs of English language learners as described in the following section (Freeman & Long, 1994).

Motivation

The learner's motivation to interact with a second language through various means of communication is generally accepted to be the most valuable component of language learning (Van den Buren, 2006; Willis, 1996). Dörnyei (2002) defines motivation not as an emotive substance but as a distinct process made up of three phases: pre-actional, actional and post-actional. The pre-actional phase is where motivation is created through the setting of clear and distinct goals with the goal-setting serving as a springboard into action. Environment stimulation and progress checks help the learner to determine further action throughout the actional phase. During the post-actional phase the learners engage in metacognition, analyzing what components of the task were motivating and how these components can play a role in future activities.

To promote motivation, Dörnyei (2002) maintains that the instructional activities should capture the learner's desire to succeed despite growing levels of complexity. The learner should be able to stay focused on instructional goals and experience strong feelings of success at their accomplishment (Crookes & Schmidt, 1991; Laufer & Hulstijn, 2001). Language learners should also be so motivated to communicate in the second language that they put aside the fear of making mistakes and seeming foolish (Freeman & Long, 1994).

Cultural Consideration

The discussion of cultural consideration for English language learners actually refers to two separate issues: the culture of the school and classroom (Cazden, 1986; Gibbons, 2006) and the cultural background of the English language learner (Reyes & Vallone, 2008). In this section, ELL instructional needs surrounding school and classroom culture will be briefly addressed. Culture, in the broadest sense, encompasses beliefs, norms and accepted behaviors that form a group identity (Peregoy & Boyle, 1997). Classroom culture, therefore, is influenced by the explicit or implied presence of several groups: students, teachers, school, community and so forth. These spheres of influence shape classroom culture and impact interaction efforts between teachers/students and students/ students in various ways. As their cultural backgrounds are extremely different from those prevalent in American schools, English language learners will not only struggle to acquire language skills and academic content but need to develop the social ability to adjust to school culture (Hawkins, 2005). Cazden (1986) points out that the struggle to communicate is present even after students use basic language successfully because communication is governed by different sociocultural rules. This communication breakdown is especially evident within the concept of *wait time* – the time a speaker waits for a response. Studies have found that the amount of *wait time* and its implied conversational rules, such as interruptions and number of speakers, highly varies from culture to culture (Bauman & Scherzer, 1974; Ochs & Schieffelin, 1984; Shultz, Erikson & Florio, 1982). Furthermore, *wait time* and other communication rules vary depending on the instructional activity taking place in the classroom (Mehan, 1979). ELL students are responsible for unraveling this cultural tapestry. When they do so and become comfortable in the routines and culture of a classroom, maximum language learning and academic success can be achieved (Peregoy & Boyle, 1997).

Representational Gestures

Representational gestures are gestures taken from the speaker's mental picture of a language term and are not part of an official language system such as American Sign Language (Church, Nolley, & Mahootian, 2004). Gestures are powerful communication aids for ELL students because these help students in a lexical search process for the unknown vocabulary term. For example, a flat hand aimed lower to the ground while a speaker says 'short' can help the ELL student mentally locate the term in his or her native tongue, connecting the term in the second language to the term in his or her first language (Church et al, 2004). A student learning a second language has already amassed a body of concepts and ideas with labels attached in the first language. Therefore, he or she acquires a new label in the second language for the previously known concepts. These connected labels, or common underlying proficiencies, represent a large portion of language structural characteristics that Germanic and Romantic languages, in particular, share (Johns & Torrez, 2001). Gestures visually aid in the finding of these common underlying proficiencies.

Vocabulary

An ELL student will run across two basic types of language within the school community (Cummins, 1989). Gibbons (1991) labels these playground language for interpersonal communication and classroom language for academic learning. ELL students may struggle for many years to master classroom language vocabulary comparable to that of a native speaker. To complicate matters further, Freeman and Freeman (2004) explain that classroom language comprises of academic vocabulary that is content-specific (e.g. thermometer, square root, timeline) and vocabulary that is academically broad (e.g. either/or, exam, highlight). Teachers can use contextualization to aid in acquiring academic vocabulary by introducing this language using manipulatives, visual aids, and real-based problems (Van den Branden, 2006). When academic language is not easily contextualized, ELL students must be exposed to as broad a range of texts, language forms and communications exploring the ways scientists, mathematicians, and other fields use language to exchange knowledge in their areas of expertise (Hawkins, 2004).

INSTRUCTIONAL STRATEGIES IN THE ELL CLASSROOM

Collaborative Learning

English language learners greatly benefit from small group learning activities, promoting student growth in three areas emphasized by second language acquisition theories: input, interaction and knowledge contextualization (McGroarty, 1993). Cooperative learning is a teaching strategy that organizes students into collaborative small groups so that learning goals are achieved (Peregoy & Boyle, 1997). Small groups place ELL students in constant negotiations for meaning by pressuring learners to communicate through repetition and

paraphrasing. Furthermore, this repeated input of information occurs within the context of the academic curriculum, helping English language learners to cement both their comprehension of language and understanding of domain concepts (Reyes & Vallone, 2008).

Several studies have documented the key role cooperative learning plays in the second language acquisition process by allowing ELLs to process both verbal and non-verbal communication, aiding comprehensible input (Swain, 1985; Freeman & Freeman, 2001). Collaboration also pressures language learners to reproduce the information and vocabulary acquired through various mediums – depending on the task at hand, fostering a cyclical process of learning: negotiation of meaning, comprehensible input, acquisition, representation leading to re-negotiation of meaning. In fact, Gibbons (2006) argues that collaborative tasks strengthen language learning by their advocacy of interaction, reflection, integration and comparison of knowledge and language. In the absence of native speakers, the benefits of cooperative learning also extend to interactions between English language learners themselves. Research findings confirm that second language interaction is just as beneficial for exchanges between two non-native speakers as they are for native speaker and non-native speaker exchanges. In fact, exchanges between non-native speakers alone may promote stronger learning experiences since communication breakdowns occur more frequently and must be addressed and corrected by the learners themselves (Porter, 1983; Pica & Doughty, 1985; Varonis and Gass, 1985).

Scaffolding

Scaffolding, a series of steps that help students analyze the process by which ideas are formed (McKenzie, 2000), helps English language learners strengthen understanding of academic language, connect prior learning to new concepts, process information effectively and become independent learners (Cummings, 1989; Fradd & Lee, 1999; Israel, 2002). Teachers of English language learners must help students connect what they know to newer academic experiences, 'bridging' both worlds and addressing the wide disparity in ELL backgrounds on different academic topics (Cummings, 1989; Hawkins, 2004; Reyes & Vallone, 2008). To scaffold learning, teachers oftentimes use verbal strategies such as summarizing, rewording and exemplifying use of academic vocabulary. Even so, academic language might be more successfully developed if teachers scaffold the mental process of language acquisition by modeling their own mental processing in 'think-alouds,' – actions that demonstrate how to approach problem-solving using metacognition (Rea & Mercuri, 2006). Studies have shown that language learners that are specifically taught how to process information in this way are more successfully able to process information on their own. These studies also explain that without instruction on how to process information using strategies, ELL students may not engage in these mental tasks (Benati, 2001; Israel 2002; Pressley & Afflerbach, 1995). Researchers go on to suggest that information processing be further modeled using a "fish bowl strategy" where a teacher leads two students in modeling the mental process aloud, afterwards engaging all students in a group discussion over the experience with the rest of the class (Rea & Mercuri, 2006). Language learners who develop learning strategies are not only better equipped to deal with academic demands but also may become life-long learners (Freeman & Long, 1991).

Incorporating Student Culture

Incorporating student culture addresses curriculum and activity designs that fully integrate the cultural background of its students (Ovando, Combs & Collier, 2006). This integration can be achieved through culture studies, assignments that provide students the opportunity to interview relatives and draw upon cultural knowledge (Doherty

et al, 2003). Access to these funds of knowledge help ELL students contextualize academic information so that it is relatable to their daily lives and more easily retrieved down the road (Moll, Amanti, Neff & Gonzalez, 1992). The inclusion of culture studies provides a fuller picture of the ELL student as an individual, one that is involved in a myriad of relationships and activities outside of the classroom. The presence of this picture can foster deeper and more meaningful linguistic exchanges due to students' perceptions of their contributions as valued in the classroom (Moll et al, 1992; Doherty et al, 2003). Freeman and Freeman (1994) further emphasized the value of culture studies as alternative assessment tools which comprise of a broader range of skills including oral presentations and development of visuals.

FREE AND OPEN SOURCE WEB 2.0 AS EDUCATIONAL TOOLS IN ELL INSTRUCTION

Computer Assisted Language Learning (CALL), in the last decade, has evolved from focus on a specific technology or piece of software to an interactive multi-modal environment where technology is but one of many components (Bloch, 2008). The broadening of CALL's identity is perhaps in response to the impact of technology on language itself. Linguists and SLA researchers note time and again that language use in internet and multimedia technologies provides an entirely new experience, and that the ability to communicate effectively using these technologies is an essential component of being literate in the current century (Crystal, 2001; Kress, 2003; Rassool, 1999). The newest wave of technology tools marking students and educators as participants today is known simply as *Web 2.0*, a label created to express the characteristics of these next-generation technologies (Stauffer, 2008).

The interactional characteristics of Web 2.0 technologies and the ease with which these can be personalized by users make them ideally suited for providing the building blocks for language learning. These technologies provide communication opportunities revolving around the achievement of common goals and comprehensible input (Peregoy & Boyle, 1997). From the processing perspective, using Web 2.0 tasks as vehicles for language instruction allow ELL students to be engaged in the content area and language learning in an environment that lowers the affective filter (e.g. anxiety) (Reyes & Vallone, 2008). Interactionists, such as Long (1985), promote the use of tasks that require communication and language-use in a realistic context, away from the focus of linguistic drills. Web 2.0 and other multimedia projects aptly fit these criteria. Aside from being highly interactive, technology-based tasks can be highly motivating and highly personalized – an advantage from a naturalist perspective on second language acquisition (Almeida-Soares, 2008; Van den Branden, 2006). Several researchers have suggested that second language learners acquire language skills more effectively when they are focused on using language as a way to exchange information that only the learners have (McGroarty, 1993; Pica, 1987; Porter, 1986). By using Web 2.0 technologies as components of group-based tasks, teachers offer ELL students a myriad of opportunities to engage in conversation that is essential to completing the given task emphasizing the sharing of responsibility and collaboration (McGroarty, 1993).

Perhaps the most beneficial characteristic of Web 2.0 tools in today's economic climate is that many are freely available. Free and open source describe a wide range of tools that allow the user freedom to modify source code, create new versions based on the original code, redistribute and mash up (combine) with other tools (Coar, 2006). For the purposes of this chapter, the open source tools identified will contain some but not all of these qualities. To narrow the scope even further, we will focus on three of the most commonly

known Web 2.0 technologies available: weblogs, wikis and podcasting.

Blogs

Blogs have been identified as an excellent means to introduce ELL students to idiomatic conversation and social interactions within the target culture (Penrod, 2007). The ability to engage in these types of conversations through the web along with the comments and feedback from native speakers are especially motivating to language learners, who, because of the sense of play involved in using blogs, can experience writing as a pleasurable activity (Gibbons, 2006; Van den Branden, 2006). Peregoy & Boyle (1997) have noted that previously unmotivated students become excited about writing when the concept of wide readership is introduced. This public audience spurs ELL bloggers to consider how their texts might influence readers and their responses. Blogs, having begun as online journals and diaries, inspire story-telling in their users (Penrod, 2007). Through storytelling, English language learners can experience higher self-esteem and motivation as their cultural backgrounds and experiences are woven into the curriculum, positively impacting the affective-filter (Reyes & Vallone, 2008). The type of electronic literacy fostered by Web 2.0 technologies is especially evident within the blogosphere, where student writers must consider how best to organize images, links, colors, audio, and layouts, in the realization that the right message cannot be shared through text alone (Penrod, 2007). While blogging, language learners are, therefore, struggling to create meaning using language in a productive way. Perhaps unaware, the ELL student also records grammatical errors and patterns in his or her writing that can be used for reinforced negative evidence, such as corrective feedback (Peregoy & Boyle, 1997).

The Landmark Project hosts a variety of online resources created with the K-12 classroom in mind. Its blogging feature, Blogmeister, can be as restricted or as global as the creator desires. To help develop a readership or to keep students aware of new posts, the site also offers a free blog tag generator and a feed creator tool. Blogmeister can be visually modified to a certain extent, but its purpose is found in the "thousands of teachers who have discovered the value of classroom blogging, both as an avenue for their communications, but also as a tool for giving voice to what their students are learning and how they are learning" (Warlick, 2009). The terms and conditions of Blogmeister prohibit students from creating and maintaining class or individual blogs, and a school code is required for registration.

Wordpress is an open-source publishing platform that can be used to create blogs and websites. Its site boasts that wordpress is "completely customizable and can be used for almost anything," including web design for Coca-Cola, GE, Ford, Best-Buy and Samsung (Wordpress, 2009). Due to its extremely stable code and its vast community of users and resources, Wordpress is a good option for K-12 organizations that are looking for district-wide tools and have the capacity to host resulting products on its servers. For individualized use by a teacher or group of students, Wordpress offers web-hosted blogs with customizable templates at wordpress.com. Its security features

Figure 1. Screen shot of Class Blogmeister registration and home page (© 2009. The Landmark Project. Used with permission.)

Figure 2. Screen shot of the discussion settings for I Heart Green, a blog hosted on Wordpress.com (© 2009. Wordpress.org. Used with permission.)

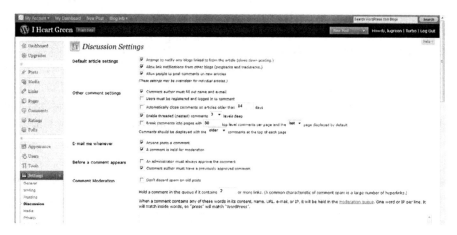

allow for moderating of comments and restricted readership.

Blogger, part of the large Google family of web tools, is perhaps the most user-friendly of the three blogging tools. Anyone can register using a Google account and in a matter of minutes, begin blogging. Blogger templates are now customizable and can be modified using html. Its security settings rival those of Blogmeister without the burden of obtaining a school code or identification. An advantage of Blogger is that it can be used in conjunction with other Google applications or partners such as Flickr, Youtube, Google Sites, Google Video and Google Wiki necessitating only one google account (Blogger, 2009). Blogger allows you to upload all manner of audio and video files, however the authors have found that it has trouble uploading video files larger than 19MB.

Wikis

Wikis, and the shared editing feature they uniquely possess, have become popular platforms for collaborative writing projects in schools, businesses and pop culture due to their simplistic structure and system of networked pages (Ebershbach, Glaser & Heigl, 2006). The technical attributes of wikis are simple and easy to use. Students are usually able to complete wiki projects maintaining focus on the curriculum content and interactions as opposed to software issues. The user-friendliness of wikis is reflected in its real time editing, links, automatically-generated menus and user control over navigation (Ebersbach, et al, 2006). This same user-friendliness simplifies the set-up of more complex and cognitively demanding assignments without the overload of technical issues. More importantly, wikis allow for the interconnection between various multimedia elements and technological information units, such as photos, texts, websites and other resources (Van den Branden, 2006).

Studies on second language learning within the framework of socialization reflect the construction of "shared understanding" that ELL students undergo when working or writing together; a struggle that encompasses not only the initial arrival at understanding, but the continued reshaping and negotiation process to refine it (Mitchell & Myles, 1998, Willet, 1995). These studies have also concluded that not only are language skills expanding during collaborative revision and editing (Samway, 1987; Urzúa, 1987) but writ-

Figure 3. Screen shot of Blogger advertising its ease-of-use and features (© 2009. Google. Used with permission.)

ten constructions of knowledge, such as these electronic maps of networked thinking, generate multiple communication events where comprehensible input is provided, a boon to language development (Peregoy & Boyle, 1997).

There are numerous wiki tools available. Wikispaces and PB Works both offer wikis free of charge to educators. It is possible to create accounts for students without student email addresses – a plus for elementary educators. Each allows file uploads of up to a total of 10MB. Wikispaces generates funds through ad placements, however, at the request of educators, it will remove any ads from these accounts. Google Wiki and Wetpaint are both completely free. Wetpaint can be more customized than the restrictive Google Wiki and is ad free for educators. Those who are attempting to select an appropriate wiki tool can begin their search at WikiMatrix, a comprehensive website that allows the user to select wikis based on a comparison matrix, a wiki choice wizard and advanced search criteria (CosmoCode, 2005).

Podcasting

Podcasts are made up of audio and video media that can be accessed and played over an internet connection by a personal computer, or downloaded

to a portable media player (Copley, 2007). Podcasts are a unique type of online media because of their use of RSS – Really Simple Syndication. RSS technology allows the user to subscribe to a podcast in very much the same way as one might program a digital video recorder to record new broadcasts of a favorite television show. Any time the user updates his or her player, new content is uploaded (McCarty, 2005; Sloan, 2005). Because of the versatility of podcast delivery modes (e.g. computers, mp3 players, cell-phones), and the RSS feature, podcasts are available at any time and any place (Copley, 2007). There are two common ways in which to use this category of Web 2.0 tools in the classroom: (1) as a pre-made instructional resource or (2) as a student-centered project (King & Gura, 2007). As an educational resource, podcasts provide many scaffolding advantages for English language learners: (1) students become aware of the content ahead of time, (2) key terms and vocabulary can be introduced beforehand, (3) the control feature allows students to start, stop or pause the flow of information when necessary; and (4) students have the power to replay the information, as well as discuss with others so as to make sense of any confusing content (Saville-Troike, 2006).

Figure 4. Screen shot of WikiMatrix demonstrating results provided by the wiki choice editor (© 2009. Cosmo Code, Inc. Used with permission.)

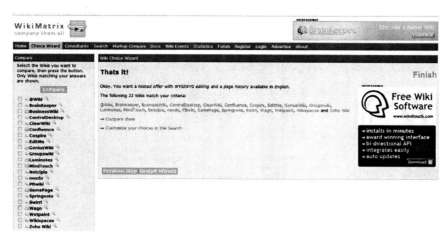

As student-led projects, podcasts promote watching, listening, speaking, reading and writing while developing a product, language skills that mutually support and develop each other (Peregoy & Boyle, 1997). Peregoy and Boyle (1997) argue that development in one of these four areas fosters development in the other three, especially between reading and oral vocabulary. Although it might be supposed that student-led projects would result in poor examples of heavily-accented audio, Flowerdew (1994) concludes that familiar accents are actually more helpful to second language learners as the phonological pronunciation is more easily recognized.

Video podcasts combine the audio production of a podcast with digital video edited for streaming on a site, such as a blog – giving rise to the term vlogging (King & Gura, 2007). Video podcasts present a distinct advantage in that language use is embedded within context, demonstrating that language terms and their meanings change with the identity of the speaker and the situation in which the term is used (Ekcman, 1995; Wagener, 2006). In experiencing instruction in a cultural context, ELL students are introduced, in non-formal ways, to the process of developing social skills necessary for interaction with English-speaking peers (Gutierrez, et al, 1999). Other accepted practices for ELL instruction that are possible through a video podcast are the use of representational gestures, and captioned text, supporting reading skills (Johns & Torrez, 2001). Video podcasts are an excellent vehicle through which students can promote their own language and cultural background, building up strong identities and healthy self-esteem (Reyes & Vallone, 2008). Student generated video podcasts reflect the culture and characteristics of its student creators. Subjects such as folk stories, oral histories and interviews all serve to connect the backgrounds of ELL students to the novel culture of the classroom, bridging both languages and helping English language learners value their own contributions to the classroom (Eckman, 1995).

There are a vast amount of free and open source software for creating, editing and disseminating audio and video podcasts. Blogger, in combination with Feedburner, can be used to quickly create a podcast feed. Skype, a well-known voice-over-internet-protocol, offers free applications that can be installed within its platform. Pamela and Supertintin are two popular applications that record both audio and video conversations. Unfortunately, the quality of these recordings is dependent on the quality of the installed hardware of conversation participants. For audio recordings that can be edited for superior quality, the open-source software, Audacity, is well-known for its powerful capability and wide range of features (Audacity, 2009).

Vodcasts can be easily created using Microsoft Photostory 3 or iPhoto. Although these are not cross-platform tools, they are intuitive and available without additional purchase. Both generate photo journals that are easily published to play on small screens. Once completed, these video podcasts can simply be uploaded to a blog or wiki. Free movie file converters are also available that will compress videos so that these are easily played back on mp3 players and cell phones. The Videora iPod converter provides a wide range of converters searchable by brand and screen size (Videora, 2009). Due to the potential for copyright violation, it would behoove educators to carefully consider Fair Use Guidelines, any school district policies and permission guidelines when using tools such as Videora.

CONCLUSION

The number of ELL students representing various backgrounds, cultures, and experiences with different instructional needs are rapidly increasing in K-12 schools. In order to provide equal learning opportunities, the individual needs of those students should be carefully addressed. Previous research and practices address several effective

Figure 5. Screen shot of Audacity running on Windows platform. (Image printed under the terms of the General Public License).

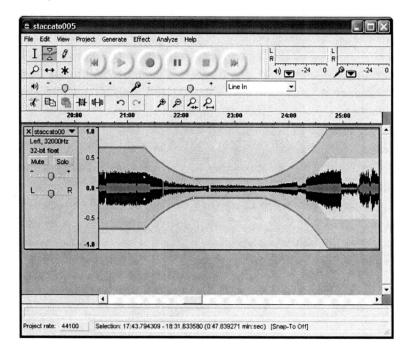

second language teaching practices aimed at improving ELL instruction. These practices, most being student centered strategies, emphasize the importance of developing instruction that takes into consideration the ELL student's cultural background, prior knowledge, motivation, social and linguistic needs. However, teachers face a daunting task when attempting to implement these strategies in the main stream classroom. Free and open source Web 2.0 tools may offer teachers

Figure 6. Screen shot of the Videora conversion options available in the Classic option. (© 2009. Red Kawa. Used with permission.)

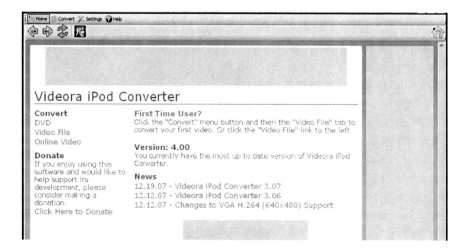

the ability to rise to this challenge in order to help ELL students develop into strong language learners by addressing the unique characteristics and instructional needs of this student population while minimizing financial concerns. While the chapter addresses pedagogical issues and use of Web 2.0 tools in the ELL classroom, the techniques and resources discussed within are applicable to a number of other content areas.

Open source Web 2.0 tools provide functionalities and convenience in applying effective instructional strategies when meeting the particular needs of ELL students. Web 2.0 applications can be effective teaching and learning tools as they allow active student participation, production, collaboration, and reflection. For teachers, these tools allow them to implement project based learning activities, distribute instructional materials, observe student product and progress, and provide feedback and scaffolding. By focusing on the particular characteristics Web 2.0 technologies possess, as opposed to the technologies themselves, teachers can select the appropriate tools that would directly impact ELL instruction by helping ELL students (as well as all other classroom members) develop academic, social and technological literacy.

REFERENCES

Aguilar-Rosell, F. (2007). Top of the pods – in search of a podcasting "pedagogy" for language learning. *Computer Assisted Language Learning*, *20*(5), 471–492. doi:10.1080/09588220701746047

Almeida-Soares, D. (2008). Understanding class blogs as a tool for language development. *Language Teaching Research*, *12*(4), 517–533. doi:10.1177/1362168808097165

Audacity. (2009). Audacity: Free audio editor and recorder. Retrieved August 12, 2009, from Audacity Website: http://audacity.sourceforge.net/

Barton, D., Hamilton, M., & Ivanič, R. (2000). *Situated literacies: Reading and writing in context*. London: Routledge.

Bloch, J. (2008). *Technologies in the second language composition classroom*. Ann Arbor, MI: University of Michigan Press.

Brown, A., & Green, T. (2008). Video podcasting in perspective: The history, technology, aesthetics, and instructional uses of a new medium. *Journal of Educational Technology Systems*, *36*(1), 3–17. doi:10.2190/ET.36.1.b

Capps, R., Fix, M., Murray, J., Ost, J., Passel, J., & Herwantoro, S. (2005). *The new demography of America's schools: Immigration and the no child left behind act*. Washington, DC: The Urban Institute.

Cazden, C. (1986). Classroom discourse. In Wittrock, M. C. (Ed.), *Handbook of research on teaching* (pp. 432–463). New York: Macmillan.

Church, R. B., Nolley, S., & Mahootian, S. (2004). The role of gesture in bilingual education: Does gesture enhance learning? *International Journal of Bilingual Education and Bilingualism*, *7*(4), 303–319. doi:10.1080/13670050408667815

Coar, K. (2006, July 7). The open source definition. Retrieved August 15, 2009, from Open Source Initiative Web site: http://www.opensource.org/docs/osd

Collier, V. P. (1989). How long? A synthesis of research on academic achievement in a second language. *TESOL Quarterly*, *23*(3), 509–531. doi:10.2307/3586923

Copley, J. (2007). Audio and video podcasts of lectures for campus-based students: Production and evaluation of student use. *Innovations in Education and Teaching International*, *44*(4), 387–399. doi:10.1080/14703290701602805

CosmoCode. (2005). Welcome to the Wiki Choice Wizard! Retrieved August 12, 2009, from WikiMatrix: Compare The All! at http://www.wikimatrix.org/wizard.php

Crystal, D. (2001). *Language and the internet.* Cambridge: Cambridge University Press.

Cummins, J. (1981). The role of primary language development in promoting educational success for language minority students. In California State Department of Education (Ed.), *Schooling and language minority students: A theoretical framework* (pp. 3-49). Los Angeles: Evaluation, Dissemination, and Assessment Centre, California State University.

Cummins, J. (1994). Primary language instruction and the education of language minority students. In California State Department of Education (Ed.), *Schooling and language minority students: A theoretical framework* (2nd ed.) Los Angeles: Evaluation, Dissemination, and Assessment Center, California State University.

Cummins, P. (1989). Video and the French teacher. *French Review, 62*(3), 411–426.

Eckman, F. R. (Ed.). (1995). *Second language acquisition theory and pedagogy.* Mahwah, NJ: Lawrence Erlbaum Associates.

Flowerdew, J. (Ed.). (1994). *Academic listening: Research perspectives.* Cambridge, UK: Cambridge University Press.

Freeman, D. E., & Long, M. H. (1991). *An introduction to second language acquisition research.* New York: Longman.

Freeman, Y. S., & Freeman, D. E. (2004). Preview, view, review: Giving multilingual learners access to the curriculum. In Hoyt, L. (Ed.), *Spotlight on comprehension: Building a literacy of thoughtfulness.* Portsmouth, NH: Heinemann.

Gee, J. P. (2000). New people in new worlds: Networks, the new capitalism, and schools. In Cope, B., & Kalantzis, M. (Eds.), *Multiliteries: Literacy learning and the design of social futures* (pp. 43–68). London: Routledge & Kegan Paul.

Gibbons, P. (2006). *Bridging discourses in the ESL classroom: Students, teachers and researchers.* Sidney, Australia: Continuum.

Google. (1999). Blogger: Create your free blog. Retrieved August 12, 2009, from Blogger at http://www.blogger.com/start

Gutierrez, K. D., Baguedano, P., Alvarez, H., & Chiu, M. (1999). Building a culture of collaboration through hybrid language practices. *Theory into Practice, 38*(2), 87–93. doi:10.1080/00405849909543837

Hall, C. (1995). Formal linguistics and the mental representation: Psycholinguistic contributions to the identification and explanation of morphological and syntactic competence. *Language and Cognitive Processes, 10*(2), 169–187. doi:10.1080/01690969508407092

Hawkins, M. R. (2004). Researching English language and literacy development in schools. *Educational Researcher, 33*(3), 365–384. doi:10.3102/0013189X033003014

Hawkins, M. R. (2005). ESL in elementary education. In Hinkel, E. (Ed.), *Handbook of research in second language teaching and learning* (pp. 25–44). Mahwah, NJ: Lawrence Erlbaum Associates.

Johns, K. M., & Torrez, N. (2001). *Helping ESL learners succeed.* Bloomington, IN: Phi Delta Kappa Educational Foundation.

King, K. P., & Gura, M. (2007). *Podcasting for teachers.* Charlotte, NC: Information Age Publishing.

Kramsch, C. (1993). *Context and culture in language teaching.* Oxford: Oxford University Press.

Krashen, S. (1982). *Principles and practices in second language acquisition*. Oxford: Pergamon Press.

Kress, G. (2003). *Literacy in the new media age*. London: Routledge. doi:10.4324/9780203164754

Lacina, J. (2004). Promoting language acquisitions: Technology and English language learners. *Childhood Education, 81*(2), 113–115.

Long, M. H. (1996). The role of the linguistic environment in second language acquisition. In Ritchie, W. C., & Bhatia, T. J. (Eds.), *Handbook of second language acquisition* (pp. 413–468). New York: Academic Press. doi:10.1016/B978-012589042-7/50015-3

Long, M. H. (2007). *Problems in SLA*. Mahwah, NJ: Lawrence Erlbaum Associates.

Long, M. H., & Porter, P. (1985). Group work, interlanguage talk, and second language acquisition. *TESOL Quarterly, 18*(2), 207–227. doi:10.2307/3586827

Mackey, A., Oliver, R., & Leeman, J. (2003). Interactional input and the incorporation of feedback: an exploration of NS-NNS and NNS-NNS adult and child dyads. *Language Learning, 53*(1), 35–56. doi:10.1111/1467-9922.00210

McCarty, S. (2005). Spoken internet to go: Popularization through podcasting. *The JALT CALL Journal, 2*(1), 67–74.

McGroaty, M. (1993). Cooperative learning and language acquisition. In Holt, D. (Ed.), *Cooperative learning: A response to linguistic and cultural diversity*. Washington, DC: Centre for Applied Linguistics.

Mitchell, R., & Myles, F. (1998). *Second language learning theories*. New York: Arnold.

Moll, L., Amanti, C., Neff, D., & Gonzalez, N. (1992). Funds of knowledge for teaching: using a qualitative approach to connect homes and classrooms. *Theory into Practice, 31*(2), 132–141. doi:10.1080/00405849209543534

National Governers Association. (2008). *The fiscal survey of states*. Washington, D. C.: National Association of State Budget Officers.

Oliver, R. (1995). Negative feedback in child NS/NNS conversations. *Studies in Second Language Acquisition, 17*(2), 459–482. doi:10.1017/S0272263100014418

Peregoy, S. F., & Boyle, O. F. (1997). *Reading, writing, & learning in ESL: A resource book for K-12 teachers*. New York: Longman.

Pica, T., & Doughty, C. (1985). Input and interaction in the communicative language classroom: A comparison of teacher-fronted and group activities. In Gass, S., & Madden, C. (Eds.), *Input in second language acquisition* (pp. 115–132). Rowley, MA: Newbury House.

Porter, P. (1983). Variations in the conversations of adult learners of English as a function of the proficiency level of participants. Unpublished doctoral dissertation, Stanford University, California.

Rassool, N. (1999). *Literacy for sustainable development in the age of information*. Clevedon, UK: Multilingual Matters.

Reyes, S. A., & Vallone, T. L. (2008). *Constructivist strategies for teaching English language learners*. Thousand Oaks, CA: Corwin Press.

Saville-Troike, M. (2006). *Introducing second language acquisition*. New York: Cambridge University Press.

Swain, M. (1985). Communicative competence: Some roles of comprehensible input and comprehensible output in its development. In Gass, S. M., & Madden, C. G. (Eds.), *Input in second language acquisition* (pp. 235–253). Rowley, MA: Newbury House.

Toohey, K. (2000). *Learning English at school: Identity, social relations and classroom practice*. Clevedon, UK: Multilingual Matters LTD.

Towell, R., & Hawkins, R. (1994). *Approaches to second language acquisition*. Pennsylvania, PA: Multilingual Matters LTD.

U. S. Department of Education. (2004). No child left behind. Retrieved September 6, 2008, from U. S. Department of Education Web site: http://www.ed.gov/nclb/landing.jhtml

U. S. Department of Education. (2006). Public elementary and secondary students, staff, schools and school districts: School year 2003-04. Retrieved September 21, 2009, from National Center for Education Statistics at http://nces.ed.gov/pubsearch/pubsinfo.asp?pubid=2006307.

Van den Branden, K. (2006). Introduction: Task-based language teaching in a nutshell. In Van den Branden, K. (Ed.), *Task-based language education: From theory to practice* (pp. 1–16). Cambridge: Cambridge University Press. doi:10.1017/CBO9780511667282.002

Varonis, E., & Gass, S. (1985). Nonnative/nonnative conversations: A model for negotiation of meaning. *Applied Linguistics*, 6(1), 71–90. doi:10.1093/applin/6.1.71

Wagener, D. (2006). Promoting independent learning skills using video on digital language laboratories. *Computer Assisted Language Learning*, 19(4/5), 279–286. doi:10.1080/09588220601043180

Warlick, D. (2009). Class blogmeister: Learning as conversation. Retrieved August 12, 2009, from The Landmark Project at http://classblogmeister.com/

ADDITIONAL READING

Aguilar-Rosell, F. (2007). Top of the pods – in search of a podcasting "pedagogy" for language learning. *Computer Assisted Language Learning*, 20(5), 471–492. doi:10.1080/09588220701746047

Almeida-Soares, D. (2008). Understanding class blogs as a tool for language development. *Language Teaching Research*, 12(4), 517–533. doi:10.1177/1362168808097165

Bloch, J. (2008). *Technologies in the second language composition classroom*. Ann Arbor, MI: University of Michigan Press.

Brown, A., & Green, T. (2008). Video podcasting in perspective: The history, technology, aesthetics, and instructional uses of a new medium. *Journal of Educational Technology Systems*, 36(1), 3–17. doi:10.2190/ET.36.1.b

Crystal, D. (2001). *Language and the internet*. Cambridge: Cambridge University Press.

Cummins, J. (1994). Primary language instruction and the education of language minority students. In California State Department of Education (Ed.), *Schooling and language minority students: A theoretical framework* (2nd ed.) Los Angeles: Evaluation, Dissemination, and Assessment Center, California State University.

Doherty, R. W., Hilberg, R. S., Pinal, A., & Tharp, R. G. (2003). Five standards and student achievement. *NABE Journal of Research and Practice*, 1(1), 1–24.

Eckman, F. R. (Ed.). (1995). *Second language acquisition theory and pedagogy*. Mahwah, NJ: Lawrence Erlbaum Associates.

Freeman, D. E., & Long, M. H. (1991). *An introduction to second language acquisition research*. New York: Longman.

Gutierrez, K. D., Baguedano, P., Alvarez, H., & Chiu, M. (1999). Building a culture of collaboration through hybrid language practices. *Theory into Practice*, 38(2), 87–93. doi:10.1080/00405849909543837

Hennessy, S., & Murphy, P. (1999). The potential for collaborative problem solving in design and technology. *International Journal of Technology and Design Education, 9*(1), 1–36. doi:10.1023/A:1008855526312

Hodges, C. B., Stackpole-Hodges, C. L., & Cox, K. M. (2008). Self-efficacy, self-regulation, and cognitive style as predictors of achievement with podcast instruction. *Journal of Educational Computing Research, 38*(2), 139–153. doi:10.2190/EC.38.2.b

Jonassen, D., Howland, J., Marra, R., & Crismond, D. (2008). *Meaningful learning with technology* (3rd ed.). Upper Saddle River, NJ: Pearson Education.

King, K. P., & Gura, M. (2007). *Podcasting for teachers*. Charlotte, NC: Information Age Publishing.

Kress, G. (2003). *Literacy in the new media age*. London: Routledge. doi:10.4324/9780203164754

Lacina, J. (2004). Promoting language acquisitions: Technology and English language learners. *Childhood Education, 81*(2), 113–115.

Long, M. H., & Porter, P. (1985). Group work, interlanguage talk, and second language acquisition. *TESOL Quarterly, 18*(2), 207–227. doi:10.2307/3586827

McGroaty, M. (1993). Cooperative learning and language acquisition. In Holt, D. (Ed.), *Cooperative learning: A response to linguistic and cultural diversity*. Washington, DC: Centre for Applied Linguistics.

Nelson, L. M. (1999). Collaborative problem solving. In Reigeluth, C. M. (Ed.), *Instructional-design theories and models: A new paradigm of instructional theory* (*Vol. II*, pp. 241–267). Mahwah, NJ: Lawrence Erlbaum Associates.

Nie, M., Cashmore, A., & Cane, C. (2008) *The educational value of student generated podcasts*. In: ALT-C 2008 Rethinking the digital divide, 9 - 11 September 2008, Leeds, UK.

Peregoy, S. F., & Boyle, O. F. (1997). *Reading, writing, & learning in ESL: A resource book for K-12 teachers*. New York: Longman.

Reyes, S. A., & Vallone, T. L. (2008). *Constructivist strategies for teaching English language learners*. Thousand Oaks, CA: Corwin Press.

Shamburg, C. (2009). *Student-powered podcasting: Teaching for 21st century learning*. Eugene, OR: ISTE.

Van den Branden, K. (2006). Introduction: Task-based language teaching in a nutshell. In Van den Branden, K. (Ed.), *Task-based language education: From theory to practice* (pp. 1–16). Cambridge: Cambridge University Press. doi:10.1017/CBO9780511667282.002

Wagener, D. (2006). Promoting independent learning skills using video on digital language laboratories. *Computer Assisted Language Learning, 19*(4/5), 279–286. doi:10.1080/09588220601043180

KEY TERMS AND DEFINITIONS

Affective-Filter: The social and emotional factors involved in language learning: level of anxiety in the learning environment, level of student motivation and level of self-confidence and self-esteem (Krashen, 1985).

BICS: Basic Interpersonal Communication Skills, or playground language (Cummins, 1989)

CALPS: Cognitive Academic Learning Skills, or academic language that is content specific (Cummins, 1989).

Comprehensible Input: Communication that is clearly understood so that it can be acquired by the language learner (Long, 1981).

Input: A cyclical process where the negotiation of meaning forces input to become more comprehensible so that it can be acquired by the language learner (Long, 1981).

Negative Evidence: A stated correction or rephrasing of an incorrectly formatted statement (Gibbons, 2006).

Negotiation of Meaning: An exchange in communication where the language learner and the native speaker engage in gesturing, paraphras-

ing and gentle correction to arrive at a mutual understanding (Long & Porter, 1985).

Positive Evidence: Any modeling of correct target language utterances (Gibbons, 2006).

Recasts: Verbal cues provided by native speakers that model the correct usage of the target language. (Mackey, Oliver, & Leeman, 2003).

Representational Gestures: Gestures taken from the speaker's mental picture of a language term that are not part of an official language system such as American Sign Language (Church, Nolley, & Mahootian, 2004).

Compilation of References

A Memorandum on Lifelong Learning. (2000, October 30). Commission of the European Communities. *A Memorandum on Lifelong Learning.* Brussels, 2000. Retrieved June 4, 2010 from www.bologna-berlin2003. de/pdf/MemorandumEng.pdf.

Abel, R. (2006, June 29). *Best practices in open source in higher education.* Retrieved May 26, 2009, http://www.a-hec.org/open_source_state.html

Aguilar-Rosell, F. (2007). Top of the pods – in search of a podcasting "pedagogy" for language learning. *Computer Assisted Language Learning, 20*(5), 471–492. doi:10.1080/09588220701746047

Aher, T. C., & Repman, J. (1994). The effects of technology on online education. *Journal of Research on Computing in Education, 26*(4), 537–546.

Akpinar, Y. (2008). Validation of a learning object review instrument: Relationship between ratings of learning objects and actual learning outcomes. *Interdisciplinary Journal of E-Learning and Learning Objects, 4,* 291–302.

Akpinar, Y. & Simsek, H. (2007). Should K–12 teachers develop learning objects? Evidence from the field with K–12 students. *International Journal of Instructional Technology and Distance Learning, 4*(3).31–44.

Albury, D. (2005). Fostering innovation in public services. *Public Money & Management, 25*(1), 51–56.

Alexander, B. (2009). Apprehending the future: Emerging technologies, from science fiction to campus reality. *EDUCAUSE Review, 44*(3), 12–29.

Allbritton, D. W. (2003). Using open-source solutions to teach computing skills for student research. *Behavior Research Methods, Instruments, & Computers, 35*(2), 251–254.

Allen, E., Cartwright, R., & Reis, C. (2003). Production programming in the classroom. *Proc. of the 34-th SIGCSE technical symposium on Computer science education* (pp. 89-93) Reno, Nevada, USA, 2003.

Allen, I., & Seaman, J. (2008). *Staying the course: Online education in the United States, 2008.* Retrieved May 18, 2009, http://www.sloan-c.org/publications/survey/index.asp

Allison, D., DeBlois, P., & EDUCAUSE Current Issues Committee. (2008). *Current issues survey report, 2008.* Retrieved May 18, 2009, from http://www.educause.edu/EDUCAUSE+Quarterly/EDUCAUSEQuarterlyMagazineVolum/CurrentIssuesSurveyReport2008/162861

Almeida, J., Krueger, J., Eager, D., & Vernon, M. (2001, June). Analysis of Educational Media Server Workloads. In *Proceedings of the 11th International Workshop on Network and Operating System Support for Digital Audio and Video (NOSSDAV 2001).*

Almeida-Soares, D. (2008). Understanding class blogs as a tool for language development. *Language Teaching Research, 12*(4), 517–533. doi:10.1177/1362168808097165

Amare, N. (2006). To Slideware Or Not To Slideware: Students' Experiences With PowerPoint Vs. Lecture. *Journal of Technical Writing And Communication, 36*(3), 297–308. doi:10.2190/03GX-F1HW-VW5M-7DAR

Amelung, C. (2005). *A Context-based Activity Notification Framework for Developers of Computer Supported Collaborative Environments.* Unpublished doctoral dissertation. University of Missouri-Columbia.

American Association of Univeristy Professors (AAUP). (2009). *Informal glossary of AAUP terms and abbreviations.* Retrieved May 27, 2009, from http://www.aaup.org/AAUP/about/mission/glossary.htm

Angier, N. (2007). *The Canon A Whirligig Tour of the Beautiful Basics in Science.* New York: Mariner Book.

Anido, L. E., Fernández, M. J., Caeiro, M., Santos, J. M., Rodríguez, J. S., & Llamas, M. (2002). Educational metadata and brokerage for learning resources. *Computers & Education, 38,* 351–374. doi:10.1016/S0360-1315(02)00018-0

Annis, L., & Jones, C. (1995). Student portfolios: Their objectives, development, and use. In Associates, P. S. (Ed.), *Improving College Teaching* (pp. 181–190). Bolton: Anker.

Antonenko, P., Toy, S., & Niederhauser, D. (2004). Modular Object-Oriented Dynamic Learning Environment: What Open Source Has to Offer. In Contemporary Instruction Concepts. Retrieved September 22, 2009, from http://contempinstruct.com/books/open%20source%20moodle.pdf.

Arbaugh, J. B. (2000). Virtual classroom characteristics and student satisfaction with internet-based MBA courses. *Journal of Management Education, 24*(1), 32–54. doi:10.1177/105256290002400104

Atkins, D., Brown, J., & Hammond, A., (2007, February). *A Review of the Open Educational Resources (OER) Movement: Achievements, Challenges, and New Opportunities.* Report to The William and Flora Hewlett Foundation, Menlo Park, CA.

Audacity. (2009). Audacity: Free audio editor and recorder. Retrieved August 12, 2009, from Audacity Website: http://audacity.sourceforge.net/

Bain, K., & Zimmerman, J. (2009). Understanding Great Teaching. *Peer Review Emering Trends and Key Debates in Undergraduate Education, 11*(2), 9–12.

Bannan-Ritland, B., Dabbagh, N., & Murphy, K. (2000). Learning object systems as constructivist learning environments: Related assumptions, theories and applications. In Wiley, D., (Ed.), *The Instructional Use of Learning Objects.* Agency for Instructional Technology and the Association for Educational Communications and Technology. http://reusability.org/read/

Barber, M., & Mourshed, M. (2007). *How the world's Best Performing School Systems Come Out on Top.* Washington, DC: McKinsey & Company.

Barnes, D. (1989). *Active Learning.* Leeds: University of Leeds TVEI Support Project.

Barrett, H. C. (2000). Create your own electronic portfolio. *Learning and Leading with Technology, 27,* 14–21.

Barton, D., Hamilton, M., & Ivanič, R. (2000). *Situated literacies: Reading and writing in context.* London: Routledge.

Bartsch, R. A., & Cobern, K. M. (2003). Effectiveness of PowerPoint Presentations in Lectures. *Computers & Education, 41*(1), 77–87. doi:10.1016/S0360-1315(03)00027-7

Baytak, A. (in press). Web 2.0; open opportunities for Turkish universities. *Proceedings of The Academic Informatics 2009 Conference.*

Beauvois, M. (1998). Conversations in slow motion: Computer-mediated communication in the foreign language classroom. *Canadian Modern Language Review, 54*(2), 198–217. doi:10.3138/cmlr.54.2.198

Beck, K. (1999). *Extreme Programming Explained; Embrace Change.* Addison-Wesley Longman Publishing.

Bednar, A., Cunningham, D., Duffy, T., & Perry, J. (1992). Theory into Practice: How Do We Link? In T. M. Duffy I D.H. Jonassen, (Eds.), *Constructivism and the Technology of Instruction.* (pp. 17-31). New Jersey: Lawerence Erlbaum Associates, Publishers.

Beizer, D. (2008). *5 tech tools with lasting appeal.* Retrieved June 1, 2009, from http://fcw.com/articles/2008/08/29/5-tech-tools-with-lasting-appeal.aspx

Benkler, Y. (2005). *Common Wisdom: Peer Production of Educational Materials*. Retrieved from http://www.benkler.org/Common_Wisdom.pdf

Benson, R., & Palaskas, T. (2006). Introducing a new learning management system: An institutional case study. *Australasian Journal of Educational Technology, 22*(4), 548–567.

Berg, A., & Korcuska, M. (2009). *Sakai Courseware Management*. The Official Guide.

Berge, Z. L. (1998). Conceptual frameworks in distance training and education. In Schreiber, D., & Berge, Z. (Eds.), *Distance training: How innovative organizations are using technology to maximize learning and meet business objectives* (pp. 19–36). San Francisco: Jossey-Bass.

Berge, Z. (2001). *Concerns of Online Teachers in Higher Education*. Retrieved from http://www.emoderators.com/zberge/iste98.html

Bergquist, W., & Pawlak, K. (2008). *Engaging the six cultures of the academy*. San Francisco: Jossey-Bass.

Berlinger, Y. (2009). What is web 3.0?: The psychological experience of using the internet is undergoing slow but constant change. *Web 2.0 Journal.* Retrieved May 15, 2009 from http://web2.sys-con.com/node/236036

Berners-Lee, T., Hendler, J., & Lassila, O. (2001). The semantic web. *Scientific American.* Retrieved May 16, 2009 from http://www.scientificamerican.com/article.cfm?id=the-semantic-web

Blanchard, A. L. (2000). *Virtual behavior settings: A framework for understanding virtual communities*. Unpublished doctoral dissertation, Claremont Graduate University, Claremont, CA.

Bloch, J. (2008). *Technologies in the second language composition classroom*. Ann Arbor, MI: University of Michigan Press.

Blokzijl, W., & Naeff, R. (2004). The Instructor as Stagehand: Dutch Student Responses to PowerPoint. *Business Communication Quarterly, 67*(1), 70–78. doi:10.1177/1080569903262046

Blood, R. (2002). *The weblog handbook: Practical advice on creating and maintaining your blog*. Cambridge, MA: Perseus Publishing.

Bonaccorsi, A., & Rossi, C. (2003). Why open source software can succeed. *Research Policy, 32*, 1243–1258. doi:10.1016/S0048-7333(03)00051-9

Bonk, C. (2009). *The world is open: How web technology is revolutionizing education*. San Francisco: Jossey-Bass.

Bonwell, C., & Eison, J. (1991). *Active Learning: Creating Excitement in the Classroom*. Washington, D.C.: Jossey-Bass.

Borko, H. (2004). Professional development and teacher learning: Mapping the terrain. *Educational Researcher, 33*(8), 3–15. doi:10.3102/0013189X033008003

Bower, M. (2008). Affordance analysis-matching learning tasks with learning technologies. *Educational Media International, 45*(1), 3–15. doi:10.1080/09523980701847115

Bower, B. (2001). Distance education: Facing the faculty challenge. *Online Journal of Distance Learning Administration, 4*(2). Retrieved June 21, 2009, from http://www.westga.edu/~distance/ojdla/summer42/bower42.html

Brancheau, J. C., Janz, B. D., & Wetherbe, J. C. (1995). *Key Issues in Information Systems Management: A Shift Toward Technology Infrastructure*. Boulder, CO: University of Colorado Graduate School of Business.

Bretthauer, D. (2002). Open source software: A history. *Information Technology and Libraries, 21*(1), 3–10.

Brittain, S., Glowacki, P., Van Ittersum, J., & Johnson, L. (2006). Podcasting lectures. *EDUCAUSE Quarterly, 29*(3), 24–31.

Brown, J. S., & Adler, R. P. (2008). Minds on fire: Open education, the long tail, and learning 2.0. *EDUCAUSE Review, 43*(1), 16–32.

Brown, A., & Green, T. (2008). Video podcasting in perspective: The history, technology, aesthetics, and instructional uses of a new medium. *Journal of Educational Technology Systems, 36*(1), 3–17. doi:10.2190/ET.36.1.b

Bruner, J. (1990). *Acts of Meaning*. Boston, MA: Harvard University Press.

Bruner, J. (1987). Proglogue to the English edition. In L.S. Vygostsky, *Collected works* (Vo.1., pp.1-16) (R. Rieber & A. Cartom, Eds.: N. Minick, Trans). New York: Plenum.

Buchan, J., & Swann, M. (2007). A Bridge too Far or a Bridge to the Future? A case study in online assessment at Charles Sturt University. *Australasian Journal of Educational Technology, 23*(3), 408–434.

Buchan, J. (2008a, September 9-11). *Rethinking management strategies for the online learning environment*. Paper presented at the ALT-C Rethinking the Digital Divide Conference, Leeds, UK. Retrieved from http://csusap.csu.edu.au/~jbuchan/html/publications.htm

Buchan, J. (2008b, December 2008). Tools for survival in a changing educational technology environment. In *Where are you now in the landscape of educational technology? Proceedings ASCILITE Melbourne 2008 Conference*, Melbourne, Australia.

Buchan, J. (2009a). Putting ourselves in the big picture: a sustainable approach to project management for e-learning. *Journal of Distance Education.*

Buchan, J. (2009b). Putting ourselves in the big picture: a sustainable approach to project management for e-learning. *Journal of Distance Education.*

Buchan, J. F., & Buchan, A. J. (2003). Lessons from nature: developing an adaptive management model for sustaining quality learning environments. In *Proceedings of the 16th Biennial Forum Conference on Open and Distance Learning*. Retrieved August 8, 2007, from http://odlaa.une.edu.au/publications/2003Proceedings/pdfs/buchan.pdf

Burdt, C., & Bassett, E. (2005). *Open source in Higher Education: Decision-making for open source adoptions*. Boston: Eduventures.

Bureau of Labor Statistics. (2008). *Human resources, training, and labor relations managers and specialists*. Retrieved from http://www.bls.gov/oco/ocos021.htm#training

Bureau of Labor Statistics. (2008). *Instructional Coordinators*. Retrieved May 4, 2009, from http://www.bls.gov/oco/ocos269.htm#outlook

Business Readiness Rating. (2006). *Business readiness rating for open source*. Retrieved June 2, 2009, from http://www.openbrr.org/wiki/index.php/BRRWhitepaper

Cambell, G. (2005). There is something in the air: Podcasting in education. *EDUCAUSE Review, 40*(6), 32–47.

Cambridge, B. L. (2001). *Electronic portfolios as knowledge builders*. Washington, D.C.: American Association for Higher Education.

Cameron, K., & Ettington, D. (1988). The conceptual foundations of organizational culture. In Smart, J. (Ed.), *Higher education: Handbook of theory and research* (pp. 356–396). New York: Agathon.

Camp, J. S. (2007, May/June). Top 10 IT Issues. *EDUCAUSE Review, 42*, 12–32.

Cañas, A. J., Carff, R., Hill, G., Carvalho, M., Arguedas, M., Eskridge, T. C., et al. Concept Maps: Integrating Knowledge and Information Visualization. Retrieved April 8, 2007 from http://cmap.ihmc.us/Publications/ResearchPapers/ConceptMapsIntegratingKnowInfVisual.pdf.

Canas, R. (2009). *OSS watch national software survey 2008*. Retrieved June 5, 2009, from Open source Software Advisory Service: http://www.oss-watch.ac.uk/resources/

Canton, J. (2006). *The extreme future: The top trends that will reshape the world for the next 5, 10, and 20 years*. New York: Penguin Group.

Capps, R., Fix, M., Murray, J., Ost, J., Passel, J., & Herwantoro, S. (2005). *The new demography of America's schools: Immigration and the no child left behind act*. Washington, DC: The Urban Institute.

Carmean, C., & Haefner, J. (2003). Next-generation course management systems. *EDUCAUSE Quarterly, 26*(1), 10–13.

Carmichael, P., & Honour, L. (2002). Open source as appropriate technology for global education. *International Journal of Educational Development, 22*(1), 47–53. doi:10.1016/S0738-0593(00)00077-8

Carnevale, D. (2007, June 22). The most poisonous force in technology. *The Chronicle of Higher Education, 53*(42), A37.

Carrington, D., & Kim, S.-K. (2003). Teaching software design with open source software. *Proc. of 33-rd ASEE/IEEE Frontiers in Education Conf.*,(pp. 9-14). November 2003.

Carroll, J. M., Neale, D. C., Isenhour, P. L., Rosson, M. B., & McCrickard, D. S. (2003). Notification and awareness: Synchronizing task-oriented collaborative activity. *International Journal of Human-Computer Studies, 58,* 313–322. doi:10.1016/S1071-5819(03)00024-7

Caruso, J., & Salaway, G. (2008). *The ECAR study of undergraduate students and information technology, 2008.* Boulder, CO: EDUCAUSE Center for Applied Research.

Casserly, C., & Smith, M. (2006). The Promise of Open Educational Resources. *Change Magazine, 38*(5), 8–17. doi:10.3200/CHNG.38.5.8-17

Castro, F., Vellido, A., Nebot, A., & Mugica, F. (2007). Applying Data Mining Techniques to e-Learning Problems. In Jain, L., Tedman, R., & Tedman, D. (Eds.), *Evolution of Teaching and Learning Paradigms in Intelligent Environment.* New York: Springer. doi:10.1007/978-3-540-71974-8_8

Cazden, C. (1986). Classroom discourse. In Wittrock, M. C. (Ed.), *Handbook of research on teaching* (pp. 432–463). New York: Macmillan.

Cebeci, Z., & Tekdal, M. (2006). Using podcasts as audio learning objects. *Interdisciplinary Journal of Knowledge and Learning Objects, 2,* 47–57.

Chan, M. (2003). Technology and the teaching of oral skills. *CATESOL Journal, 15,* 51–57.

Chao, I. (2008). Moving to Moodle: Reflections two years later. *EDUCAUSE Quarterly, 31*(3), 46–52.

Chauhan, A. (2004). Open source and open standards in higher education. *ACET Journal of Computer Education and Research, 2*(1), 1–3.

Chen, C., Hsieh, Y., & Hsu, S. (2007). Mining learner profile utilizing association rule for web-based learning diagnosis. *Expert Systems with Applications, 33*(1). doi:10.1016/j.eswa.2006.04.025

Chen, H., Wigand, R. T., & Nilan, M. (1999). Flow activities on the Web. *Computers in Human Behavior, 15*(5), 585–608. doi:10.1016/S0747-5632(99)00038-2

Christensen, C. M., Horn, M. B., & Johnson, C. W. (2008). *Disrupting Class: How Disruptive Innovation Will Change the Way the World Learns.* New York: McGraw-Hill.

Christenson, C., & Overdorf, M. (2000). Meeting the Challenge of Disruptive Change. *Harvard Business Review,* (March-April): CK-12. Retrieved from http://www.ck12.org.

Church, R. B., Nolley, S., & Mahootian, S. (2004). The role of gesture in bilingual education: Does gesture enhance learning? *International Journal of Bilingual Education and Bilingualism, 7*(4), 303–319. doi:10.1080/13670050408667815

Chyung, S. Y. (2001). Systematic and systemic approaches to reducing attrition rates in online higher education. *American Journal of Distance Education, 15*(3), 36–49. doi:10.1080/08923640109527092

Clarey, J. (2008). How to implement an effective e-learning 2.0 strategy. Retrieved May 8, 2009 from http://www.brandon-hall.com/publications/learning2.0/learning2.0.shtml

Clark, E. J., & Eynon, B. (2009). E-portfolios at 2.0--Surveying the field. *Peer Review, 11*(1), 18–23.

Clark, R. E. (1994). Media will never influence learning. *Educational Technology Research and Development, 42*(2), 21–29. doi:10.1007/BF02299088

Cleary, Y., & Marcus-Quinn, A. (2008). Using a virtual learning environment to manage group projects: A case study. *International Journal on E-Learning, 7*(4), 603–621.

Coar, K. (2006, July 7). The open source definition. Retrieved August 15, 2009, from Open Source Initiative Web site: http://www.opensource.org/docs/osd

Cocea, M. (2006). Extendibility of educational systems to include a learner-adaptive motivational module. In R. Vasile, R. Kimari, & D. Andone (Eds.), *Proceedings of the 12th NETTIES (Networking Entities) International Conference: The Future of E: Advanced Educational Technologies for a Future e-Europe* (pp. 195-198). Timisoara, Romania: Orizonturi Universitare.

Coffey, J. W. (2005). A meta-cognitive tool for courseware development, maintenance, and reuse. *Computers & Education, 48*(4), 548–566. doi:10.1016/j.compedu.2005.03.008

Colins, P. H. (1990). *Black Feminist Thought*. New York: Routledge.

Collier, V. P. (1989). How long? A synthesis of research on academic achievement in a second language. *TESOL Quarterly, 23*(3), 509–531. doi:10.2307/3586923

Collis, B., & Strijker, A. (2004). Technology and human issues in reusing learning objects. *Journal of Interactive Media in Education, 4*, 1–32. http://www-jime.open.ac.uk/2004/4/.

Commonwealth of Virginia. Governor Kaine Launches Virginia Physics Flexbook: Open content web tool to provide supplemental 21st century physics materials for Virginia teachers. Office of the Governor. Released: March 16, 2009. Retrieved October 20, 2009 from http://www.governor.virginia.gov/MediaRelations/NewsReleases/viewRelease.cfm?id=897

Computer Museum. (2006). *Russian Virtual Computer Museum*, M. A. Lavrentev. Retrieved June 4, 2010 from http://computer-museum.ru/english/galglory_en/Lavrentev.htm

Copley, J. (2007). Audio and video podcasts of lectures for campus-based students: Production and evaluation of student use. *Innovations in Education and Teaching International, 44*(4), 387–399. doi:10.1080/14703290701602805

Coppola, C. (2005). Understanding the open source portfolio Retrieved June 10, 2009, from http://www.rsmart.com/assets/understandingOSP_Dec2005.pdf

Coppola, C., & Neelley, E. (2004). Open source – opens learning: Why open source makes sense for education. *The r-smart group.* Retrieved September 9, 2009, from http://www.rsmart.com/assets/OpenSourceOpensLearningJuly2004.pdf

Cornelius, B. (2006). *OSS watch survey 2006.* Retrieved June 5, 2009, from http://www.oss-watch.ac.uk/studies/survey2006/

CosmoCode. (2005). Welcome to the Wiki Choice Wizard! Retrieved August 12, 2009, from WikiMatrix: Compare The All! at http://www.wikimatrix.org/wizard.php

Cowan, N. (2001). The magical number 4 in short-term memory: A reconsideration of mental storage Capacity. *The Behavioral and Brain Sciences, 24*(1), 87–113. doi:10.1017/S0140525X01003922

Crittenden, J. (1992). *Beyond Individualism: Reconstituting the Liberal Self.* New York: Oxford University Press.

Crystal, D. (2001). *Language and the internet.* Cambridge: Cambridge University Press.

Cuban, L. (2001). *Oversold & underused: Computers in the classroom.* Cambridge, MA: Harvard University Press.

Cuban, L. (1986). *Teachers and machines: Classroom use of technology,* New York: Teachers College Press. Dils, K. (1999). The use of technology to reach the various learning styles of middle school history and social studies students. *Journal of the Association for History & Computing, 2*(3). Retrieved June 1, 2008, from http://mcel.pacificu.edu/jahc/jahcII3/index.htmlhttp://mcel.pacificu.edu/jahc/jahcII3/index.html

Cummins, P. (1989). Video and the French teacher. *French Review, 62*(3), 411–426.

Cummins, J. (1981). The role of primary language development in promoting educational success for language minority students. In California State Department of Education (Ed.), *Schooling and language minority students: A theoretical framework* (pp. 3-49). Los Angeles: Evaluation, Dissemination, and Assessment Centre, California State University.

Cummins, J. (1994). Primary language instruction and the education of language minority students. In California State Department of Education (Ed.), *Schooling and language minority students: A theoretical framework* (2nd ed.) Los Angeles: Evaluation, Dissemination, and Assessment Center, California State University.

Dabbagh, N. (2004). Distance learning: Emerging pedagogical issues and learning designs. *Quarterly Review of Distance Education, 5*(1), 37–49.

Dabbagh, N., & Bannan-Ritland, B. (2005). *Online learning: Concepts, strategies, and application*. Upper Saddle River, NJ: Pearson Education, Inc.

Dalziel, J. (2003). Open standards versus open source in e-learning. *EDUCAUSE Quarterly, 26*(4), 4–7.

Darling-Hammond, L., Holtzman, D., Gatlin, S. J., & Heilig, J. V. (2005). Does teacher preparation matter? Evidence about teacher certification, Teach for America, and teacher effectiveness. *Education Policy Analysis Archives, 13*(42).

Dean, M. W. (2008). Put your videos on other people's ipods. *O'Reilly Media*. Retrieved May 3 from2009, http://digitalmedia.oreilly.com/2008/09/04/youtube-rss-ipod-tutorial.html

Dean, P., & Leinonen, T. (2003). ITCOLE final report. Technical Report IST-2000-26249, European Commission, ITCOLE Project. Retrieved from http://www.euro-cscl.org/site/itcole/

Dede, C. (1996). The evolution of distance education: Emerging technologies and distributed learning. *American Journal of Distance Education, 10*(2), 4–36. doi:10.1080/08923649609526919

Delivering Success to Ohio's High Schools (2009), The KnowledgeWorks School Improvement Efforts, Building High-Performing High Schools, and Impact on Student Achievement. *The KnowledgeWorks Foundation*, January 2009.

DeNuei, D., & Dodge, T. (2006). Asynchronous learning networks and student outcomes: The utility of online learning components in hybrid courses. *Journal of Instructional Psychology, 33*(4), 256–259.

Design-Based Research Collective. (2002). Design-based research: An emerging paradigm for educational inquiry. *Educational Researcher, 32*(1), 5–8. doi:10.3102/0013189X032001005

Dewey, J. (1938). *Experience and Education*. London: Collier Macmillian Publishers.

Dewey, B. I., & DeBlois, P. B., & EDUCAUSE Current Issues Committee. (2006, May/June). Top-10 IT Issues 2006. *EDUCAUSE Review, 41*, 58–79.

Dewey, J. (1916). *Democracy and Education*. New York:Macmillan Company. (Macmillan Paperback Edition 1961.)

Dholakia, U. M. (2006). *What Makes an OE Program Sustainable?* OECD papers on CERI—Open Educational Resources Program. Paris, France

Diller, K., & Phelps, S. (2008). Learning outcomes, portfolios and rubrics, oh my! Authentic assessment of an information literacy program. *Libraries and the Academy, 8*(1), 75–88.

DiNucci, D. (1999). Fragmented future. *Print, 53*(4), 32.

Dobretsov, N. L. (2001). "Triangle of Lavrentev": the principles of science organization in Siberia. *Bulletin of the Russian Academy of Sciences, 71*(5), 428–436.

Dollinger, M. (2000). Materials engineering and the challenge of teaching history in the community college. *The History Teacher, 34*(1), 9–20. doi:10.2307/3054370

Dolonen, J. (2006). Empirical study of learning design. Retrieved from http://calibrate.eun.org/shared/data/calibrate/deliverables/D3p1_v2.pdf

Domine, V. (2006). Online pedagogy: Beyond digital "chalk and talk.". *Academic Exchange Quarterly, 10*(1), 48–51.

Doppen, F. H. (2004). Beginning Social Studies Teachers' Integration of Technology in the History Classroom. *Theory and Research in Social Education, 32*(2), 248–279.

Dougiamas. (November 1998). A Journey into Constructivism. In Dougiamas. Retrieved September 21, 2009, from http://dougiamas.com/writing/constructivism.html.

Dourish, P., & Bellotti, V. (1992). Awareness and coordination in shared workspaces. In *Proceedings of the Conference on Computer-Supported Cooperative Work,* Toronto, Canada.

Downes, S. (2001). Learning objects: Resources for distance education worldwide. *International Review of Research in Open and Distance Learning, 2*(1). http://www.irrodl.org/index.php/irrodl/issue/view/11.

Downes, S. (2005). E-learning 2.0. *eLearn Magazine.* Retrieved May 11, 2009 from http://www.elearnmag.org/subpage.cfm?section=articles&article=29-1

Doyle, B. (2006). When to wiki, when to blog. *E-Content: Digital Content Strategies and Resources.* Retrieved May 5, 2009 from http://www.econtentmag.com/Articles/ArticlePrint.aspx?ArticleID=16900

Duffy, T., & Jonassen, D. (1992). Constructivism: New implications for instructional technology. In Duffy, T. (Ed.), *Constructivism and the technology of instruction: A conversation* (pp. 1–16). Hillsdale, NJ: Lawrence Erlbaum Associates.

Dunlap, J., & Lowenthal, P. (2009). Tweeting the night away: Using Twitter to enhance social presence. *Journal of Information Systems Education, 20*(2).

Dunlap, J., Wilson, B., & Young, D. (2002, June 24-29). Xtreme learning control: Examples of the open source movement's impact on our educational practice in a university setting. In *Proceedings of the ED-MEDIA 2002 World Conference on Educational Multimedia, Hypermedia & Telecommunications* (pp. 2-7).

Durando, M. (2008). Project final report. CALIBRATE, IST-028025, European Commission. Retrieved from http://calibrate.eun.org/shared/data/calibrate/deliverables/CALIBRATEFinalReport.pdf

Duval, E., Forte, E., Cardinaels, K., Verhoeven, B., Durm, R. V., & Hendrikx, K. (2001). The Ariadne knowledge pool system. *Communications of the ACM, 44*(5). doi:10.1145/374308.374346

Ebner, M. (2007). E-learning 2.0 = e-learning 1.0 + web 2.0? *The 2nd International Conference on availability, reliability and security* (pp. 1235-1239). Los Alamitos: IEEE Computer Society.

Eckman, F. R. (Ed.). (1995). *Second language acquisition theory and pedagogy.* Mahwah, NJ: Lawrence Erlbaum Associates.

Edirisingha, P., & Salmon, G. (2007). IMPALA podcast models: some examples. Retrieved May 7, 2009 from http://www2.le.ac.uk/projects/impala/documents/IMPALA_podcast_models

EDUCAUSE Constituent Group. (2008, October 20). *2008 Openness Constituent Group Meeting.* Retrieved June 1, 2009, from http://www.educause.edu/wiki/Openness

EDUCAUSE CORE Data Service. (2007). *Fiscal year 2007 summary report.* Retrieved May 27, 2009, from http://net.educause.edu/apps/coredata/reports/2007/

EduTools. (2009). *Welcome to EduTools.* Retrieved May 27, 2009, from http://www.edutools.info/index.jsp?pj=1

Edwards, K. (2001). Epistemic communities, situated learning and open source software development. In *Proceedings of the Workshop on Epistemic Cultures and the Practice of Interdisciplinarity,* Trondheim, Norway. Retrieved September 9, 2009, from http://opensource.mit.edu/papers/kasperedwards-ec.pdf

Egbert, J. (1999). Classroom practice: Practical assessments in the CALL classroom. In Egbert, J., & Hanson-Smith, E. (Eds.), *CALL environments: Research, practice, and critical issues* (pp. 257–271). Alexandria, VA: TESOL.

Erickson, T., & Kellogg, W. A. (2003). Social Translucence: Using Minimalist Visualizations of Social Activity to Support Collective Interaction. In Höök, K., Benyon, D., & Munro, A. (Eds.), *Designing Information Spaces: The Social Navigation Approach* (pp. 17–42). New York: Springer.

Eriskon, E. H. (1968). *Identity: Youth and Crisis*. New York: W.W. Norton, &Co.

Escrig-Tena, A., & Bou-Llusar, J. (2005). A model for evaluating organizational competencies: An application in the context of a quality management initiative. *Decision Sciences*, *36*(2), 221–257. doi:10.1111/j.1540-5414.2005.00072.x

Eynon, B. (2009). It helped me see a new me: ePortfolio, learning and change at LaGuardia Community College Retrieved June 12, 2009, from http://www.academiccommons.org/commons/essay/eportfolio-learning-and-change

Felder, R. M. (1990). Meet Your Students: 2. Susan and Glenda. *Chemical Engineering Education*, *24*(1), 7–8.

Felder, R. M. (1994). Meet Your Students: 5. Edward and Irving. *Chemical Engineering Education*, *28*(1), 36–37.

Felder, R. M. (1988). Learning and teaching styles in engineering education. Retrieved April 8, 2007 from http://www.ncsu.edu/felder-public/Papers/LS-1988.pdfhttp://www.ncsu.edu/felder-public/Papers/LS-1988.pdf

Ferdig, R. E., & Trammell, K. D. (2004). Content delivery in the "blogosphere". *The Journal: Transforming Education through Technology*. Retrieved May 16, 2009 from http://www.thejournal.com/articles/16626/

Fernandez, L. (2008). An antidote for the faculty-IT divide. *EDUCAUSE Quarterly*, *31*(1), 7–9.

Ferret, L. J. (2006). Wikis and e-learning. In Berman, P. (Ed.), *E-learning concepts and techniques* (pp. 73–74). Bloomsburg, PA: Bloomsburg University.

Ferster, B., Hammond, T., & Bull, G. (2006). Primary Access: Creating Digital Documentaries in the Social Studies Classroom. *Social Education*, *70*(3), 147–150.

Fletcher, G. (2009). Signs of a Significant Disruption in the Traditional Textbook Model. *T.H.E. Journal*, February 2009 News. Retrieved September 29, 2009, from http://thejournal.com/articles/2009/02/25/signs-of-a-significant-disruption-in-the-traditional-textbook-model.aspx

Fletcher, G. (2009a). The Disruption of the Traditional Textbook Model Continues. *T.H.E. Journal*. Retrieved September 29, 2009, from http://thejournal.com/Articles/2009/06/24/The-Disruption-of-the-Traditional-Textbook-Model-Continues.aspx

Flewelling, J. (2002). From language lab to multimedia lab: Oral language assessment in the new millennium. In C. M. Cherry (Ed.), *Dimension: Proceedings of the Southern Conference on Language Teaching*, (pp. 33-42). Valdosta, GA: SCOLT Publications.

Flowerdew, J. (Ed.). (1994). *Academic listening: Research perspectives*. Cambridge, UK: Cambridge University Press.

Forte, E. N., Forte, M. H. K. W., & Duval, E. (1997). The ARIADNE Project (part 1): Knowledge pools for computer-based and telematics-supported classical, open and distance education. *European Journal of Engineering Education*, *22*(1), 61–74. doi:10.1080/03043799708923438

Foster, P., Tonkyn, A., & Wigglesworth, G. (2000). Measuring spoken language: A unit for all reasons. *Applied Linguistics*, *21*, 354–375. doi:10.1093/applin/21.3.354

Frambach, R., & Schillewaert, N. (2002). Organizational innovation adoption: A multilevel framework of determinants and opportunities for future research. *Journal of Business Research*, *55*(2), 163–176. doi:10.1016/S0148-2963(00)00152-1

Franklin, T., & van Harmelen, M. (2007). Web 2.0 for content for learning and teaching in higher education. *JISC: Supporting education and research*. Retrieved May 1, 2009 from http://www.jisc.ac.uk/media/documents/programmes/digitalrepositories/web2-content-learning-and-teaching.pdf

Freeman, D. E., & Long, M. H. (1991). *An introduction to second language acquisition research*. New York: Longman.

Freeman, Y. S., & Freeman, D. E. (2004). Preview, view, review: Giving multilingual learners access to the curriculum. In Hoyt, L. (Ed.), *Spotlight on comprehension: Building a literacy of thoughtfulness*. Portsmouth, NH: Heinemann.

Freemind. (n.d.). Retrieved from http://freemind.source-forge.net/http://freemind.sourceforge.net

Friedman, T. (2006). *The world is flat: A brief history of the twenty-first century (updated and expanded edition)*. New York: Farrar, Straus, and Giroux.

Frielick, S. (2004). Beyond constructivism: An ecological approach to e-learning. In *Beyond the comfort zone: Proceedings of the 21st ASCILITE Conference* (pp. 328-332). Perth, Australia: University of Western Australia.

Friesen, N. (2004). Three objections to learning objects and e-learning standards. In McGreal, R. (Ed.), *Online Education Using Learning Objects* (pp. 59–70). London: Routledge.

Fuchs, I. (2008). Challenges and opportunities of open source in higher education. In Katz, R. (Ed.), *The tower and the cloud: Higher education in the age of cloud computing* (pp. 150–157). Boulder, CO: EDUCAUSE.

Fuhrman, C. P. (2006, July). Appreciation of software design concerns via open-source tools and projects. *Proc. of 10-th Workshop on Pedagogies and Tools for the Teaching and Learning of Object Oriented Concepts,*(at ECOOP 2006). Nantes, France, July 2006.

Futernick, K. (2007, October). Study Examines Why Teachers Quit and What Can Be Done. *District Administration*, *43*(10), 16.

Gallaher, M., & Petrusa, J. (2006). Innovation in the U.S. service sector. *The Journal of Technology Transfer*, *31*(6), 611–628. doi:10.1007/s10961-006-0018-4

García, E., Romero, C., Ventura, S., & Castro, C. (2006). Using rules discovery for the continuous improvement of e-learning courses. In *Proceedings of the International Conference Intelligent Data Engineering and Automated Learning,* (pp. 887-895). Burgos, Spain.

Gardner, H. (2008). *5 Minds for the Future*. Boston, MA: Harvard Business Press.

Gareis, E. (2007). Active Learning: A Power point Tutorial. *Business Communication Quarterly*, *70*(4), 462–466. doi:10.1177/10805699070700040304

Gaudioso, E., & Talavera, L. (2006). Data mining to support tutoring in virtual learning communities: Experiences and challenges. In Romero, C., & Ventura, S. (Eds.), *Data mining in e-learning, Advances in Management Information Series* (*Vol. 4*, pp. 207–226). Southampton, UK: WitPress. doi:10.2495/1-84564-152-3/12

Gee, J. P. (2000). New people in new worlds: Networks, the new capitalism, and schools. In Cope, B., & Kalantzis, M. (Eds.), *Multiliteries: Literacy learning and the design of social futures* (pp. 43–68). London: Routledge & Kegan Paul.

Geser, G. (2007). Open educational practices and resources — OLCOS roadmap 2012. OLCOS. Retrieved from http://www.olcos.org/english/roadmap/

Ghosh, R. (2006, June 14). *Who is behind open source? Presentation at the Gartner Open Source Summit, Barcelona, Spain*. Retrieved June 5, 2009, from http://www.flossproject.org/papers/20060614/RishabGHOSH-gartner2.pdf

Gianella, A. F. (1916). The Use of Flash Cards for Drill in French. *Modern Language Journal*, *1*(3), 96–99. doi:10.2307/313582

Gibbons, P. (2006). *Bridging discourses in the ESL classroom: Students, teachers and researchers*. Sidney, Australia: Continuum.

Gill, T. (2006). The memory grid: A glass box view of data representation. *Journal of Information Systems Education*, *17*(2), 119–129.

Gilligan, C. (1993). *In a Different Voice*. Cambridge, MA: Harvard University Press.

Glasser, B. G., & Strauss, A. L. (1967). *The discovery of grounded theory*. Chicago: Aldine.

GNU Operating System. (2009). *The free software definition*. Retrieved September 9, 2009, from http://www.gnu.org/philosophy/free-sw.html

Goggins, S., Laffey, J., & Tsai, I.-C. (2007). *Cooperation and groupness: Community formation in small online collaborative groups*. Paper presented at the ACM Group Conference.

Goldman, J. P. (1991, April). Balancing School Sports and Academics. *Education Digest*, *56*(8), 67–70.

Gonsalves, A. (2003). The Linux alternative. *Technology & Learning*, *23*, 9–12.

Google. (1999). Blogger: Create your free blog. Retrieved August 12, 2009, from Blogger at http://www.blogger.com/start

Gov. Schwarzenegger Announces One of Nation's Largest Textbook Publishers Among Those Participating in Free Digital Textbook Initiative (June 16, 2009) [Press Release] *Office of the Governor Arnold Schwarzenegger*. Retrieved, October 22, 2009 from http://gov.ca.gov/press-release/12542/

Graham, P. (2005). Web 2.0. *Paul Graham*. Retrieved April 29, 2009 from http://www.paulgraham.com/web20.html

Grainne, C., & Dyke, M. (2004). What are the affordances of information and communication technololgies. *ALT-J: Research in Learning*, *12*(2), 113–124.

Green, K. (2008). *The 2008 national survey of information technology in U.S. higher education*. Encino, CA: The Campus Computing Project.

Green, K. C. (2004). *Campus computing 2004: The 15th national survey of computing and information technology in American higher education*. Encino, CA: The Campus Computing Project.

Greene, M. (1988). *The Dialectic of Freedom*. New York: Teachers College Press.

Greene, M. (1995). *Releasing the Imagination*. San Francisco, California: Jossey-Bass.

Gross, R., & Acquisti, A. (2005). Information revelation and privacy in online social networks (the facebook case). In S. C. di Vimercati, & R. Dingledine (Eds.), *The 2005 ACM Workshop on Privacy in the Electronics Society* (pp. 71-80). New York: ACM Press.

Gruver, M. (2009). Time well spent? Teacher learning debated in Wyoming, *The Associated Press*. March 11, 2009.

Guba, E. G., & Lincoln, Y. S. (1981). *Effective evaluation*. San Francisco: Jossey-Bass.

Guhlin, M. (2007). The Case for Open Source. *techLearning*. February 15, 2007

Gutierrez, K. D., Baguedano, P., Alvarez, H., & Chiu, M. (1999). Building a culture of collaboration through hybrid language practices. *Theory into Practice*, *38*(2), 87–93. doi:10.1080/00405849909543837

Hai-Peng, H., & Deng, L. (2007). Vocabulary acquisition in multimedia environment. *US-China Foreign Language*, *5*(8), 55–59.

Hall, C. (1995). Formal linguistics and the mental representation: Psycholinguistic contributions to the identification and explanation of morphological and syntactic competence. *Language and Cognitive Processes*, *10*(2), 169–187. doi:10.1080/01690969508407092

Halse, G., & Terzoli, A. (2002). *Open source in South African schools: Two case studies*. Retrieved September 9, 2009, from http://www.schoolnetafrica.net/fileadmin/resources/Open_Source_in_South_African_Schools.pdf

Hannafin, M. J., & Land, S. M. (1997). The foundations and assumptions of technology-enhanced, student-centered learning environments. *Instructional Science*, *25*, 167–202. doi:10.1023/A:1002997414652

Hara, N., & Kling, R. (2000). Student distress in web-based distance education course. *Information Communication and Society*, *4*(3), 557–579. doi:10.1080/13691180010002297

Hargadon, S. (2006, October 23*). Interview with Martin Dougiamas, creator of Moodle*. Retrieved September 9, 2009, from http://www.stevehargadon.com/2006/10/interview-with-martin-dougiamas.html

Hargreaves, A., & Shirley, D. (2008, October). The Fourth Way of Change. *Educational Leadership*, *66*(2).

Harknett, R. J., & Cobane, C. T. (1997). Introducing Instructional Technology to International Relations. *Political Science and Politics*, *30*, 496–500. doi:10.2307/420130

Hart, T. (2003). *Open source in education*. Retrieved September 9, 2009, from http://www.portfolio.umaine.edu/~hartt/OS%20in%20Education.pdf

Hartman, K., Neuwirth, C., Kiesler, S., Sproull, L., Cochran, C., Palmquist, M., & Zabrow, D. (1995). Patterns of social interaction and learning to write: Some effects of network technologies. In Berge, Z., & Collins, M. (Eds.), *Computer-mediated communication and the online classroom* (pp. 47–78). Creskill, NJ: Hampton Press, Inc.

Harvard University. (1999). Authorship guidelines. *Harvard University Medical School*. Retrieved May 14, 2009 from http://www.hms.harvard.edu/integrity/authorship.html

Hawkins, M. R. (2004). Researching English language and literacy development in schools. *Educational Researcher*, *33*(3), 365–384. doi:10.3102/0013189X033003014

Hawkins, M. R. (2005). ESL in elementary education. In Hinkel, E. (Ed.), *Handbook of research in second language teaching and learning* (pp. 25–44). Mahwah, NJ: Lawrence Erlbaum Associates.

Haymes, T. (2008). The three-e strategy for overcoming resistance to technological change. *EDUCAUSE Quarterly*, *31*(4), 67–69.

Heery, R. (2009). Digital repositories roadmap review: towards a vision for research and learning in 2013. *JISC*. Retrieved from http://www.jisc.ac.uk/media/documents/themes/infoenvironment/reproadmapreviewfinal.doc

Herbert, M. (2001). *Open source in education: An overview*. Retrieved September 9, 2009, from http://people.redhat.com/mherbert/papers/RHPaper1.pdf

Herman, I. (2008). Semantic web activity statement. *W3C Semantic Web*. Retrieved May 12 from 2009, http://www.w3.org/2001/sw/Activity.html

Herman, I. (2008). W3C semantic web activity. *W3C Semantic Web*. Retrieved May 12, 2009 from http://www.w3.org/2001/sw/

Higher Learning Commission. (2003). Handbook of accreditation 3rd. Retrieved June 8, 2009, from http://www.ncahlc.org/download/Handbook03.pdf

Hignite, K. (2004, August). *An open mind on open source*. Retrieved May 25, 2009, from http://www.nacubo.org/Business_Officer_Magazine/Magazine_Archives/August_2004/An_Open_Mind_on_Open_Source.html

Hill, C., & Jones, G. (2001). *Strategic management theory-An integrated approach*. Boston: Houghton Mifflin.

Hofstede, G. (1980). *Culture's consequences: International differences in work related values*. Thousand Oaks, CA: Sage Publications, Inc.

Honebein, P. (1996). Seven goals for the design of constructivist learning environments. In Wilson, B. (Ed.), *Constructivist learning environments: Case studies in instructional design* (pp. 11–24). Englewood Cliffs, NJ: Educational Technology Publications.

Huang, J., Newell, S., Galliers, R., & Pan, S. (2003). Dangerous liaisons? Component based development and organizational subcultures. *IEEE Transactions on Engineering Management*, *50*(1), 89–99. doi:10.1109/TEM.2002.808297

IEEE. (2002). IEEE 1484.12.1-2002, *Learning Object Metadata standard. Final draft, IEEE Standards Department*.Retrieved from http://ltsc.ieee.org/wg12/files/LOM_1484_12_1_v1_Final_Draft.pdf

Ingram, D., Louis, K. S., & Schroeder, R. G. (2004). Accountability policies and teacher decision-making: Barriers to the use of data to improve practice. *Teachers College Record, 106*(6), 1258–1287. doi:10.1111/j.1467-9620.2004.00379.x

Inoue, Y. (2009). Linking self-directed lifeline learning and e-learning: Priorities for institutions of higher education. In Stansfield, M., & Connolly, T. (Eds.), *Institutional Transformation Through Best Practices in Virtual Campus Development: Advancing E-learning Policies* (pp. 22–37). Hershey, PA: IGI Global.

Inside Higher Ed. (2009, June 29). *US Push for Free Online Courses*. Retrieved September 9, 2009, from http://www.insidehighered.com/news/2009/06/29/ccplan

Iyer, H. (2003). Web-based instructional technology in an information science classroom. *Journal of Education for Library and Information Science, 44*(5), 296–315.

Jafari, A. (2004). The sticky ePortfolio system: Tackling challenges and identifying attributes. *EDUCAUSE Review, 39*(4), 38–49.

Jaffee, D. (2003). Virtual transformation: Web-based technology and pedagogical change. *Teaching Sociology, 31*(2), 227–236. doi:10.2307/3211312

Jalongo, M. R. (2003). Editorial: On behalf of children: Lessons from Japan: Reflective, collaborative planning for instruction. [PD.]. *Early Childhood Education Journal, 31*, 81–84. doi:10.1023/B:ECEJ.0000005431.20794.52

Johns, K. M., & Torrez, N. (2001). *Helping ESL learners succeed*. Bloomington, IN: Phi Delta Kappa Educational Foundation.

Johnson, J. (2000). Levels of success in implementing information technologies. *Innovative Higher Education, 25*(1), 59–76. doi:10.1023/A:1007536402952

Johnson, W. (2003). Using agent technology to improve the quality of web-based education. In Zhong, N., & Liu, J. (Eds.), *Web Intelligence*. New York: Springer.

Johnson, L. F. (2003). Elusive vision: Challenges impeding the learning object economy. *New Media Consortium*. http://archive.nmc.org/pdf/Elusive_Vision.pdf

Joint Information Systems Committee. (2008). *Open source software: briefing paper*.

Kamal, M. (2006). IT innovation adoption in the government sector: Identifying the critical success factors. *Journal of Enterprise Information Management, 19*(2), 192–222. doi:10.1108/17410390610645085

Kamel Boulos, M. N., Maramba, I., & Wheeler, S. (2006). Wikis, blogs and podcasts: A new generation of web-based tools for virtual collaborative clinical practice and education. *BMC Medical Education, 6*. Retrieved April 28, 2009, from http://www.biomedcentral.com/1472-6920/6/41/

Kanuka, H., Rouke, L., & Laflamme, E. (2007). The influence of instructional methods on the quality of online discussions. *British Journal of Educational Technology, 38*, 260–271. doi:10.1111/j.1467-8535.2006.00620.x

Kárpáti, A. (2008). Final evaluation report. CALIBRATE, IST-028205, European Commission. http://calibrate.eun.org/shared/data/calibrate/deliverables/D4_3_Evaluation_ReportFinal.pdf

Karsak, E., & Ozogul, C. (2009). An integrated decision making approach for ERP system selection. *Expert Systems with Applications, 36*(1), 660–667. doi:10.1016/j.eswa.2007.09.016

Ke, W., & Wei, K. (2008). Organizational culture and leadership in ERP implementation. *Decision Support Systems, 45*(2), 208–218. doi:10.1016/j.dss.2007.02.002

Kegan, R. (1982). *The Evolving Self*. Cambridge, MA: Harvard University Press.

Kelly, M. (2001). Using new media to teach East European history. *Nationalities Papers, 29*(3), 499–507. doi:10.1080/00905990120073735

Khristianovich, S.A., Lavrentev, M.A. & Lebedev, S.A. (1956, February 14). Actual tasks of scientific work organization. Pravda, 14.02.1956.

Kim, A. (2002). Open source presents benefits to educators. *T.H.E. Journal, 30*(1), 1–3.

King, K. P., & Gura, M. (2007). *Podcasting for teachers.* Charlotte, NC: Information Age Publishing.

Kitchen, S., Finch, S., & Sinclair, R. (2007). Harnessing technology schools survey 2007. National *Centre for Social Research (Nat-Cen).* http://partners.becta.org.uk/index.php?section=rh&rid=14110

Koohang, A., & Harman, K. (2005). Open source: A metaphor for e-learning. *Informing Science Journal, 8,* 75–86.

Korcuska, M. (2009). Sakai Product Council announcement: Sakaiproject.

Kornblith, G. J. (2003). Textbooks and Teaching - Editors' Introduction: More than Bells and Whistles? Using Digital Technology to Teach American History. *The Journal of American History, 89*(4), 1456–1457.

Kotter, J. P., & Cohen, D. S. (Eds.). (2002). *The heart of change.* Boston: Harvard Business School Press.

Kottke, J. (2003). It's "weblog" not "web log". *Kottke. org.* Retrieved May 2, 2009 from http://www.kottke.org/03/08/its-weblog-not-web-log

Kozma, R. (1994). A reply: Media and methods. *Educational Technology Research and Development, 42*(3), 11–14. doi:10.1007/BF02298091

Kozna, R. B., & Johnston, J. (1991). The Technological Revolution Comes to the Classroom. *Change, 23*(1), 10–22.

Kramsch, C. (1993). *Context and culture in language teaching.* Oxford: Oxford University Press.

Krashen, S. (1981). *Second Language Acquisition and Second Language Learning.* New York: Pergamon Press.

Krashen, S. (1982). *Principles and practices in second language acquisition.* Oxford: Pergamon Press.

Kress, G. (2003). *Literacy in the new media age.* London: Routledge. doi:10.4324/9780203164754

Krish Inc. (2009). Web 2.0 design. *Krish Inc: From evolution to acumen.* Retrieved April 29 from 2009, http://www.krishinc.com/web-design-development-services-india/web2.0-design.html

Kuliamin, V. V. (2007). *Software Engineering. Component-based Approach.* Moscow: INTUIT-Binom.

Lacina, J. (2004). Promoting language acquisitions: Technology and English language learners. *Childhood Education, 81*(2), 113–115.

Laffey, J., Amelung, C., & Goggins, S. (2009). A context awareness system for online learning: Design based research. *International Journal on E-Learning, 8*(3), 313–330.

Laffey, J., Lin, G., & Lin, Y. (2006). Assessing social ability in online learning environments. *Journal of Interactive Learning Research, 17*(2), 163–177.

Laffey, J., & Musser, D. (2006). Shadow net Workspace: An open source intranet for learning communities. *Canadian Journal of Learning and Technology, 32*(1).

Laffey, J., Musser, D., Remidez, H., & Gottdenker, J. (2003). Networked systems for schools that learn. *Communications of the Association of Computer Machinery, 46*(9), 192–200.

Laffey, J., & Amelung, C. (in press). Using notification systems to create social places for online learning. In Dumova, T., & Fiordo, R. (Eds.), *Handbook of Research on Social Interaction Technologies and Collaboration Software: Concepts and Trends.* Hershey, PA: IGI Global.

Laffey, J., & Musser, D. (1996). Designing a journal system for learning from field experience in teacher education. *Technology and Teacher Education Annual,* 649-653.

Lakhan, S., & Jhunjhunwala, K. (2008). Open source software in education. *EDUCAUSE Quarterly, 31*(2), 1–11.

Lambert, H. (2008). Managing risk and exploiting opportunity. *EDUCAUSE Review, 43*(6), 36–37.

Lambert, H. (2005). *Collaborative open source software: Panacea or pipe dream for higher education?* Retrieved May 26, 2009, from http://www.educause.edu/ir/

Lambert, H. D. (2004, October 19). *Collaborative Open Source software: Panacea or pipe dream for higher education?* Paper presented at the 2004 EDUCAUSE Conference, Denver, CO.

Lane, L. (2008). Toolbox or trap? Course management systems and pedagogy. *EDUCAUSE Quarterly, 31*(3), 4–6.

Langer, J. (2001). Succeeding against the odds in English. *English Journal, 91*(1), 37–42. doi:10.2307/821652

Larose, D. T. (2006). *Data mining methods and models.* Hoboken, NJ: Wiley-Interscience.

Lave, J., & Wenger, E. (1990). *Situated Learning: Legitimate Periperal Participation.* Cambridge, UK: Cambridge University Press.

Lavrentev, M.A. (1971, February 13) Highways of Siberian science. Izvestia, 13.02.1971.

Lazzari, M., & Betella, A. (2007). Towards guidelines on educational podcasting quality: Problems arising from a real world experience. In Smith, M. J., & Salvandy, G. (Eds.), *Human interface and the management of information. Interacting in information environments* (pp. 404–412). Berlin: Springer. doi:10.1007/978-3-540-73354-6_44

Leinonen, T. (2005). Urinal as a learning object. http://flosse.dicole.org/?item=urinal-as-a-learning-object

Leinonen, T., Toikkanen, T., & Silfvast, K. (2008). Software as hypothesis: Research-based design methodology. In *The Proceedings of Participatory Design Conference 2008.* New York: ACM.

Levy, M., & Hubbard, P. (2005). Why call CALL "CALL"? *Computer Assisted Language Learning, 18*(3), 143–149. doi:10.1080/09588220500208884

Lifton, R. (1993). *The Protean Self.* New York: Basic Books.

Lin, Y., & Laffey, J. (2006). Exploring the relationship between mediating tools and student perception of interdependence in a CSCL environment. *Journal of Interactive Learning Research, 17*(4), 385–400.

Lin, Y. W., & Zini, E. (2008). Free/libre open source software implementation in schools: Evidence from the field and implications for the future. *Computers & Education, 50*(3), 1092–1102. doi:10.1016/j.compedu.2006.11.001

Lin, Y., Lin, G., Liu, P., Huang, X., Shen, D., & Laffey, J. (2006). *Building a social and motivational framework for understanding satisfaction in online learning.* Paper presented at the Annual Conference of American Educational Research Association, San Francisco.

Lipponen, L. (2002). Exploring foundations for computer-supported collaborative learning. In G. Stahl (Ed.), *The Computer-supported Collaborative Learning 2002 Conference: Computer support for collaborative learning: Foundations for a CSCL community* (pp. 72-81). Hillsdale: Erlbaum.

Long, M. H. (2007). *Problems in SLA.* Mahwah, NJ: Lawrence Erlbaum Associates.

Long, M. H., & Porter, P. (1985). Group work, interlanguage talk, and second language acquisition. *TESOL Quarterly, 18*(2), 207–227. doi:10.2307/3586827

Long, M. H. (1996). The role of the linguistic environment in second language acquisition. In Ritchie, W. C., & Bhatia, T. J. (Eds.), *Handbook of second language acquisition* (pp. 413–468). New York: Academic Press. doi:10.1016/B978-012589042-7/50015-3

Lorenzo, G., & Ittelson, J. (2005a). *An Overview of E-Portfolios*: Educause Learning Initiative.

Lorenzo, G., & Ittelson, J. (2005b). *Demonstrating and Assessing Student Learning with E-Portfolios.* Educause Learning Initiative.

Lowry, R. B. (1999). Electronic Presentation of Lectures—Effect Upon Student Performance. *University Chemistry Education, 3*(1), 18–21.

Lyons, J. F. (2004). Teaching U.S. History Online: Problems and Prospects. *The History Teacher, 37*(4), 447–456. doi:10.2307/1555549

Lyotard, J. F. (1991). *The Postmodern Condition: A Report on Knowledge.* Minneapolis, MN: University of Minnesota Press.

Mackey, A., Oliver, R., & Leeman, J. (2003). Interactional input and the incorporation of feedback: an exploration of NS-NNS and NNS-NNS adult and child dyads. *Language Learning, 53*(1), 35–56. doi:10.1111/1467-9922.00210

MacIntyre, P. D. (1999). Language Anxiety: A Review of the Research for Language Teachers. In Young, D. J. (Ed.), *Affect in Foreign Language and Second Language Learning. A Practical Guide to Creating a Low-anxiety-Classroom Atmosphere* (pp. 24–45). Boston: McGraw-Hill College.

MacManus, R. (2007). E-learning 2.0: All you need to know. *Read Write Web.* Retrieved April 28, 2009 from http://www.readwriteweb.com/archives/e-learning_20_all_you_need_to_know.php

Mader, S. (2006). Wiki vs. blog. *Business Blog Wire.* Retrieved May 6, 2009 from http://www.businessblogwire.com/2006/03/stewart_mader_wiki_vs_blog.html

Margaryan, A., & Littlejohn, A. (2008). Repositories and communities at cross-purposes: issues in sharing and reuse of digital learning resources. *Journal of Computer Assisted Learning, 24*(4), 333–347. doi:10.1111/j.1365-2729.2007.00267.x

Markov, Z., & Larose, D. T. (2007). *Data mining the web: Uncovering patterns in web content, Structure, and Usage.* Hoboken, NJ: Wiley-Interscience.

Marra, R. M., & Jonassen, D. H. (2001). Limitations of online courses for supporting constructive learning. *Quarterly Review of Distance Education, 2*(4), 303–317.

Martin-Blas, T., & Serrano-Fernandez, A. (2009). The role of new technologies in the learning process: Moodle as a teaching tool in physics. *Computers & Education, 52*(1), 35–44. doi:10.1016/j.compedu.2008.06.005

Materu, P. (2004). Open Source Courseware: A Baseline Study. *The World Bank*, Washington, DC. MIT's Open-CourseWare. Retrieved from http://ocw.mit.edu

Matthew, T., Levstik, D., & Levstik, L. S. (1991). *Teaching and Learning History. Handbook of Research on Social Studies Teaching and Learning.* New York: Macmillan.

Matthews, K. (2006). Research into podcasting technology including current and possible future uses. Retrieved May 8, 2009 from http://mms.ecs.soton.ac.uk/2007/papers/32.pdf

Mayer, R. E. (2003). Elements of a science of e-learning. *Journal of Educational Computing Research, 29*(3), 297–313. doi:10.2190/YJLG-09F9-XKAX-753D

Mazzoni, D., & Dannenberg, R. (2000). *Audacity* [software]. Pittsburg, PA: Carnegie Mellon University.

McCarty, S. (2005). Spoken internet to go: Popularization through podcasting. *The JALT CALL Journal, 2*(1), 67–74.

McCormick, R. (2003). Keeping the pedagogy out of learning objects. EARLI. http://celebrate.eun.org/eun.org2/eun/Include_to_content/celebrate/file/KeepingPedagogyOutOfLOs3v2.doc

McGrath, O. (2008b). Open Educational Technology: Tempered Aspirations. In Iiyoshi, T., & Kumar, M. S. V. (Eds.), *Opening Up Education: The Collective Advancement of Education through Open Technology, Open Content, and Open Knowledge* (pp. 13–26). Cambridge, MA: MIT Press.

McGrath, O. (2005, November 6-9). Gauging adoptability: a case study of e-portfolio template development. In *Proceedings of the 33rd Annual ACM SIGUCCS Conference on User Services,* Monterey, CA (pp. 214-217). New York: ACM.

McGrath, O. (2006, November 5-8). Balancing act: community and local requirements in an open source development process. In *Proceedings of the 34th Annual ACM SIGUCCS Conference on User Services,* Edmonton, Alberta, Canada (pp. 240-244). New York: ACM.

McGrath, O. (2007, October 7-10,). Seeking activity: on the trail of users in open and community source frameworks. In *Proceedings of the 35th Annual ACM SIGUCCS Conference on User Services,* Orlando, Florida (pp. 234-239). New York: ACM.

McGrath, O. (2008a, October 19-22). Insights and surprises from usage patterns: some benefits of data mining in academic online systems. In *Proceedings of the 36th Annual ACM SIGUCCS Conference on User Services Conference,* Portland, OR (pp. 59-64). New York: ACM.

McGreal, R. (2005). Copyright wars and learning objects. *Interactive Technology and Smart Education, 2,* 141–153. doi:10.1108/17415650580000039

McGreal, R. (2007). A typology of learning object repositories. *Athabasca University.* http://hdl.handle.net/2149/1078

McGroaty, M. (1993). Cooperative learning and language acquisition. In Holt, D. (Ed.), *Cooperative learning: A response to linguistic and cultural diversity.* Washington, DC: Centre for Applied Linguistics.

McKeachie, W. J. (1954). Student-Centered versus Instructor-Centered Instruction. *Journal of Educational Psychology, 45,* 43–50. doi:10.1037/h0060215

Means, B., Toyama, Y., Murphy, R., Bakia, M., & Jones, K. (2009). *Evaluation of evidence- based practices in online learning: A meta-analysis and review of online learning studies.* Washington, DC: U.S. Department of Education. Retrieved September 19, 2009, from http://www.ed.gov/rschstat/eval/tech/evidence-based-practices/finalreport.pdf

Merholz, P. (1999). Post on October 12, 1999. *Peterme.com.* Retrieved April 30, 2009 from http://web.archive.org/web/19991013021124/http://peterme.com/index.html

Milne, A. J. (2007). Entering the Interaction Age: Implementing a Future Vision for Campus Learning Spaces. *EDUCAUSE Review, 42*(1), 12–31.

Minaei-Bidgoli, B. (2005). *Data Mining for a Web-Based Educational System.* Unpublished doctoral dissertation, Michigan State University.

Minaei-Bidgoli, B., Kashy, A., Kortemeyer, G., & Punch, W. (2004). Optimizing classification ensembles via a genetic algorithm for a web-based educational system. In *Proceedings of the Joint International Association For Pattern Recognition (IAPR) Workshops on Syntactical and Structural Pattern Recognition (SSPR 2004) and Statistical Pattern Recognition (SPR 2004),* Lisbon, Portugal.

Minaei-Bigdoli, B., & Tan, P. Kortemeyer, G., & Punch, W.F. (2006) Association analysis for a web-based educational system. In C. Romero & S. Ventura (Eds.), *Data mining in e-learning* (pp. 139-156). Southampton, UK: Wit Press.

Mitchell, R., & Myles, F. (1998). *Second language learning theories.* New York: Arnold.

Molina, P., & EDUCAUSE Evolving Technologies Committee. (2006). Pioneering new territory and technologies. *EDUCAUSE Review, 41*(5), 112–135.

Moll, L., Amanti, C., Neff, D., & Gonzalez, N. (1992). Funds of knowledge for teaching: using a qualitative approach to connect homes and classrooms. *Theory into Practice, 31*(2), 132–141. doi:10.1080/00405849209543534

Monge, S., Ovelar, R., & Azpeitia, I. (2008). Repository 2.0: Social dynamics to support community building in learning object repositories. *Interdisciplinary Journal of E-Learning and Learning Objects, 4.*

Montalbano, E. (2009). Forrester: Microsoft office in no danger from competitors. *PC World.* Retrieved September 9, 2009, from http://www.pcworld.com/businesscenter/article/166123/forrester_microsoft_office_in_no_danger_from_competitors.html?tk=nl_dnx_h_crawl

Moodle. Retrieved June 15, 2009 from http://docs.moodle.org/en/About_Moodlehttp://docs.moodle.org/en/About_Moodle

Moore, A. H. (2002). Lens on the future: Open source learning. *EDUCAUSE Review, 37*(5), 43–51.

Moore, M. G. (2003). This book in brief: Overview. In Moore, M. G., & Anderson, W. (Eds.), *Handbook of distance education* (pp. xiii–xxiii). Mahwah, NJ: Lawrence Erlbaum Associates, Inc.

Morelli, R., Tucker, A., Danner, N., De Lanerolle, T. R., Ellis, H. J. C., & Izmirli, O. (2009). Revitalizing computing through fee and open Source software for humanity. *Communications of the ACM, 52*(8), 67–75. doi:10.1145/1536616.1536635

Morgan, G. (2003). *Faculty use of course management systems.* Boulder, CO: EDUCAUSE Center for Applied Research (ECAR).

Moyle, K. (2003). *Open source software and Australian school education: An introduction.* Retrieved September 9, 2009, from http://www.educationau.edu.au/jahia/webdav/site/myjahiasite/shared/papers/open_source.pdf

Multimedia Educational Resources for Learning and Online Teaching (Merlot). http://www.merlot.org

Musser, D., Laffey, J., & Lawrence, B. (2000). Center for echnology Innovation in Education, University of Missouri-Columbia. In Branch, R., & Fitzgerald, M. A. (Eds.), *Educational Media and Technology Yearbook* (*Vol. 25*, pp. 89–95). Engelwood, CO: Libraries Unlimited, Inc.

Myers, J. (1991). Cooperative learning in heterogeneous classes. *Cooperative Learning, 11*(4).

National Center for Education Statistics. (2000). *Teachers' tools for the 21st century. A report on teachers' use of technology.* Washington, DC: Author.

National Center for Education Statistics. (2009). *Fast Facts.* Retrieved May 28, 2009, from http://nces.ed.gov/fastfacts/index.asp?faq=FFOption6#faqFFOption6

National Governers Association. (2008). *The fiscal survey of states.* Washington, D. C.: National Association of State Budget Officers.

National Standards in Foreign Language Education Project. (1999). *Standards for foreign language learning in the 21st century.* Yonkers, NY: Author.

Nations, D. (2009). What are web widgets?: How can I use a web widget? *About.com: Web Trends.* Retrieved May 6, 2009 from http://webtrends.about.com/od/widgets/a/what_is_widget.htm

Navica. (2008). *Choosing the right open source product: Don't leave it to chance.* Retrieved June 5, 2009, from http://www.navicasoft.com/pages/osmm.htm

NCES. (2006). Revenues and Expenditures for Public Elementary and Secondary Education 2005-2006. *National Center for Education Statistics.* Retrieved October 11, 2009, from http://nces.ed.gov/pubs2008/expenditures/index.asp

Nederlof, H. (2009). A crib sheet for selling Sakai to traditional management. In Lumsden, J., Mangarole, S., & Shanker, A. (Eds.), *Sakai Courseware management. The official guide* (pp. 369–384). Birmingham, UK: Packt Publishing.

Novak, T. P., Hoffman, D. L., & Yung, Y. F. (2000). Measuring the Customer Experience in Online Environments: A Structural Modeling Approach. *Marketing Science, 19*(1), 22–42. doi:10.1287/mksc.19.1.22.15184

O'Dell, R. (2002). Using Open Source in Education. *T.H.E. Focus.* Retrieved September 9, 2009, from http://www.thejournal.com/thefocus/12.cfm

O'Hara, K. J., & Kay, J. S. (2003). Open source software and computer science education. *J. Comput. Small Coll., 18*(3), 1–7.

O'Reilly, T. (2005). What is 2.0: Design patterns and business models for the next generation of software. *O'Reilly Media.* Retrieved April 28, 2009 from http://www.oreillynet.com/pub/a/oreilly/tim/news/2005/09/30/what-is-web-20.html

Obendhain, A., & Johnson, W. (2004). Product and process innovation in service organizations: The influence of organizational culture in higher education institutions. *Journal of Applied Management and Entrepreneurship, 9*(3), 91–113.

Ochoa, X., & Duval, E. (2009). Quantitative analysis of learning object repositories. *IEEE Transactions on Learning Technologies, 2*(3), 226–238. doi:10.1109/TLT.2009.28

OECD. (2007) Giving Knowledge for Free: The emergence of Open Educational Resources. *Center for Educational Research and Innovation.* Retrieved September 22, 2009, from http://www.sourceoecd.org/education/9789264031746

O'Laughlin, N., & Borkowski, E. (2008, October 29). *Transitioning learning management systems: Making the move at the enterprise level.* Retrieved June 5, 2009, from http://www.educause.edu/Resources/Browse/OpenSource/17546

Oliver, R. (1995). Negative feedback in child NS/NNS conversations. *Studies in Second Language Acquisition, 17*(2), 459–482. doi:10.1017/S0272263100014418

Open Educational Resources. (2008). *Wikipedia.* Retrieved September 22, 2009 from http://en.wikipedia.org/wiki/Open_educational_resources

Open Source Initiative. (2006, July 7). *The open source definition.* Retrieved May 1, 2009, from http://www.opensource.org/docs/osd

OpenCourseWare. Retrived June 15, 2009 from http://web.mit.edu/ocwhttp://web.mit.edu/ocw

O'Reilly, T. (2009). *What is Web 2.0? Design patterns and business models for the next generation of software.* Retrieved September 23, 2009, from http://oreilly.com/web2/archive/what-is-web-20.html

Ortutay, B. (2009). Fast-growing facebook's user base hits 200 million. *Yahoo! Finance.* Retrieved May 21, 2009 from http://finance.yahoo.com/news/Fastgrowing-Facebooks-user-apf-14886318.html?v=6

OsFlash. Retrieved June 15,2009 from http://osflash.orghttp://osflash.org

Owyang, J. (2009). A collection of social network stats for 2009. *Web Strategy by Jeremiah Owyang.* Retrieved May 20, 2009 from http://www.web-strategist.com/blog/2009/01/11/a-collection-of-soical-network-stats-for-2009/

Ozkan, B. (2008). *How to effectively use free and open source software in education.* Paper presented at the World Conference on E-Learning in Corporate, Government, Healthcare, and Higher Education 2008 Chesapeake VA.

Palfrey, J., & Gasser, U. (2008). *Born digital: Understanding the first generation of digital natives.* New York: Basic Books.

Papastergiou, M. (2006). Course management systems as tools for the creation of online learning environments: Evaluation from a social constructivist perspective and implications for their design. *International Journal on E-Learning, 54*(4), 593–622.

Parker, K. R., & Chao, J. T. (2007). Wiki as a teaching tool. *Interdisciplinary Journal of Knowledge and Learning Objects, 3*, 57–72.

Parker, M. (2000). *Organisational culture and identity: Unity and division at work.* London: Sage Publications, Ltd.

Pavlicek, R. (2000). *Embracing Insanity.* Indianapolis, IN: Sams.

Pedler, M., Burgoyne, J., & Boydell, T. (1997). *The Learning Company: A strategy for sustainable development* (2nd ed.). London: McGraw-Hill.

Pedroni, M., Bay, T., Oriol, M., & Pedroni, A. (2007, March). Open source projects in programming courses. *ACM SIGCSE Bulletin, 39*(1), 454–458. doi:10.1145/1227504.1227465

Peet, M. (2008). *Creating Institutional Pathways for Transformation and Change: Educating for Leadership and Social Innovation.* Paper presented at the Annual Meeting for the Association for the Study of Higher Education.

Peet, M. (in press). The integrative knowledge portfolio process: A program guide for educating reflective practitioners and lifelong learners, from http://services.aamc.org/30/mededportal/servlet/segment/mededportal/information/

Peregoy, S. F., & Boyle, O. F. (1997). *Reading, writing, & learning in ESL: A resource book for K-12 teachers.* New York: Longman.

Perkins, D., & Hartman, J. *(October,2007).* Transparent Teaching: An Open- Source code for student learning. *Presentation at the Annual Geological Society Meeting. Colorado, Denever.*

Perry, W. (1970). *Forms of Intellectual and Ethical Development in the College Years: A Scheme.* New York: Holt, Rinehart, and Winston.

Petrenko, A. K., Petrenko, O. L., & Kuliamin, V. V. (2008). Research Organizations in IT Education. *ISP RAS Proceedings, 15,* 41–50.

Petrides, L., & Jimes, C. (2008). Building open educational resources from the ground up: South Africa's free high school science texts. *Journal of Interactive Media in Education, 7.* http://jime.open.ac.uk/2008/07/.

Petrides, L., Nguyen, L., Jimes, C., & Karaglani, A. (2008). Open educational resources: inquiring into author use and reuse. *International Journal of Technology Enhanced Learning, 1*(1), 98–117. doi:10.1504/IJTEL.2008.020233

Petrides, L. (2006). Creating Knowledge Building and Sharing Capacity through Case Study Development. *The Institute for the Study of Knowledge Management in Education.* October 3, 2006.

Petrides, L. (2008). OER Case Study Framework. *The Institute for the Study of Knowledge Management in Education.* Retrieved September 20, 2009, from http://wiki.oercommons.org/mediawiki/index.php/OER_Case_Study_Framework

Piaget, J. (1973). *To Understand is to Invent.* New York: Grossman.

Pica, T., & Doughty, C. (1985). Input and interaction in the communicative language classroom: A comparison of teacher-fronted and group activities. In Gass, S., & Madden, C. (Eds.), *Input in second language acquisition* (pp. 115–132). Rowley, MA: Newbury House.

Picciano, A. (2002). Beyond student perceptions: Issues of interaction, presence, and performance in an online course. *Journal of Asynchronous Learning Networks, 6*(1), 21–40.

Picciano, A. G., & Seaman, J. (2008). *K-12 online learning: A 2008 follow-up of the survey of U.S. school district administrators.* The Sloan Consortium.

Pierson, M., & Cozart, A. (2005). Novice Teacher Case Studies: A Changing Perspective on Technology during Induction Years. In C. Crawford et al. (Eds.), *Proceedings of Society for Information Technology and Teacher Education International Conference 2005* (pp. 3332-3337). Chesapeake, VA: AACE.

Põldoja, H., Leinonen, T., Väljataga, T., Ellonen, A., & Priha, M. (2006). Progressive Inquiry Learning Object Templates (PILOT). *International Journal on E-Learning, 5*(1), 103–111.

Porter, P. (1983). Variations in the conversations of adult learners of English as a function of the proficiency level of participants. Unpublished doctoral dissertation, Stanford University, California.

President's Information Technology Advisory Committee. (2000, October). Developing open source software to advance high end computing: Report to the president. Arlington, VA: National Coordination Office for Information Technology Research and Development. Retrieved September 3, 2009, from http://www.nitrd.gov/pubs/pitac/pres-oss-11sep00.pdf.

Priest, G. (1999). *Learn fast. Go fast.* Retrieved May 18, 2009, from http://internettime.com/Learning/articles/LearnfastGofast2.pdf

Project Service Centre. (2009). *Roles and responsibilities.* Retrieved February 16, 2009, from http://www.csu.edu.au/division/psc/roles-and-responsibilities/

Putland, G. (2006). *Blogs, Wikis, RSS and there's more? Web 2.0 on the march. Education.au Limited.* Retrieved May 21, 2007, from http://www.educationau.edu.au/jahia/Jahia/home/pid/337

Putnam, R. (2000). *Bowling alone*. New York: Simon & Schuster.

Raack, R. C., Smith, A. M., & Raack, M. L. (1973). The Documentary Film in History Teaching: An Experimental Course. *The History Teacher*, *6*(2), 281–294. doi:10.2307/491726

Ragains, P. (1995). Four variations on Drueke's active learning paradigm. *Research Strategies*, *13*(1), 40–50.

Rassool, N. (1999). *Literacy for sustainable development in the age of information*. Clevedon, UK: Multilingual Matters.

Raymond, E. S. (2001). *The cathedral and the bazaar: Musings on Linux and open source by an accidental revolutionary*. Cambridge, MA: O'Reilly.

Raymond, E. (1999). *The cathedral and the bazaar*. Retrieved September 9, 2009, from http://www.catb.org/~esr/writings/cathedral-bazaar/cathedral-bazaar/

Rebecchi, M. (2004b). *Strategic Approaches to e-Learning: Delivering Quality*. The Charles Sturt University Experience.

Rebecchi, M. (2004a). *Implementation of a Commercial Virtual Learning Environment at Charles Sturt University*.

Recker, M. M., & Dorward, J. (2004). Discovery and use of online learning resources: Case study findings. *Journal of Educational Technology & Society*, *7*(2), 93–104.

Reed, J. H. (1998). *Effect of a model for critical thinking on student achievement in primary source document analysis and interpretation, argumentative reasoning, critical thinking dispositions, and history content in a community college history course*. Unpublished doctoral dissertation, University of South Florida, Florida.

Reich, R. (1992). *The work of nations: Preparing ourselves for 21st century capitalism*. New York: Alfred A. Knopf, Inc.

Remidez, H., Laffey, J., & Musser, D. (2001). Open Source and the diffusion of teacher education software. *Technology and Teacher Education Annual*, *3*, 2774–2778.

Remidez, H., Laffey, J., & Musser, D. (2001). Open source and the diffusion of teacher education software. In J. Price, et al. (Eds.), *Proceedings of Society for Information Technology and Teacher Education International Conference 2001* (pp. 2774-2778). Chesapeake, VA: AACE

Reschke, W., & Aldag, R. (2000, August). *The business case for culture change*. Retrieved May 20, 2009, from http://www.greatorganizations.com/culturestudy.htm

Resta, P., & Laferriere, T. (2007). Technology in support of collaborative learning. *Educational Psychology Review*, *19*(1), 65–83. doi:10.1007/s10648-007-9042-7

Reyes, S. A., & Vallone, T. L. (2008). *Constructivist strategies for teaching English language learners*. Thousand Oaks, CA: Corwin Press.

Richards, P. (2001). MIT to make nearly all course materials available free on the World Wide Web, Retrieved June 15, 2009, from http://web.mit.edu/newsoffice/nr/2001/ocw.htmlhttp://web.mit.edu/newsoffice/nr/2001/ocw.html.

Richardson, H., & Ward, R. (2005). *Developing and Implementing a Methodology for Reviewing E-portfolio Products*. The Centre for Recording Achievement.

Risinger, C. F. (2006). Using Blogs in the Classroom: A New Approach to Teaching Social Studies with the Internet. *Social Education*, *70*(3), 130–132.

Rogers, E. (1995). *Diffusion of innovations* (4th ed.). New York: The Free Press.

Romero, C., & Ventura, S. (2007). Educational data mining: A survey from 1995 to 2005. *Expert Systems with Applications*, *33*(1). doi:10.1016/j.eswa.2006.04.005

Romero, C., Ventura, S., & Garcia, E. (2008). Data mining in learning management systems: Moodle case study and tutorial. *Computers & Education*, 51.

Roof, S., & Frazier, G. (1962). Note: An IBM 704 computer program for computing bartlett's test of homogeneiety of variance. *Biometrics*, *18*(2), 251–252. doi:10.2307/2527464

Rovai, A. P. (2002). Development of an instrument to measure classroom community. *The Internet and Higher Education, 5*(3), 197–211. doi:10.1016/S1096-7516(02)00102-1

Safayeni, F., Derbentseva, N., Cañas, J., & Concept Maps, A. A Theoretical Note on Concepts and the Need for Cyclic Concept Maps. Retrieved April 8, 2007, from http://cmap.ihmc.us/Publications/ResearchPapers/Cyclic%20Concept%20Maps.pdfhttp://cmap.ihmc.us/Publications/ResearchPapers/Cyclic%20Concept%20Maps.pdf

Safran, C., Helic, D., & Gütl, C. (2007). E-learning practices and web 2.0. In M. Aurer (Ed.), *The 10th International Conference on Interactive Computer Aided Learning* (pp. 1(8)-8(8)). Kassel: Kassel University Press.

Salmon, G. (2006). *E-tivities: The key to active online learning. London.* Sterling, VA: RoutledgeFalmer.

Saville-Troike, M. (2006). *Introducing second language acquisition.* New York: Cambridge University Press.

Schachter, R. (2009). Digital Classrooms Take Flight. District Administration. *The Magazine for School District Management.* October 2009.

Schein, E. (1985). *Organizational culture and leadership.* San Francisco: Jossey-Bass.

Schroeder, U., & Spannagel, C. (2006). Supporting Active Learning Process. *International Journal on E-Learning, 5*(2), 245–264.

Schwaber, K., & Beedle, M. (2001). *Agile Software Development with Scrum.* Upper Saddle River, NJ: Prentice Hall.

Schwartz, J. (2005). The Participation Age. *IT Conversations Legacy Programs.* Recorded April 4, 2005.

Sclater, N. (2008). *Large-scale open source e-learning systems at the Open University UK.* Boulder: EDUCAUSE Center for Applied Research (ECAR).

Scott, J. L. (2004) *Graduate students' perceptions of online classroom community: A quantitative research study.* Unpublished doctoral dissertation, Capella University, Columbia.

Seixas, P. (1993). Popular Film and Young People's Understanding of the History of Native American-White Relations. *The History Teacher, 26*(3), 351–370. doi:10.2307/494666

Sen, R. (2007). A strategic analysis of competition between open source and proprietary software. *Journal of Information Management Systems, 24*(1), 233–257. doi:10.2753/MIS0742-1222240107

Sen, A., Dacin, P. A., & Pattichis, C. (2006). Current trends in web data analysis. *Communications of the ACM, 49*(11), 85–91. doi:10.1145/1167838.1167842

Senge, P. (1990). *The Fifth Discipline.* London: Century Business.

Shin, N. (2006). Online learner's flow experience: an empirical study. *British Journal of Educational Technology, 37*(5), 705–720. doi:10.1111/j.1467-8535.2006.00641.x

Siemens, G. (2004). ePortfolios Retrieved June, 11, 2009, from http://www.elearnspace.org/Articles/eportfolios.htm

Smart, J., & St. John, E. (1996). Organizational culture and effectiveness in higher education: A test of the "culture type" and "strong culture" hypothesis. *Educational Evaluation and Policy Analysis, 18*(3), 219–241.

Smith, K. (2006). Case study III - Higher education culture and the diffusion of technology in classroom instruction. In Metcalfe, A. (Ed.), *Knowledge management and higher education* (pp. 222–241). Hershey, PA: Idea Group, Inc.

Smith, P., Rudd, P., & Coghlan, M. (2008). Harnessing technology: Schools survey 2008. National Foundation for Educational Research. http://partners.becta.org.uk/index.php?section=rh&rid=15952

Sowe, S. K., & Stamelos, I. G. (2007). Involving software engineering students in open source software projects: Experiences from a pilot study. *Journal of Information Systems Education, 18*(4), 425–436.

Stang, K., & Street, C. (2007). Tech Talk for Social Studies Teachers: The Jamestown Colony: Access and Technology. *Social Studies, 98*(3), 88–89. doi:10.3200/TSSS.98.3.88-89

Stephens, R. P. (2005). Using Technology to Teach Historical Understanding. *Social Education, 69*(3), 151–154.

Stepp-Greany, J. (2002). Student perceptions on language learning in a technological environment: Implications for the new millennium. *Language Learning & Technology, 6*(1), 165–180.

Stunden, A. (2003). The muscles, aches, and pains of open source. *EDUCAUSE Review, 38*(6), 100–101.

Su, F., & Beaumont, C. (2008). Student perceptions of e-learning with a wiki. *SOLSTICE Conference 2008: E-learning and learning environments for the future, 1*. Retrieved May 19, 2009, from http://www.edgehill.ac.uk/solstice/Conference2008/documents/Session5_FrankSu_000.pdf

Suthers, D. (2006). Technology affordances for intersubjective meaning making: A research agenda for CSCL. *International Journal of Computer-Supported Collaborative Learning, 1*(3), 315–337. doi:10.1007/s11412-006-9660-y

Swain, M. (1985). Communicative competence: Some roles of comprehensible input and comprehensible output in its development. In Gass, S. M., & Madden, C. G. (Eds.), *Input in second language acquisition* (pp. 235–253). Rowley, MA: Newbury House.

Szabo, A., & Hastings, N. (2000). Using IT in the Undergraduate Classroom: Should We Replace the Blackboard with Power Point. *Computers & Education, 35*(3), 175–188. doi:10.1016/S0360-1315(00)00030-0

Szulik, M. J. (2007). Open for change. *EDUCAUSE Review, 42*(1), 4–5.

Tallent-Runnels, M. K., Thomas, J. A., Lan, W. Y., Cooper, S., Ahern, T. C., & Shaw, S. M. (2006). Teaching courses online: A review of the research. *Review of Educational Research, 76*(1), 93–135. doi:10.3102/00346543076001093

Tan, W. T. (2007). *Free/open source software: education.* Retrieved August 20, 2009, from http://www.iosn.net/education/foss-education-primer/fossPrimer-Education.pdf

Teacher Education Accreditation Council. (2009). Quality principles for teacher education programs Retrieved June 8, 2009, from http://www.teac.org/?page_id=170

Thacker, C. (2007). Podcasts in education. *Macinstruct.* Retrieved May 7, 2009, from http://www.macinstruct.com/node/43

The Sakai Foundation. (2009). *Sakai.* Retrieved August 10, 2009, 2009, from http://sakaiproject.org/portal

Thomas, J., & Mullaly, M. (2008). Implementation. In *Researching the value of project management* (pp. 145–186). Newton Square, PA: Project Management Institute, Inc.

Thorp, D. B. (2005). Using Technology to Teach Historical Understanding. *Social Education, 69*(3), 151–154.

Tierney, W. (1988). Organizational culture in higher education: Defining the essentials. *The Journal of Higher Education, 59*(1), 2–21. doi:10.2307/1981868

Tinker, R. (2000). *Ice machines, steamboats, and education: Structural change and educational technologies.* Paper presented at the Secretary's Conference on Educational

Toikkanen, T., & Leinonen, T. (2006). Distributed design and development using agile methods and Trac. In *VTT Symposium 241. The 7th International Conference on eXtreme Programming and Agile Processes in Software Engineering,* (pp. 85–86). Espoo, Finland. VTT.

Tong, T. (2004). *Free/open source software in education.* Retrieved September 9, 2009, from http://www.iosn.net/education/foss-educationprimer/fossPrimer-Education.pdf

Toohey, K. (2000). *Learning English at school: Identity, social relations and classroom practice.* Clevedon, UK: Multilingual Matters LTD.

Tosh, D., & Werdmuller, B. (2004). E-portfolios and weblogs: One vision for ePortfolio development. Retrieved September 21, 2006 from http://www.eradc.org/papers/ePortfolio_Weblog.pdf

Towell, R., & Hawkins, R. (1994). *Approaches to second language acquisition.* Pennsylvania, PA: Multilingual Matters LTD.

Townsend, R. B. (2006). Historians Teach More And Larger Classes, But Make Less Use of Technology. *Perspectives: American Historical Association Newsletter*, *44*(4), 18–23.

Trentin, G. (2000). The apprentice historian: studying modern history with the help of computers and telemetric. *International Journal of Educational Telecommunications*, *6*(3), 213–225.

Trice, H., & Beyer, J. (1993). *The cultures of work organizations*. Upper Saddle River, NJ: Prentice Hall.

Tuomi, I. (2006), Open Educational Resources: What they are and why do they matter. Retrieved October 10, 2009, from http://www.meaningprocessing.com/personalPages/tuomi/articles/OpenEducationalResources_OECDreport.pdf

TypingWeb. (2009). TypingWeb Features. *TypingWeb: Free Online Typing Tutor.* Retrieved May 13, 2009, from http://classic.typingweb.com/typingtutor/features.php

U. S. Department of Education. (2004). No child left behind. Retrieved September 6, 2008, from U. S. Department of Education Web site: http://www.ed.gov/nclb/landing.jhtml

U. S. Department of Education. (2006). Public elementary and secondary students, staff, schools and school districts: School year 2003-04. Retrieved September 21, 2009, from National Center for Education Statistics at http://nces.ed.gov/pubsearch/pubsinfo.asp?pubid=2006307.

U.S. Department of Education. (2009, June 26). *Analysis of controlled studies shows online learning enhances classroom instruction.* Retrieved September 9, 2009, http://www.ed.gov/news/pressreleases/2009/06/06262009.html
van Rooij, S. (2007). Open source software in US higher education: Reality or illusion? *Education & Information Technologies, 12*(4), 191-209.

Umbach, P. D. (2007). Faculty cultures and college teaching. In Perry, R., & Smart, J. (Eds.), *The scholarship of teaching and learning in higher education: An evidence-based perspective* (pp. 263–317). New York: Springer. doi:10.1007/1-4020-5742-3_8

UNESCO. (2002). Forum on the impact of open courseware for higher education in developing countries. Final report, UNESCO. http://www.wcet.info/resources/publications/unescofinalreport.pdf

Unicon (2009). Sakai Collaboration and Learning Environment. Retrieved June 10, 2009, from http://www.unicon.net/opensource/sakai

United Nations General Assembly Resolution. (A/55/2) September 8, 2000. *United Nations Millennium Declaration.* Retrieved June 2, 2009, from http://www.un.org/millennium/declaration/ares552e.pdf

Uys, P. (2009). *Change and innovation strategies during the implementation of an open source LMS: an Australian case study. Research, Reflections and Innovations in Integrating ICT in Education.* Paper presented at the V International Conference on Multimedia and ICT in Education (m-ICTE2009), Lisbon, Portugal.

Uys, P., & Morton-Allen, M. (2007). *A suggested methodological framework for evaluating and selecting an open source LMS.* Retrieved June 5, 2009, from http://www.csu.edu.au/division/landt/interact/documents/2007%2006%2007%20Sakai%20Amsterdam%20Presentation%20FINAL.ppt

Van Assche, F., & Vuorikari, R. (2006). A framework for quality of learning resources. In Ehlers, U., & Pawlowski, J. (Eds.), *European Handbook for Quality and Standardization in E-Learning*. Berlin, Germany: Springer. doi:10.1007/3-540-32788-6_29

Van Assche, F., & Massart, D. (2004). Federation and brokerage of learning objects and their metadata. In *Fourth IEEE International Conference on Advanced Learning Technologies (ICALT'04)* (pp.316–320).

Van den Branden, K. (2006). Introduction: Task-based language teaching in a nutshell. In Van den Branden, K. (Ed.), *Task-based language education: From theory to practice* (pp. 1–16). Cambridge: Cambridge University Press. doi:10.1017/CBO9780511667282.002

van Rooij, S. W. (2007). Open Source software in US higher education: Reality or illusion? *Education and Information Technologies, 12*(4), 191–209. doi:10.1007/s10639-007-9044-6

van Rooij, S. W. (2009). Adopting Open-Source Software Applications in US Higher Education: A Cross-Disciplinary Review of the Literature. *Review of Educational Research, 79*(2), 682. doi:10.3102/0034654308325691

Vanijja, V., & Supattathum, M. (2006). *Statistical analysis of e-learning usage in a university.* Paper presented at the Third International Conference on eLearning for Knowledge-based Society (eLearningAP 2006), Bangkok, Thailand.

Varonis, E., & Gass, S. (1985). Nonnative/nonnative conversations: A model for negotiation of meaning. *Applied Linguistics, 6*(1), 71–90. doi:10.1093/applin/6.1.71

Villano, M. (2006). Open source vision. *Campus Technology, 19*(11), 26–36.

Volle, L. (2005). Analyzing oral skills in voice e-mail and online interviews. *Language Learning and Technology, 9*(3), 146-163. Retrieved June 2, 2009, from http://llt.msu.edu/vol9num3/volle/

Von Meier, A. (1999). Occupational cultures as a challenge to technological innovation. *IEEE Transactions on Engineering Management, 46*(1), 101–114. doi:10.1109/17.740041

Vrasidas, C. (2004). Issues of pedagogy and design in e-learning systems. In *Proceedings of the 2004 ACM Symposium on Applied Computing* (pp. 911-915).

Vygotsky, L. S. (1978). *Mind in Society.* Cambridge, MA: Harvard University Press.

Wagener, D. (2006). Promoting independent learning skills using video on digital language laboratories. *Computer Assisted Language Learning, 19*(4/5), 279–286. doi:10.1080/09588220601043180

Wallace, L., Keil, M., & Rai, A. (2004). How software project risk affects project performance: An investigation of the dimensions of risk and an exporatory model. *Decision Sciences, 35*(2), 289–321. doi:10.1111/j.00117315.2004.02059.x

Wang, W., & Zaiane, O. R. (2002, September 2-6). Clustering web sessions by sequence alignment. In *Proceedings of the 13th International Workshop on Database and Expert Systems Applications DEXA* (pp. 394-398). Washington, DC: IEEE Computer Society.

Warger, T. (2002). The open-source movement. *EDUTECH Report, 18*(2), 18-20. Retrieved September 9, 2009, from http://net.educause.edu/ir/library/pdf/eqm0233.pdf

Warlick, D. (2009). Class blogmeister: Learning as conversation. Retrieved August 12, 2009, from The Landmark Project at http://classblogmeister.com/

Watson, R. T., Boudreau, M., York, P. T., & Greiner, M. (2008). Opening the classroom. *Journal of Information Systems Education, 19*(1), 75–85.

Watson, J., Gemin, B., & Ryan, J. (2008). Keeping [*Online Learning: A Review of State-Level Policy and Practice.* Evergreen, CO: Evergreen Consulting Associates.]. *Pacing and Clinical Electrophysiology,* K-12.

Weaver, D., Spratt, C., & Nair, C. (2008). Academic and student use of a learning management system: Implications for quality *Australasian Journal of Educational Technology, 24*(1), 30-41.

Weber, S. (2004). *The success of open source.* Cambridge, MA: Harvard University Press.

Wedemeyer, C. (1974). Characteristics of open learning systems. In *Open Learning Systems.* Washington: National Association of Educational Broadcasters.

Wellman, B., & Gulia, M. (1999). Virtual communities as communities: Net surfers don't ride alone. In Smith, M., & Kollock, P. (Eds.), *Communities in cyberspace* (pp. 163–190). Berkeley, CA: Routledge.

Wellman, B. (1999). The network community: An introduction to networks in the global village. In Wellman, B. (Ed.), *Networks in the global village* (pp. 1–48). Boulder, CO: Westview Press.

Wenger, E. (2009). *Communities of practice.* Retrieved August 13, 2009, from http://www.ewenger.com/theory/index.htm

Wenglinsky, H. (2002). The Link between Teacher Classroom Practices and Student Academic Performance. *The entity from which ERIC acquires the content, including journal, organization, and conference names, or by means of online submission from the author.Education Policy Analysis Archives*, v10 n12 Feb 2002.

Wentling, T. L., Waight, C., Gallaher, J., La Fleur, J., Wang, C., & Kanfer, A. (2000). *e-Learning - A review of the literature.* Retrieved May 18, 2009, from http://learning.ncsa.uiuc.edu/papers/elearnlit.pdf

Wheeler, B. (2004). Open source 2007: How did this happen? *EDUCAUSE Review, 39*(4), 12–27.

Wheeler, B. (2007). Open source 2010: Reflections on 2007. *EDUCAUSE Review, 42*(1), 48–67.

Wheeler, B., & DeStefano, J. (2007, July-August). *Mitigating the risks of big systems.* Retrieved June 5, 2009, from http://www.nacubo.org/Business_Officer_Magazine/Magazine_Archives/July-August_2007/Mitigating_the_Risks_of_Big_Systems.html

Whitehurst, J. (2009). Open source: narrowing the divide between education, business and community. *EDUCAUSE Review, 44*(1), 70–71.

Wikipedia (2009). Blog. *Wikipedia, the free encyclopedia.* Retrieved May 11, 2009, from http://en.wikipedia.org/wiki/Blog

Wikipedia (2009). Electronic learning. *Wikipedia, the free encyclopedia.* Retrieved May 21, from 2009, http://en.wikipedia.org/wiki/E-learning

Wikipedia (2009). Podcast. *Wikipedia, the free encyclopedia.* Retrieved May 15, 2009, from http://en.wikipedia.org/wiki/Podcast

Wikipedia. (2009). *Open Source.*

Wikipedia: The free encyclopedia. (2009, September 5). FL: Wikimedia Foundation, Inc. Retrieved September 5, 2009, from http://www.wikipedia.org

Wiley, D. (2000). Connecting learning objects to instructional design theory: A definition, a metaphor, and a taxonomy. In Wiley, D.,(Ed.) *The Instructional Use of Learning Objects*, chapter 1. Agency for Instructional Technology and the Association for Educational Communications and Technology. http://reusability.org/read/

Wiley, D. (2003). Learning objects: Difficulties and opportunities. http://opencontent.org/docs/lo_do.pdf

Wiley, D. (2006), On the Sustainability of Open Educational Resource Initiatives in Higher Education, *OECD Centre for Educational Research and Innovation (CERI).* Retrieved October 20, 2009, from http://www.oecd.org/edu/oer

Wiley, D. A. (2000). *Connecting learning objects to instructional design theory: A definition, A metaphor, and A taxonomy.* Retrieved May 27, 2009, from http://reusability.org/read/chapters/wiley

Williams van Rooij, S. (2007a). Open source software in higher education: Reality or illusion? *Education and Information Technologies, 12*(4), 191–209. doi:10.1007/s10639-007-9044-6

Williams van Rooij, S. (2007b). Perceptions of open source versus commercial software: Is higher education still on the fence? *Journal of Research on Technology in Education, 39*(4), 433–453.

Williams, D. (2007). Blogging definitions: Types of blogs. *Web design, SEO, blog marketing and social media marketing for your business.* Retrieved May 20, 2009, from http://www.webdesignseo.com/blogging-terms/blogging-definitions-types-of-blogs-part-2.php

Wilson, T. (2008). New ways of mediating learning: Investigating the implications of adopting open educational resources for tertiary education at an institution in the United Kingdom as compared to one in South Africa. *International Review of Research in Open and Distance Learning, 9*(1).

Wilson, B. (1996). What is a constructivist learning environment? In Wilson, B. (Ed.), *Constructivist learning environments: Case studies in instructional design* (pp. 3–10). Englewood Cliffs, NJ: Educational Technology Publications.

Winn, W., & Snyder, D. (1996). Cognitive perspectives in psychology. In Jonassen, D. H. (Ed.), *Handbook of research in educational communications and technology* (pp. 112–142). New York: Macmillan.

Wolf, K., & Dietz, M. E. (1998). Teaching portfolios: Purposes and possibilities. *Teacher Education Quarterly, 25*(1), 9–22.

Woodrow, L. (2006). Anxiety and speaking English as a second language. *RELC Journal, 37*(3), 308–328. doi:10.1177/0033688206071315

Woolf, B. (2006). Wiki vs. blog. *E-Content: IBM Developer Works.* Retrieved May 5, 2009, from http://www.ibm.com/developerworks/wikis/display/woolf/Wiki+vs.+Blog

Woolsey, K. (2008). Where is the new learning? In Katz, R. (Ed.), *The tower and the cloud: Higher education in the age of cloud computing* (pp. 212–218). Boulder, CO: EDUCAUSE.

Working with Open Source. (2004, March)... *EDUTECH Report, 20*(3), 1–7.

Yang, S. C. (2003). Learner-generated oral history: spanning three centuries project. *Computers in Human Behavior, 19*(3), 299–318. doi:10.1016/S0747-5632(02)00060-2

Yang, S. C. (2007). E-critical/thematic doing history project: Integrating the critical thinking approach with computer-mediated history learning. *Computers in Human Behavior, 23*(5), 2095–2112. doi:10.1016/j.chb.2006.02.012

Yengin, I. (2006). *Role of computer assisted active learning system in history of civilization teaching,* Unpublished master thesis, University of Bahcesehir, Istanbul.

Young, J. (2002). 'E-Portfolios' Could Give Students a New Sense of Their Accomplishments. *The Chronicle of Higher Education, 48*(26).

Zastrocky, M., Harris, M., & Lowendahl, J. (2008). *E-learning for higher education: Are we reaching maturity?* Stamford, CT: Gartner Group.

Zellmer, M. B., Frontier, A., & Pheifer, D. (2006, November). What Are NCLB's Instructional Costs? *Educational Leadership, 64*(3), 43–46.

Zhang, D., & Nunamaker, J. (2003). Powering e-learning in the new millenium: An overview of e-learning and enabling technology. *Information Systems Frontiers, 5*(2), 207–218. doi:10.1023/A:1022609809036

Zhou, G., & Xu, J. (2007). Adoption of educational technology ten years after setting strategic goals: A Canadian university case. *Australasian Journal of Educational Technology, 23*(4), 508–528.

About the Contributors

Betül Özkan Czerkawski serves as the assistant professor of educational technology and program director at University of Arizona South (USA). Prior to joining the faculty at the USA, she has worked in Long Island University and University of West Georgia as faculty coordinator of instructional technology and assistant professor of educational technology research, respectively. Dr. Czerkawski holds a MA and PhD in Instructional Design and Development and BA in Italian Philology. She completed her post-doctoral study in Iowa State University where she also served as a project manager for a Fulbright Grant. Her research interests include technology integration in teaching and learning, design of online learning environments, and emerging educational technologies. Dr. Czerkawski has presented and published widely on E-Learning in the past decade.

* * *

Utku Köse was born on March 26, 1985 in Afyon, Turkey. He was educated at Gazi Anatolian Profession High School (Department of Computer-Software) and entered Gazi University in 2004. He graduated as a faculty valedictorian in 2008 with a BS in computer education. Now, he is a research assistant at the Distance Education Vocational School, Afyon Kocatepe University, Turkey. His research interests focus on distance education and electronic learning applications, blended learning, virtual learning environments, online / virtual laboratories, new learning / teaching models, mobile / wireless technologies, animation and 3D systems, artificial intelligence techniques (fuzzy logic and artificial neural networks) and cryptography.

Kim Huett is self-professed "technogeek" and an instructor of technology integration at the University of West Georgia in Carrollton, Georgia. She holds the MS in Secondary Education from Texas A&M University at Corpus Christi and BA degrees in English and Spanish from the University of Texas at Austin. She has taught English and Spanish classes, is certified in K-12 technology at all levels and has taught Spanish for the Texas Virtual School. She is currently pursuing her Educational Specialist degree in Instructional Technology. Her research interests include FOSS and K-12 online learning environments as well as the impact of emerging technologies on educational outcomes. She presents regularly at *American Journal of Distance Education* and *Quarterly Review of Distance Education*.

Jason H. Sharp is an Assistant Professor of Computer Information Systems at Tarleton State University in Stephenville, Texas. He received the PhD from the University of North Texas and the MS and BS from Tarleton State University. His publications appear in *The DATA BASE for Advances in Information Systems* and the *Information Systems Education Journal*. He has presented papers at multiple conferences including the *International Conference on Information Systems, Americas Conference on Information Systems, International Conference on Extreme Programming and Agile Processes in Software Engineering, Conference on Information Systems Applied Research*, and the *Information Systems Educators Conference*. His current research interests include component-based software development, agile development methods, flexible and distributed information systems development, globally distributed agile teams, and the use of open source software in education.

Jason B. Huett is an Assistant Professor of Media and Instructional Technology at the University of West Georgia. He presents internationally on a topics concerning distance education and online learning. He is a member of noted editorial boards, and serves as a consultant for several virtual schools, universities, and the state of Georgia. He was a featured researcher at the 2006 *AECT International Convention* in Dallas, Texas and has published numerous articles—including two award-winning publications—in journals such as *The American Journal of Distance Education, Quarterly Review of Distance Education,* the *Information Systems Education Journal, and TechTrends.* He also has several book chapters in print as well as new book: *Learning and Instructional Technologies for the 21st Century: Visions of the Future.* His other research interests include FOSS, online communications, constructivist learning, distance learner motivation, collaborative learning, standards for distance education, systems approaches to distance learning environments, and K-12 technology integration. He is also trying to find his calm little center.

Gladys Palma de Schrynemakers is the assistant provost of Long Island University's Brooklyn Campus. Among diverse administrative contributions to the Campus, Dr. Schrynemakers co-chaired the recent, highly successful Middle States accreditation process and has won nearly $4.1 million in grants and awards. She serves as director of CSTEP, a student enrichment program to encourage science careers among students of diverse racial and ethnic backgrounds, and Principle Investigator for Project QUEST (Quality Undergraduate Expanded Science Training), a program which seeks to prepare students to enter STEM research fields. She directs the Brooklyn Campus Outcomes Assessment efforts for both the academic and co-curricular departments and units. During a 20-year career at Long Island University, she holds the rank of adjunct full professor and also has taught a range of graduate and undergraduate courses. Currently, she teaches an Urban Studies graduate seminar titled, "Cinema and the City." Dr. Schrynemakers holds a doctorate from Columbia University and master's degrees from Columbia University, C. W. Post and City College.

Shahron Williams van Rooij is assistant professor in the Instructional Technology program for the College of Education & Human Development at George Mason University. Dr. Williams van Rooij teaches courses in the e-Learning graduate certificate program using course formats that model the various e-Learning delivery modes and emphasizing the application of instructional design principles and learning theories to e-Learning in both educational and training settings. Dr. Williams van Rooij has more than twenty years of corporate experience, ten of which are in the design, development and marketing of software systems for higher education. Her research is currently focused on the role of open source software systems to achieve enterprise-wide efficiencies and construct an integrated learning environment that serves both the academic and business sides of higher education. Dr. Williams van Rooij is also a Project Management Professional (PMP®) credentialed by the Project Management Institute (PMI).

Barbara (Bobbi) Kurshan has honed her vision of *"what can be"* using technology while supporting the growth of new education companies and developing innovative software products. She currently serves as the President of Educorp Consultants Corporation, where she provides strategic consulting in the areas of education, technology and innovation and the Executive Vice President of WorldSage, a consortium of higher education institutions in the EU. As the past Executive Director of Curriki she helped to build one of the most innovative and robust global open source education communities. Curriki is a non-profit, social entrepreneurship organization that supports the development and free distribution of open source educational materials to improve education worldwide. Dr. Kurshan has previously served as the Co-CEO of Core Learning an education investment fund and the Chief Academic Officer of bigchalk. She currently serves on the Board of several education companies. Dr. Kurshan has been involved with education and technology for over 30 years. She developed the first children's software products for Microsoft and also created award-winning products for McGraw-Hill, Apple, CCC (Pearson) and others. As a professor, she helped students research the impact of technology on learning. Numerous publishing credits include topics that explore women's attitudes toward technology, how kids learn using computers, and new ways of learning through understanding. Dr. Kurshan received her EdD in Curriculum and Instruction with a concentration in Educational Technology and an MS in Computer Science from Virginia Tech University, and a Bachelor of Science in Mathematics from Newcomb College, Tulane University.

Peter Levy has more than 15 years of experience working in the cross-section of technology and education. Peter began his career as an analyst for Jupiter MediaMetrix and has worked in a range of leadership roles in strategy, product development and business development for Scholastic, bigchalk and Wireless Generation. Since 2003, Peter has been the Principal of Levy Associates, an educational technology consulting company providing strategic planning, business development, marketing and product development services. Peter works with companies and organizations to develop research-based approaches to planning and implementing growth based on effective partnerships, strategic marketing and outreach and innovative product positioning. In addition to his for-profit clients, Peter has worked extensively with Curriki, where he directed all of the partnership agreements with for-profit publishers, not-for-profit organizations and Ministries of Education. His current practice now includes helping other publishers devise effective open source strategies. Some notable articles and reports published include: the Online Learning chapter of the *SIAA Trends Report for Education Technology, 2010,* the cover story, "Curriki and the Open Educational Resources Movement" in *Multimedia and Internet@ Schools Magazine,* May/June 2009 as well as several analyst reports on the K–12, post secondary and corporate training markets for the New York office of the Canadian Consulate.

Anne Schreiber Anne Schreiber has over 20 years experience as a multi-media publisher, product designer and educator. She is currently the Vice President of Education Content and Curriculum at Common Sense Media, a not-for-profit organization that helps children, their teachers and their families navigate the world of multi-media and life in an online, connected culture. Common Sense Media has developed extensive curriculum in Digital Citizenship, Internet Safety and Research and Information Literacy. Anne's successful career includes: Chief Academic Officer at Curriki, an organization dedicated to the creation of validated, open source K-12 curricula, Vice President of Product at the Grow Network/McGraw-Hill, Publisher at Scholastic, Vice President of Content and Programming at bigchalk, and Managing Editor of Time Warner's parenting Web site, "ParentTime." Anne created and directed the science content for the award-winning "The Magic School Bus" television series and "Scholastic Science Place" as well as the highly successful beginning literacy system, "WiggleWorks". Publishing credits include more than a dozen books for young children. Anne began her career as an elementary school teacher, developing staff and student enrichment programs. Anne did both her undergraduate and graduate work in Curriculum and Instruction and Science Education at Cornell University.

Janet Buchan (BSc, Dip.Ed, MEd.) is an instructional designer, educational technologist and Manager of an Educational Design and Media team at Charles Sturt University, NSW, Australia. She is active in the innovation and implementation of new educational technologies and has researched and published in the areas of educational management, designing digital media, online assessment, blended and flexible learning. Her PhD research looks at developing resilience and managing change in contemporary e-learning, or technology enhanced learning environments.

Alexey V. Khoroshilov is a researcher of Institute for System Programming, Russian Academy of Sciences. Khoroshilovs is an Assistant Professor of Faculty of Computational Mathematics and Cybernetics of Lomonosov Moscow State University. He graduated from Moscow State University in 2000, in 2004 get PhD in Mathematics from Institute for System Programming. Conducts lectures and practical classes in Moscow State University. His main research interests are test automation, requirements analysis, operating systems test methods.

Victor V. Kuliamin is a senior Researcher of Institute for System Programming, Russian Academy of Sciences. Kuliamin is an Associate Professor of Faculty of Computational Mathematics and Cybernetics of Lomonosov Moscow State University. He graduated from Moscow State University in 1995, in 2000 get PhD in Mathematics from Moscow State University. He also conducts lectures in Moscow State University. Main research interests are model based testing, software verification methods.

Alexander K. Petrenko is a leading Researcher, head of Software Engineering department in Institute for System Programming, Russian Academy of Sciences. He is a Professor of Faculty of Computational Mathematics and Cybernetics of Lomonosov Moscow State University. Petrenko graduated from Moscow Institute of Electronic Machinery in 1974, in 1983 get PhD in Computer Science from Keldysh Institute of Applied Mathematics, in 2003 get Doctor of Sciences degree from Institute for System Programming. He also conducts lectures in Moscow State University. His main research interests: formal methods of software engineering, test automation, software quality assurance, software development processes.

Olga L. Petrenko is an Associate Professor of Moscow Open Education Institute. Petrenko graduated from Moscow Institute of Electronic Machinery in 1973, in 1984 get PhD in History of Science from Institute of History of Science and Technology, Russian Academy of Sciences. Olga conducts lectures and training courses in Moscow Institute of Open Education and several Moscow education centers. Petrenko's main research interests: active learning, collaborative and participatory learning, building active learning process.

Vladimir V. Rubanov is head of department for Operating Systems at the Institute for System Programming of the Russian Academy of Sciences (ISPRAS). Vladimir holds M.Sc. degree with honors from the Moscow Institute of Physics and Technology (Phystech) and PhD in Computer Science from

ISPRAS. Since 2001, Vladimir has been leading the biggest industrial projects of ISPRAS with both Russian and foreign partners in the field of operating systems, software verification and tools for embedded systems. Currently, Vladimir leads the Russian Linux Verification Center (linuxtesting.org) at ISPRAS, which is aimed at ensuring high quality and compatibility of Linux, an open source operating system, through developing open standards and advanced testing and verification technologies.

Owen McGrath works for Educational Technology Services at the University of California (UC) Berkeley. Currently, he manages technical operations for UC Berkeley's learning management and coursecasting environments. During his career at UC Berkeley, he has led development and support efforts in multimedia courseware and collaborative on-line tools. Previously, he was also a research consultant with the Knowledge Media Lab (KML) of The Carnegie Foundation for the Advancement of Teaching. He has a Ph.D. in education from UC Berkeley and bachelor's degrees in English and computer science.

Stein Brunvand is an Assistant Professor in Educational Technology at the School of Education at the University of Michigan-Dearborn. He earned his Masters of Arts in Educational Technology in 2003 and his PhD in Learning Technologies in 2005 from the University of Michigan. Dr. Brunvand's teaching and research interest focus on the meaningful integration of technology in k-12 and higher education instruction. He is currently pursuing research that investigates the impact of fieldwork on teacher adoption and implementation of technology in the classroom.

Gail R. Luera is currently appointed as the Associate Dean in the School of Education at the University of Michigan- Dearborn where she is an Associate Professor of Science Education. She earned her doctorate at the University of Michigan-Ann Arbor; School of Natural Resources and Environment: Resource Policy and Behavior (Environmental Education). Dr. Luera has taught at Eastern Michigan University and the University of Michigan-Ann Arbor as well as for the Orange County (CA) Department of Education where she served as an acting principal for the Orange County Outdoor Science School for nine years. Dr. Luera's research interests focus very broadly on issues that influence effective teaching or student learning in many types of settings such as identifying and addressing factors that are barriers to K-12 or University faculty implementing educational innovations and researching the impact of educational technology to facilitate student learning and interaction with other students.

Tiffany Marra is the Project Manager for the University of Michigan's campus-wide Mportfolio Initiative. She is currently leading an effort to build open-source ePortfolio tools that address the learning and assessment needs of a wide variety of disciplines, schools, and stakeholders on the University of Michigan campus. She earned her PhD at the University of Michigan in Educational Technology and Learning Science in 2005, studying the effect of technology curricula on students' (particularly undergraduate women) future career choices.

Melissa Peet is the Academic Director for the Integrative Learning and ePortfolio Initiative at the University of Michigan. Dr. Peet's research focuses on understanding the types of knowledge, curriculla, and learning methods that supports students in becoming effective leaders, entrepreneurs and change agents. Dr. Peet is currently exploring the role of tacit knowledge (unconscious and informal ways of knowing) in the development of leaders, innovators and extraordinary practitioners across several fields and disciplines. She has recently developed a methodology for retrieving the tacit knowledge that evolves from peoples' experiences and is in the process of integrating this methodology with reflective learning and ePortfolio methods for use in higher education.

Tarmo Toikkanen, PsM, is a researcher in the Learning Environments research group at Media Lab, School of Art and Design, Aalto University in Helsinki Finland. His doctoral studies are located in the University of Helsinki and Aalto University. His research focus is on studying collaborative learning scenarios with the help of social network analysis and other relational methods. His background is in computer technology and he has been the technical lead in several international R&D projects, developing digital learning platforms and other software products. Most of the products have been published openly, using OSI approved open source licenses. Tarmo is an accomplished speaker, published author, and teacher trainer in the fields of educational technology, web technologies, and social media.

Jukka Purma, MA in cognitive science, is a researcher in Learning Environments Research Group at Media Lab, School of Art and Design, Aalto University in Helsinki Finland. He has eight years of experience in educational open source software, especially with Zope and Python development. He has been developing LeMill since 2006. In addition to learning environments, he is researching and developing software for novel visualizations in biolinguistics.

Teemu Leinonen is a professor of New Media Design and Learning and the Head of Department of the Media Lab, School of Art and Design, Aalto University in Helsinki Finland. Teemu Leinonen holds over a decade of experience in the field of research, design and development of web-based learning. His areas of interest and expertise covers design for learning, computer supported collaborative learning (CSCL), online cooperation, learning software design, educational planning and educational politics. Teemu's and his research group's approach to research and design of New Media and learning is theory-based but design-oriented. This means that besides the academic research papers the outcomes of the group are often software systems, software prototypes, applications and scenarios. Teemu has delivered a number of talks and presentation in national and international conferences, has given in-service courses for teachers and carried out consulting and concept design for several ICT and media companies.

Peter B. Swanson (PhD, University of Wyoming) is an Assistant Professor of Foreign Language Methods at Georgia State University. He teaches undergraduate and graduate courses in Spanish, pedagogy, and the implementation of technology in the foreign language classroom. He has published in many peer-reviewed journals such as the *Journal of Vocational Behavior, Dimension,* the *NECTFL Review,* and the *Phi Delta Kappan.* His research interests focus on assessment of oral language proficiency, foreign language teacher identity and the recruitment and retention of language educators, and teachers' sense of efficacy teaching languages. Prior to his work at Georgia State University, he taught Spanish in elementary and secondary schools in the Rocky Mountain region and won several distinguished teaching awards.

Patricia N. Early is the Language Lab Coordinator at Georgia State University. Formerly a Spanish instructor in Higher Education, she now focuses her research interests into the effective inclusion of technology into the second language curriculum, with particular interests in virtual learning spaces, the use of technology in addressing affective barriers, and technology solutions for accommodating individual learning styles. Ms Early is a member of the International Association for Language Learning

Technology, the Southeastern Association for Language Learning Technology, and previously published in Dimension, the journal of the Southern Conference on Language Teaching. She holds an MA in Spanish from Georgia State University, and at the time of this writing is working towards completion of the PhD in Instructional Technology at Georgia State University.

Quintina M. Baumann is a Spanish teacher in the Cobb County School District in Georgia. She has taught Spanish for eleven years, and is particularly interested in methods to increase student participation in the target language. While completing the action research project for her degree as Education Specialist in Foreign Language Education at Auburn University, Ms. Baumann researched the use of recording software during performance assessment tasks as a means of reducing anxiety, differentiating instruction, and increasing proficiency. She is a member of the American Council of the Teaching of Foreign Languages, as well as the Foreign Language Association of Georgia. Ms. Baumann also holds an MA in Teaching English as a Second Language from Southern Illinois University, and a BA in Spanish from Saint Louis University.

James Laffey is a Professor in the School of Information Science and Learning Technologies and a former researcher and systems developer at Apple Computer, Inc. Dr. Laffey has a PhD in Education from the University of Chicago and has won awards for the design of innovative, media-based computer systems. Through his design work and scholarship he is internationally recognized as an expert in the area of human-computer interaction. He currently teaches graduate level courses on development of systems to optimize HCI and learning, including methods to improve the social nature of online communities. He has received over $6 million of funding during the past 10 years, and is currently the principal investigator for grants from AutismSpeaks and the Institute of the Education Sciences to research and develop iSocial.

Matthew Schmidt is a PhD candidate in the School of Information Science and Learning Technologies at the University of Missouri. His current research interests focus on designing and implementing 3D virtual environments for individuals with autism spectrum disorders. He holds a BA and MA in German Language and Literature with an emphasis on Computer-Assisted Language Learning (CALL). He has designed and developed educational technologies and curricula for diverse disciplines including special education, second language acquisition, veterinary medicine, biological anthropology, nuclear engineering, and health physics. Matthew also serves as the project manager of the iSocial project to advance methods for supporting youth with ASD to learn social competencies within 3D VLEs.

Chris Amelung is the Senior Web Developer in the Center for Media and Instructional Innovation (CMI2) at Yale University. At Yale, Chris leads the development of innovative educational media and courseware for the University and his research interests include building new knowledge to support sociality and interaction in online learning environments. Chris received his Ph.D. in Information Science and Learning Technologies from the University of Missouri-Columbia in 2005. Chris is the author of the Context-aware Activity Notification System (CANS) used in a grant from the Fund for Improving Post-Secondary Education.

Dilek Karahoca is social anthropologist and interested in human computer interaction, web based education systems, and blended learning methodologies. She has articles about hospital information systems, tourism information systems, education information systems in SCI, and engineering index. She has a book, *Management Information Systems* as a co-author with Adem Karahoca. She has already supervised 10 Master of Science students' projects.

Adem Karahoca is head of Software Engineering Department of Engineering Faculty at Bahcesehir University in Istanbul. His research interests are web based learning systems and intelligent web based education tools, software standards, human computer interaction, data mining and web mining, mobile information systems and hospital information systems. He has 23 ICT related books in Turkish language. He has edited a data mining book in English. Also, he has written 10 articles that indexed in SCI and engineering index, and more than 100 proceeding papers. He has already supervised 40 Master of Science students.

İlker Yengin is currently a PHD student and teaching assistant in the College of Education and Human Sciences in University of Nebraska Lincoln. He is pursuing his PHD in the Instructional Technology area in Department of Teaching, Learning and Teacher Education. In his research Yengin has been focused on Instructional Technology and Human Computer Interaction

Huseyin Uzunboylu is currently Vice Dean of the Faculty of Education and Head of Computer Education & Instructional Technologies Department at the Near East University. In addition, he is a part time instructor at the Bahcesehir University in Turkey. His research interests are in the field of web-based education, learning management systems, m-learning, e-learning, collaborative learning and knowledge management systems. Huseyin Uzunboylu has 28 scientific articles presented and published in the international conferences. He also has 2 published books and 2 books' chapters; moreover he has 21 articles that 7 of them are within the covered of SSCI index. In addition, he is an editor-in-chief of the Cypriot Journal of Educational Sciences

Lucilia Green is an Instructional Technology doctoral student and part-time graduate instructor in the College of Education at Texas Tech University. Having served as a K-12 classroom teacher and school librarian for almost ten years, she now teaches Applications of Technology in Education, a course geared towards preservice teachers. In partnership with other instructors, she is also currently developing a standard curriculum and hybrid version of this course for distance delivery. Ms. Green's research interests include the use of Web 2.0 technologies to enhance instruction, blended learning, universal instructional design and technology integration at the K-12 level.

Fethi Inan is an assistant professor of Instructional Technology in the College of Education at Texas Tech University. His research interests include technology integration programs and practice in K-12 schools, individualized web-based learning environments, preservice teacher practice and professional development and instructional applications of emerging technologies.

Index

A

academic references 40
accessibility 75, 85, 86
Acculturation Theory 225
acquisition-learning 224
action awareness 189
action-oriented learning 42
active history teaching 203
active learning 40, 42, 43
activity awareness 187, 189, 191, 193, 195
adaptive learning environments 120
ARIADNE project 148
Asynchronous JavaScript and XML (AJAX) 6
Audacity 168, 172, 173, 174, 175, 176, 177,
178, 179, 180, 181, 183, 184, 185
audio language 170

B

blended courses 187
blended learning 47, 52, 208, 216
blog 3, 4, 5, 6, 7, 9, 12, 13, 16, 17, 18, 19, 20,
21, 22, 222, 223, 229, 230, 235, 238
Bloom's Taxonomy 43
bonding mechanisms 59

C

Chief Academic Officer (CAO) 58, 60, 62, 74
Chief Information Officer (CIO) 62, 63, 64, 74,
classroom-based learning 189
classroom computers 169, 171
classroom instruction 57, 71
cognitive skills 111
collaborative 75, 77, 78, 80, 82, 83, 85, 86, 88,
89

Collaborative Learning Environment (CLE)
92, 93, 94, 95, 97, 98, 99, 102, 103, 106,
107
collaborative OER 147, 151
collaborative work 3, 187
commercial education 57
communication rules 226
community of practice (CoP) 24, 32, 34, 95,
96, 106, 107
community source model 93, 103
community source software 92, 93, 103
Computer Assisted Language Learning (CALL)
170, 171, 185, 222, 228, 235, 237, 238,
239
computer assisted learning systems (CALS)
203, 204, 205, 207, 208, 209, 215
computer geeks 27
computer generation 24
computing systems 190
constructivism 170
Content (courseware) Management Systems
(CMS) 93
Context-aware Activity Notification System
(CANS) 187, 190, 191, 192, 193, 195,
196, 197, 198, 199
cooperative strategies 77
course activity 188
course evaluations 134
course management system (CMS) 42, 47, 57,
63, 68, 70, 187, 188, 189, 190, 191, 192,
193, 196, 197, 198, 204, 216
Creative Commons (CC) 150, 153, 155, 166
critical thinking 203, 205, 206, 207, 210, 215,
218, 219
cultural backgrounds 226, 229

CPSIA information can be obtained at www.ICGtesting.com
Printed in the USA
BVOW050235110412

287354BV00007B/37/P